CRITICAL
MEDIA
STUDIES

WITHDRAWN

About the Authors

ELINOR CHRISTOPHER

Brian L. Ott (*right*) is Professor of Media Studies at Colorado State University. His previous books include *The Small Screen: How Television Equips Us to Live in the Information Age* (Wiley-Blackwell, 2007) and *It's Not TV: Watching HBO in the Post-Television Era* (co-edited, Routledge, 2008). He currently serves as editor for the *Western Journal of Communication*. In his spare time, Brian enjoys playfully making fun of people who read Lostpedia.com and like Whoopi Goldberg movies.

Robert L. Mack received his Master of Arts in Communication Studies from Colorado State University in 2009. He is currently a Ph.D. student in Communication Studies at The University of Texas, Austin. His scholarly interests concentrate on theories of how things come to "mean," including discourse studies, psychoanalysis, and critical cultural studies. He also enjoys Agatha Christie murder mysteries, the theory forums at Lostpedia.com, and movies where Whoopi Goldberg evades danger in large, metropolitan cities.

Brian L. Ott and
Robert L. Mack

⟨W⟩WILEY-BLACKWELL

A John Wiley & Sons, Ltd., Publication

This edition first published 2010
© 2010 Brian L. Ott and Robert L. Mack

Blackwell Publishing was acquired by John Wiley & Sons in February 2007. Blackwell's publishing program has been merged with Wiley's global Scientific, Technical, and Medical business to form Wiley-Blackwell.

Registered Office
John Wiley & Sons Ltd, The Atrium, Southern Gate, Chichester, West Sussex, PO19 8SQ, United Kingdom

Editorial Offices
350 Main Street, Malden, MA 02148-5020, USA
9600 Garsington Road, Oxford, OX4 2DQ, UK
The Atrium, Southern Gate, Chichester, West Sussex, PO19 8SQ, UK

For details of our global editorial offices, for customer services, and for information about how to apply for permission to reuse the copyright material in this book please see our website at www.wiley.com/wiley-blackwell.

The right of Brian L. Ott and Robert L. Mack to be identified as the authors of this work has been asserted in accordance with the Copyright, Designs and Patents Act 1988.

Wiley also publishes its books in a variety of electronic formats. Some content that appears in print may not be available in electronic books.

Designations used by companies to distinguish their products are often claimed as trademarks. All brand names and product names used in this book are trade names, service marks, trademarks or registered trademarks of their respective owners. The publisher is not associated with any product or vendor mentioned in this book. This publication is designed to provide accurate and authoritative information in regard to the subject matter covered. It is sold on the understanding that the publisher is not engaged in rendering professional services. If professional advice or other expert assistance is required, the services of a competent professional should be sought.

Library of Congress Cataloging-in-Publication Data

Ott, Brian L.
    Critical media studies : an introduction / Brian L. Ott and Robert L. Mack.
       p. cm.
    Includes bibliographical references and index.
    ISBN 978-1-4051-6185-5 (alk. paper) — ISBN 978-1-4051-6186-2 (pbk. : alk. paper)
1. Mass media.   I. Mack, Robert L., 1985–   II. Title.
    P90.O88 2010
    302.23 — dc22
                                                                          2009018572

A catalogue record for this book is available from the British Library.

Set in 10.5/13pt Minion by Graphicraft Limited, Hong Kong
Printed in Singapore by Ho Printing Singapore Pte Ltd

01   2010

Contents

A Shout Out!

Work on this book, originally titled *Critical Media Studies: An Introduction, or A Student's Guide to Fabulous Dinner Conversation*, began nearly 2 years ago. In the ensuing time, it has undergone significant changes and development, not the least of which was a shortening of its title. Apparently, "some" thought that the phrase *dinner conversation* might be misleading. We, however, remain convinced that it would have been an effective way to target the *Food Network* demographic. Although we harbor no hard feelings about this change, we do hope that readers will discuss the book over dinner (or any meal, including tea time: hello to our British readers!) and that the ensuing conversation will be fabulous.

Another significant development has been the book's cover art. Initially we wanted an image of two squirrels "doing it" . . . a metaphor, of course, for the often frenzied exchange that occurs between media producers and consumers. But, as with the title, more sensible heads prevailed, resulting in the equally enticing image of Tokyo at night. We, nevertheless, would like to thank our colleague, Dr Greg Dickinson, for taking said picture of the squirrels and almost losing a finger in the process. Our own fingers remain crossed for the second edition.

Despite our disappointment that the squirrel-on-squirrel image was not selected, we believe that the existing cover is equally appropriate to the themes raised in the book. The bright, but blurry lights of the city invite readers to study the image more closely just as *Critical Media Studies* asks readers to study the media more closely. Likewise, the array of colors that comprise the image reflect the array of perspectives contained in the book, each shedding their own light on the media.

We are deeply indebted to the sensible heads mentioned above for both their assistance and support. In particular, we would like to express our gratitude to the team at Wiley-Blackwell, especially Elizabeth Swayze, Senior Editor, Margot Morse, Senior Editorial Assistant, and Desirée Zicko, Marketing Manager. Their advice and guidance at every stage of the production process has been invaluable. We feel fortunate to have had such a dynamic, creative, and thoughtful team guiding us. We also wish to thank Dave Nash for his assistance in securing various copyright permissions. Finally, we extend a special thanks to Nik Prowse, our freelance project manager, for his hard work on formatting the manuscript and careful attention to detail. Since it is cliché to say that any remaining mistakes are solely our own, we instead locate the blame squarely with the Illuminati.

Cheers,
Brian and Rob
May 8, 2009

1 Introducing Critical Media Studies

How We Know What We Know

Everything we know is learned in one of two ways.[1] The first way is *somatically*. These are the things we know through direct sensory perception of our environment. We know what some things look, smell, feel, sound, or taste like because we personally have seen, smelled, felt, heard, or tasted them. One of the authors of this text knows, for example, that "Rocky Mountain oysters" (bull testicles) are especially chewy because he tried them once at a country and western bar. In short, some of what we know is based on first-hand, unmediated experience. But the things we know through sensory perception make up a very small percentage of the total things we know. The vast majority of what we know comes to us a second way, *symbolically*. These are the things we know *through* someone or something such as a parent, friend, teacher, museum, textbook, photograph, radio, film, television, or the internet. This type of information is mediated, meaning that it came to us via some indirect channel or **medium**. The word medium is derived from the Latin word *medius*, which means "middle" or that which comes between two things: the way that television and the Discovery Channel might come between us and the ocean floor, for instance.

   In the past 30 seconds, those who have never eaten Rocky Mountain oysters now know they taste chewy, as that information has been communicated to them through, or mediated by, this book. When we stop to think about all the things we know, we suddenly recognize that most of what we know is mediated. We know something about China even if we have never been there; we know something about Napoleon Bonaparte although he died long before we were born; we may, thanks to the crime drama *CSI*, even know something about the particulars of conducting a homicide investigation even though we probably never have conducted one ourselves. Prior to the advent of modern mass media, people were the primary medium or conduit through which information passed. This method of transmitting information had several significant limitations. Since messages were communicated by people, information was tied to human modes of transportation and thus traveled very slowly, especially over great distances like continents and oceans. Moreover, as a message circulated, it often passed through multiple channels (people), each of which altered it, if only slightly. There was, at this time, no way to efficiently communicate a uniform message to a large audience in distant places. What distinguishes modern mass media like print and television from personal media like humans and hand-written letters, then, are precisely their unique capacity to address large numbers of people in remote locations simultaneously.

Critical Media Studies is about the social and cultural consequences of that revolutionary capability. Recognizing that the mass media are, first and foremost, communication technologies that increasingly mediate both what we know and how we know, this book surveys a variety of perspectives for evaluating and assessing the role of mass media in our daily lives. Whether it be listening to an iPod while walking across campus, sharing pictures with friends on MySpace or Facebook, receiving the latest sports scores via your cell phone, sharing your favorite YouTube video over email, or settling in for the most recent episode of *Grey's Anatomy*, the mass media are regular fixtures of everyday life. But before beginning to explore the specific and complex roles that the mass media play in our lives, it is worth looking, first, at who they are, where they originated, and how they have developed.

Who Are the Mass Media?

As we have seen, *media* is a broad term that includes a diverse array of communication technologies such as human beings, cave drawings, smoke signals, letters, the telegraph, the telephone, books, magazines, newspapers, radio, film, television, iPods, cell phones, video games, and computers to name just a few. This book, however, is principally concerned with **mass media**, or those communication technologies that have the *potential* to reach a large audience in remote locations. What distinguishes mass media from personal media, then, is not merely audience size. While a graduation speaker or musician may address as many as 40,000 people at once in a stadium, for instance, neither one is mass mediated because the audience is not remote. Now, of course, if a 50 Cent concert is being broadcast live via satellite, those watching at home on their TVs or streaming it live over the internet are experiencing it through mass media. Simply put, mass media collapse space and transcend physical distance. Working from this definition, we have organized the mass media into four sub-categories: print media, motion picture and sound recording, broadcast media, and new media. These categories, like all acts of classification, are arbitrary, meaning that they emphasize certain features of the media they group together at the expense of others. Nonetheless, we offer these categories as one way of conceptually organizing mass communication technologies.

Print media

In an electronically saturated world like the one in which we live today, it is easy to overlook the historical legacy and contemporary transformations of print media, the first mass medium. German printer Johannes Gutenberg invented the movable-type printing press in 1450, sparking a revolution in the ways that human beings could disseminate, preserve, and ultimately relate to knowledge. Printed materials before the advent of the press were costly and rare, but the invention of movable type allowed for the (relatively) cheap production of a diverse array of pamphlets, books, and other items. This flourishing of printed materials touched almost every aspect of human life. Suddenly knowledge could be recorded for future generations in libraries or religious texts, and social power increasingly hinged upon literacy and ownership of printed materials. Most importantly, the press allowed for an unprecedented circulation of knowledge to far-flung cities across Europe. Although still limited by class distinctions, access to information from outside of one's immediate context was a real possibility. Mass media was born.

Not long after the settlement of Jamestown in the USA in 1607, the colonies established their first printing press. Located in Cambridge, Massachusetts, the press was printing popular religious tracts such as the *Bay Psalm Book*, a 148-page collection of English translations of Hebrew, by 1640.[2] Although much of the early printing in the colonies was religion-oriented, novels such as *Robinson Crusoe* (1719) and *Tom Jones* (1749), imported from England, were also popular. Religious tracts were eventually followed by almanacs, newspapers, and magazines. The most well-known early almanac, *Poor Richard's Almanac*, which included information on the weather along with some political opinions, was printed from 1733 to 1757 by Benjamin Franklin in Philadelphia. Although various cities had short-lived or local non-daily newspapers in the 1700s, the New York *Sun*, which is considered the first successful mass-circulation newspaper, did not begin operations until 1833.[3] The failure of earlier newspapers is often attributed to the fact that they were small operations run by local printers. It was not until newspapers began using editors and receiving substantial financial backing – first from political parties and later from wealthy elites like Joseph Pulitzer and William Randolph Hearst – that the newspaper industry mushroomed.

During the nineteenth and twentieth centuries, the newspaper industry experienced explosive growth. This continued until 1973 when "U.S. newspapers had reached a combined aggregate circulation of 63 million copies daily."[4] At the time, this reflected a daily newspaper for about 92 percent of US households. Since 1973, however, newspaper circulation has steadily declined. By 2005, the total circulation of weekday newspapers had fallen to 55.3 million or about 49 percent of US households. In

Table 1.1   Number of magazine titles in the USA

	1990	1995	2000	2006
Number of titles	23,786	28,682	31,024	22,106

Source: *National Directory of Magazines, 2004* and *2007*; Oxbridge Communications.

Table 1.2   Average circulation of top 10 magazines* in 2006 and 1997 in the USA

Publication	2006		1997	
	Average circulation	Rank	Average circulation	Rank
Reader's Digest	10,094,284	1	15,062,549	1
Better Homes and Gardens	7,627,046	2	7,609,962	4
National Geographic	5,072,478	3	9,012,597	3
Good Housekeeping	4,675,281	4	4,691,510	6
Ladies' Home Journal	4,136,462	5	4,551,892	7
Time – Weekly News Magazine	4,082,740	6	4,153,069	10
Woman's Day	4,014,278	7	4,303,377	8
Family Circle	4,000,887	8	5,079,305	5
People	3,786,360	9	3,559,006	11
TV Guide	3,499,746	10	13,137,106	2
Total circulation of top 10	50,989,562		71,160,373	

Source: Audit Bureau of Circulations. *Data exclude magazines whose circulation is tied to membership benefits (i.e. *AARP The Magazine*, *AARP Bulletin*, and *AAA Westways*).

many ways, the history of the magazine industry in the US closely mirrors that of the newspaper industry. It began somewhat unsteadily, underwent tremendous growth, and is currently in a period of decline. The first US magazine, *American Magazine*, was published in 1741. But the magazine boom did not really begin until the mid-nineteenth century. And though the industry continued to experience growth throughout the twentieth century, it has begun to suffer a decline in both the total number of titles (Table 1.1) and circulation (Table 1.2) since 2000.

As Table 1.1 illustrates, the total number of magazine titles in the US declined by nearly 29 percent from 2000 to 2006. Moreover, as Table 1.2 shows, the combined circulation of the top 10 magazines in 2006 is roughly 20 million less than the combined circulation of those same 10 magazines 9 years earlier. Despite declining readership in the newspaper and magazine industries, the book publishing industry would suggest that Americans are still reading. In 2004, an impressive 195,000 new titles were published in the USA, more than 2.5 times the number of new titles published in 1996. Book sales, too, are strong, as an estimated 3 billion books were sold in the USA in 2005.

Motion picture and sound recording

Sound recording and motion pictures may seem like an odd pairing at first, but their histories are deeply intertwined thanks in large part to Thomas Edison. In the span of 15 years, Edison and his assistant, William Kennedy Laurie Dickson, created what would later develop into the first two new mass media since print. Edison's first invention, of the phonograph in 1877, was a device that played recorded sound, and his second, the kinetoscope in 1892, was an early motion picture device that showed short, silent films in peep-show fashion to individual viewers. But Edison's goal was to synchronize audio and visual images into a film projector that would allow for more than one viewer at a time. Although sound film did not become possible until the early 1920s, improvements in film projection, namely the development of the vitascope, gave rise to the silent film era in the meantime. The eventual synchronization of sound and film launched talking pictures, or "talkies." The first commercially successful, feature-length talkie was a musical film, *The Jazz Singer*, in 1927. Hollywood was about to enter its Golden Age of the 1930s and 1940s, in which "the studios were geared to produce a singular commodity, the feature film."[5]

With the motion picture industry firmly established, sound recording was now receiving independent attention and the record industry began to dominate the music industry, which had previously been involved primarily in the production of sheet music. By the start of the twentieth century, profits from the sale of sound recordings quickly eclipsed profits from the sale of sheet music. This shift was fueled in large part by the continuous development of cheap and easily reproducible formats such as magnetic tape in 1926, long-playing (LP) records in 1948, compact or audio cassettes in 1963, optical or compact discs (CDs) in 1982, and lossy bit-compression technologies such as MPEG-1 Audio Layer 3 (MP3s) in 1995. With the exception of magnetic tape for sound recording, which was invented by German engineer Fritz Pfleumer, and Columbia Records' LP, Sony and Phillips are responsible for the previously mentioned recording formats, as well as the Betamax (1975), laserdisc (1978), Video2000 (1980), Betacam (1982), Video8 (1985), Digital Audio Tape (1987), Hi8 (1989), CD-i (1991), MiniDisc (1992), Digital Compact Disc (1992), Universal Media Disc (2005), Blu-ray Disc (2006), and DVD (as part of the 1995 DVD Consortium) formats. Several of these more recent formats have had implications for the motion picture industry, as they allow for the playback and recording of movies on DVD players and computers at home.

Broadcast media

The development of broadcast technologies changed the media landscape once again. Instead of media physically having to be distributed to stores or shipped to audiences as books, magazines, and newspapers are, or audiences physically having to travel to the media as in the case of film, media could now directly be brought to

Table 1.3 Number of commercial broadcast stations in the USA

	1950	1960	1970	1980	1990	2000	2006
AM radio stations	2,118	3,539	4,323	4,589	4,987	4,685	4,754
FM radio stations	493	815	2,196	3,282	4,392	5,892	6,266
TV stations: UHF and VHF	47	515	677	734	1,092	1,288	1,376

Source: US Census Bureau, *The 2007 Statistical Abstract*, and the Federal Communications Commission. Data exclude educational broadcast stations.

audiences over public airwaves. This was an important development because it freed mass media from transportation for the first time in history. We have excluded the electrical telegraph (1830s) because, like the telephone (1870s), it is better classified as a personal medium than a mass medium. Radio came on the scene first, experimenting with transmissions as early as the 1890s and making scheduled broadcasts in the 1920s. But television followed shortly thereafter with Philo T. Farnsworth, a Mormon from the small farm community of Rigby, Idaho, applying for the first television patent in 1927 and CBS launching the first TV schedule in 1941. Not only do radio and television share an overlapping technological history, but they also share an overlapping professional history, as many of TV's early stars came from radio. After the Federal Communications Commission (FCC) sorted out broadcast frequencies for radio in 1945 and TV in 1952, commercial broadcast stations spread rapidly (see Table 1.3).

The tremendous growth in the number of commercial radio and television stations since 1950 suggests a strong consumer demand for their output. This perception is reinforced by the data on radio and TV ownership and usage. Census data from 2004 indicate that 99 percent of US households have a radio and 98.2 percent have a television set. To put this in perspective, consider that over 4 million more US households own a television than a telephone. On average, homes are equipped with eight radios and two and a half television sets. But radio and television are more than just staggeringly widespread. They also receive impressive use. "In 1999," Todd Gitlin observed, "a television set was on in the average American household more than seven hours a day . . . [and] the average individual watched about four hours a day, not counting the time the set was on but the individual in question was not watching."[6] Radio usage is difficult to calculate, as we listen to the radio at work, at home, in cars, and while working out. Suffice to say, Americans spend a significant amount of time with radio and television.

Before turning to the fourth and final category of mass media, two recent developments with regard to radio and television need to be addressed: satellite (subscription) radio and cable (wired) television. In many ways, these developments are analogous. Both technologies charge for content, include some content that cannot be broadcast over public airwaves, and trouble the traditional understanding of broadcast media. Satellite radio and, increasingly, cable television employ a digital signal, which qualifies them for inclusion in the category of new media. That having been said, not all cable television is digital, and satellite radio, which uses a digital signal, is broadcast. As such, neither technology fits neatly into the category of broadcast or new media. Confusion over how to categorize satellite radio and cable TV has not stopped either one from being successful, however. From 1970 to 2004, for instance, the number of US households with cable television has grown from 7 to nearly 70 percent. In North America, there are currently two satellite radio providers, XM Radio, which has over 8 million subscribers (23 percent growth from the previous year), and Sirius Radio, which has nearly 7 million subscribers (61 percent growth from the previous year). As these data suggest, cable television and satellite radio are growing in patrons quickly and dramatically.

New media

New media is the broadest and, hence, most difficult of the four categories of mass media to delimit and define. Though we offer a definition from Lev Manovich, even he is aware of its problematic nature: "new media are the cultural objects which use digital computer technology for distribution and circulation."[7] One difficulty with this definition is that what it includes must continuously be revised as computing technology becomes a more common mode of distribution. The development of digital television, film, photography, and e-books, for instance, would place them in the category of new media along with the internet, websites, online computer games, and internet capable mobile telephony. The ever-expanding character of this category raises a second problem, which can be posed as a question; will it eventually come to include all media and therefore be a meaningless category? The likely answer is yes, for reasons we will discuss later under the topic of convergence. But for the time being, it remains a helpful way to differentiate it from traditional print, celluloid film, and broadcast radio and television. As long as there are mass media that exist as something other than 0s and 1s, new media will remain a useful and meaningful category.

The history of new media begins with the development of the microprocessor or computer chip. Introduced in 1971, the world's first commercial microprocessor, the 4-bit Intel 4004, executed about 60,000 calculations a second. By the early 1990s, the 486 microprocessor, which was typical of computers at the time, could perform 54 million calculations per second. Intel's Pentium Pro, introduced in 1995, increased performance yet again to roughly 250 million calculations per second. But computers were not only rapidly becoming more powerful, they were also rapidly becoming more connected. Developed initially as a communication technology for the US Department of Defense, the internet began to catch the public's attention in the 1970s when its potential for sending personal electronic messages (emails) became evident. But it was the development of a graphic-based user interface and common network protocols in the early 1990s that popularized the internet by transforming it into the hypertextual platform we know now as the World Wide Web.

Table 1.4 Percentage of US households with select new media

	Percentage of US households			
	1997	2000	2003	2006
Personal computer	36.6	51.0	61.8	68.0
Internet connection	18.6	41.5	54.6	73.0
Broadband connection: DSL and cable	N/A	4.5	19.9	42.0
Mobile telephony*	20.0	39.0	54.0	73.0

Source: Pew Internet & American Life Project. *Reflects national penetration rate as estimated by the Federal Communications Commission.

At the turn of the millennium, experts estimated that there were more than 8 billion web pages, a number that was doubling at the time every 6 months.[8] With the infrastructure in place, the cost of computing technology declining, and the ability of ordinary people to become mass producers of information, the adoption of new media in the USA has been swift over the past decade (see Table 1.4).

And even though cell-phone adoption in the US lags behind many European countries, mobile telephony boasts one of the fastest penetration rates of any communication technology in history. It also signals, as we will see shortly, one of the most important trends shaping contemporary mass media today.

Living in Postmodernity

As the previous section illustrates, the mass media develop and change over time. It is important, therefore, to study them in historical context. Since the focus of this book is on *contemporary* mass media, this section reflects on the character of the contemporary historical moment. The present era has variously been described as the information age, the third wave, post-industrial society, the space age, and postmodernity. While none of these labels is without its shortcomings, we prefer the term postmodernity to refer to the contemporary moment given its wide use by media scholars. **Postmodernity** describes the historical epoch that began to emerge in the 1960s as the economic mode of production in most Western societies slowly shifted from goods-based manufacturing to information-based services. In the transition from modernity to postmodernity, the mass production of standardized, durable goods such as automobiles and toasters has steadily given way to the reproduction of highly customizable soft goods such as iTunes libraries and cell phone plans. As the mass media have both contributed to and been transformed by this historical transition, the remainder of this section explores five key trends animating the mass media in postmodernity.

Convergence

The previous section organizes the media into four categories as a way of sketching a brief history of mass communication technologies. Ironically, the first major trend in the mass media today involves the erasure of such boundaries. Increasingly, contemporary media reflect *convergence*, the tendency of formerly diverse media to share a common, integrated platform. As strange as it may seem in light of the prevalence of streaming video, internet radio, and online newspapers today, convergence is a relatively recent phenomenon that was considered visionary in the early 1980s when Nicholas Negroponte and others at the MIT Media Lab began exploring multimedia systems. Before media convergence could become a reality, it had to overcome two major obstacles. First, the noise associated with analog signals such as those used in television and radio broadcasting generated message distortion and decay over long distances. This problem was solved through digitization, which reduces distortion by relying on bits rather than a continuous signal. Second, bandwidth limitations prevented large data packets, such as video, from being transmitted quickly and easily over a communication channel. But improved data-compression techniques along with bandwidth expansions have made possible the real-time transmission of large data packets over communication channels. As these technical hurdles have been overcome, convergence has accelerated.

Mobility

Historically, mass media have not been very mobile. If you wanted to see a film, you had to go to the theater. If you wanted to watch your favorite television show, you had to do so in the privacy of your own home. Even print media such as books, magazines, and newspapers were limited in their mobility, as their size and weight significantly restricted the amount of printed material one was likely to carry around. But the development of powerful microprocessors and wireless technology is rapidly changing all this, and today, instead of going to media, media can come to or go with us virtually anywhere. As one of the book's authors typed this paragraph, for instance, he was sitting in his favorite café, listening to his iTunes, and working on his laptop. When he needed to track down a source, he simply connected wirelessly to the University library and downloaded the article directly to his hard drive. Indeed, in the past 2 years, this author has stopped going to the library altogether. Even when he requires a book that does not exist electronically (yet!), he logs on to his computer and simply has it delivered straight to his office. As technology becomes more and more portable, media are being transformed from home appliances into personal (and fashion) accessories. In light of this trajectory, the next evolution will likely see media go from being something we wear to something we download directly through cybernetic implants.

Fragmentation

Despite its continued use, the phrase mass media is rapidly becoming a misnomer. The *mass* in mass media has traditionally referred to the large, undifferentiated, anonymous, and passive audience addressed by television, radio, and print's standardized messages. But a tremendous proliferation of media content, if not ownership, has led to specialization and niche marketing. What Alvin Toffler has called the "de-massification" of media has been underway since at least the early 1970s. Decreasing production costs have greatly altered the economics of the media industry, reducing the necessity for standardization. The result has been a dramatic increase in media channels and a fragmentation of output that caters to the increasing diversity of the consuming public.[9] Whereas once there were only three television networks, which could not fill 24 hours of programming, today there are hundreds of networks as well as premium cable services with around-the-clock programming. Television is not unique, either: the print media and radio have witnessed a similar proliferation of specialty outlets. General-purpose magazines such as *The Saturday Evening Post* and *Life* that dominated the magazine industry in the 1960s had been replaced by 4,000 special-interest magazines by 1980.[10] The internet, of course, reflects the most fragmented medium, delivering a dizzying array of content. Even an online bazaar like amazon.com has country-specific portals and employs tracking software, or so-called cookies, that record user preferences to create a highly customized shopping experience. As this technology improves, we can count on media becoming more and more tailored to individual tastes.

Globalization

Globalization is *the* buzzword of the moment: a concept that has captured the interest of academics, business leaders, and politicians alike.[11] Even as the world has become increasingly fragmented by specialized interests, it has simultaneously become more global as well. *Globalization* is a complex set of social, political, and economic processes in which the physical boundaries and structural policies that previously reinforced the autonomy of the nation state are collapsing in favor of instantaneous and flexible worldwide social relations. While globalization is multidimensional, we wish to focus chiefly on economic globalization. In the past few decades, the spread of capitalism has fueled the rise of multinational corporations who wish to profit from untapped "global markets." Hence, these corporations aggressively support free-trade policies that eliminate barriers such as trade tariffs between national and international markets. For the mass media, which are owned and controlled almost exclusively today by multinational corporations, globalization creates opportunities to bring their cultural products to distant local markets. This fact has raised fears about *cultural imperialism*, the imposition of one set of cultural values on other cultures. The process is dialectical or bi-directional, however. Local markets are influencing the products and thinking of the very companies targeting them, leading to concern that cultural difference is being eradicated in favor of one large hybridized culture.

Simulation

Although the concept of simulation can be traced back to the ancient Greeks, its current cultural cache is due principally to the French theorist Jean Baudrillard and his book *Simulacra and Simulation*. "Simulation," Baudrillard writes, "is the generation by models of a real without origin or reality: a hyperreal."[12] According to Baudrillard, Western societies, and "America" in particular, are increasingly characterized by simulation because the real and the imaginary (i.e. images or representations) have imploded. This argument is premised on (in Baudrillard's words) the *precession* of simulacra, which suggests that the image has evolved from being a good representation of an external reality, to a distorted representation of an external reality, to a mask that conceals the absence of a basic reality, to bearing no relation to any reality at all.[13] The matter of simulation is an important one, as the mass media are the key social institutions fueling this social phenomenon. The media, for instance, endlessly produce and reproduce images of love, violence, and family (to name only a few) that no longer point or refer to some external reality. Rather, they exist only as images of images for which there is no original. Simulation suggests that the media no longer represent, if they ever did, our social world; they construct a realer-than-real space that *is* our social world.

Why Study the Media?

Perhaps the most important reason to study mass media today is because of their sheer ubiquity. In the transition to postmodernity, mass media have gone from being one institution among many within our cultural environment to being the very basis of our cultural environment. The further back in history one travels, the less central mass media are to social life and the more central are other social institutions such as the family, the church, the school, and the state. But today, these social institutions have been subsumed by, and are largely filtered through, the mass media. More than ever before, the mass media have replaced families as caretakers, churches as arbiters of cultural values, schools as sites of education, and the state as public agenda-setters. In the introduction, we explored the two ways we know things, somatically and symbolically (directly and indirectly). Not only do we know most things symbolically, but the media represent an ever-expanding piece of the total symbolic pie of social mediators. Table 1.5 summarizes the number of hours the average American spends with select media each year.

As Table 1.5 indicates, though we may gradually be changing which media we use, the mass media remain a significant socializing force in contemporary society. **Socialization** describes the process by which persons – both individually and

Table 1.5 Hourly use of select media per person per year in the USA

	2000	2002	2004	2006
Publishing industry				
Daily newspapers	201	194	188	179
Books	107	109	108	106
Magazines	135	125	124	122
Motion picture and sound recording				
Cinema (does not include home video)	12	14	12	12
Recorded music	258	200	185	175
Broadcast industry				
Broadcast television	793	719	678	684
Cable and satellite television	674	800	868	871
Broadcast and satellite radio	942	991	986	975
New media				
Internet	104	147	176	190
Video games	64	70	77	82

Source: US Census Bureau, *The 2007 Statistical Abstract*, table 1110.

collectively – learn, adopt, and internalize the prevailing cultural beliefs, values, and norms of a society. Because all social institutions are mediators, they all contribute to socialization. When information passes through a channel or medium, it is translated from direct sensory experience into a set of symbols. Since symbols are selective, privileging some aspects of the thing being represented at the expense of others, they function as filters. Language is perhaps the most obvious example of how symbols operate as filters. When you listen to a friend tell a story or read about history in a textbook, you are not experiencing the events being described directly. You are only experiencing them symbolically. The words you hear or read are representations of the event you are learning about, not the actual event itself. This is why two accounts of the same event, while potentially very similar, are never identical. Stories are inevitably filtered through the symbols, and therefore the perspective, of the storyteller. As society's main storytellers, the mass media filter virtually every aspect of our world, shaping both *what* we learn and *how* we learn.

What we learn

Mediated messages are comprised of content and form. Broadly speaking, the content influences what we learn and the form influences how we learn. Both content and form are central to the socializing function of the mass media, though content has typically been given more attention. *Content* refers to the informational component of a message, to the specific details, facts, ideas, and opinions communicated through mass media. Audiences are often consciously aware of the content of mediated messages. We know, for instance, that when we watch the evening news we are learning specifics about our world. In one viewing of the MSNBC news program *Countdown with Keith Olbermann*, one author learned that Iraqi insurgents had blown up a Sunni mosque, that Scooter Libby had been denied his request to delay his incarceration, and that Paris Hilton had found God in prison. It should probably be noted at this point that the content of a message need have neither use-value nor truth-value to be classified as informational. As both misinformation and disinformation would suggest, fairness and accuracy are not defining attributes of information. Information need only be *meaningful*, as opposed to gibberish, to count as information.

The content of the mass media matters for several reasons. First, by choosing to include or cover some topics and to exclude or ignore others, the media establish which social issues are considered important and which are considered unimportant. Simply put, the mass media largely determine what we talk and care about. Second, content lacking a diversity of views and opinions significantly limits the scope of public debate and deliberation on matters of social importance. Unpopular and dissenting viewpoints are essential to a healthy democracy, however, as they often reframe issues in fresh, productive ways. Third, because media content is communicated using symbols and all symbols are selective, media content is necessarily biased. The language and images used to inform, educate, and entertain you also convey selective attitudes and beliefs. In short, the content of the mass media socializes us to care about some issues and not others, to see those issues from some perspectives and not others, and to adopt particular attitudes toward the perspectives it presents.

How we learn

Whereas content refers to the informational component of a message, *form* describes the cognitive component of a message. Form can be thought of as the way a message is packaged and delivered. The packaging of a message is a consequence, first, of the medium and, second, of the genre or class. Every medium or communication technology packages messages differently.[14] The unique ways that a message is packaged influence how we process it. In other words, communication mediums train our conscious to think in particular ways, not *what* to think, but *how* to think. Media scholars generally agree, for instance, that the way we interpret and make sense of language differs radically from the way we interpret and makes sense of images. Whereas language is highly temporal and thus favors a sequential or linear way of knowing,[15] images are decidedly spatial and hence privilege an associative or non-linear way of knowing. A simple way to confirm this difference is to place a page of printed text next to an image. While the printed text only makes sense when the words are read in succession, the elements within the image can be processed simultaneously.

Because the medium of a message conditions how one processes the informational elements within a message, some media scholars contend that message form is a more fundamental and important socializing force than message content. This position is most famously associated with Marshall McLuhan, who succinctly claimed, "The medium is the message." Given the transition to postmodernity, in which the image has steadily replaced the word as the prevailing form in mass media (even print media such as magazines and newspapers are increasingly filled with pictures), the belief that young people today are cognitively different than their parents is rapidly gaining adherents. If media guru Douglas Rushkoff is correct, then television and MTV along with video games and the internet may account for everything from the invention and popularity of snowboarding to the emergence and spread of attention deficit disorder. As such, critical media scholars must attend not only to what the mass media socialize us to think, but also to how they socialize us to think.

Doing Critical Studies

As powerful socializing agents that shape what and how we know ourselves and our world, it is vital that we study the mass media critically. **Critical studies** is an umbrella term used to describe an array of theoretical perspectives which, though diverse, are united by their skeptical attitude, humanistic approach, political assessment, and activist orientation. Before turning to the individual perspectives that comprise critical studies, let us examine the four key characteristics they share in greater detail.

Attitude: skeptical

The theoretical perspectives that comprise critical studies all begin with the assumption that there is more at stake in mass media than initially meets the eye. To a layperson, for instance, what gets reported on the evening news may appear to be an objective retelling of the day's major events. But to the critical scholar, the production of news is a complex process shaped by the pragmatic need to fill a 1-hour time block every day, as well as to garner high ratings. These factors, in large part, determine what counts as news, how the news is produced, and what the news looks like. The various perspectives within Critical Media Studies approach the news with *skepticism*, then, not as a way of debunking it, but as a way of understanding the pressures and practices that constrain it. Some critics refer to this skeptical attitude as a "hermeneutics of suspicion."[16] Hermeneutics describes a mode of interpretation grounded in close analysis. So, a hermeneutics of suspicion would be a mode of close analysis with a deep distrust of surface appearances and "common-sense" explanations.

Approach: humanistic

Universities, like many other cultural institutions, are divided into various units and departments. Though the precise divisions may vary some from one institution to another, one common way of organizing disciplines and departments is into the categories of the natural sciences, social sciences, and humanities. These categories, while neither rigid nor entirely discrete, reflect a set of general distinctions concerning subject matter, outlook, and method (i.e. procedure of investigation). Whereas the natural sciences seek to understand the physical world by empirical and "objective" means, for instance, the humanities aim to understand historical and social phenomena by interpretive and analytic means. To say that critical studies are broadly humanistic, then, is to associate them with a particular set of questions and a general approach to answering those questions. Critical studies are, first and foremost, modes of criticism "which have as their determinate goal the improvement of society."[17] Humanistic criticism emphasizes self-reflection, critical citizenship, and democratic principles;[18] it involves "thinking about freedom and responsibility and the contribution that intellectual pursuit can make to the welfare of society."[19] Because of the subjective element of humanistic criticism, the knowledge it creates is never complete, fixed, or finished.[20]

Assessment: political

In many scholarly arenas, the final step in research is the objective reporting of one's findings (usually in an academic journal). But critical studies are interested in the practical and political implications of those findings, and thus entail judgment. Although there is no universal criterion for leveling political judgments across individual studies of the mass media, critical studies are generally concerned with determining whose interests are served by the media, and how those interests contribute to domination, exploitation, and/or asymmetrical relations of power. Research in this tradition interrogates how media create, maintain, or subvert particular social structures, and whether or not such structures are just and egalitarian. A Feminist study of television sitcoms, for instance, would examine how the representation of male and female characters in such programs functions to reinforce or challenge gender and sexual stereotypes. Critical studies view society as a complex network of interrelated power relations that symbolically privilege and materially benefit some individuals and groups over others. The central aim of critical scholarship is to evaluate the media's role in constructing and maintaining particular relationships of power.

Action: social activism

One of the most unique and controversial characteristics of critical studies are their commitment to social activism. Critical studies operate on the premise that scholarship should be action oriented, that scholars have a social responsibility not only to identify injustice, but also to confront and challenge it. Many media scholars who work within the critical studies paradigm belong to media-reform organizations such as Fairness and Accuracy in Reporting (FAIR), the Media Education Foundation, Media Democracy in Action, Free Press, the Action Coalition for Media Education, the Center for Creative Voices in Media, and countless others. Critical studies' scholars believe that it is incumbent upon citizens and not just the government to hold big media accountable. Social activism can take many forms from boycotts and culture jamming to producing alternative media and supporting independent media outlets.

Key Critical Perspectives

In an effort to assist students in evaluating the media critically, this book examines, explains, and applies 11 critical perspectives, each of which is rooted in a different social theory. **Theory** is an explanatory and interpretive tool that simultaneously enables and limits our understanding of the particular social product, practice, or process under investigation. The term theory derives from the Greek word *theoria*, which refers to vision, optics, or a way of seeing. Since, as Kenneth Burke notes in *Permanence and Change*, "Every way of seeing is also a way of not seeing,"[21] no theory is without limitations. The authors believe that since every theory has biases and blind spots that no theory ought to be treated as the final word on any subject. Theory is most useful when it is used and understood as a partial explanation of the phenomenon being studied. Students are strongly encouraged to take each perspective seriously, but none as infallible or universal. The 11 critical perspectives in this book have been grouped in three clusters based upon whether their primary focus is on media industries, messages, or audiences. A brief examination of those three theory clusters will serve as a chapter overview for the book.

Media industries: Marxist, Organizational, and Pragmatic

Part 1 of *Critical Media Studies* examines media industries and their practices of production, paying particular attention to the economic, corporate, and governmental structures that enable and constrain how mass media operate. Chapter 2 explores the media from a Marxist theoretical perspective by examining the ways that capitalism and the profit-motive influence media-ownership patterns and marketing practices. Chapter 3 approaches the media from an Organizational perspective by focusing on the work routines and professional conventions within media industries. Chapter 4, the final chapter in the first part, investigates media industries from a Pragmatic perspective, exploring how laws and regulations impact media products.

Media messages: Rhetorical, Cultural, Psychoanalytic, Feminist, and Queer

Part 2 of the book centers on media messages, and concerns how the mass media communicate ideas, ideologies, and models of identity. Chapter 5 utilizes a

Rhetorical perspective to illuminate how the various structures within media texts work to influence and move audiences. Chapter 6 reflects a Cultural perspective and investigates how the media convey ideologies about matters such as class and race that, in turn, shape cultural attitudes toward various social groups. Chapter 7 adopts a Psychoanalytic perspective, considering parallels between media messages and the unconscious structures of the human psyche. Chapter 8 approaches media from a Feminist perspective, highlighting the complex ways that media influence our cultural performances of gender, whereas Chapter 9 adopts a Queer perspective to illustrate how media contribute to our attitudes about sexuality.

Media audiences: Reception, Erotic, and Ecological

In Part 3, *Critical Media Studies* turns to media consumption and use to illuminate how audiences derive diverse meanings, pleasures, and symbolic equipment from the mass media. Employing a Reception approach, Chapter 10 explores how audiences interpret media and use those interpretations in their everyday lives. Chapter 11 focuses on an Erotic perspective, demonstrating the wide range of pleasures, both dominant and subversive, that audiences find in media. Chapter 12 concludes Part 3 by offering an Ecological perspective: one that seeks to demonstrate the practical resources that audiences find in media for confronting and resolving personal and social problems.

SUGGESTED READING

Allen, R.C. (ed.) *Channels of Discourse, Reassembled: Television and Contemporary Criticism*, 2nd edn. Chapel Hill, NC: University of North Carolina Press, 1992.

Berger, A.A. *Media Analysis Techniques*, 3rd edn. Thousand Oaks, CA: Sage Publications, 2004.

Croteau, D. and Hoynes, W. *Media/Society: Industries, Images, and Audiences*, 3rd edn. Thousand Oaks, CA: Pine Forge Press, 2003.

Devereux, E. *Understanding the Media*, 2nd edn. Thousand Oaks, CA: Sage Publications, 2007.

Durham, M.G. and Kellner, D.M. (eds) *Media and Cultural Studies: KeyWorks*, revised edn. Malden, MA: Blackwell, 2006.

Grossberg, L., Wartella, E.A., Whitney, D.C., and Wise, J.M. *MediaMaking: Mass Media in a Popular Culture*, 2nd edn. Thousand Oaks, CA: Sage Publications, 2006.

Marris, P. and Thornham, S. *Media Studies: a Reader*, 2nd edn. New York: New York University Press, 2000.

Stevenson, N. *Understanding Media Cultures: Social Theory and Mass Communication*, 2nd edn. Thousand Oaks, CA: Sage Publications, 2002.

Storey, J. *An Introduction to Cultural Theory and Popular Culture*, 2nd edn. Athens, GA: University of Georgia Press, 1998.

Strinati, D. *An Introduction to Theories of Popular Culture*. New York: Routledge, 1994.

Taylor, L. and Williams, A. *Media Studies: Texts, Institutions and Audiences*. Malden, MA: Blackwell, 1999.

Williams, K. *Understanding Media Theory*. London: Arnold, 2003.

NOTES

1. S.I. Hayakawa, *Language in Thought and Action* (New York: Harcourt, Brace and Company, 1941), 31–33.

2. J. Cullen, *The Art of Democracy: a Concise History of Popular Culture in the United States* (New York: Monthly Review Press, 1996), 23–4.

3. Cullen, 48.

4. A. Toffler, *Future Shock* (New York: Random House, 1970), 174.

5. T. Schatz, The Return of the Hollywood Studio System, in *Conglomerates and the Media*, E. Barnouw et al. (eds) (New York: The New Press, 1997), 73–106.

6. T. Gitlin, *Media Unlimited: How the Torrent of Images and Sounds Overwhelms Our Lives* (New York: Metropolitan Books, 2001), 15–16.

7. L. Manovich, New Media from Borges to HTML, in *The New Media Reader*, N. Wardrip-Fruin and N. Montfort (eds) (Cambridge, MA: The MIT Press, 2003), 16–17.

8. F. Biocca, New Media Technology and Youth: Trends in the Evolution of New Media. *Journal of Adolescent Health* 27, 2000, 23.

9. Toffler, 249.

10. J. Naisbitt, *Megatrends: Ten New Directions Transforming Our Lives* (New York: Warner Books, 1982), 99–100.

11. M. Waters, *Globalization*, 2nd edn (New York: Routledge, 1995), 1.

12. J. Baudrillard, *Simulacra and Simulation,* trans. S.F. Glaser (Ann Arbor, MI: University of Michigan Press, 1994), 1.

13. Baudrillard, 6.

14. J.W. Chesebro and D.A. Bertelsen, *Analyzing Media: Communication Technologies as Symbolic and Cognitive Systems* (New York: The Guilford Press, 1996), 22.

15. M. Stephens, *The Rise of the Image the Fall of the Word* (New York: Oxford University Press, 1998), 78–9.

16. According to Paul Ricoeur, the hermeneutics of suspicion is "a method of interpretation which assumes that the literal or surface-level meaning of a text . . . is an effort to conceal the political interests which are served by the text. The purpose of interpretation is to strip off the concealment, unmasking those interests" [D.G. Myers, Hermeneutics of Suspicion, in *Glossary of Biblical Interpretation* (College Station, TX: Texas A&M University, 1999), www-english.tamu.edu/ pers/fac/myers/hermeneutical_lexicon.html; accessed December 14, 2008]. Ricoeur writes, "Hermeneutics seems to me to be animated by this double motivation: willingness to suspect, willingness to listen; vow of rigor, vow of obedience" [P. Ricoeur, *Freud and Philosophy: an Essay on Interpretation* (New Haven, CT: Yale University Press, 1970), 27; see also pp. 32–3)].

17. H. Hardt, *Critical Communication Studies: Communication, History and Theory in America* (New York: Routledge, 1992), x.

18. E.W. Said, *Humanism and Democratic Criticism* (New York: Columbia University Press, 2004).

19. Hardt, xi.

20. Said, 12.

21. K. Burke, *Permanence and Change,* revised edn (Los Altos, CA: Hermes Publications, 1954), 49.

Part I

Media Industries:
Marxist, Organizational,
and Pragmatic Perspectives

2 Marxist Analysis

When the cult television classic *My So-Called Life* premiered on ABC in the late summer of 1994, critics hailed it as "the first TV show to get adolescence right."[1] The show followed the daily life of 15-year-old Angela Chase (Claire Danes) and offered what many critics considered a poignant, realistic glimpse into the world of high school. However, the show faced a number of problems from the outset that resulted in its cancellation only 19 episodes later. On top of the fact that ABC executives time slotted *Life* against NBC's hit *Friends*, the show was primarily directed at a teen demographic and "could fetch only a paltry $50,000 per commercial spot."[2] Despite a massive fan letter-writing campaign dubbed Operation Life Support, the show succumbed to the financial demands of the market before it even completed its first season.

The brief rise and fall of *My So-Called Life* is an important reminder to all media consumers about the power of the economy in shaping media content. Though the show was hugely popular among viewers and critics alike, the simple fact that it could not fetch top-dollar advertising eventually led to its demise. In many ways this case study illustrates the critical perspective in media studies commonly referred to as Marxist analysis. Roughly speaking, Marxist media scholars look at the effects of ownership and economics on the production and distribution of media content. Books, films, and television shows do not just spontaneously occur: all are created as products to be bought and sold in a greater system of commodity exchange. Marxist scholars are interested in how this notion of media content as "product" in turn shapes the way it looks and circulates.

We begin this chapter with an overview of Marxist theory before turning our attention to contemporary patterns of media ownership, with a particular focus on how industry moves toward increasing consolidation and incorporation diminish competition and encourage standardization of the mass media. These effects are fully taken up in the latter half of the chapter, where we analyze how the capitalistic profit-motive inspires particular production methods that result in far-reaching social consequences.

Marxism: an Overview

Marxism is both a theory and a social and political movement rooted in the idea that "society is the history of class struggles." Its origins lie in the work of Karl Marx and Friedrich Engels, who collaborated on *The German Ideology* in 1845 (though it was not published until long after their deaths) and the *Communist Manifesto* in 1848. Marx, who was born in Prussia in 1818, is the more well known of the two due, in part, to his single-authored works, including *The Poverty of Philosophy* (1847), *Theories of Surplus Value* (1860), *Capital* (1867), *A Contribution to the Critique of Political Economy* (1859), and *Economic and Philosophic Manuscripts of 1844*, which was published posthumously in 1930. The central premise of Marxism is that the mode of production in society (or underlying economic structure) determines the social relations of production (or class structure). This theory understands and makes sense of the world through the perspective of **historical materialism**.

Marx believed that the material world (i.e. natural phenomena and processes) precedes human thought: that the external, concrete, material conditions of social existence determine or *ground* consciousness. In this way, Marxism is *materialist*, as opposed to idealist: a philosophy positing that ideas determine social existence. He also believed that the material conditions of societies change over time, and thus must be viewed in *historical* context. As Marx explains in the Preface to *A Contribution to the Critique of Political Economy*:

> In the social production of their existence, men [*sic*] inevitably enter into definite relations, which are independent of their will, namely relations of production appropriate to a given stage in the development of their material forces of production. The totality of these relations of production constitutes the economic structure of society, the real foundation, on which arises a legal and political superstructure and to which correspond definite forms of social consciousness. The mode of production of material life conditions the general process of social, political and intellectual life. It is not the consciousness of men that determines their existence, but their social existence that determines their consciousness.[3]

Marxism, then, holds that social consciousness, as encoded in institutions such as culture (art and media), religion, education, politics, and the judicial system, which Marx collectively referred to as the **superstructure**, reflects or mirrors the material conditions of society, which he termed the economic **base**. Marx's famous base/superstructure model is sometimes represented in the following manner:

(social) superstructure
—————————————————
(economic) base

For Marx, the superstructure and the social institutions that comprise it operate in the realm of ideas or *ideology*. Thus, to understand the ruling ideas (dominant ideology) in society, one needs to attend to the material mode of production in society. As Marx and Engels explain in *The German Ideology*:

> The ideas of the ruling class are in every epoch the ruling ideas: i.e. the class which is the ruling *material* force of a society is at the same time its ruling *intellectual* force. The class which has the means of material production at its disposal, consequently also controls the means of mental production. . . . The ruling ideas are nothing more than the ideal expression of the dominant material relations, the dominant material relations grasped as ideas.[4]

The mode of production within any society, according to Marx, is characterized by two aspects: its "forces [or means] of production" such as the land, natural resources, and technology needed to produce material goods, and its "relations of production" such as labor practices and ownership (of property, company shares, or the ways goods are distributed). For Marx, a society based on a capitalist mode of production is inherently exploitive because it creates two classes, a working or proletariat class and a ruling class or bourgeoisie.

Since the bourgeoisie owns and controls the means of production in society, the only commodity that the proletariat has to sell is its labor. According to Marx, the ruling class exploits the economic value (i.e. labor) of the working class to increase surplus value or profits. But the capitalist system in many countries has changed dramatically since Marx developed his Labor Theory of Value, and the division of labor that produced such a harsh divide between the haves and the have nots in the past has been replaced by a system that sustains a large middle class, the petty or petite bourgeoisie, of small business owners and white-collar workers (i.e. lawyers, doctors, professors, etc.). Their ideological domination—and it is domination (e.g. the middle class still behaves in a manner that sustains the ruling elite)—appears to be less grounded in their working conditions. This has led most contemporary Marxist critics and scholars to reject *deterministic* models, which they label "vulgar Marxism," that see the superstructure as having no autonomy from the economic base. While Marxist critics are still interested in who owns and controls the means of production in society, they also recognize that ideology can and does influence material conditions. Thus, for them, the process is much more dialectical than unidirectional, and it is this dialectic which they wish to understand.

Table 2.1   Consumer spending on select media per person per year ($ in billions)

	2000	2002	2004	2006
Publishing industry				
Daily newspapers	51.93	53.00	51.62	48.97
Books	85.84	87.64	89.67	91.27
Magazines	47.54	46.86	46.88	47.59
Motion picture and sound recording				
Cinema	32.64	39.59	38.76	39.11
Recorded music	61.04	52.47	49.39	45.77
Broadcast industry				
Cable and satellite television	189.45	224.30	255.36	282.92
Broadcast and satellite radio	–	0.07	1.15	4.68
New media				
Internet	49.47	85.84	113.48	138.83
Video games	27.89	32.34	32.94	36.13

Source: US Census Bureau, *The 2007 Statistical Abstract*, table 1110. Numbers reflect actual values and have not been adjusted for inflation.

The prevailing ideology of capitalism is known as the **profit-motive**—the continuous desire to increase capital. Contemporary Marxist critics, many of whom adopt the label political economists, investigate both the prevailing patterns of media ownership and how the logic of capital, or profit-motive, influences media business practices. There is good reason to do so, as the mass media are big business. According to Ben Bagdikian in *The New Media Monopoly*, US Americans were spending approximately $800 billion a year on media products in 2002.[5] It is especially interesting to note *how* consumers divided their spending. The US Census Bureau estimates that revenue for just the broadcasting and telecommunications industry was over $485 billion in 2002. Add to that $246 billion in revenue for the publishing industry and another $78 billion for the motion-picture and sound-recording industries, and the picture slowly comes into focus. Table 2.1 summarizes precisely where and how much money Americans have been spending on select media since 2000. To put these numbers into perspective, consider that in 2002 the average US household was spending more money on media ($1,782) than on clothing, footwear, and other apparel products and services combined ($1,694).

Patterns of Media Ownership

Adopting a historical materialist perspective, Marxist analysis of mass media begins by examining the means and relations of production under *contemporary* capitalism, or what Marxist critic Fredric Jameson calls "late" capitalism. Like all economic systems, capitalism changes over time. The information-based service economy of the twentieth-first century is substantially different than the industrial-based manufacturing economy of the nineteenth and twentieth centuries. It is vital, therefore, to consider how the media industry is organized and controlled today. Toward that end, this section investigates four current and deeply intertwined patterns of media ownership: concentration, conglomeration, integration, and multinationalism.

Concentration

The ownership of mass media is more highly concentrated today than at any other time in history. **Concentration** reflects an organizational state in which the ownership and control of an entire industry, such as the mass media, is dominated by just a few companies. This is also sometimes referred to as an *oligopoly*, as opposed to a monopoly in which one company dominates an entire industry (e.g. Microsoft's domination of the software industry). Oligopolies reduce competition by making it all but impossible for small, independent, or start-up companies to survive in the marketplace. The big companies typically buy up the small companies or drive them out of business. Once an industry becomes highly concentrated, the few remaining companies function more like partners or a cartel than competitors. They each control such a large piece of the industry pie that the other companies do not constitute a real threat. Such is the current state of mass media, which have gone from being dominated by 20 companies just 20 years ago to being dominated by five today. Time Warner, Disney, Viacom, News Corporation, and Bertelsmann comprise the first tier of corporate media giants, or what Ben Bagdikian calls "the Big Five".[6] Whereas these last two companies are not US-based, their vast ownership of US media clearly qualifies them for inclusion on this list. We should also note that as of December 31, 2005, Viacom Inc. split into two publicly traded companies, Viacom and CBS Corporation. Former CEO Sumner Redstone is the chairman of both companies and still controls 71 percent of the voting stock in each. Throughout this chapter, "Viacom" refers to the new, post-2005 Viacom unless specified otherwise.

Although there are certainly other large, profitable media corporations, such as General Electric, Sony, AT&T, Vivendi, Clear Channel, Gannett, and Knight-Ridder, they are clearly second-tier media companies whose percentage of the total media profits pale in comparison to the Big Five. As a way of demonstrating the domination of the Big Five, let us consider the scope and power of Time Warner, the largest media company in the world. Time Warner became the largest media corporation in January 2000 following its merger with American Online, which combined their $163 billion and $120 billion respective net worths. Currently, Time Warner is comprised of seven major divisions – AOL, Time Warner Cable, Warner Bros. Entertainment, New Line Cinema, Time Inc., Turner Broadcasting System, and Home Box Office – each of which owns dozens of brands and companies.

In 2006, Warner Home Video (a subsidiary of Warner Bros. Entertainment) captured 18.3 percent, or nearly one-fifth, of all US consumer spending on DVDs and VHS, the most of any studio. As the largest magazine publisher in both the USA and UK and the third largest in Mexico, Time Inc. – with its more than 130 magazine titles – earned 18.4 percent of the total advertising revenues generated by domestic magazines. Time Warner estimates that 50 percent of all American adults read at least one of their magazines every month, and that more than 100 of its magazines are sold in the USA every minute! Time Warner Cable is currently the second largest cable operator in the USA, and Turner Broadcasting System is the number one mobile provider of news (CNN), the number one news and information site online (CNN.com), and number one cable news network in unique viewers (CNN/US). Since 2001, Time Warner has cleared over $3 billion on home entertainment, licensing, and merchandising exclusively from the *Lord of the Rings* trilogy. Time Warner dominates not only in profits, but also in awards. In 2006, it collected six Academy Awards, including Best Picture for *The Departed* and Best Animated Feature for *Happy Feet*, three National Magazine Awards from the American Society of Magazine Editors, three Golden Globe Awards, five Peabody Awards for excellence in broadcasting, and 26 prime-time Emmy Awards. Time Warner is, to say the least, a considerable force within the media industry (see Figure 2.1).

Conglomeration

A second prevailing and closely related pattern of media ownership is **conglomeration**, the corporate practice of accumulating multiple, though not necessarily media, companies and businesses through startups, mergers, buyouts, and takeovers. Whereas concentration describes the media industry as a whole and its increasing consolidation into the hands of fewer and fewer corporations, conglomeration describes the particular structure of the corporations themselves. Some scholars reserve the term conglomerate to describe large corporations whose media holdings reflect only one dimension of their overall corporate portfolio. A corporation like General Electric, which manufactures home appliances and light bulbs but also owns NBC, the USA Network, Sci-Fi Channel, Bravo, MSNBC, and Universal Pictures, offers a prime example. Such a distinction may be outdated, however, as media-only conglomerates are among some of the most powerful corporations in the world. Thus, we regard each of the Big Five media corporations as conglomerates even though the majority of their holdings are restricted to media.

Let us take a closer look at how a media giant like the Walt Disney Company becomes a conglomerate. Like many conglomerates, the Walt Disney Company has rather humble origins, having been started as a small animation studio in 1923 by brothers Walt and Roy Disney. Early success at Walt Disney Studios (originally Disney Brothers Cartoon Studio) led to the formation of three other companies in 1929, Walt Disney Enterprises, Disney Film Recording Company, and Liled Realty and Investment Company. These companies later merged under the name Walt Disney Productions in 1938. In an effort to expand its business, the company began

Time Warner (2007)

AOL LLC	Amateur Gardening	Uncut
AOL	Amateur Photographer	Volksworld
AOL Europe	Angler's Mail	VW Camper & Bus
AOL Canada	Gage & Aviary Birds	VW Golf Plus
Advertising.com	Garavan Magazine	Wallpaper
AIM	Chat	Web User
CompuServe	Chat – It's Fate	Wedding
GameDaily.com	Classic Boat	What Digital Camera
ICQ	Country Homes & Interiors	What's On TV
Lightingcast	Country Life	Woman
MapQuest	Cycle Sport	Woman & Home
Moviefone	Cycling Weekly	Woman's Own
Netscape	Decanter	Woman's Weekly
Relegence	Essentials	World Soccer
Spinner.com	European Boat Builder	Yachting Monthly
TMZ.com	Eventing	Yachting World
Truveo	Golf Monthly	Your Yacht
Userplane	Guitar	TIME INC. SOUTH PACIFIC
	Hair	Bride To Be
TIME INC.	Hi Fi News	English Woman's Weeldy
All You	Homes & Gardens	In Style Australia
Business 2.0	Horse	Practical Parenting
Entertainment Weeldy	Horse & Hound	TIME Australia
Essence	Ideal Home	Who
Fortune	In Style (UK)	GRUPO EDITORIAL EXPANSION
Fortune Asia	International Boat Industry	Ambientes
Fortune Europe	Land Rover World	Audi Magazine
FSB: Fortune Small Business	Livingetc	Balance
Golf	Loaded	Chilango
In Style	MBR-Mountain Bike Rider	EXP
Money	MinWorld	Expansion
People	Model Collector	IDC
People en Español	Motor Boat & Yachting	Life and Style
Real Simple	Motor Boats Monthly	Manufactura
Sports Illustrated	Motor Caravan Magazine	Obras
Sports Illustrated For Kids	NME	Quién
StyleWatch	Now	Vuelo
This Old House	Nuts	Yachts
TIME For Kids	Park Home & Holiday Caravan	In Style Mexico
TIME Asia	Pick Me Up	TIME INC. BUSINESS UNITS
TIME Atlantic	Practical Boat Owner	Media Networks, Inc.
TIME Canada	Practical Parenting (UK)	Synapse Group, Inc.
TIME U.S.	Prediction	Targeted Media, Inc.
SOUTHERN PROGRESS CORPORATION	Racecar Engineering	Time Customer Service
Coastal Living	Rugby World	Time Inc. Content Solutions
Cooking Light	Ships Monthly	Time Inc. Licensing & Syndication
Cottage Living	Shoot Monthly	Time Inc. Interactive
Health	Shooting Times	Time Inc. Home Entertainment
Southern Accents	Soaplife	Time Inc. Studios
Southern Living	Sporting Gun	Time Warmer Retail Sales & Marketing
Sunset	Stamp Magazine	JOINT VENTURES
Oxmoor House	SuperBike Magazine	Avantages
Southern Living at Home	The Field	European Magazines Ltd.
Sunset Books	The Golf†	Evarn
IPC MEDIA	The Railway Magazine	Hachette Filpacchi Expansion
25 Beautiful Homes	The Shooting Gazette	
25 Beautiful Kitchens	TV & Satellite Week National	HOME BOX OFFICE, INC.
4X4	TV easy	HBO
Aeroplane Monthly	TVTimes	HBO On Demand

Figure 2.1   Time Warner brands and supporting organizations. Source: *Building Brands for a Digital World, 2007 Profile.* Time Warner, May 2007.

Cinemax
Cinemax On Demand
HBO Video
HBO Mobile
HBO Independent Productions
HBO Domestic and International Program
    Distribution
HBO On Demand International
Israel
United Kingdom
HBO Mobile International
United Kingdom
Ireland
Belgium
Netherlands
Germany
Austria
Switzerland
Italy
Spain
South Africa
South Korea
JOINT VENTURES
Picturehouse
THISJUSTIN.com
HBO Adria
HBO Asia
HBO Brasil
HBO Czech
HBO Hungary
HBO India
HBO Ole
HBO Poland
HBO Romania
El Latin America Channel

TURNER BROADCASTING SYSTEM,
    INC.
ACCSelect.com
Adult Swim
AdultSwim.com
Boomerang
Boomerang.com
Cartoon Network
Cartoon Network
Asia Pacific
Cartoon Network Europe
Cartoon Network
Cartoon America
Cartoon Network Studios
Cartoonnetwork.com
CartoonnetworkYA.com
CNN/U.S.
CNN Airport Network
CNN en Español
CNN en Español Radio
CNN Headline News
CNN Headline News in Asia Pacific
CNN Headline News in Latin America
CNN International
CNN Mobile
TBS

TBS.com
TCM Asia Pacific
TCM Canada
TCM Europe
TCM Classic Hollywood in Latin America
TCM.com
TheSmokingGun.com
TNT HD
TNT Latin America
TNT.tv.com
Toonami
Turner Classic Movies
Turner Network Television
Veryfunnyads.com
Williams Street Studio
JOINT VENTURES
Cartoon Network Japan
Cartoon Network Korea
CNN+
CETV
CNNj
CNNMoney.com
CNN Turk
CNN.de (German)
CNN.com.jp (Japanese)
Zee/Turner
Boing
CNN-IBN

NEW LINE CINEMA CORPORATION
New Line Cinema
New Line Distribution
New Line Home Entertainment
New Line International Releasing
New Line Marketing
New Line Merchandising/Licensing
New Line Records
New Line New Media
New Line Television
New Line Theatricals

WARNER BROS. ENTERTAINMENT INC.
WARNER BROS. PICTURES
WARNER BROS. PICTURES
    INTERNATIONAL
WARNER INDEPENDENT PICTURES
WARNER BROS. TELEVISION GROUP
Warner Bros. Television
Warner Bros. Domestic Television Distribution
Warner Bros. Domestic Cable Distribution
Warner Bros. International Television
    Distribution
Warner Bros. Arimation (Looney Tunes, Hanna-
    Barbera)
Telepictures Productions
Warner Horizon Television
The CW Television Network
Kids' WBI on The CW
WARNER BROS. HOME ENTERTAINMENT
    GROUP
Warner Home Video
Warner Bros. Advanced Digital Services

Warner Bros. Digital Distribution
Warner Bros. Interactive Entertainment (Warner
    Bros. Games)
Warner Premiere
Warner Bros. Technical Operations
WARNER BROS. CONSUMER PRODUCTS
WARNER BROS. INTERNATIONAL CINEMAS
WARNER BROS. STUDIO FACILITIES
WARNER BROS. THEATRE VENTURES
DC COMICS
    MAD Magazine
    Vertigo
    WildStorm

TIME WARNER CABLE INC.
Time Warner Cable
Road Runner High Speed Online
Digital Phone
Time Warner Cable Business Class
Time Warner Cable Media Sales
OPERATING DIVISIONS
Time Warner Cable Albany
Time Warner Cable Austin (includes Waco)
Time Warner Cable Buffalo
Time Warner Cable Charlotle
Time Warner Cable Eastern Carolina (Raleigh,
    Wilmington)
Time Warner Cable Greensboro
Time Warner Cable Kansas City
Time Warner Cable Los Angeles
Time Warner Cable Mid-Ohio (Columbus)
Time Warner Cable National (based in Derwer,
    CO, nonclustered systems)
Time Warner Cable New England (Portland, ME)
Time Warner Cable New York & New Jersey
Time Warner CableNorth Texas (Dallas)
Time Warner Cable Northeast Ohio (Akron &
    Cleveland)
Oceanic Time Warner Cable (Hawaii)
Time Warner Cable Rochester
Time Warner Cable San Antonio
Time Warner Cable San Diego
Time Warner Cable South Carolina (Columbia)
Time Warner Cable Southwest Ohio (Cincinnati,
    Dayton)
Time Warner Cable Southwest (El Paso,
    Haringen, Corpus Christi, et al.)
Time Warner Cable Syracuse
Time Warner Cable Wisconsin (Miwaukee &
    Green Bay)
LOCAL CHANNELS
Capital News 9 – Albany, NY
MetroSports – Kansas City, MO
MetroWeather – Kansas City, MO
News 8 – Austin, TX
News 10 Now – Syracuse, NY
News 14 – Carolina-Charlotte, Raleigh, and
    Greensboro, NC
NY1 News – New York, NY
NY1 Noticias – New York, NY
R News – Rochester, NY
SportsNet – New York

Figure 2.1 *Continued*

Table 2.2 Annual revenues for the Walt Disney Company ($ in millions)

	2002	2003	2004	2005	2006
Media networks	9,733	10,941	11,778	13,207	14,638
Parks and resorts	6,465	6,412	7,750	9,023	9,925
Studio entertainment	6,691	7,364	8,713	7,587	7,529
Consumer products	2,440	2,344	2,511	2,127	2,193
Total revenues	**25,329**	**27,061**	**30,752**	**31,944**	**34,285**

Source: The Walt Disney Company, *2006 Annual Report.*

designing its theme parks in 1952 and formed Buena Vista Distribution to distribute Disney's feature films 2 years later. But Walt Disney Productions did not become The Walt Disney Company until February of 1986, by which time it also included the Disney Channel and a new film label, Touchstone Pictures. Under the leadership of Michael Eisner, the company conducted a series of key acquisitions in the 1990s, including independent film distributor Miramax in 1993 and perhaps more importantly Capital Cities/ABC, a $19 billion transaction, in 1996.[7] During the 1990s, it also established Hyperion, a book-publishing division. By decade's end, the Walt Disney Company had grown into a global empire with powerful interests in all four of the mass media industries.

In 2004, Disney narrowly escaped a hostile takeover attempt by Comcast, an event that contributed to Michael Eisner's replacement as CEO by Bob Iger the following year. Shortly after Iger assumed the reins, Disney acquired Pixar Animation Studios in a transaction worth $7.4 billion. "Disney's performance during Iger's first year," reports the company's website, "was stellar, with record revenues, record cash flow and record net earnings for fiscal year 2006."[8] Presently, Disney is organized into four major business segments: studio entertainment (Walt Disney Pictures, Touchstone Pictures, Miramax Films, Buena Vista Home Entertainment, Lyric Street Records, Hollywood Records), parks and resorts (Disneyland, Walt Disney World, Disney Cruise Line, and Disney Club Vacation resorts), consumer products (Disney Toys, Hyperion Books, The Baby Einstein Company, DisneyStore.com), and media networks (ABC Television Network, the Disney Channel, ESPN Inc., Buena Vista Worldwide Television, and the Walt Disney Internet Group). As Table 2.2 indicates, since its modest beginnings, the Walt Disney Company has grown into a very profitable media conglomerate.

Integration

Media conglomerates are by definition integrated. **Integration** is an ownership pattern in which the subsidiary companies or branches within a corporation are strategically interrelated. Corporations can be integrated vertically, horizontally, or both. *Vertical integration* describes a corporation that owns and controls various aspects of production and distribution *within* a single media industry. Vertical integration can significantly increase the profits associated with a media product by allowing the "parent" corporation to oversee all stages of its development, everything from production and marketing to distribution and exhibition. A media conglomerate that owns record copyrights, record labels, sound production companies, and record clubs or stores would possess strong vertical integration in the music industry, for instance, and thus profit at each of these stages. The filmed entertainment division at Viacom offers a concrete example of vertical integration. In 1972, Paramount Pictures produced the Oscar-winning film *The Godfather*, which grossed $134 million in the USA by 1973. But domestic box office receipts are far from the end of the story. Today, Paramount Home Entertainment markets and distributes the film on DVD, Worldwide Television Distribution negotiates its broadcast on TV, and Famous Music licenses the use of its soundtrack. All of these companies are part of the Paramount Pictures Corporation, a wholly owned subsidiary of Viacom.

The popular, conspiracy-driven TV drama, *The X-Files* (1993–2002), provides a second example of the benefits of vertical integration. The Fox Broadcasting Company produced the show, which then aired in first-run production on the Fox network. In addition to the profits generated by its initial airing, Twentieth Television, a division of Fox Television, syndicated three rounds of reruns on local Fox affiliates and other stations, collecting an additional $35 million a year. Meanwhile, FX, one of Fox's numerous cable networks, also aired the show in rerun, generating $69 million more in annual profits. In total, Fox's yearly profits from *The X-Files*, after subtracting production costs of course, exceeded $180 million dollars,[9] a rather impressive figure when one considers it was only one television show from one company owned by Rupert Murdoch's Australian-based media conglomerate News Corporation.

Horizontal integration describes an ownership pattern in which a corporation dominates one stage in the production process (or at the same level in the value chain). This typically takes one of two forms. Some firms achieve horizontal integration through ownership of multiple outlets in one medium, thereby reducing competition. A company like News Corporation, which owns 35 Fox television stations, several of which are in the same markets, for instance, would be considered horizontally integrated. If a company controlled all or nearly all the radio stations, TV stations, or newspapers within a market, then it would have a horizontal *monopoly* in that market.[10] As we will see in Chapter 4, the 1996 Telecommunications Act, which eliminated or relaxed many ownership restrictions in the USA, has increased this form of integration. Another way for a corporation to achieve horizontal integration is to own and control companies *across* the various media industries, but typically at the same level of production, distribution, or exhibition.[11] This corporate structure is sometimes referred to alternatively as *cross-media ownership*. Like vertical integration, horizontal integration can have tremendous financial benefits, namely by enhancing synergy, a concept we will explore shortly. As Table 2.3 demonstrates, all of the Big Five media conglomerates are horizontally integrated.

Table 2.3 Horizontal integration of the Big Five

	Print media	Film and sound	Broadcast media	New media
Time Warner (Richard Parsons, CEO)	Warner Books, DC Comics, *People*, *Time*, *Sports Illustrated*, *In Style*	Warner Brothers Studios, New Line Cinema, Atlantic Records, Elektra	CNN, HBO, TBS, TNT, Cinemax, Cartoon Network	AOL, Netscape, MapQuest, CompuServ
Disney (Bob Iger, CEO)	Hyperion Books, *Discover*, *Jane*, *Family PC*	Walt Disney Pictures, Buena Vista, Dimension Films, Miramax, Touchstone	ABC, A&E, the History Channel, E! Entertainment, ESPN, Lifetime	Disney Mobile, ESPN.com, ABC.com, Go.com, Movies.com
Viacom (Philippe Dauman, CEO)	Simon & Schuster (until the split with CBS on December 31, 2005)	Paramount Pictures, DreamWorks Studios, MTV Films, Famous Music	Comedy Central, MTV, VH1, BET, Nickelodeon, Spike TV, CMT, TV Land, and CBS (until 2005)	IFILM, Atom Entertainment, Shockwave, Xfire, RateMy-Professors.com, Harmonix
Bertelsmann (Reinhard Mohn, CEO)	Random House, Doubleday, Bantam, Fodor's Travel Guides	BMG Music, Columbia, Arista, Epic, RCA, Jive Records	RTL Television (Germany), M6 (France), Five (UK)	Arvato Mobile (Europe's leading mobile provider)
News Corp (Rupert Murdoch, CEO)	HarperCollins, Zondervan, *TV Guide*, *New York Post*, *The Times* (UK)	Blue Sky Studios, Fox Searchlight, 20th Century Fox, MySpace Records	FOX, My Network TV, FX Networks, BSkyB (UK)	DirectTV, MySpace, Photobucket, Grab.com

Multinationalism

A fourth pattern of contemporary media ownership is **multinationalism**, or a corporate presence in multiple countries, allowing for the production and distribution of media products on a global scale. Multinationalism should not be confused with globalization, however. As we saw in Chapter 1, globalization is a complex set of economic and political processes, and while globalization may be contributing to the rise of multinational corporations, it cannot be reduced to this ownership trend. Multinational media conglomerates, or TNCs (short for transnational corporations) as they are sometimes called, do not simply (re)distribute a static, prepackaged product developed in one locale to various countries around the globe, nor do they completely re-invent the proverbial wheel each time. National differences in regulatory policies as well as cultural values means that TNCs often partner with national media companies to produce and distribute media that will be successful in that country or region. In some cases, the "foreign" companies owned by TNCs are former local or independent media that they have simply bought out.

For most media conglomerates, international markets represent potential profits that are just too tempting to resist.

The German-based Bertelsmann, which is made up of six divisions, RTL Group, Random House, Gunter + Jahr, MBG, Arvada, and Direct Group, provides an excellent example of a powerful multinational media conglomerate. Consider the scope of Bertelsmann's broadcasting production and distribution company, RTL Group, the largest in Europe.

> RTL Group's content production arm, Fremantle Media produces more than 10,000 hours of programming every year. In 22 countries, Fremantle Media creates and produces a range of award-winning programmes including primetime drama, serial drama, entertainment, factual and comedy. With programming rights in about 150 countries, Fremantle Media is also the largest independent TV distribution company outside the United States.[12]

Like RTL Group, Bertelsmann's book publishing division, Random House – the world's largest general-interest book publisher – is a global company that prides itself on being decentralized.

> The publisher presents a broad spectrum of editorial voices supplied by more than 100 publishing imprints in 16 countries. These include historic publishing houses such as Doubleday and Alfred A. Knopf (USA); Ebury and Transworld (UK); Plaza & Janés (Spain); Sudamericana (Argentina) and Goldmann (Germany). Random House empowers each of its publishers with autonomy and independence from outside interference, thus ensuring the greatest diversity for its publishing.[13]

Bertelsmann's global reach in the book-publishing industry is mirrored by News Corporation's massive newspaper empire, Time Warner's domination in the magazine industry, Viacom's MTV networks, which reach over 496 million households in 162 countries, and Disney's worldwide resorts, theme parks, and toy-merchandizing capability. As an examination of contemporary ownership patterns reveals, the media industry in the USA is overwhelmingly concentrated among five fully integrated, multinational conglomerates.

Strategies of Profit Maximization

As we have just seen, ownership and control of the mass media is driven by a profit-motive. But ownership alone does not guarantee financial success. Thus, the few multinational conglomerates that dominate the media industry utilize a series of strategies to maximize profits. We are using the term *strategy* here in a very specific way consistent with the French sociologist Michel de Certeau. For de Certeau, strategies are the exclusive domain of the "strong" or subjects of will and power. "A strategy," he writes, "assumes a place that can be circumscribed as *proper* (*propre*) and thus serve as the basis for generating relations with an exterior distinct from it (competitors, adversaries, "clientèles," "targets," or "objects" of research)."[14] de Certeau contrasts strategies with tactics, which he defines as the everyday practices used by the "weak" to resist domination (tactics will be explored in Chapter 11). The distinction between strategies and tactics hinges on ownership; only those who have a "place" to stockpile their winnings can carry out strategies. The six main strategies of profit maximization in the media industry today include cross-development, advertising, spectacle, the logic of safety, joint ventures, and niche marketing.

Cross-development

The first key strategy of media conglomerates is cross-development, or the involvement of multiple subsidiary companies in the development, production, and distribution of a media brand for the purpose of "exploiting it for all the profit possible."[15] Cross-development, which media executives commonly refer to as *synergy*, is made possible because of horizontal integration. Since each of the Big Five engages in cross-development regularly, the examples are virtually endless. Time Warner, which owns DC Comics and publishes over 900 comic book titles, for instance, frequently has "DC Comics' characters appear in comic book live-action and animated series, direct-to-video releases, collectors' books, online entertainment, licensing and marketing deals, consumer products, graphic novels and feature films."[16] Characters such as Superman and Batman, who started out as comic book heroes, have both repeatedly found their way onto the big screen in feature films produced and distributed by Warner Bros. Entertainment. The television series *Smallville*, which also taps the Superman mythology, is produced by Warner Bros. Television and airs on the Warner Bros. network. Similarly, the Academy Award-winning 1989 film *Batman*, which grossed a record-setting (at the time) $40,489,746 during its opening weekend, was released in conjunction with two albums.[17] The first was Prince's *Batman* soundtrack on Warner Brothers Records, which debuted at number one on the Billboard 200 charts and went multi-platinum, selling 11 million copies worldwide. The second album, also released on Warner Bros. Records, featured the original score composed by Danny Elfman.

Increasingly, the summer blockbuster lies at the heart of cross-promotional efforts. In fact, big-budget films often only get made today if they can demonstrate strong cross-promotional potential. Typically, this means a film that will appeal to a wide audience and can be marketed to children through toy lines and the fast-food industry. While perhaps no media conglomerate has perfected this formula better than Disney, one of the best examples comes from MCA/Universal. We are speaking, of course, about the 1993 mega hit *Jurassic Park*. Created by Steven Spielberg and based on the Michael Crichton book by the same name, *Jurassic Park* cost Universal Studios a whopping $56 million to produce.[18] So, MCA/Universal could not take any chances and undertook a $65 million licensing and promotional campaign, which involved making deals with over 100 companies from Kenner and Kellogg's to SEGA and Ocean Software to market 1,000 products.[19] The marketing hype paid off and *Jurassic Park* cleared a record $50 million its first weekend, eclipsed $100 million in 9 days, and eventually grossed over $350 million in the USA and Canada. But as Thomas Schatz notes, "It's overseas box-office performance was even stronger, and together with its huge success on video cassette [distributed by MCA/Universal Home Video], pay-cable, and other ancillary markets pushed the film's revenues to well over a billion dollars."[20] The film's international success was due in part to screenings of the film's trailer in Japan through Panasonic, a company owned by Matsushita Electric Industrial Co. and the parent corporation of MCA/Universal. Nor did the profits end with the film. In 1996, a year after the Canadian media conglomerate Seagrams purchased MCA/Universal from Matsushita, Jurassic Park – The Ride opened at Universal Studios Hollywood, boosting attendance at the park by 40 percent compared with the previous year.

Advertising

Advertising, the practice of pitching products or services to consumers, has long been a staple of the media industry. Since their creation, US newspapers and magazines have been subsidized in large part by advertisements, while the broadcast media generate nearly all of their revenue from advertising. On July 1, 1941, CBS launched the first TV schedule with 15 hours of weekly programming, including two 15-minute news programs Monday through Friday. That same day, WNBT (later NBC) aired the first television commercial (for Bulova watches) during a Dodgers/Phillies game. By 1949, advertisers were spending $12 million a year on television advertising alone, a number that jumped to $128 million in just two short years.[21] In the mid-1960s, a typical 30-second ad spot during a national prime-time TV series cost about $20,000–$25,000.[22] Today, that same spot costs anywhere from $100,000 to $420,000, depending on the show's ratings.[23] But the cost of these spots pale in comparison to those for special events like the Super Bowl. During the 1999 Super Bowl, for instance, advertisers paid $1.6 million on average for a 30-second spot; with the Fox network selling 58 minutes of ad time, one game generated about $93 million in advertising revenue.[24]

Over time, the cost of producing network television has increased, so the TV industry has constantly had to devise new ways of increasing ad revenue. One of the earliest solutions was to shorten the length of the ad spots themselves. In 1965, every network television commercial was a full 60 seconds in length, but 10 years later only 6 percent were a minute long. By cutting ad spots in half to 30 seconds, networks were able to double the number of ads they could sell. But the price was not cut in half. So, two 30-second ads cost more than one 60-second spot had. Ad spots have continued to get shorter and many spots today are only 15 seconds in length.[25] Meanwhile, the total amount of advertising time has steadily grown, while the length of network shows has been trimmed. In 1999, the typical "1-hour" show had been cut to 44 minutes, and the average "half-hour" show had been shortened to 21 minutes.[26] This means that roughly 30 percent of all TV time is taken up by commercials. With the advent of new technologies such as the VCR and remote control that allowed for commercial "zapping," advertisers complained that they were not getting what they paid for, namely consumer eyeballs.

So, television adapted yet again, first, by reducing the length of the commercial break between two programs or sometimes eliminating it altogether as a way of preventing viewers from leaving to take a bathroom break between shows. In addition to creating more, shorter commercial breaks, the networks began to sell *product placements*. Instead of characters in television using or wearing generic products, networks began to charge companies to promote their products by highlighting labels and name brands, or simply having characters mention a brand. Films, which until recently did not have commercials, had pioneered the in-text ad much earlier with famous product placements such as Coca-Cola in *Blade Runner* and Reese's Pieces in *E.T.: The Extra-Terrestrial*. Today, if you can make out a brand in television or film, then chances are it's a paid advertisement. Disney, however, has taken product placement to a whole new level. Rather than promoting brands within its media, the media itself is the brand being advertised. Children's television programs such as the animated series, *My Friends Tigger and Pooh*, on the Disney Channel function as one long advertisement for the Winnie-the-Pooh brand and related merchandise. Recent Disney films such as *Toy Story* and *Cars* (both from Pixar) and *The Chronicles of Narnia* and *Pirates of the Caribbean* all work similarly to sell everything from T-shirts and sleeping bags to furniture and baby food. Nor is Disney shy about is use of media to sell Disney-related merchandise. According to their *2006 Annual Report*:

> The Disney Fairies franchise, launched in 2005, is already captivating girls around the world with successful new best-selling books like *Rani in the Mermaid Lagoon* and *Disney Fairies* magazines in Europe. Coming up, audiences will hear Tinker Bell speak for the very first time in *Tinker Bell*, the movie from DisneyToon Studios, which will bring to life the amazing world of Disney Fairies in computer-animation and will be supported with a broad consumer products line at major retailers around the world. . . .
>
>   Celebrating its 15th season on-air in 2007, *Power Rangers* ranks as a Top 3 action brand in toys, while *Cars* was the most successful film merchandise program since *The Lion King*. *Pirates of the Caribbean* was also successful and DCP [Disney Consumer Products] will now leverage the film as a year round franchise. With great entertainment and original content from Buena Vista Games (BVG), like the highly anticipated *Spectrobes*, DCP can now reach boys of all ages.[27]

Advertising in the media is so pervasive that one media scholar, Dallas Smythe, argues that the only commodity really sold in the media today is audiences. Massmedia audiences are sold to advertisers and advertisers expect to get what they are paying for. So, the media industry has developed increasingly clever ways to package us (see Niche marketing, below) for quick and easy delivery to their primary customers: the advertisers.

Spectacle

Originally published in France in 1967, Guy Debord's *The Society of the Spectacle* is regarded as one of the most important works of political and cultural theory in modernity. In its opening pages, Debord explains:

> Understood in its totality, the spectacle is both the outcome and the goal of the dominant mode of production. It is not something *added* to the real world—not a decorative element, so to speak. On the contrary, it is the very heart of society's real unreality. In all its specific manifestations—news or propaganda, advertising or the actual consumption of entertainment—the spectacle epitomizes the prevailing mode of social life. It is the omnipresent celebration of a choice *already made* in the sphere of production, and the consummate result of that choice.[28]

For Debord, our whole society has become little more than *spectacle*—mere exhibition and display. Through the endless reproduction of shocking images, be they of sex or violence, and glitzy promotions, the media collapses news into entertainment and entertainment into life. The production of a hyper-sensational world through spectacle ensures that viewers will attend to media. After all, its depiction of life is more dramatic and interesting than life itself. Consider gangsta rap's creation of what Debord calls a "real unreality," in which multi-million dollar artists who drive luxury automobiles, cover themselves in bling, and work for transnational media conglomerates rap about gang violence, growing up in the hood, and stickin' it to "the man." While all of these are very real social phenomena, gangsta rap glamorizes them, pimps them as commodities, as lifestyles, that can be attained and lived at the level of style and appearance. Life imitates art, which imitates nothing at all.

The power of spectacle to create a real unreality was driven home for one of this book's authors one night while tuned to the local Fox affiliate in Denver, Colorado. He had been watching *The Simpsons* or some other hyper-real Fox show, but became hypnotized by a station promo that ran during nearly every commercial break. He kept hearing, in a local anchor's familiar voice, the words: "Ron has a nuclear bomb buried in his back yard. There are bombs buried all over Colorado. Find out where tonight at 11." This so-called "news" wanted him to believe that digging a hole to plant a tree in his backyard could potentially cause a nuclear holocaust. The promo was designed to elicit one response (aside from soiling oneself): fear. Now, as a media critic, he knew he was being manipulated, scared into watching the news. But despite such reflexivity, not to mention the fact that he never watches Fox news, the idea was so outrageous, so spectacular that he stayed tuned over 2 hours waiting for the news. The story, which did not run until 38 minutes into the news program, was about a few missile silos in a remote part of Colorado than had been built in the 1960s during the Cold War. While the silos still housed intercontinental ballistic missiles, they were, of course, under the constant protection of the US military. In retrospect, the author realizes it must have been a particularly slow news day. With nothing "real" to promote – no reason for him to stay up and watch the news – the station relied on spectacle, the realer-than-real, to ensure that he would anyway. And the news is not alone. Increasingly, our whole media environment is starting to look like an episode of the *Jerry Springer Show*.

Logic of safety

The most fundamental rule of the profit-motive is "nothing succeeds like success." So, when a concept or formula meets with (financial) success, media conglomerates exploit it again and again. Since this practice is rooted in risk avoidance, it is known as the logic of safety. Media conglomerates are typically reluctant to try anything original, innovative, or edgy. The cost of trying something new only to see it fail is simply not worth the risk. Instead, the big media conglomerates have perfected the art of imitation, which comes in three basic flavors: sequels, remakes, and spin-offs. Movies are especially costly to make. In 2002, the average cost to produce a Hollywood feature film was $58.8 million, and it cost another $30.6 million to market it.[29] If a studio is going to invest that kind of money upfront, then they want a guarantee of success, or at least as close to a guarantee as they can get. Thus, when a film like *Rush Hour*, produced by New Line Cinema (Time Warner) in 1998, grosses $141 million at the box-office (USA only) and another $54 million in video rentals, you can bet there is going to be a sequel, regardless of whether or not the first film was any good. And when the sequel, *Rush Hour 2* (2001), grosses $226 million in domestic box-office receipts, eclipsing the original, it will be a trilogy (at least!). *Rush Hour 3* was released during summer 2007.

The first *Rush Hour* was itself already a rehash of a tired Hollywood formula, the buddy-cop film. Sometimes film production companies recycle not only the generic formula, but the story and characters as well in the form of a remake. Paramount's 2001 *Vanilla Sky*, for instance, is a remake of the 1997 Spanish film *Abre los Ojos*. A few more well-known remakes include *King Kong* (1933/2005), *The Manchurian Candidate* (1962/2004), *Freaky Friday* (1976/2003), and *Psycho* (1960/1998). Filmscroll.com reports that remakes are on the rise, increasing from 25 in 2002 to 44 in 2006.[30] Nor are remakes limited to the film industry. Remakes in the music industry are almost as numerous as the artists themselves. A few examples include *NSYNC's remake of "Just Got Paid" (Johnny Kemp), No Doubt's remake of "Hateful" (The Clash), Puff-Daddy's remake of "Break My Stride" (Matthew Wilder), Nirvana's remake of "The Man Who Sold The World" (David Bowie), Nine Inch Nails' remake of "Dead Souls" (Joy Division), and Limp Bizkit's remake of "Faith" (George Michael).

Although television also produces remakes – it's especially well known for adapting successful British shows like *The Office*, *Pop Idol* (becoming *American Idol*), and *Who Wants to be a Millionaire?* – the more common strategy is what sociologist Todd Gitlin calls "recombinancy." Television is a particularly formulaic media. Not only can audiences count on popular genres such as the game show, drama, situation comedy, and reality TV, but they can also count on sub-genres with very specific traits. Prime time would simply not be complete without a medical drama, crime drama, legal drama, and police drama, for instance. In many instances, when a show is nearing the end of its run, producers will simply create a spin-off that focuses on a popular or even secondary character from the original. *All in the Family* spun off *The Jeffersons*, *Mary Tyler Moore* spun off *Lou Grant*, *Happy Days* spun off *Lavern & Shirley*, and *Dallas* spun off *Knots Landing* to name just a few. More recently, when a show has been particularly successful, producers simply spun-off additional versions of the same thing, as has happened with *CSI* and *Law and Order*.

But regardless of whether it's movie sequels, music remakes, or television spin-offs, they all share the logic of safety. Indeed, when "innovation" does emerge in the media industry, it is typically because a small, independent producer has "broken the rules." When this occurs, the "emergent rules" are quickly co-opted and endlessly reproduced by the large conglomerates, or the smaller company is simply bought-out. This is precisely what happened at Miramax. After the unlikely success of controversial films like *sex, lies, and videotape* (1989), *Tie Me Up! Tie Me Down!* (1990), and *The Crying Game* (1992), Disney acquired Miramax in 1993. Releasing future films such as *Pulp Fiction* (1994) under the Miramax label allowed Disney to branch into more risqué film making without endangering its wholesome, family image.

Joint ventures

Given the high costs of television, sound, and film production, media conglomerates often undertake joint ventures to reduce financial risks. By splitting the costs of a new venture, neither corporation has to bear the full financial burden should the venture fail. "The dominant five media conglomerates," noted Bagdikian in 2004, "have a total of 141 joint ventures, which makes them business partners with each other."[31] Prior to the late 1980s, a 24-hour all-comedy cable network had never been tried in the USA. So, it was hardly a surprise when Time Warner's The Comedy Channel merged with Viacom's HA! to form Comedy Central in 1991. For 12 years, both companies retained 50 percent ownership in the network. As it turns out, Comedy Central went on to become a huge success and when Viacom eventually purchased Time Warner's share in 2003, it cost them $1.2 billion. Another reason media conglomerates may join forces is to expand their control in one particular industry. In 2004, for instance, BMG Entertainment (a Bertelsmann company) joined forces with Sony Music Entertainment (a Sony company) to form Sony BMG Music Entertainment and, thereby, join EMI, Universal, and Warner as one of the Big Four record companies. According to the Bertelsmann website:

> Sony BMG Music Entertainment [is] a joint venture between Bertelsmann and Sony. With legendary labels such as Arista, Columbia Records, Epic Record, Jive, and RCA Records, Sony BMG's vast catalog includes some of the most important recordings in history and spans genres ranging from hiphop, country, and classical, to gospel,

pop and rock. The company's core competency is discovering and developing artists, and bringing their music to audiences worldwide through a variety of products and distribution channels. Sony BMG is home to local artists and international superstars, including Beyoncé, Justin Timberlake, Christina Aguilera, The Fray, Dido, Carrie Underwood, Alicia Keys and Bob Dylan. The company is headquartered in New York and is owned in equal parts by Bertelsmann AG and the Sony Corporation of America.[32]

The merger also reportedly allowed the companies to cut up to 2,000 jobs, saving Sony BMG nearly $350 million a year. Such cooperation is not unusual, especially when one considers that the major media conglomerates have *interlocking directorates*. Each of the media conglomerates is overseen by a board of directors and often an individual will sit on multiple boards, making them interlocked. The people deciding what is good for one media conglomerate, then, are likely to be some of the same people deciding what is good for another. The result is joint ventures.

Niche marketing

A sixth and final strategy of profit maximization employed by media conglomerates is *niche marketing*, or the targeting of a specific segment of the public that shares particular but known demographic traits. Niche marketing is commonly characterized as *narrowcasting* to distinguish it from *broad*casting, a model that targeted a large, anonymous, and undifferentiated audience. The financial benefit of niche marketing is twofold. First, if a media corporation can deliver a niche audience that is highly sought after, then it can charge a premium for advertising. Say, for instance, a retail business sells skateboards and the business knows from past experience that the vast majority of its customers are ages 12–22 and skewed slightly toward males. The Fox network could charge this business much more for a 30-second advertising spot than say CBS, where 54 percent of its prime-time viewers are over 50.[33] Even highly rated programs like CBS's *60 Minutes* are probably not a good place to advertise skateboards. Similarly, NBC, which boasts the largest percentage of viewers who earn over $75,000 a year, would be the most logical place to advertise luxury automobiles. In the past, advertising rates were closely tied to audience share. But in this model, many viewers may not have been part of the target demographic an advertiser wished to reach. As media corporations increasingly target narrower audiences, they can charge much more for advertising.

A second advantage of niche marketing is that it allows media corporations to attract and reach previously untapped markets. As the tastes of some viewers and listeners run counter to popular tastes, these audiences were largely disinterested in the messages propagated by the old broadcast model. Thanks to new media technologies such as the internet and satellite, however, highly specialized content can now be delivered to even the most remote places. Historically, the size of a town dictated how many radio stations it had, and therefore how diversified the choice of formats was. A smaller market might only receive three radio stations such as hits, rock, and country. XM radio, by contrast, features 69 different music channels in addition to its news, talk, sports, and entertainment programming, and is available anywhere. Although the music on XM radio is currently commercial-free, this will likely change. When new media are introduced into the marketplace, they frequently court customers with the promise of little or no advertising. But after building a customer base, media moguls generally let advertisers in. Cable television, which started out largely commercial-free, is now saturated with advertising.

Consequences of Ownership Patterns and Profit Maximization

In any capitalist society, the patterns and strategies discussed in this chapter may not seem surprising or abnormal. We are, of course, socialized from birth to see capitalism not as *one possible* economic system, but as *the only* economic system. In such a context, the desire to accumulate wealth appears to be intrinsic and instinctive rather than constructed and learned. But when culture is transformed into nature (i.e. made to seem natural), we do not stop to question it. We do not ask, why does it matter that the media industry is highly concentrated? Or what difference does it make that the major media conglomerates operate according to a logic of safety? The remainder of this chapter begins with a reminder that late capitalism is only one structural (i.e. economic) possibility and that the patterns of ownership and strategies of profit maximization that emerge in relation to it have significant social and political consequences that affect our lives. Three implications in particular warrant our attention: the reduction of diversity, the restriction of democratic ideals, and the spread of cultural imperialism.

Reduces diversity

Concentration, which severely restricts competition, integration, which leads to the development of some projects and not others, and the logic of safety, which drastically limits creativity, collectively result in the homogenization of media. Despite the plethora of media outlets and the apparent array of choices today, media products such as music, television, and film are overwhelmingly similar in form and content. The uniformity of media has long been recognized by media scholars and can be traced back to the *Frankfurt School*, an institute for social research established in Weimar, Germany in 1923. The Frankfurt tradition found its way to the USA in the 1930s when German scholars immigrated there following the rise of National Socialism in Germany. Influenced by Marxism, scholars such as Herbert Marcuse, Theodor Adorno, and Max Horkheimer saw the mass media and popular culture as rigid, formulaic, highly standardized, and clichéd. They argued that media's unending sameness had a pacifying effect on audiences, eliminating the possibility for critical thought, and thereby producing our very consciousness. Though the Frankfurt School has been critiqued for promoting the idea of *false consciousness*, the belief that the masses are duped into blindly accepting the prevailing ideology, their criticisms of standardization are not entirely without merit.

While examples of standardization can be found in any of the media industries, the music industry and especially pop music provides a compelling example. In 1941, Adorno argued that popular music was successful because it was simultaneously standardized (i.e. it was all the same and therefore required no thought or effort to enjoy) and pseudo-individualized (i.e. it was cloaked in false appearance of uniqueness). Explained Adorno:

> The necessary correlate of musical standardization is pseudo-individualization. By pseudo-individualization we mean endowing cultural mass production with the halo of free choice or open market on the basis of standardization itself. Standardization of song hits keeps the customers in line by doing their listening for them, as it were. Pseudo-individualization, for its part, keeps them in line by making them forget that what they listen to is already listened to for them, or "pre-digested."[34]

If Adorno's critique sounds overly harsh, allow us to cite an example. In 1997, three brothers from Tulsa, Oklahoma, known collectively as Hanson, became a pop sensation with their song, "MMMBop," which quickly rocketed to number one. Featuring scintillating lyrics such as "In an mmm bop they're gone. In an mmm bop they're not there/Until you loose your hair. But you don't care," MMMBop appeared with 12 other songs (four more of which were hits) on the album *Middle of Nowhere*, which has sold over 10 million copies worldwide. Hanson, along with the near-endless iteration of boy bands and pop queens like Britney Spears, Christina Aguilera, and Avril Lavigne, would suggest that musical innovation and diversity are not only atypical, but also unnecessary for success.

Restricts democracy

A second social consequence of ownership patterns and profit-maximization strategies in the media industry is the decline of democratic ideals. Democracy is premised on the notion of egalitarianism, the free and open exchange of ideas, and the participation of diverse publics.

But until the relatively recent development and spread of new media, it was virtually impossible for ordinary citizens to share their ideas and opinions with large, remote audiences. Thus, only those who owned and controlled the means of production truly had a "public" voice. Even as access is gradually becoming more democratic through personal and political blogs, for instance, the major media conglomerates continue to function as powerful *gatekeepers*. Gatekeeping is a filtering practice that determines what makes it into the media and what does not. Media such as radio, television, and film remain almost entirely inaccessible to ordinary citizens. And even more democratic media platforms such as YouTube, MySpace, and Facebook are being bought up by the major conglomerates. Often, what starts out as creative, independent art is later co-opted for corporate profit.

By controlling what is included in (and thus excluded from) both news and entertainment media, the major media conglomerates also exercise an *agenda-setting* function. Agenda-setting refers to the power of the media to influence what people are concerned with or care about. By covering some news stories and not others, or by treating some scenarios, themes, and issues in entertainment media and not others, the media greatly influence what the public regards as important. The idea of agenda-setting asserts that media do not influence *what* audiences think, so much as they influence what audiences think *about*. Typically, agenda-setting is discussed in relation primarily to the news media. But entertainment media also exercise an agenda-setting function. The sheer prevalence of cop shows and crime dramas ensures that violence will be viewed as a serious social concern, while the absence of environmental dramas has the opposite effect. Sex and violence are seen as social concerns, in part, because there is so much sex and violence in the media. Meanwhile, the ongoing genocide in Darfur is of little concern to many US Americans because it receives little to no attention in the media.

In addition to gatekeeping and agenda-setting, the major media conglomerates exercise an important *framing* function. Framing describes the viewpoint or perspective that is employed by the news and entertainment media when covering social and political issues. Just as the lens of a camera frames its subject, media frames create particular windows through which audiences view issues. The news media's repeated framing of political issues around a conservative/liberal or left/right binarism, for instance, greatly limits the scope of public debate by marginalizing non-centrist or alternative perspectives. During political campaigns, third-party candidates are rarely taken seriously by the media. The naming and hence framing of third-party candidates as "on the fringe" works to ensure that they will remain there. Similarly, as we will see in the next chapter, when the news media frame a public tragedy such as a shooting as the random act of a madman, it obscures the underlying social conditions that may have contributed to the tragedy, thereby severely undercutting the possibility of changing or improving those conditions. In short, the gatekeeping (filtering), agenda-setting (focusing), and framing (structuring) functions of the major media conglomerates consistently undermine democratic principles and ideals.

Fuels cultural imperialism

A third consequence of contemporary ownership patterns and profit-maximization strategies many observers warn is *cultural imperialism*. Cultural imperialism describes the exporting of US values and ideologies around the globe, usually to the detriment of local culture and national sovereignty. While local culture certainly inflects upon and influences the media products such as television, film, and music imported from predominantly US-centered media conglomerates, the cultural imperialism hypothesis is rooted in the idea of unequal flow. This idea holds that while cultural beliefs and values are flowing in both directions the inward flow is so much greater than the outward flow that over time it causes cultural erosion in poorer countries with less-developed media industries. In some cases, exposure to outside cultural values can have devastating effects on local cultures. There was a significant rise in infant deaths in a number of countries in Africa, for instance, when mothers switched from breast-feeding to bottle-feeding after seeing it repeatedly featured in European and US television programs and advertising. The mixing of infant formula with unsanitary water in this particular region resulted in an epidemic.[35] Furthermore, given the financial resources behind the Big Five, it is often difficult for independent, local production companies to compete with multinational conglomerates. The increasing concentration of highly integrated media companies along with the drive to make profit is clearly not without significant social consequences.

Conclusion

This chapter has looked at the effects of ownership patterns and profit-motive on the creation and circulation of media texts. Though largely masked by their sheer complexity in contemporary society, the means of production ultimately determine the shape and content of media in a Marxist framework. Formed through multiple mergers and buyouts, the five major conglomerations that dominate the media industry look to maximize profit whenever possible, leading to a strange combination of standardization and spectacularization in media content as a result of the hegemonic logic of safety. At the same time, the industry's increasing ability to cross-promote and advertise media content drives this fairly uniform product to almost every corner of the Earth. The widespread cultural influence, in turn, restricts democracy, reduces content diversity, and increases the cultural capital of the countries that produce the majority of media today.

If, while reading this chapter, you felt somewhat overwhelmed or depressed at the utter control of the industry presented in the Marxist perspective, you are not alone. Marxist critique is certainly an important contribution to media studies, and indeed one of the oldest, but it is not complete in its ability to understand how the media industry functions. As we will see in the next two chapters, other factors like conventions and government regulations also help shape media content. Media industries represent a special kind of contemporary business, in that they are often in the service of both profit and art, and a strictly economic analysis will always be partial in its ability to explain the inner workings of these increasingly visible companies.

MEDIA LAB 1: DOING MARXIST ANALYSIS

OBJECTIVE

The aim of this lab is to utilize Marxist principles to analyze the media. Specifically, students will investigate how *patterns of ownership* and the profit-motive shape the content and form of select magazines.

ACTIVITY

- Divide class into small groups of 4–5 students each.
- Supply each group with a Time Warner publication such as *People*, *In Style*, *Sports Illustrated*, *Entertainment Weekly*, or *Time*.
- Ask students to record their answers to the following questions.
  1 How, if at all, are the ownership patterns of concentration, conglomeration, integration, and multi-nationalism reflected in the magazine?
  2 Give three specific examples of cross-promotion in the magazine. Hint: use Figure 2.1 from this chapter.
  3 What role does advertising play in the magazine? How is it incorporated? Cite three specific examples.
  4 How does the style, design, and layout of the magazine reflect a profit-motive? Cite six specific examples. Please include discussion of spectacle and the logic of safety.

SUGGESTED READING

Bagdikian, B.H. *The New Media Monopoly*. Boston: Beacon Press, 2004.

Barnouw, E. *Conglomerates and the Media*. New York: New Press, 1997.

Croteau, D. and Hoynes, W. *The Business of Media: Corporate Media and the Public Interest*, 2nd edn. Thousand Oaks, CA: Pine Forge Press, 2006.

Gandy, Jr, O.H. The Political Economy Approach: a Critical Challenge. *Journal of Media Economics* 1992; 5: 23–42.

Garnham, N. *Capitalism and Communication: Global Culture and the Economics of Information*. Newbury Park, CA: Sage Publications, 1990.

Garnham, N. Contributions to a Political Economy of Mass-communication. In *Media, Culture and Society: a Critical Reader*, R. Collins, J. Curran, N. Garnham, P. Scannell, P. Schesinger, and C. Sparks (eds), pp. 9–32. Newbury Park, CA: Sage Publications, 1986.

Golding, P. and Murdock, G. Culture, Communications, and Political Economy. In *Mass Media and Society*, J. Curran and M. Gurevitch (eds), pp. 15–32. New York: Edward Arnold, 1991.

Herman, E. and Chomsky, N. *Manufacturing Consent: The Political Economy of the Mass Media*. New York: Pantheon, 1988.

Horkheimer, M. and Adorno, T.W. *Dialectic of Enlightenment*. Translated by J. Cumming. New York: Continuum, 2001.

Jhally, S. The Political Economy of Culture. In *Cultural Politics in Contemporary America*, I. Angus and S. Jhally (eds), pp. 65–81. New York: Routledge, 1989.

Marx, K. (with Engels, F.) *The German Ideology including Theses on Feuerbach and Introduction to the Critique of Political Economy*. Amherst, NY: Prometheus Books, 1998.

McChesney, R.W. *Corporate Media and the Threat to Democracy*. New York: Seven Stories Press, 1997.

McChesney, R.W. *Rich Media, Poor Democracy: Communication Politics in Dubious Times*. New York: The New Press, 1999.

McChesney, R.W. *The Problem of the Media: U.S. Communication Politics in the 21st Century*. New York: Monthly Review Press, 2004.

McChesney, R.W. *Communication Revolution: Critical Junctures and the Future of Media*. New York: The New Press, 2007.

Mosco, V. and Wasko, J. *The Political Economy of Information*. Madison, WI: University of Wisconsin Press, 1988.

Murdoch, G. Large Corporations and the Control of the Communications Industries. In *Culture, Society and the Media*, M. Gurevitch, T. Bennett, J. Curran, and J. Woollacott (eds), pp. 118–50. New York: Routledge, 1982.

Schiller, H.I. Not Yet the Post-imperialist Era. *Critical Studies in Mass Communication* 1991; 8: 13–28.

Symthe, D.W. *Dependency Road: Communications, Capitalism, Consciousness and Canada*. Norwood, NJ: Ablex, 1981.

Wasko, J. *How Hollywood Works*. Thousand Oaks, CA: Sage Publications, 2003.

Williams, R. *Problems in Materialism and Culture: Selected Essays*. London, Verso: 1980.

NOTES

1. R. Gehr, My So-Called Strife, *The Village Voice*, vol. 39, no. 50, December 13, 1994, 57.

2. J. Jensen, Life As We Knew It: Looking Back at My So-Called Life—How ABC's Angsty Gem Set the Tone for Teen Dramas, *Entertainment Weekly*, issue 782/783, September 10, 2004, 126–32, www.ew.com/ew/article/0,,692296,00.html (accessed December 10, 2008).

3. K. Marx, *Selected Writings*, L.H. Simon (ed.) (Indianapolis, IN: Hackett Publishing Company, 1994), 211.

4. K. Marx (with F. Engels), *The German Ideology including These on Feuerbach and Introduction to the Critique of Political Economy* (Amherst, New York: Prometheus Books, 1998), 67.

5. B.H. Bagdikian, *The New Media Monopoly* (Boston: Beacon Press, 2004), 29.

6. Bagdikian, 30–50.

7. *Company History*, The Walt Disney Company, http://corporate.disney.go.com/corporate/complete_history_6.html (accessed December 14, 2008).

8. *Company History*, The Walt Disney Company, http://corporate.disney.go.com/corporate/complete_history_7.html (accessed Decemeber 14, 2008).

9. J.L. Roberts, TV Turns Vertical, *Newsweek*, October 19, 1998, 54–6, www.newsweek.com/id/93520 (accessed December 10, 2008).

10. R.W. McChesney, *Rich Media, Poor Democracy: Communication Politics in Dubious Times* (New York: The New Press, 1999), 16.

11. D. Croteau and W. Hoynes, *Media/Society: Industries, Images, and Audiences* (Thousand Oaks, CA: Pine Forge Press, 2003), 40, 45.

12. *RTL Group – Quality Entertainment on all Stations*, Bertelsmann – Media Worldwide, www.bertelsmann.com/bertelsmann_corp/wms41/bm/index.php?ci=168&language=2&pagesize=A&pagecolor=normal (accessed December 14, 2008).

13. *Random House – Number One in the World of Book Publishing*, Bertelsmann – Media Worldwide, www.bertelsmann.com/bertelsmann_corp/wms41/bm/

index.php?ci=24&language=2&pagesize=A& pagecolor=normal (accessed December 14, 2008).

14. M. de Certeau, *The Practice of Everyday Life*, trans. Steven Rendall (Berkeley: University of California Press, 1984), xix.

15. McChesney, 91.

16. *Building Brands for a Digital World, 2007 Profile*, Time Warner (2007), 14.

17. For an extended analysis of the Batman brand and franchise, see E.R. Meehan, in "Holy Commodity Fetish, Batman!": The Political Economy of a Commercial Intertext, in *The Many Lives of Batman: Critical Approaches to a Superhero and His Media*, R.E. Pearson and W. Uriccho (eds) (New York: Routledge, 1991), 47–65.

18. Crichton's book was published in 1990 by Alfred A. Knopf, Inc., an imprint owned by the New York based-publishing house Random House. At the time, Random House was still an independent publisher. But it was acquired by media giant Bertelsmann in 1998.

19. P.H. Broeske, The Beastmaster: Steven Spielberg Keeps a Tight Rein on His Dino Epic, "Jurassic Park," *Entertainment Weekly*, issue 161, May 12, 1993, www.ew.com/ew/article/0,,305858,00.html (accessed December 14, 2008).

20. T. Schatz, The Return of the Hollywood Studio System, in *Conglomerates and the Media*, E. Barnouw *et al.* (eds) (New York: The New Press, 1997), 74.

21. S.J. Baran, *Introduction to Mass Communication: Media Literacy and Culture*, 2nd edn (New York: McGraw Hill, 2001), 346.

22. R. Campbell, *Media & Culture: an Introduction to Mass Communication*, 2nd edn (Boston: Bedford/ St Martins, 2000), 415.

23. R. Campbell, C.R. Martin, and B. Fabos, *Media & Culture: an Introduction to Mass Communication*, 6th edn (Boston: Bedford/St. Martin's, 2009), 402.

24. Campbell, 344.

25. Baran, 347–8.

26. K. Alexander, TV Networks Trim Shows to Make Time for Ads, *Fort Collins Coloradoan*, September 18, 1999, D11.

27. *The Walt Disney Company 2006 Annual Report*, The Walt Disney Company (2006), 34.

28. G. Debord, *The Society of the Spectacle*, trans. D. Nicholson-Smith (New York: Zone Books, 1995), 13.

29. J. Wasko, *How Hollywood Works* (Thousand Oaks, CA: Sage Publications, 2003), 33.

30. Hollywood Remake or Hollywood Mistake? *Filmscroll*, September 23, 2006, www.filmscroll.com/?p=45 (accessed August 1, 2007).

31. Bagdikian, 9.

32. BMG – A Passion for Music, Bertelsmann – Media Worldwide, www.bertelsmann.com/bertelsmann_ corp/wms41/bm/index.php?ci=26&language=2& pagesize=A&pagecolor=normal (accessed August 1, 2007).

33. R. Grover, Must-See TV for Left-Handed Men Under 30: ABC, CBS, and NBC are Increasingly Watched by Niche Viewers, *Business Week* December 14, 1998, 104.

34. T.W. Adorno (with the assistance of G. Simpson), On Popular Music: 1941, in *On Record: Rock, Pop, and the Written Word*, S. Frith and A. Goodwin (eds) (London: Routledge, 2000), 308.

35. Baran, 551.

3 Organizational Analysis

In 1999, the California-based pop punk band Blink-182 reached the number one spot on the US Modern Rock chart with the song, "All the Small Things," off of their album *Enema of the State*. The song's accompanying music video, which was directed by Marcos Siega, parodied various pop videos by artists such as the Backstreet Boys, *NSYNC, and 98 Degrees. Blink-182's "All the Small Things" music video – a nominee for MTV's Video of the Year in 2000 – derives its humor by flaunting and exaggerating the established aesthetic codes of music videos, especially those employed in the pop videos of boy bands. Were it not for the recognizability of those codes (i.e. camera angles, shot framing, editing, etc.) by audiences, the video would seem both strange and un-amusing. As with most mainstream media products, music videos are highly formulaic, and thus lend themselves to easy parody. Given the infinite array of artistic and aesthetic styles that could be used to make music videos, why is it that they are so homogenous? Drawing on Marxist theory, the previous chapter suggested that one possible answer lies in the logic of safety, and the desire to guarantee success (i.e. profits) by minimizing risk. This chapter examines an alternate, though not necessarily mutually exclusive, explanation rooted in analysis of organizational and professional cultures.

Media scholars employing an Organizational perspective seek to understand "why media organizations, a specific medium, or the mass media institution produces the kinds of content it does."[1] In other words, these scholars understand that an organization is more than the mere arrangement of disparate parts. The manner in which media industries and institutions arrange themselves directly influences the kinds of content they produce. We begin this chapter by tracing the most import-ant aspects of an Organizational perspective, attending to the structures, processes, and conventions of organizations, as well as to the process of professionalization. Each of these concepts helps us better understand how the various facets of an organization come together to form an integrated whole. The latter half of the chap-ter undertakes an extended analysis of work in a specific industry, the news media, as a way of demonstrating the key role that work practices play in shaping media products. Contrary to popular belief, we contend that the news is not an objective retelling of the day's events, but rather a highly selective text structured by organ-izational demands.

Organizational Theory: an Overview

Work is a central feature of daily life, particularly in the USA, where workers put in the longest work hours of any industrialized nation. According to the Economic Policy Institute, the average US American worker worked 39.6 hours a week for 47.1 weeks in 2004. This means that the typical worker is working nearly 2,000 hours per year. With so much time spent at work, it is important to understand what happens there, and how what happens there influences an organization's services and products. Our work lives are most centrally defined by whom we work with and for. Collectively, employers and employees comprise **organizations**: a system (network) of ordered relationships and coordinated activities directed toward specific goals.[2] At a film studio such as Paramount, for instance, there are writers, producers, directors, actors, editors, sound crews, make-up artists, etc. engaged in scripting, shooting, editing, and marketing a particular film. Paramount, like any other organization, has two basic dimensions: structure and process.[3] *Structure* describes the underlying framework that shapes an organization over time, and includes three key elements: hierarchy, differentiation and specialization, and for-malization. *Hierarchy* refers to the specific arrangement of job roles and positions based upon authority within an organization. Inevitably, some persons or groups have more decision-making power than others within an organization, and thus are central to both the creation and maintenance of a particular corporate culture. The second structural element of organizations, *differentiation and specialization*, accounts for the division of companies into units, departments, and positions, each of which performs specific tasks. To the extent that these tasks require a unique set of skills and training, the positions within an organization are filled by professionals. **Professionals** are individuals who possess expertise in a particular area or field that allows them to accomplish the distinctive tasks of their position. A book editor, for example, is a professional with specialized training and credentials in proofread-ing and copyediting. The third structural element of organizations is *formalization*, or the degree to which specific practices must conform to accepted organizational and professional conventions. We will discuss the topic of conventions in greater depth shortly, but first let us consider the second major dimension of organizations: process.

If structure represents the underlying framework of an organization, then *process* reflects the actual substance built upon that framework. Structure and process can be likened to Kenneth Burke's notion of "container and thing contained."[4] Although a container has an identifiable shape and form, its contents can very greatly. The contents are, of course, always shaped and thus constrained to some extent by the container. So, while every organizational member, as an individual, engages in unique behaviors and actions (i.e. process), such behaviors and actions are always constrained, which is to say limited, by hierarchy, differentiation and specialization, and formalization (i.e. structure). The media critic who adopts an Organizational approach or perspective is interested in the precise ways that structure and process mutually influence one another within a media organization. One productive way of getting after that relationship is by analyzing the communicative practices that occur within organizations and how those practices create and maintain a particular organizational culture.

Assessing communicative practices

Every organization develops a unique **organizational culture**: the set(s) of norms and customs, artifacts and events, and values and assumptions that emerge as a consequence of organizational members' communicative practices. In this section, we outline five ways to study an organization's culture: performance, narrative, textual, management, and technology. Before examining these various lenses, however, we wish to stress that communicative practices are dynamic, contingent, and transactional, meaning that they are not static, universal, or bounded, but complex, improvisational, and continuous. To understand an organizational culture, then, one must look at its communicative practices in local, social, and historical contexts, including why, when, where, and how they occur, as well as whether or not they are ignored, legitimated, and/or challenged by organizational members.

1   *Performance.* Performances are expressive (i.e. productive and purposeful) displays (i.e. both process and product) that carry symbolic significance (i.e. meaning and implication) in a particular context.[5] Four important types of organizational performance include ritual, sociality, politics, and enculturation.[6] *Ritual* performances are those personal or organizational behaviors that members engage in on a regular or routine basis. One of the authors of this book, for instance, drinks coffee every morning as he reads his email. This is a personal ritual because it is not necessitated by his job. Such personal rituals are sometimes known as trademark performances because they are strongly associated with particular members. Organizational rituals by contrast, such as attending weekly faculty meetings, involve routine behaviors that are necessitated by or expected within a specific workplace environment. Given the near "sacred" character of some

organizational rituals, they can be particularly revealing of an organization's culture. *Sociality*, a second type of performance, refers to the codes of etiquette that are enacted with regard to friendliness, small talk, joking, and privacy within an organization. *Politics* are performed differently in every organization and influence the type and degree of independence, negotiating, and coalition building that are acceptable. A fourth common type of organizational performance, *enculturation*, emphasizes those "communicative performances wherein the newcomer learns the social knowledge and skills of the culture."[7] Although *narratives* are also a type of organizational performance, we have chosen to treat them separately given their unique complexity and importance.

2   *Narratives*. Stories are a ubiquitous feature of organizations, and the stories members tell about their workplace experiences are another way to evaluate the endless (re)creation of an organization's culture. Since stories are inherently selective, what does and does not get storied speaks to an organization's values and norms, as does the frequency with[8] and manner in which stories are told. Narratives can be classified as personal, collegial, or corporate. Personal stories are those that convey individual subjective experiences; collegial stories are those told about other organizational members, and corporate stories are those told about the organization itself. Each of these story types can function to affirm or discourage certain attitudes and activities within a culture. Narratives that glorify the success of an action or event invite emulation, while those that recount or accentuate failure sound a cautionary tone.[9]

3   *Textual*. Another means of examining an organization's culture is through the texts – written or electronic documents such as company bylaws, policy manuals, procedure handbooks, training manuals, office memos, newsletters, mission statements, reports, etc. – it produces. The purpose of formal texts like those just mentioned is to explicitly identify what are considered to be acceptable and unacceptable actions and activities within an organization. Given the origin and relative permanence of such documents, they tend to represent and reinforce managerial perspectives. Not all texts created within an organization are formal, however. Graffiti, personal employee notes, and "private" emails are all examples of informal, more spontaneous, texts. Whereas formal texts espouse the managerial or company "line," informal texts communicate the views of those in the "trenches." One way of understanding an organization's culture, then, is by examining the differences and similarities between formal and informal texts, between espoused and enacted views. If, for example, a parody of the company newsletter was circulated widely among employees, it might suggest that the newsletter is seen as little more than managerial propaganda.

4   *Management*. A fourth lens through which to evaluate an organization's culture is a managerial perspective. This approach concerns how "organizational culture is developed and directed by managers for the purpose of improving operating efficiencies, enhancing the bottom line, or creating satisfied customers."[10] Though this perspective, which conceives of organizations principally as businesses, emerged initially as a way to assist managers in achieving success by

implementing strategies that enhance productivity, performance, and profits, it can be used by critical organizational scholars to evaluate the political consequences of managerial practices. Drawing upon Marxist principles concerning the influence of economic imperatives on corporate culture, for instance, scholars might examine how specific management structures (i.e. the level and flexibility of hierarchy) and practices (i.e. hiring, assessment, promotion) influence both the character of products produced and the quality of employee's lives (i.e. pay, benefits, respect, voice, support, working conditions, etc.) within a particular organization.

5   *Technology.* In the context of an increasingly post-industrial and global economy, information technology (IT) has come to play a central role in the contemporary workplace. From networked communications to data storage and retrieval, IT is vital to the everyday operation of an ever-expanding array of organizations. Consequently, organizational scholars need to examine the ways in which technology structures work activities, as well as "influences organizational members' work roles and work relationships."[11] The quick and easy access to information on wire services, for instance, has decreased the need for news organizations, especially local affiliates, to produce their own news, thereby altering journalists' daily routines (i.e. how they gather and package news). Technology is not so much a tool for doing one's job more effectively or efficiently today, as it is the very environment in which one does their job. In remaking the workplace environment, technology has fundamentally altered the skills required to perform some jobs. Indeed, the decreasing cost and increasing availability of IT is directly related to the rise of citizen journalism.

Studying performances, narratives, texts, management, and technology are all ways for scholars to evaluate and assess how communicative practices mediate the tension between structure and process within an organization. The structure/process dialectic is not exclusively an internal dynamic, however. Organizations must also respond to external pressures such as the professional culture that prepares members to work in a profession. Organizational cultures and professional cultures are not the same thing.[12] Whereas an organizational culture is always unique to a specific organization and its practices, a professional culture may extend across a wide array of organizations. A **professional culture**, then is set(s) of norms and customs, artifacts and events, and values and assumptions that emerge as a consequence of formal training (i.e. education, apprenticeships, internships, etc.), membership and participation (i.e. professional associations, conferences, workshops, licenses, etc.), and recognition (i.e. industry awards and honors) within a profession. While an attorney in the USA works at a specific law firm (or organizational culture), she or he must also earn a juris doctorate (JD degree) from a law school accredited by the American Bar Association and be licensed by the bar association where one practices law (or professional culture). To appreciate why workers carry out their jobs as they do, then, requires an understanding of both organizational and professional conventions.

Characteristics of conventions

Conventions describe the norms that govern the technical and creative choices made by workers in the execution of their duties, art, or craft. For media workers, conventions influence everything from how one dresses and whom one eats lunch with to the way a news anchor reads news copy and a cameraperson frames particular shots. As these examples suggest, conventions operate at various levels, including a unit or departmental level, corporate level, and finally occupational or professional level. If it were not for conventions, workers would confront a virtually infinite array of options in how to carry out their job-related tasks. Thus, employees internalize and abide by conventions as a matter of practicality. Given the centrality conventions play in how workers carry out their jobs, it is worth considering the chief characteristics and consequences of conventions in greater detail. Conventions are motivated, shared, naturalized, resilient, and directive.

1   *Motivated.* Though conventions may appear to be arbitrary and capricious, they typically develop out of some pragmatic need even if that need is as simple as efficiency or the desire for a sense of community, belonging, and group cohesion. In the academic department of this book's authors, for example, faculty members playfully address one another as "professor," instead of by their first names. This communicative practice heightens the sense of community among faculty by creating identification between those members of the department who have doctorate degrees. Feelings of belonging always depend, in part, upon exclusion. The term "professor" fosters this feeling by distinguishing faculty from students, staff, and administrators. Conventions, then, are motivated rather than random. There is some purpose behind them even if that purpose is not immediately self-evident.

2   *Shared.* Although most of the practices in which people engage are purposeful, not all practices – even routine practices – become conventions. For practices to function as norms, they must be internalized by other employees. Simply put, conventions are shared. Creating and maintaining a curriculum vitae (i.e. detailed academic resumé) is a professional convention that academics share. The fact that an individual professor within an academic department routinely uses Microsoft PowerPoint to lecture does not make that practice a convention, as other professors can present course material however they choose to. The use of PowerPoint is a personal practice, not something one does *because* one is a professor.

3   *Naturalized.* A third characteristic of conventions is that they are naturalized and thus largely invisible. Since conventions are "the norm," workers tend to adopt and abide by them unconsciously and unreflectively. When persons act in accordance with the prevailing norms, their behaviors appear to be "natural" rather than "cultural." A common professional convention among students is raising their hand to ask a question. Despite the fact that this book's authors have never once asked students to raise their hands when they have questions,

they have all blindly accepted this behavior as convention(al) and norm(al). We are willing to bet that those same students do not raise their hands when they have questions for their friends at dinner, as the conventions of friendship differ from those of education.

4 *Resilient.* Conventions typically endure over time, often as much out of tradition as anything else. The comment, "That's just the way we've always done it," which utilizes an appeal to tradition for instance, is a fairly common response to the question, "Why do you do it that way?" Though conventions are relatively resilient or stable, they are neither fixed nor static. Indeed, as organizational demands change, so too do conventions. As we will see shortly, the rise of new conventions partially accounts for why today's news media looks very different than the news media of just 40 years ago. One of the factors scholars who employ an Organizational approach to studying the media ought to consider, then, is why and under what circumstances conventions change.

5 *Directive.* Finally and perhaps most significantly, conventions are *directive.* They sanction or authorize some practices and behaviors, and discourage or disapprove of others. In other words, conventions function not as mere suggestions for possible courses of action, but as unspoken guidelines or rules for the correct or appropriate action. Because of their motivated, shared, naturalized, resilient, and directive character, conventions – be they organizational or professional – have a significant impact on daily workplace practices and consequently on the services and products offered by media companies. Before illustrating this through a specific case study, we briefly reflect on the process of professionalization.

Professionalization

The existence and operation of professional conventions leads to **professionalization**: the process by which an individual with free will and choice is transformed (i.e. socialized) into an ideological subject (i.e. professional) whose behaviors and actions reaffirm one's status as a professional. Simply stated, professionalization is the internalization of professional conventions as common sense. Consider the "training" of a professional film director like Martin Scorsese, for instance. Although Scorsese's interest in film goes back to his childhood, his formal training did not begin until he was a student at NYU's prestigious film school. We say "formal training," as the mere act of watching films had already begun to educate and professionalize him. Having graduated with an MFA in film directing in 1966, Scorsese now had the professional credentials to begin making Hollywood films. The combination of his personal style (process) with his professional training (structure) has led to a career of critically acclaimed films and most recently an Academy Award for Best Director of *The Departed* (2006). In short, Scorsese was taught a set of filmmaking conventions, which allowed him to become a professional film maker and hence reproduce those conventions in his own work, for which he was recognized as outstanding in his field. None of this is to suggest that Scorsese is not a talented film maker, only to highlight that what counts as "excellence" in film making depends to a large extent on an adeptness with professional conventions.

This brief account of Scorsese's career highlights several interconnected dimensions of professional socialization. Once professional norms harden into common sense, arising often as a consequence of the profit-motive or as a matter of practicality, they establish the standards by which a profession measures quality and competence. These standards, in turn, serve as guides for making hires, conducting annual evaluations, determining promotions, and dispensing awards and recognition. The more fully one has been professionally socialized through one's education and training, the more likely one is to get a job. After all, one already possesses the skills that have been deemed valuable and necessary. Similarly, once in a position, the more one is able to conform to existing professional conventions, the more likely one is to be rewarded with money, promotions, responsibilities, recognition, and praise. Professionals, then, have many powerful incentives to adopt and follow professional conventions even if they are consciously unaware of them. Most professions also have professional societies to which their members belong. These societies generate literature, conduct studies, and host conventions that all function to further reinforce professional conventions. They, in effect, perform the socializing role performed early in one's career by formal education.

The News Media: an In-Depth Case Study

To better understand the ways that media organizations constrain the practices and hence the products of media workers, the remainder of this chapter undertakes a detailed case study of the news media. This section begins by recounting the historical development of the press in the USA, including its professionalization, before turning to a detailed examination of the causes, character, and consequences of journalistic conventions. The news media or "press" have a long and storied history in the USA, one that extends back to Colonial America. The colonies' first newspapers, which began to appear in the late 1600s, bore little resemblance to the newspapers of today. They were typically large, one-sided, single sheets, which earned them the nickname *broadsides*. Broadsides and the multi-page newspapers to follow were often overtly political and more than a little critical of the British crown. *Public Occurrences, Both Foreign and Domestic*, the first newspaper published in the USA, for instance, was banned after only a single issue – published on September 25, 1690 – because the government objected to Boston publisher Benjamin Harris's unfavorable depiction of British rule. Such setbacks did not deter upstart publishers, however, and during the 1700s colonial broadsides and newspapers were instrumental in challenging British authority and decree and fostering colonial solidarity. The "No *Stamped Paper* to be had" broadside (Figure 3.1), for instance, reported on colonial efforts to repeal the greatly despised 1765 Stamp Act, which

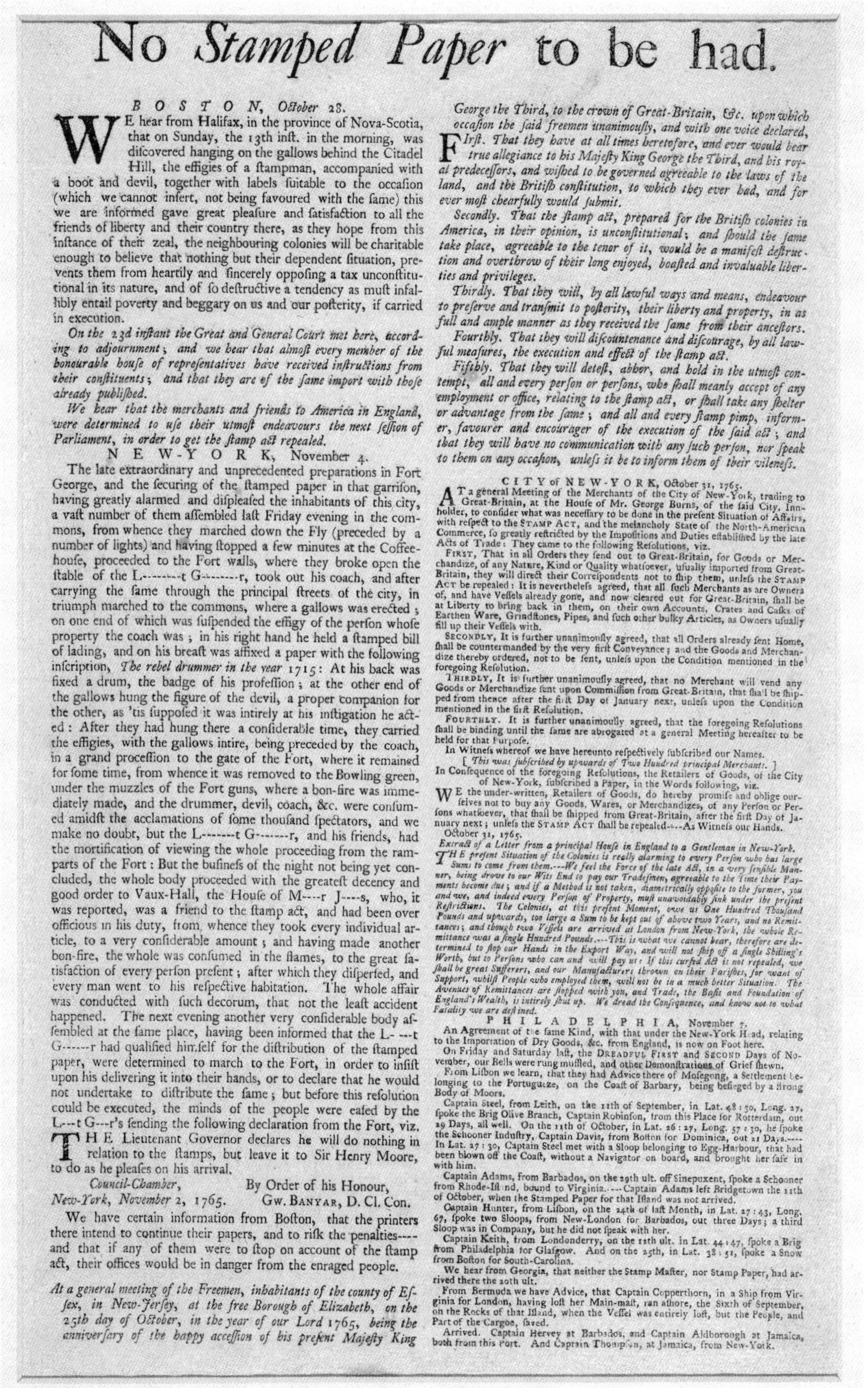

No *Stamped Paper* to be had.

B O S T O N, October 28.

WE hear from Halifax, in the province of Nova-Scotia, that on Sunday, the 13th inſt. in the morning, was diſcovered hanging on the gallows behind the Citadel Hill, the effigies of a ſtampman, accompanied with a boot and devil, together with labels ſuitable to the occaſion (which we cannot inſert, not being favoured with the ſame) this we are informed gave great pleaſure and ſatisfaction to all the friends of liberty and their country there, as they hope from this inſtance of their zeal, the neighbouring colonies will be charitable enough to believe that nothing but their dependent ſituation, prevents them from heartily and ſincerely oppoſing a tax unconſtitutional in its nature, and of ſo deſtructive a tendency as muſt infallibly entail poverty and beggary on us and our poſterity, if carried in execution.

On the 23d inſtant the Great and General Court met here, according to adjournment; and we hear that almoſt every member of the honourable houſe of repreſentatives have received inſtructions from their conſtituents; and that they are of the ſame import with thoſe already publiſhed.

We hear that the merchants and friends to America in England, were determined to uſe their utmoſt endeavours the next ſeſſion of Parliament, in order to get the ſtamp act repealed.

N E W-Y O R K, November 4.

The late extraordinary and unprecedented preparations in Fort George, and the ſecuring of the ſtamped paper in that garriſon, having greatly alarmed and diſpleaſed the inhabitants of this city, a vaſt number of them aſſembled laſt Friday evening in the commons, from whence they marched down the Fly (preceded by a number of lights) and having ſtopped a few minutes at the Coffee-houſe, proceeded to the Fort walls, where they broke open the ſtable of the L--------t G--------r, took out his coach, and after carrying the ſame through the principal ſtreets of the city, in triumph marched to the commons, where a gallows was erected; on one end of which was ſuſpended the effigy of the perſon whoſe property the coach was; in his right hand he held a ſtamped bill of lading, and on his breaſt was affixed a paper with the following inſcription, *The rebel drummer in the year* 1715: At his back was fixed a drum, the badge of his profeſſion; at the other end of the gallows hung the figure of the devil, a proper companion for the other, as 'tis ſuppoſed it was intirely at his inſtigation he acted: After they had hung there a conſiderable time, they carried the effigies, with the gallows intire, being preceded by the coach, in a grand proceſſion to the gate of the Fort, where it remained for ſome time, from whence it was removed to the Bowling green, under the muzzles of the Fort guns, where a bon-fire was immediately made, and the drummer, devil, coach, &c. were conſumed amidſt the acclamations of ſome thouſand ſpectators, and we make no doubt, but the L-------t G-------r, and his friends, had the mortification of viewing the whole proceeding from the ramparts of the Fort: But the buſineſs of the night not being yet concluded, the whole body proceeded with the greateſt decency and good order to Vaux-Hall, the Houſe of M---r J----s, who, it was reported, was a friend to the ſtamp act, and had been over officious in his duty, from whence they took every individual article, to a very conſiderable amount; and having made another bon-fire, the whole was conſumed in the flames, to the great ſatisfaction of every perſon preſent; after which they diſperſed, and every man went to his reſpective habitation. The whole affair was conducted with ſuch decorum, that not the leaſt accident happened. The next evening another very conſiderable body aſſembled at the ſame place, having been informed that the L- ---t G------r had qualified himſelf for the diſtribution of the ſtamped paper, were determined to march to the Fort, in order to inſiſt upon his delivering it into their hands, or to declare that he would not undertake to diſtribute the ſame; but before this reſolution could be executed, the minds of the people were eaſed by the L---t G---r's ſending the following declaration from the Fort, viz.

THE Lieutenant Governor declares he will do nothing in relation to the ſtamps, but leave it to Sir Henry Moore, to do as he pleaſes on his arrival.

Council-Chamber, By Order of his Honour,
New-York, November 2, 1765. Gw. BANYAR, D. Cl. Con.

We have certain information from Boſton, that the printers there intend to continue their papers, and to riſk the penalties---- and that if any of them were to ſtop on account of the ſtamp act, their offices would be in danger from the enraged people.

At a general meeting of the Freemen, inhabitants of the county of Eſſex, in New-Jerſey, at the free Borough of Elizabeth, on the 25th day of October, in the year of our Lord 1765, being the anniverſary of the happy acceſſion of his preſent Majeſty King George the Third, to the crown of Great-Britain, &c. upon which occaſion the ſaid freemen unanimouſly, and with one voice declared,

FIrſt. That they have at all times heretofore, and ever would bear true allegiance to his Majeſty King George the Third, and his royal predeceſſors, and wiſhed to be governed agreeable to the laws of the land, and the Britiſh conſtitution, to which they ever had, and for ever moſt chearfully would ſubmit.

Secondly. That the ſtamp act, prepared for the Britiſh colonies in America, in their opinion, is unconſtitutional; and ſhould the ſame take place, agreeable to the tenor of it, would be a manifeſt deſtruction and overthrow of their long enjoyed, boaſted and invaluable liberties and privileges.

Thirdly. That they will, by all lawful ways and means, endeavour to preſerve and tranſmit to poſterity, their liberty and property, in as full and ample manner as they received the ſame from their anceſtors.

Fourthly. That they will diſcountenance and diſcourage, by all lawful meaſures, the execution and effect of the ſtamp act.

Fifthly. That they will deteſt, abhor, and hold in the utmoſt contempt, all and every perſon or perſons, who ſhall meanly accept of any employment or office, relating to the ſtamp act, or ſhall take any ſhelter or advantage from the ſame; and all and every ſtamp pimp, informer, favourer and encourager of the execution of the ſaid act; and that they will have no communication with any ſuch perſon, nor ſpeak to them on any occaſion, unleſs it be to inform them of their vileneſs.

C I T Y of N E W-Y O R K, October 31, 1765.

AT a general Meeting of the Merchants of the City of New-York, trading to Great-Britain, at the Houſe of Mr. George Burns, of the ſaid City, Innholder, to conſider what was neceſſary to be done in the preſent Situation of Affairs, with reſpect to the STAMP ACT, and the melancholy State of the North-American Commerce, ſo greatly reſtricted by the Impoſitions and Duties eſtabliſhed by the late Acts of Trade: They came to the following Reſolutions, viz.

FIRST, That in all Orders they ſend out to Great-Britain, for Goods or Merchandize, of any Nature, Kind or Quality whatſoever, uſually imported from Great-Britain, they will direct their Correſpondents not to ſhip them, unleſs the STAMP ACT be repealed: It is nevertheleſs agreed, that all ſuch Merchants as are Owners of, and have Veſſels already gone, and now cleared out for Great-Britain, ſhall be at Liberty to bring back in them, on their own Accounts, Crates and Caſks of Earthen Ware, Grindſtones, Pipes, and ſuch other bulky Articles, as Owners uſually fill up their Veſſels with.

SECONDLY, It is further unanimouſly agreed, that all Orders already ſent Home, ſhall be countermanded by the very firſt Conveyance; and the Goods and Merchandize thereby ordered, not to be ſent, unleſs upon the Condition mentioned in the foregoing Reſolution.

THIRDLY, It is further unanimouſly agreed, that no Merchant will vend any Goods or Merchandize ſent upon Commiſſion from Great-Britain, that ſhall be ſhipped from thence after the firſt Day of January next, unleſs upon the Condition mentioned in the firſt Reſolution.

FOURTHLY. It is further unanimouſly agreed, that the foregoing Reſolutions ſhall be binding until the ſame are abrogated at a general Meeting hereafter to be held for that Purpoſe.

In Witneſs whereof we have hereunto reſpectively ſubſcribed our Names.

[*This was ſubſcribed by upwards of Two Hundred principal Merchants.*]

In Conſequence of the foregoing Reſolutions, the Retailers of Goods, of the City of New-York, ſubſcribed a Paper, in the Words following, viz.

WE the under-written, Retailers of Goods, do hereby promiſe and oblige ourſelves not to buy any Goods, Wares, or Merchandizes, of any Perſon or Perſons whatſoever, that ſhall be ſhipped from Great-Britain, after the firſt Day of January next; unleſs the STAMP ACT ſhall be repealed----As Witneſs our Hands.

October 31, 1765.

Extract of a Letter from a principal Houſe in England to a Gentleman in New-York.

THE preſent Situation of the Colonies is really alarming to every Perſon who has large Sums to come from them.---We feel the Force of the late Act, in a very ſenſible Manner, being drove to our Wits End to pay our Tradeſmen, agreeable to the Time their Payments become due; and if a Method is not taken, diametrically oppoſite to the former, you and we, and indeed every Perſon of Property, muſt unavoidably ſink under the preſent Reſtrictions. The Colonies, at this preſent Moment, owe us One Hundred Thouſand Pounds and upwards, too large a Sum to be kept out of above two Years, and no Remittances; and though two Veſſels are arrived at London from New-York, the whole Remittance was a ſingle Hundred Pounds.---This is what we cannot bear, therefore are determined to ſtop our Hands in the Export Way, and will not ſhip off a ſingle Shilling's Worth, but to Perſons who can and will pay us: If this curſed Act is not repealed, we ſhall be great Sufferers, and our Manufacturers thrown on their Pariſhes, for want of Support, whilſt People who employed them, will not be in a much better Situation. The Avenues of Remittances are ſtopped with you, and Trade, the Baſis and Foundation of England's Wealth, is intirely ſhut up. We dread the Conſequence, and know not to what Fatality we are deſtined.

P H I L A D E L P H I A, November 7.

An Agreement of the ſame Kind, with that under the New-York Head, relating to the Importation of Dry Goods, &c. from England, is now on Foot here.

On Friday and Saturday laſt, the DREADFUL FIRST and SECOND Days of November, our Bells were rung muffled, and other Demonſtrations of Grief ſhewn.

From Liſbon we learn, that they had Advice there of Moſegong, a Settlement belonging to the Portugueze, on the Coaſt of Barbary, being beſieged by a ſtrong Body of Moors.

Captain Steel, from Leith, on the 11th of September, in Lat. 48 : 30, Long. 27, ſpoke the Brig Olive Branch, Captain Robinſon, from this Place for Rotterdam, out 29 Days, all well. On the 11th of October, in Lat. 26 : 27, Long. 57 : 30, he ſpoke the Schooner Induſtry, Captain Davis, from Boſton for Dominica, out 21 Days.---- In Lat. 27 : 30, Captain Steel met with a Sloop belonging to Egg-Harbour, that had been blown off the Coaſt, without a Navigator on board, and brought her ſafe in with him.

Captain Adams, from Barbados, on the 29th ult. off Sinepuxent, ſpoke a Schooner from Rhode-Iſland, bound to Virginia.----Captain Adams left Bridgetown the 11th of October, when the Stamped Paper for that Iſland was not arrived.

Captain Hunter, from Liſbon, on the 24th of laſt Month, in Lat. 27 : 43, Long. 67, ſpoke two Sloops, from New-London for Barbados, out three Days; a third Sloop was in Company, but he did not ſpeak with her.

Captain Keith, from Londonderry, on the 12th ult. in Lat. 44 : 47, ſpoke a Brig from Philadelphia for Glaſgow. And on the 25th, in Lat. 38 : 51, ſpoke a Snow from Boſton for South-Carolina.

We hear from Georgia, that neither the Stamp Maſter, nor Stamp Paper, had arrived there the 20th ult.

From Bermuda we have Advice, that Captain Copperthorn, in a Ship from Virginia for London, having loſt her Main-maſt, ran aſhore, the Sixth of September, on the Rocks of that Iſland, when the Veſſel was entirely loſt, but the People, and Part of the Cargoe, ſaved.

Arrived. Captain Hervey at Barbados, and Captain Aldborough at Jamaica, both from this Port. And Captain Thompſon, at Jamaica, from New-York.

Figure 3.1 "No *Stamped Paper* to be had" broadside.
LIBRARY OF CONGRESS.

required all colonial newspapers to carry a stamp tax designed to generate revenue for the British government. The Stamp Act along with British efforts to suppress anti-government views and sentiments, which included shutting newspapers down, partially accounts for why the framers of the US Constitution were committed to guaranteeing a "free press" following the American Revolution. The belief in an independent press, free from governmental regulation and interference, is what earned the news media its reputation as the Fourth Estate. As Thomas Jefferson famously wrote:

> I am persuaded myself that the good sense of the people will always be found to be the best army. They may be led astray for a moment, but will soon correct themselves. The people are the only censors of their governors: and even their errors will tend to keep these to the true principles of their institution. To punish these errors too severely would be to suppress the only safeguard of the public liberty. The way to prevent these irregular interpositions of the people is to give them full information of their affairs thro' the channel of the public papers, and to contrive that those papers should penetrate the whole mass of the people. The basis of our governments being the opinion of the people, the very first object should be to keep that right; and were it left to me to decide whether we should have a government without newspapers, or newspapers without a government, I should not hesitate a moment to prefer the latter.[13]

Jefferson's statement suggests that he saw newspapers as vital to an informed public and thus to a healthy democracy.

As newspapers spread and flourished following the American Revolution, they remained decidedly political. In fact, many newspapers were openly sympathetic toward or even funded by particular political parties and interests: a journalistic model known as the *partisan press*. This trend continued until about the mid-1800s when newspapers, in an attempt to appeal to broader audiences, slowly began to temper their partisan messages in favor of human-interest stories. It was also during this period that six New York newspapers established the first major news wire, the Associated Press (AP), in an effort to exchange news and information more efficiently. This shift along with the relatively inexpensive cost of papers contributed to an explosion of dailies, and triggered fierce competition. Consequently, journalism (especially following the Civil War) became increasingly fascinated with scandal, corruption, and sensational headlines: a practice that came to be called *muckraking* as a result of its fondness for dredging up "muck." The trend toward salacious, personality-centered, entertainment-oriented, soft news only increased as newspapers aggressively competed for readers and advertisers. One of the most famous and nasty competitions occurred in New York between William Randolph Hearst's *Morning Journal* and Joseph Pulitzer's *New York World*. As these and other local rivals battled for greater shares of the marketplace, quality journalism committed to covering hard news was replaced by *yellow journalism*: a style that lacked any sense of social responsibility and privileged sensational and even fabricated stories and photos.

Although yellow journalism was prevalent as well as profitable throughout the late 1800s, by the turn of the century it was slowly being challenged by a more responsible model of journalism: one that eschewed tabloid news, sensational stories, publicity stunts, and excessive commercialism in favor of the impartial reporting of information regarded as vital to the public. This shift was due in large part to the increasing professionalization of journalism: a process that "included the founding of journalism schools and professional organizations as well as the formulation of several codes of ethics, such as the one drawn up by the American Society of Newspaper Editors in 1923."[14] Journalistic practices were also influenced by the publication of Walter Lippmann's *Liberty and the News* in 1920. Lippmann, a well-known essayist and editor, wrote that "the present crisis of western democracy is a crisis in journalism" because "there is no steady supply of trustworthy and relevant news."[15] Writing in a broadly libertarian tradition, Lippmann was an ardent advocate for the journalistic standard of **objectivity**, or the reporting of facts in an impartial manner. Although objectivity existed as a journalistic ideal long before Lippmann, he was vital to its widespread adoption as a professional norm following World War I.

Further professionalization of journalism in the twentieth century was fueled by two interrelated factors: growing concern over the possibility of government regulation and the advocacy of social responsibility theory. Fears among newspaper owners and editors that the government might attempt to regulate the press were far from unfounded. The Federal Radio Commission (FRC), for instance, had been established in 1927 to regulate radio following arguments by Commerce Secretary Herbert Hoover that the airwaves belong to the people and therefore ought to serve the "public interest." Mounting pressure for newspapers to submit to similar regulatory efforts ultimately led to the formation of the Hutchins Commission on Freedom of the Press in 1942.

The Commission, which was funded by Time Inc. CEO Henry Luce and headed by University of Chicago President Robert Maynard Hutchins, sought to address the question, "Is the freedom of press in danger?"[16] Comprised of academics from Yale University and the University of Chicago, whom Hutchins had appointed, the Commission on Freedom of the Press released its final 133-page report, *A Free and Responsible Press*, in 1947. In its report, the Hutchins Commission advocated a code of social responsibility for the press that included five basic services:

1   a truthful, comprehensive, and intelligent account of the day's events in a context which gives them meaning,
2   a forum for the exchange of comment and criticism,
3   the projection of a representative picture of the constituent groups in society,
4   the presentation and clarification of the goals and values of the society,
5   full access to the day's intelligence.

Response to the report was both swift and harsh, especially from journalists and editors who resented the implication that they were not doing their jobs. Despite the indignant response of the press, however, the report had a significant influence on academic thinking, and a "social responsibility" model soon became the standard in journalism schools around the country. The adoption and teaching of a common journalistic model (and, hence, set of practices) fueled the professionalization of the field, and paved the way for the rise of "accredited" journalism schools. One way to understand the history of journalism in the USA, then, is to see it as a story about the gradual transformation of journalists from independent, civic-minded, "ink-stained wretches to college-educated professionals."[17]

News organizations and journalistic conventions

Having reviewed some of the key developments in the history and evolution of journalism, we can now turn our attention to the modern-day news organization and ask how its organizational structure and processes shape the daily output of the media product we know as "news." Ideally, the **news** ought to provide the public with accurate and reliable information that assists them in better exercising their civic duties in a democratic society. In reality, however, the news is more often, explains Lance Bennett, "what newsmakers (politicians and other political actors) promote as timely, important, or interesting from which news organizations select, narrate, and package for transmission (via communication technologies) to people who consume it."[18] In other words, the news is produced (like any other commodity) not discovered (like knowledge). To understand the sizeable gap between the ideal and the actuality of what constitutes the news, we must examine the specific professional conventions that govern how news is gathered and reported. Like all conventions, the conventions of news *gathering* and *reporting* did not emerge arbitrarily. They are responses to specific situational demands.

The two major situational constraints on news gathering are the "news hole" and the "news whole," both of which are influenced heavily by the profit-motive discussed in Chapter 2. The *news hole*, or the necessity to deliver the news every day at the same time (i.e. to "fill the hole"), is one of the most powerful institutional forces in journalism and it has resulted in a series of concrete organizational practices and routines. The need to produce the news every day by a specific deadline is a heavy burden for both local and national news outlets. To meet the daily demand for news created by the news hole, journalists rely upon a series of standardized practices for collecting the news that include journalistic beats, news agencies, and punditry and press releases. **Journalistic beats** are the places and institutions where "news" is "expected" to occur on any given day, such as police stations and courthouses. These institutions comprise the criminal/legal beat, for instance, and are reliable sources of news. According to Herbert Gans, national news in the USA is overwhelmingly dominated by five beats: incumbent presidents, presidential candidates, leading federal officials, state and local officials, and alleged and actual violators of laws and mores.[19] The reason the news is dominated by a steady stream of stories about crime and politicians, then, is not because these topics and figures are inherently newsworthy, but because news organizations assign reporters to these beats. Mark Fishman describes how this journalistic practice influences what counts as "news" and what does not:

> Some happenings in the world become public events. Others are condemned to obscurity as the personal experience of a handful of people. The mass media, and in particular news organizations, make all the difference. . . . [A] crucial part of the newsmaking process—the routine work of beat reporters—[. . .] determines what becomes a public event and what becomes a nonevent. . . . [R]eporters' "sense of events," their methods for seeing the newsworthiness of occurrences, are based on schemes of interpretation originating from and used by agency officials within the institutions beat reporters cover. Nonevents are specific happenings that are seen as "out of character" within the institutional settings in which they occur. . . . To seriously entertain these occurrences as potential news would force journalists to question their own methods for detecting newsworthy events.[20]

The events that are systematically excluded from public view (i.e. the so-called non-events) as a result of prevailing news-gathering conventions, then, are really nothing more than occurrences that, if reported, would call into question the legitimacy of the beats (people and institutions) that reporters depend on for news.

In addition to news organizations gathering news from the same places day after day, they also obtain news from news agencies or wire services. **News agencies** can be corporations such as Reuters that produce and sell stories to other news providers or non-profit cooperatives like the Associated Press that work with large media companies to generate news centrally and distribute it locally. Since the major news agencies generally prepare features and news packages complete with stock images and footage, the stories they provide can generally be used by news organizations with virtually no modification. This is particularly valuable to news organizations that must meet daily print and broadcast deadlines. The use of news agencies as a central means of gathering news explains, at least partially, why the major news networks inevitably cover the same stories every day. The consistency of the news across networks does not arise because various news organizations independently "discover" the same news every day, but because they all collect news from the same beats and news agencies.

A third way that news organizations gather news is through political pundits and press releases. **Punditry** describes news that is pre-packaged by politicians and their communication consultants (i.e. press advisors and public relations managers) to promote a favorable image of a politician and her or his specific policy initiatives.[21] In the interest of *image management*, consultants constantly seek to control both the news situation and message surrounding political actors. The strategies consultants employ to control the news situation are vast and sophisticated, and range from carefully staged, scripted, and acted *pseudo events* to scheduled press briefings where politicians set the agenda.[22] One of the most (in)famous pseudo events in recent history was President George W. Bush's May 1, 2003 declaration of an end

Figure 3.2
President Bush
declaring an end
to major combat
operations in Iraq.
J. SCOTT APPLEWHITE/
AP/PA PHOTOS.

to major combat operations in Iraq aboard the aircraft carrier USS *Abraham Lincoln* under a red, white, and blue banner boldly proclaiming, "Mission Accomplished" (Figure 3.2).

In addition to staging pseudo events, consultants also attempt to manage the image of a politician by controlling the news message. Consultants and pundits accomplish this by packaging their messages as clear, concise slogans, saturating the news with these slogans, and providing some form of evidence that the message is credible. This practice, which depends upon carefully constructed *sound bites*, is often referred to as *political spin*. Such pre-packaged news, though clearly biased, is attractive to journalists because it is delivered directly to them and presented in a form that is easily reportable. Bennett estimates that nearly three-quarters of all political news comes from government officials in the form of interviews, press conferences, press releases, official proceedings, and sanctioned leaks.[23] **Press releases** are strategically prepared written or recorded statements produced for news organizations to announce something that claims to be newsworthy.

Political consultants are not the only ones who use press releases as a strategy for getting carefully controlled messages picked up as news, however. Many major corporations, non-profit organizations, scientific foundations, and even fanatical cults utilize press releases as a way to promote themselves, their views, and their products. In his 2007 book, *It's Not News, It's Fark: How Mass Media Tries to Pass off Crap as News*, Drew Curtis documents that press releases are frequently picked up, oftentimes with no changes, and run as news. Curtis calls this phenomenon the "unpaid placement masquerading as actual article," and notes that it is surprisingly common.[24] Consider, for instance, annual lists such as *People*'s Sexiest Man Alive or *Time*'s 100 Most Influential People. Each year, these magazines circulate press releases about their picks, which are then reported by mainstream news organizations as news. But is the selection and announcement of Matt Damon as 2007's sexiest man alive really news or just an advertisement for *People* magazine? In a similar vein, big drug companies often release the results of "scientific studies" announcing landmark medical breakthroughs that are in actuality little more than advertisements for their latest designer drug.

Journalistic beats, news agencies, and political pundits and press releases do more than assist news organizations in filling the daily news hole, however; they also aid them in filling it completely or wholly. The *news whole* is our phrase to describe the specific amount of time or space allotted for reporting the news each day. Has it ever seemed strange to you that regardless of the events of the day, nightly national news broadcasts are always precisely 60 minutes long? This means that journalists must gather enough news every day to fill the entire news program, but not so much news that it won't fit in the program. So, how does the need to make the news "fit" daily programming schedules constrain the practices of news gathering? The chief way it does this is by influencing the selection of stories. When journalists are sent into the field to produce news packages that will later be used locally or shared through news agencies, they know that the typical television news package is only 60–90 seconds long. Before they ever became professionals, young journalists were taught the basic formulas for creating news packages in school. Consequently, events and information that do not readily lend themselves to a short, simple, dramatic, and narrative format are commonly ignored or overlooked. Complex issues, even those vital to the public, are far less likely to see the light of your television screen or the front page of your daily newspaper than matters that can easily be reported by answering the routine who, what, where, and when questions.

The strict conventions that govern news gathering are driven in large part by the profit-motive, or the desire of news organizations to produce the news cheaply and efficiently, while simultaneously appealing to the largest audience possible. Audience share is important because it determines what can be charged for advertising time and thus affects advertising revenues.[25] In short, journalists are under considerable economic pressures to find audience-grabbing stories on short deadlines with minimal resources. Consequently, the selection of news stories often has little to do with their *newsworthiness*: their social and informational value to the public. Rather than asking what really matters to people's everyday lives or what is vital for people to know to be able to effectively carry out their civic duties, journalists simply regard the public figures and institutions that comprise their regular beats as newsworthy. Hence, the news is not something that is uncovered, explored, and reported on each day; rather, it is a product or commodity manufactured by news organizations for maximum palatability and profitability. This claim is further evidenced by news-reporting conventions.

One of the perennial issues raised about the news media is its supposed political bias; we say "supposed" because the precise nature of its bias depends upon whom you ask. In *Bias: A CBS Insider Exposes How the Media Distort the News*, Bernard Goldberg argues the news media have a left-wing bias, while in *What Liberal Bias?: The Truth about Bias and the News*, Eric Alterman contends that the news media have a right-leaning bias. The problem with this debate generally, regardless of the side being argued, is that it is utterly relative. To say that the news media have a left-wing bias presumes there is an objective, apolitical position from which to judge it. The debate also assumes (incorrectly) that all news outlets have the same political bias, as though the *New York Times* and *New York Post* were identical. The question of political bias in the news is a nonsensical one, then, especially since – despite their clear political leanings – the *New York Times* and *New York Post* cover stories in remarkably similar ways. The far more insidious bias in the news is an informational, not political, one. **Informational bias** refers to how a story is structured and told, and as Lance Bennett notes, most news stories display four informational biases.

1   *Personalization.* Most news stories focus on individuals rather than institutions, and emphasize human-interest angles and emotional impact over and often at the expense of broader social contexts and political perspectives. Simply put, news stories are people-centered; they rely heavily upon interviews, first-person accounts, eye-witness testimony, and expert opinions. The focus on individual people is designed to make stories feel more personal, direct, and immediate. But by focusing on individual actors, such as the President, in a story about economic recession, for instance, audiences are encouraged to view political issues individually rather than socially. Consequently, they are more likely to blame specific political actors for social ills and less likely to understand the underlying factors and root causes of social problems.

2   *Dramatization.* The news is overwhelmingly biased toward the narrative presentation of information. Regardless of the specific issues journalists are reporting on, those issues tend to be structured as stories, "as contrasted, for example, to analytical essays, political polemics, or more scientific-style problem reports."[26] Moreover, to heighten audience interest, journalists frequently focus on the most sensational, scandalous, and shocking details of a story. The insistence on narrativizing the news has at least two significant consequences. First, since some issues are difficult to pictorialize and require sustained analysis, their dramatization leads to inaccurate or misrepresentative reporting (if they get covered at all). Second, since narratives have beginnings, middles, and endings, dramatized news has the potential to impose a clean and tidy sense of closure on complex, enduring issues.

3   *Fragmentation.* A third information bias in the news is the tendency to treat stories in isolation, ignoring their connection to other stories and the larger contexts in which they occur. Both newspapers and televised newscasts organize the news into brief, self-contained capsules. This can foster the misimpression that the world is just a series of random, unrelated events. The compartmentalization of news stories can obfuscate not only the interconnections among

stories, but also their historical significance. Fragmented news makes the world appear chaotic and unpredictable. Indeed, the prevalence of fragmented news helps to explain why the 9/11 attacks were so utterly incomprehensible to most Americans, who had no context for understanding the connections between the economic and foreign policies of the USA, and the religious zealotry of Islamic extremists. To most Americans, the attacks of September 11, 2001 on the World Trade Center and Pentagon are isolated events with no prior history or context.

4   *Authority-disorder.* The fourth and final informational bias of the news is closely related to the first three, and in particular, the way that personalized news becomes dramatized. Since personalization leads to a focus on individuals and dramatization favors the sensational, it is common to depict the individuals and parties involved in a story as in conflict or tension. This tension is typically represented as one between authority (i.e. police, government leaders, public officials) and disorder (i.e. criminals, natural disasters, terrorism). Furthermore, since the news is comprised of individual capsules that require narrative closure, the authority-disorder tension is generally resolved either in the direction of authority through the restoration of normalcy or in the direction of disorder and the cynical view that public officials are incompetent. Consider the news media framing of Hurricane Katrina, which struck the Gulf Coast and devastated New Orleans on August 28, 2005. The story was structured around a natural catastrophe (disorder) and the government's response, as represented by Michael Brown, then Director of the Federal Emergency Management Agency (FEMA). When the government was not able to quickly restore normalcy, Brown was fired for his incompetence.

In 2002, Ott and Aoki undertook a study of the print news media's coverage in the *Washington Post*, *New York Times*, and *Los Angeles Times* of the brutal murder of Matthew Shepard. Their analysis, which included 71 news articles, demonstrated that the press framed the event as a dramatic story about a frail, innocent boy named Matthew Shepard, who was mercilessly beaten and left for dead on the open Wyoming range by two monstrous, homophobic twenty-somethings, Aaron McKinney and Russell Henderson. The story found closure in the convictions of McKinney and Henderson, both of whom received life sentences in the Wyoming State Penitentiary. But by reporting the story as it did, as an isolated and unthinkable act of violence, the news media never equipped citizens to confront (or change) the broader culture of hate and intolerance that exists around sexuality in the USA. "The news media's fascination with personalities and drama over institutional and social problems," concluded Ott and Aoki, "bring[s] . . . closure *and* resolution to the larger social issues they [public tragedies] raise . . . [and does] not serve the public well as a basis for social and political action."[27]

The informational biases of personalization, dramatization, fragmentation, and authority-disorder in the news are often visual as well as linguistic. Like journalism more broadly, press photography operates according to a strict set of professional conventions. In the early 1960s, Roland Barthes published two famous

Figure 3.3 2001 Pulitzer Prize for Breaking News Photography: federal agents removing Elián González. ALAN DIAZ/AP/PA PHOTOS

studies, *The Photographic Message* and *Rhetoric of the Image*, in which he identified the distinctive visual codes of press photography and advertising photography respectively. Barthes recognized that photojournalists are trained professionals who have learned to take pictures in a particular way, namely so that they evoke strong emotion, appear to be candid, and situate the viewer in the action. Advertising photography, by contrast, creates desire or pleasure, emphasizes careful staging, and places the viewer at a distance from its subject. The noticeable difference in visual codes between photojournalism and advertising photography is a powerful reminder that no image is objective, and that editors select the images used in the news precisely because they best conform to the aesthetic norms of photojournalism. If an image is especially adept at modeling the conventions of the press photograph, then it may even win a Pulitzer Prize, such as the photograph in Figure 3.3, which dramatically depicts the Bureau of Alcohol, Tobacco and Firearms' (ATF's) forced removal of Cuban immigrant Elián González from his uncle's home in Florida. The image vividly captures the restoration of authority, and thus conveys a strong sense of closure. Indeed, within days of this photograph, the story of Elián – a story that had garnered tremendous national and international attention – had all but disappeared in the mainstream press.

Conventions of the news magazine

Up to this point, our discussion of the news media has focused primarily on print media. But television is also an important source of news in the USA. Within the

TV news industry, there are numerous news formats, ranging from the morning talk show (e.g. *Good Morning America*, *The Today Show*, *The Early Show*) and news commentary program (e.g. *The O'Reilly Factor*, *Hardball with Chris Matthews*) to the evening news (e.g. *NBC Nightly News*, *CBS Evening News*, *ABC News*) and newsmagazine (e.g. *20/20*, *Dateline NBC*, *48 Hours*, *Primetime*, *60 Minutes*). Each of these formats employs its own distinct formula for organizing and presenting information. In this section, we highlight the formal conventions of the evening newsmagazine by drawing upon Richard Campbell's landmark study, *60 Minutes and the News: A Mythology for Middle America*.

60 Minutes is one of the most successful television shows in history, having finished in Nielsen's top 10 programs a record 23 consecutive seasons. Created in 1968 by Don Hewitt, who remains the show's executive producer, *60 Minutes* has won more Emmy awards than any other news broadcast. The show combines investigative journalism with celebrity journalism, and typically consists of two or three separately produced segments. As Campbell has demonstrated, those segments generally follow one of four well-worn formulas.

1   *News as mystery*. This type of report is what many people think of when they hear the phrase "investigative reporting" because it often involves journalists with hidden cameras, who uncover wrongdoings by playing detective and surprising or ambushing interviewees. For Campbell, stories told using this formula precede in four stages: (1) the identification of key characters, who are framed as villains or criminals; (2) the search for clues of criminal violation; (3) the stalking and ultimate confrontation of the wrongdoer about his/her misdeeds; and (4) an assurance that the wrongdoers have been brought to justice, and safety has been restored. In August 2004, for instance, *60 Minutes* aired a segment titled "Doing Business with the Enemy" that uncovered major US companies such as Halliburton were conducting millions of dollars worth of business with countries that sponsor terrorism (e.g. Iran).

2   *News as therapy*. This formula places the reporter in the position of analyst or therapist, rather than detective. In his or her capacity as therapist, the journalists performs four key roles: (1) a social commentator who endows the narrative with moral meaning by placing the interview in appropriate historical, political, or cultural context; (2) an intimate confidant to whom the interviewee can reveal private, personal details; (3) as a champion of heroic characters or a foil to villainous characters; and (4) as an inquisitor, who asks tough, confrontational questions that probe deviations from popular values. Correspondent Ed Bradley's interview, titled "Being the First Man on the Moon," of the famously private Neil Armstrong about his family and fame in July 2006 is exemplary of this formula.

3   *News as adventure*. The adventure story formula features plays like a Western and the reporter as tourist or a well-informed traveler in search of drama and adventure. The reporter-tourist is portrayed in three recurring capacities: (1) as viewers' surrogate for exploring and ultimately understanding a new, unfamiliar,

or exotic locale; (2) as nostalgic traveler (in search of a simpler, uncorrupted time: a past still reflected in small-town, Middle American values) or as seeker of the authentic, natural or "real" America behind the fast-paced, high-tech modernist exterior; and (3) as protector from foreign or alien values that somehow threaten traditional, American-heartland values. The story of the Moken people, who miraculously survived the tsunami in Asia, illustrates news as adventure. In this June 2007 story, correspondent Bob Bimon traveled to a remote island off the coast of Thailand to learn the secrets of these native peoples in "Sea Gypsies Saw Signs in the Waves."

4   *News as arbitration.* A final formula used in newsmagazines is news as arbitration, which positions the reporter as referee or arbitrator. Of the four formulas, this one shares the most in common with orthodox journalism by featuring the reporter (1) as a neutral observer, (2) who defers to experts or authorities, (3) emphasizes a dialectical rather than expository structure, (4) abandons the search for a clear, unequivocal villain, and (5) resists proving narrative closure and resolution. "The Oil Sands of Alberta," which aired in June 2006, illustrates the news-as-arbitration formula. The story described the vast oil reserves in Canada and reported on the dependence on fossil fuels and environmental debates that the reserves raise, but did not take sides or suggest what the outcome of these debates will be.

Consequences of news conventions

The professionalization of the news – and more specifically the journalistic conventions involved in news gathering and reporting – has four serious consequences. First, by deciding who and what gets covered (and conversely who and what does not get covered), the news media exercise a powerful *gatekeeping* function: the ability to control access to the public. Due to the pressures on journalists to meet deadlines, some issues, events, and actors are far more likely to be reported on than others. This system privileges organizations and politicians who possess the financial and structural resources to provide newsmakers (i.e. journalists) with ready-made-news, and disadvantages alternative, independent, and less well-funded groups and citizens seeking to promote their message. In the political arena, news conventions greatly benefit the two major political parties and their candidates, while marginalizing and ostracizing third-party or independent candidates. This bias is one of the reasons why it makes little sense to debate whether the news is leftist or rightist; the blind reproduction of the two-party system means that news is overwhelmingly centrist.

An additional side-effect of gatekeeping is *agenda-setting*, or the belief that the news media do not influence *what people think* so much as they influence *what people think about*. The news media, by covering some topics and not others, establish the important topics of the day; they, in effect, set the agenda for public dialogue. Because so much of what is reported as news is a product of journalistic beats, news agencies, and political punditry and press releases, the news media significantly restrict the diversity of topics on the public's mind. For the most part, if the media is not talking about it, neither is the public. Moreover, as profit-driven entities, news outlets frequently engage in cross-promotional efforts for their parent corporations. Just before Disney released the summer blockbuster *Armageddon* (1998), for instance, ABC News (a Disney subsidiary) repeatedly ran stories about the dangers of asteroids striking the Earth. In this case, the so-called "news" functioned as little more than a film advertisement. Conversely, news outlets occasionally censor stories that could potentially hurt their corporate image such as when the President of ABC News axed a story ABC journalists were working on regarding Disney theme parks hiring known child molesters.[28]

A second and closely related consequence of news conventions is *homogenization*. Just as news-gathering conventions limit the diversity of *what* is covered, news-reporting conventions limit the diversity of *how* it is covered. "Working practices," note Taylor and Willis, "contribute to the production of similar and less innovative programs across news production.... The routines and working practices within news production therefore act to further the shared understanding of the form of news and hence also work to ensure a reproduction of both visual style and approach to content."[29] Despite the infinite number of ways a newspaper could be structured, for instance, there is a remarkable consistency in layout across US newspapers. Nor are the similarities among papers purely stylistic. Because journalists have been professionalized by their education, training, and experience, different reporters at different newspapers are likely to cover the same story the same way. The presence of multiple newspapers in one locale, then, only creates "the appearance of choice," as both what they report on and how they report on it are likely to possess greater similarities than differences.

A dramatic increase in soft news is the third major consequence of news conventions. *Soft news* describes news that is high in entertainment value, but low in educational value; this type of news is sometimes referred to as "infotainment" because it is packaged so as to make it look important and informational despite the fact that it has no intrinsic social significance. In contrast to soft news, hard news is characterized by sustained reporting on issues important to people's lives, and in a manner that equips citizens to make informed decisions on public policy and social issues. Soft news appeals to viewers primarily on an emotional level by evoking fear, concern, or outrage. Common topics of soft news include crime (especially heinous crimes like child molestation), alcohol and drugs, gangs and violence, and fires and accidents. The degree to which the news is dominated by these types of stories is sometimes referred to as the *mayhem index*. Although the mayhem index is difficult to quantify, Bennett notes that between 1993 and 1996 the number of news stories about murder on the national news networks increased by 700 percent, while during that same time period, the actual murder rate declined 20 percent.[30] No story, however, is *inherently* soft or hard news. Even crime stories can be reported as hard news if they focus on the social causes and consequences of violence, rather than on the sensational details of the crime or the tremendous grief of the victim's family. Thus, the prevalence of soft news is a result of how the news is reported, namely according to the four informational biases identified earlier in this chapter, rather than what is reported as news.

The fourth consequence of news conventions concerns the attribution of responsibility for social ills. The ways stories are framed by journalists influences how citizens understand social problems and ultimately whom they hold responsible for those problems. In his book *Is Anyone Responsible?* media scholar Shanto Iyengar argues that most news stories are framed in one of two general ways, either episodically or thematically. "The episodic news frame," according to Iyengar, "takes the form of a case study or event-oriented report and depicts public issues in terms of concrete instance."[31] The thematic news frame, by contrast, is more likely to situate social issues in a broader, abstract context and involve a "'takeout,' or 'backgrounder,' report directed at general outcomes or conditions."[32] Episodic and thematic news frames strongly influence how citizens assign responsibility for social problems. Whereas the episodic frame leads to the blaming of individuals, typically politicians, for social problems, the thematic frame tends to hold all of us accountable for social ills. Based on what we have learned in this chapter, it probably comes as no surprise that the news is dominated by episodic frames. This is because, as Bennett explains, "the (four) information biases in the news add up to news that is episodic."[33] The danger of episodic news is that it does not serve the public well as a basis for social and political action, since it frames problems as individual rather than institutional.

Conclusion

This chapter has explored the media industry from an Organizational perspective by looking at the interplay of structure and process. We learned that organizations consist of various professionals each with specialized skills and duties they have learned through formal training and actual practice. Routine work practices that are unique to a particular organization or profession are known as conventions. To illustrate how these principles actually operate, the chapter undertook a detailed analysis of the news media. Journalistic beats, news agencies, and political pundits and press releases were shown to dominate news gathering conventions, while four primary information biases (personalization, dramatization, fragmentation, and authority-disorder) were shown to govern news-reporting conventions. Although these conventions may have developed for both pragmatic and economic reasons, they commonly result in news that is narrow, homogeneous, soft, and episodic. Despite the intensive focus on the news in this chapter, professionalization exists across media industries. Popular magazines, books, music, television, and film, therefore, are no less the product of professional conventions than is the news.

MEDIA LAB 2: DOING ORGANIZATION ANALYSIS

OBJECTIVE

The purpose of this lab is to learn to analyze the media from an Organizational perspective. Specifically, students will investigate how *news-gathering* and *news-reporting conventions* shape the selection and style of news stories.

ACTIVITY

- Divide class into small groups of 4–5 students each.
- Supply each group with a copy of the university's newspaper.
- Ask students to record their answers to the following questions.
  1   Looking at the newspaper as a whole, what are the primary journalistic beats covered? Hint: A few of them may be unique to a student paper.
  2   Compare the style and layout of this newspaper to other newspapers you are familiar with. How is it similar? Different?
  3   Select one news story from the paper and identify how, if at all, the story reflects the four information biases described by Lance Bennett. Be specific in your answer. How does the language of the article reinforce particular informational biases?
  4   Is the story you selected primarily episodic or thematic in its framing? How do you know?

SUGGESTED READING

Bennett, W.L., Lawrence, R.C., and Livingston, S. *When the Press Fails: Political Power and the News Media from Iraq to Katrina*. Chicago, IL: University of Chicago Press, 2007.

Bennett, W.L. *News: the Politics of Illusion*, 6th edn. New York: Pearson Education, 2005.

Campbell, R. *60 Minutes and the News: a Mythology for Middle America*. Chicago, IL: University of Illinois, 1991.

Cheney, G., Chistensen, L.T., Zorn, Jr, T.E., and Ganesh, S. *Organizational Communication in an Age of Globalization: Issues, Reflections, Practices*. Prospect Heights, IL: Waveland Press, 2004.

Cohen, E.D. (ed.) *News Incorporated: Corporate Media Ownership and Its Threat to Democracy*. New York: Prometheus Books, 2005.

Cohen, S. and Young, J. (eds) *The Manufacture of News: Social Problems, Deviance and the Mass Media*, revised edn. Beverly Hills, CA: Sage Publications, 1981.

Curtis, D. *It's Not News, It's Fark: How Mass Media Tries to Pass Off Crap as News*. New York: Gotham Books, 2007.

Ettema, J.S. and Whitney, D.C. (eds) *Individuals in Mass Media Organizations: Creativity and Constraint*. Beverly Hills, CA: Sage Publications, 1982.

Fallows, J. *Breaking the News: How the Media Undermine American Democracy*. New York: Vintage Books, 1997.

Fenton, T. *Bad News: The Decline of Reporting, The Business of News, and The Danger To Us All.* New York: HarperCollins Publishers, 2005.

Fischman, W., Solomon, B., Greenspan, D., and Gardner, H. *Making Good: How Young People Cope with Moral Dilemmas at Work.* Boston, MA: Harvard University Press, 2004.

Gans, H.J. *Deciding What's News: a Study of CBS Evening News, NBC Nightly News, Newsweek and Time.* New York: Pantheon Books, 1979.

Gardner, H. Irresponsible work. In *Responsibility at Work: How Leading Professionals Act (And Don't Act) Responsibly*, H. Gardner (ed.), pp. 262–82. San Francisco, CA: Jossey-Bass, 2007.

Iyengar, S. *Is Anyone Responsible? How Television Frames Political Issues.* Urbana, IL: University of Chicago Press, 1991.

Keyton, J. *Communication and Organizational Culture: a Key to Understanding Work Experiences.* Thousand Oaks, CA: Sage Publications, 2005.

Leigh, R.D. (ed.) *A Free and Responsible Press: a General Report on Mass Communication: Newspapers, Radio, Motion Pictures, Magazines and Books by the Commission on Freedom of the Press.* Chicago, IL: University of Chicago Press, 1947.

Lippmann, W. *Liberty and the News.* Princeton, NJ: Princeton University Press, 2008.

McPhee, R.D. Organizational Communication: a Structural Exemplar. In *Rethinking Communication, Volume 2: Paradigm Exemplars*, B. Dervin, L. Grossberg, B.J. O'Keefe, and E. Wartella (eds), pp. 199–212. Newbury Park, CA: Sage Publications, 1989.

Merritt, D. and Rosen, J. *Imagining Public Journalism: an Editor and Scholar Reflect on the Birth of an Idea.* Indiana University School of Journalism, Roy W. Howard Public Lecture, April 13, 1995.

Ott, B.L. and Aoki, E. The Politics of Negotiating Public Tragedy: Media Framing of the Matthew Shepard Murder. *Rhetoric and Public Affairs* 2002; 5: 483–505.

Schmidt, J. *Disciplined Minds: a Critical Look at Salaried Professionals and the Soul-Battering System that Shapes Their Lives.* New York: Rowman & Littlefield Publishers, 2000.

Schudson, M. *Discovering the News: a Social History of American Newspapers.* New York: Basic Books, 1978.

Siebert, F.S., Peterson, T., and Schramm, W. *Four Theories of the Press: The Authoritarian, Libertarian, Social Responsibility, and Soviet Communist Concepts of What the Press Should Be and Do.* Urbana, IL: University of Illinois Press, 1963.

Tuchman, G. Making News by Doing Work: Routinizing the Unexpected. *Journal of Sociology* 1973; 79: 110–31.

Tuchman, G. *Making News: a Study in the Construction of Reality.* New York: Free Press, 1978.

Whitney, D.C., Sumpter, R.S., and McQuail, D. News Media Production: Individuals, Organizations, and Institutions. In *The Sage Handbook of Media Studies*, J.D.H. Downing, D. McQuail, P. Schlesinger, and E. Wartella (eds), pp. 393–410. Thousand Oaks, CA: Sage Publications, 2004.

NOTES

1. D.C. Whitney, R.S. Sumpter, and D. McQuail, News Media Production: Individuals, Organizations, and Institutions, in *The Sage Handbook of Media Studies*, J.D.H. Downing, D. McQuail, P. Schlesinger, and E. Wartella (eds) (Thousand Oaks, CA: Sage Publications, 2004), 394.

2. G. Cheney, L.T. Christensen, T.E. Zorn, Jr, and S. Ganesh, *Organizational Communication in an Age of Globalization: Issues, Reflections, Practices* (Prospect Heights, IL: Waveland Press, 2004), 7–8.

3. Cheney *et al.*, 18.

4. K. Burke, *A Grammar of Motives* (Berkeley: University of California Press, 1969), 3.

5. E. Bell, *Theories of Performance* (Thousand Oaks, CA: Sage Publications, 2008), 16–17.

6. M.E. Pacanowsky and N. O'Donnell-Trujillo, Organizational Communication as Cultural Performance, *Communication Monographs* 50, 1983, 135–44.

7. Pacanowsky and O'Donnell-Trujillo, 144.

8. "When multiple organizational members tell (and retell) similar stories, the specifics of the stories accrue and are taken as findings about artifacts, values, and assumptions of an organization's culture" [J. Keyton, *Communication and Organizational Culture* (Thousand Oaks, CA: Sage Publications, 2005), 90].

9. Pacanowsky and O'Donnell-Trujillo, 139.

10. Keyton, 93.

11. Keyton, 112.

12. Keyton, 70.

13. T. Jefferson, Amendment I (Speech and Press), Document 8, Thomas Jefferson to Edward Carrington, in *The Papers of Thomas Jefferson Vol. 5, 1781*, J.P. Boyd (ed.) (Princeton, NJ: Princeton University Press, 1952). http://press-pubs.uchicago.edu/founders/documents/amendI_speechs8.html (accessed March 31, 2009).

14. W. Fischman, B. Solomon, D. Greenspan, and H. Gardner, *Making Good: How Young People Cope with Moral Dilemmas at Work* (Boston, MA: Harvard University Press, 2004), 25.

15. W. Lippmann, *Liberty and the News* (Princeton, NJ: Princeton University Press, 2008), 2, 6.

16. R.D. Leigh (ed.). *A Free and Responsible Press: A General Report on Mass Communication: Newspapers, Radio, Motion Pictures, Magazines and Books by the Commission on Freedom of the Press* (Chicago, IL: University of Chicago Press, 1947), 1.

17. J. Straubhaar and R. LaRose, *Media Now: Communication in the Information Age*, 3rd edn. (Belmont, CA: Wadsworth Publishing, 2001), 118.

18. W.L. Bennett, *News: The Politics of Illusion* (New York: Pearson Education, 2005), 9.

19. H.J. Gans, *Deciding What's News: A Study of CBS Evening News, NBC Nightly News, Newsweek and Time* (New York: Pantheon Books, 1979), 9–11.

20. M. Fishman, News and Nonevents: Making the Visible Invisible, in *Individual in Mass Media Organizations: Creativity and Constraint*, J.S. Ettema and D.C. Whitney (eds) (Beverly Hills, CA: Sage Publications, 1982), 219.

21. This definition of punditry is specific to the USA. In other countries such as the UK, the term is less pejorative and refers to respected experts who offer valuable opinions on news events.

22. Bennett, 142–3.

23. Bennett, 125.

24. D. Curtis, *It's Not News, It's Fark: How Mass Media Tries to Pass Off Crap as News* (New York: Gotham Books, 2007), 60.

25. Bennett, 92.

26. Bennett, 46.

27. B.L. Ott and E. Aoki, The Politics of Negotiating Public Tragedy: Media Framing of the Matthew Shepard Murder, *Rhetoric and Public Affairs* 5, no. 3, 2002, 498.

28. Bennett, 99.

29. L. Taylor and A. Willis, *Media Studies: Texts, Institutions and Audiences* (Malden, MA: Blackwell Publishers, 1999), 128.

30. Bennett, 14.

31. S. Iyengar, *Is Anyone Responsible? How Television Frames Political Issues* (Urbana, IL: University of Chicago Press, 1991), 14.

32. Iyengar, 14.

33. Bennett, 53.

4 Pragmatic Analysis

In 2004, pop musician Justin Timberlake accidentally exposed the breast of fellow musician Janet Jackson for a few seconds to a televised public during the halftime show of Superbowl XXXVIII. The Federal Communication Commission (FCC) responded by fining CBS, the show's distributor, $550,000 for featuring an instance of nudity on public television. Yet when director John Cameron Mitchell released his film *Shortbus* to a relatively small number of public American theatres in 2006, the FCC did not react to the film's sexual content with fines. Although *Shortbus* features explicit depictions of heterosexual and homosexual sex acts like fellatio and masturbation, the unrated film premiered to favorable critical reviews, accrued modest box office success, and earned multiple critical film awards without any real trouble from the FCC.

Upon first glance it may appear that these actions are inconsistent. How can the momentary flash of a woman's breast receive such a hefty fine from the government while the public screening of graphic sex acts goes unsanctioned? And yet, the American public apparently shared the FCC's logic because no groups organized at the time to protest the government's seemingly inconsistent intervention into one and not the other. Given the unique contexts of each example, what framework helps us resolve this apparent conflict and understand how the wildly different reactions are both appropriate?

This chapter asks the question, what should be the government's role in media? This relationship, of course, varies greatly from society to society. In some countries, the media is state-owned, -controlled, and -run: a sort of propagandistic arm of the government. In most democratic societies, the media is "relatively" independent of the government, often performing the function of "the Fourth Estate." But even in democratic societies, government and media are not completely independent, and, indeed, the media industry favors some involvement and regulation by the government. Without government-imposed copyright laws, for instance, the film industry would be severely hurt (financially) by movie piracy.

But when and under what circumstances is regulation needed? And how much regulation is enough without being too much? In the past, attempts to answer this question have often relied on abstract principles such as free speech and public interest. Although these are certainly important principles, without some guiding theoretical framework to suggest how these concepts should be utilized in practice, it is very difficult to approach the relationship between government and media in a critical way. This is where our chapter differs from most on the subject. Rather than presenting an historical overview of government regulation as a loose theme in media studies, we offer the philosophical perspective of Pragmatism as a guiding heuristic for critically evaluating government regulation of the media. We will begin by outlining some of the major tenets and thinkers of Pragmatism before looking at how Pragmatist ideas help us better understand the process of regulation in the American media industries.

Pragmatism: an Overview

Pragmatism is the branch of philosophy that assesses truth in terms of effect, outcome, and practicality. Unlike earlier, metaphysical philosophers who viewed truth as a transcendental constant waiting to be discovered, Pragmatists claim that truth depends on the degree to which a concept or theory provides us with useful results in the process of solving problems. Metaphysical truths by their nature cannot actually be fully known, and many Pragmatists argue that believing or not believing in them has no real bearing on one's daily life. Instead, the truth of an idea or course of action (and therefore its merit) should be based on tangible results and the possible consequences of supporting or disregarding it. As a result, truth becomes a sort of label, a quality that a thing can possess or lack, and it is always dependent on contextual factors.

Pragmatism is often referred to as the only significant American contribution to world philosophy, and the connections between Pragmatism's emphasis on practicality and the American Protestant work ethic are not difficult to see. In addition, almost all key Pragmatic thinkers have come from American institutions. The philosopher Charles Saunders Peirce is credited with actually coining the term in the late nineteenth century, but other key thinkers have played a more important role in developing the philosophy into its current form. We choose to focus on three in this chapter: William James, John Dewey, and Richard Rorty.

William James (1842–1910)

William James was a Harvard professor and one of the most important early Pragmatic philosophers. In both *Pragmatism* (1907) and its sequel, *The Meaning of Truth* (1909), James in effect "founded" the American school of Pragmatism by popularizing Peirce's own obscure work on the subject (which might have otherwise been forgotten). James was among the first to stress the practical application of philosophy to one's life. "The whole function of philosophy," he writes, "ought to be to find out what definite difference it will make to you and me, at definite instants of our life, if this world formula or that world formula be the true one."[1] This focus on the consequences of individual belief is a marked quality of James's writing on Pragmatism. He believed that individuals could mature and grow by addressing personal problems through a Pragmatic lens, and he stressed a flexible moderation between extremes as the best way to achieve this goal. Pre-eminent Pragmatic scholar Cornel West sees this focus on the personal as a natural extension of James's comfortable socio-economic status: "James was preoccupied with the state of his and others' souls, not the social conditions of their lives."[2] Instead, the Pragmatic focus on larger social issues is primarily the result of the philosophical work of John Dewey.

John Dewey (1859–1952)

John Dewey is more popularly known as a great pillar in American educational theory of the twentieth century, but his theories on the nature of education are intrinsically tied to his own Pragmatic philosophy. His major works in relation to Pragmatism include *Reconstruction in Philosophy* (1919) and *The Quest for Certainty* (1929). Throughout his work Dewey situated the process of knowing and learning within the field of human activity and experience. He asserted that thought is the direct result of physical beings encountering difficulties in their daily lives and attempting to generate ways of overcoming those difficulties. For Dewey, "imaginative recovery of the bygone is indispensable to successful invasion of the future, but its status is that of an instrument."[3] In other words, we learn from past experiences in order to manage future ones. Thought, then, is practical by nature, and Dewey believed that the metaphysical focus of philosophy inappropriately divorced human thought from its roots in practical concerns. He mirrored James in his claims that philosophy should return to its original function as a tool in correcting problems.

However, Dewey importantly expanded the focus of Pragmatic thought from individual problems to larger social issues through his work on progressive education. Educational institutions at the time concentrated heavily on the rote memorization of facts and processes, a practice that Dewey found deeply troubling. Operating from a Pragmatic perspective, he claimed that educators should instead focus on training students to develop a variety of problem-solving skills in order to make them more productive and responsible citizens of a democratic society. In this way, social problems would decrease as the populace became more educated in practical, flexible ways of improving the world. These thoughts regarding Pragmatic education were instrumental in connecting individual evolution to social improvement, and in many ways his work paved the way for the tenets of Pragmatist thought we have today. However, the budding American philosophy still faced a number of conceptual problems. These problems became the focus of one of the most important scholars in contemporary Pragmatism, Richard Rorty.

Richard Rorty (1931–2007)

Richard Rorty began in the 1960s as a scholar of analytic philosophy, a branch of thought related to Pragmatism that roughly aligns philosophical work with the empiricism of the hard sciences. However, as represented in works like *Consequences of Pragmatism* (1982) and *Contingency, Irony, and Solidarity* (1989), he spent much of his career (eloquently) defending Pragmatism as a distinct philosophy and diffusing some of the perspective's perceived weaknesses. Rorty railed against the uselessness of metaphysical philosophy because he found it impossible and sterile. For Rorty, metaphysical philosophical approaches to life are uninspiring, merely the "search for a way in which one can avoid the need for conversation and deliberation and simply tick off the way things are."[4] Those who engage in Pragmatic approaches may give up the awesome search for some deeper, more complete meaning in life, but in turn they gain a more profound understanding of human systems and an appreciation for human agency.

Rorty was also an important figure in overcoming one of the key criticisms leveled against Pragmatism: relativism. **Relativism** is the belief that diverse approaches and theories related to a given subject are all equally correct. Action becomes difficult in a relativistic lens because there is no consistent truth to act upon. Because Pragmatism abandons the search for underlying truths on a topic, critics often see it as a relativist approach that cannot practically address the problems it purports to solve. However, Rorty drew an important distinction between *relativism* in the metaphysical sense and *possibilities* as they apply to the real world. Pragmatists are relativistic when it comes to metaphysical theories, in the sense that all searches for essential truth are equally valid because none of them actually makes any real difference. However, when it comes to lived experience and situations, Pragmatists entertain options only to the point that they can be discussed, tested and selected in the process of problem solving. "When such an alternative is proposed," Rorty writes, "we debate it, not in terms of categories or principles but in terms of the various concrete advantages and disadvantages it has."[5] Thus, Pragmatists avoid spinning in relativistic circles by considering and organizing multiple ideas according to their social use.

The collective ideas of James, Dewey, and Rorty regarding practical application, social utility, and informed discernment provide a foundation for a Pragmatic perspective on the government regulation of media industries. Pragmatism allows us to judge the worth of regulation according to the perceived outcomes and effects of the regulation. In a very rough sense, regulatory policy is "true," worthy or good if it clearly benefits American society or helps to concretely correct social problems. Careful consideration of many factors and deliberation between multiple options are the hallmarks of quality government regulation; engaging in such debates helps ensure that the resulting policy best meets the many needs of society. "Bad" regulation, in turn, does not provide definite social benefits or stems from constant, predetermined or uncontested truths and beliefs about the world. In a way, evaluating media regulation from a Pragmatic perspective is appropriate because it echoes Dewey's notion of "pragmatic meliorism," or the recognition of the elements present in a historical moment and a dedication to developing ways of improving them.[6] We present a formal paradigm for making these kinds of judgments below.

A Pragmatic Approach to the Government Regulation of Media

Two concepts provide the standards for evaluation within a Pragmatic approach to media: consequences and contingencies. **Consequences** refer to the clear effects of a given regulation on society at large. Generally, consequences must be beneficial to society if we are to deem the regulation a good one. Does the policy stop advertisers from misrepresenting products and potentially causing harm to significant portions of the population? Does the regulation increase the likelihood that traditionally underrepresented portions of the population share in the production of media messages? The use of consequences as a standard of judgment reflects the Pragmatic focus on the tangible results of a belief as the measure of its truth. However, it should also be apparent that the above examples are based on contemporary judgments of what actually constitutes a social benefit. After all, people have only recently recognized the increasing of diversity as an important or worthy social goal of regulation. From this example, we can see that consequences are always tied to the historical moment.

The fact that we can only make judgments about consequences as historical individuals speaks to the second standard, **contingencies**, or the factors a regulation should address as a result of context and situation. The social norms of any given moment, as well as predominant mediums or types of technology present, all form a group of contingent factors that influence the possible types of regulation. Generally, a quality regulation must adequately take into account and respond to the socio-historical factors in play during its creation. In addition, it must consider these factors within the aforementioned framework of social utility. For example, prior to the invention of the internet, no one dreamed of debating the regulation of virtual or simulated child pornography. The historical advent of the web prompted the need for this debate, and the unique opportunities presented by an online medium directed it, but the debate was still centered on the consequence of protecting children. The use of contingencies to complement our understanding of consequences mirrors the Pragmatist focus on considering and evaluating multiple options in the process of solving problems. In a sense, the best regulatory solutions are those that have beneficial consequences according to the contingencies of their historical moment.

In addition to the contingencies presented by social or historical contexts, the regulation of American media must also respond to a particular set of regular or ever-present contingencies unique to the American context. It may seem strange to you that a factor can be both regular and contingent. The Pragmatist philosophy itself hinges on a rejection of constants. However, it is important to understand that these factors are *regular in their presence* but *contingent upon one another at any given time*. In other words, government regulation must always respond to these particular factors, and the best regulations balance them, but the degree to which one is valued over the other varies from moment to historical moment.

The first set of regular contingencies is the tension between free speech and public interest. The freedoms of speech and press granted by the First Amendment of the US Constitution guarantee the open expression of ideas and the existence of media outlets beyond federal ownership and control. A media industry that is able to freely report and comment upon events functions as an informal check in the American political system. Taken together, the twin freedoms often give good reason to hold back government regulation that might impede or censor the free circulation of ideas. At the same time, a completely independent media would quickly fall apart. Prior to the government regulation of the radio industry, different private companies would often use the same airwaves and inadvertently jam one another's signal. Before the advent of government-regulated telephone service, it was often necessary for families to possess multiple telephones, one for each privately maintained phone network they subscribed to.[7] Thus, at times it is necessary for the government to intervene in the interest of the public in order to make a media industry more efficient. The resulting tension between the regular contingencies of free speech and public interest represents a uniquely American dichotomy that debates about government regulation must always consider. Typically, the dominant social norms or political climate of the age will direct which concept trumps the other in relation to regulation. Quality regulation, however, should always consider both, and later in the chapter we will look at how this philosophical tension translates into particular examples of media regulation.

The second set of regular contingencies is the interplay between government regulation and media self-regulation. These contingencies are in some ways an extension of the public-interest focus. They are based in the social responsibility theory of the press, or the notion that the media is in the service of the public and should be guided by issues of public concern. Early media legislators reasoned that airwaves were a publicly owned, finite national resource. Any industry hoping to lease this resource should have the public's interest in mind, and it became the federal government's responsibility to manage airwave use based on this principle. Through the Federal Communications Commission (FCC; which regulates broadcasting, wire, satellite, and cable services) and the Federal Trade Commission (which regulates advertising and public relations), the government has historically used the notion of public interest to decide which radio stations to license, what times questionable content can be broadcast, and more. However, at times the media industries have made the conscious decision to regulate themselves in an effort to reduce the scope of government intervention. While the FCC still controls industry aspects like broadcast licensing, many media outlets have devised their own rules in relation to best practices or questionable content. Again, like the first set of contingencies, the use of federal and industry-based regulation varies with the social and political climate, but the presence of the dialectic always informs new regulatory policy.

Overall, the central tenets of consequences and contingencies provide a Pragmatic framework from which we can evaluate the regulation of American media. Regulation is directly tied to social and historical factors, but the American context also gives rise to the regular contingencies of free speech versus public interest and government versus media self-regulation. With all of these factors to consider, it should be clear that the process of deciding upon the best form of regulation is a difficult one. Government officials and industry representatives have to balance a number of different (and sometimes competing) issues in attempting to address social problems related to the media. The remainder of this chapter will focus on some of the more prevalent issues within the American media and examples of how different bodies have responded through regulation. As you read, pay special attention to the ways in which regular contingencies find expression in specific media policies.

Issues in the Regulation of American Media

The history of American media regulation is full of many compelling topics. This section focuses on six particular thematic areas within media regulation that have rich and varied histories. We have grouped regulations into thematic areas according to the practical ends or problems that they address. Additionally, each section is followed by a brief discussion where we provide our own interpretation of the regulations in question. In this way, we hope to provide you with some initial ideas about how to critically respond to the regulation of media from a Pragmatic stance. The first three themes deal primarily with patterns of media ownership, and the last three concentrate on issues dealing with media content. The six themes are: combating monopoly, protecting intellectual property, maintaining national interest, promoting diversity, managing morality, and ensuring accuracy.

Combating monopoly

Regulations designed to prevent media monopolies have focused historically on limiting the amount of a given market that any one company can own. These policies cover broadcasting, programming, and a number of other aspects of the industry. Regulations in this tradition often work toward the practical goal of ensuring that healthy competition remains a vital part of the American media landscape.

One of the clearest historical examples of anti-monopoly regulation is the Financial Interest and Syndication Rules (often abbreviated to Fin-Syn Rules). Various television stations proliferated after the medium was introduced in the first half of the nineteenth century, but the major networks of ABC, NBC, and CBS came to dominate the airwaves during the 1950s. By enlisting many local stations throughout the country as broadcast affiliates, the networks had an unparalleled and far-reaching influence on the American public. The FCC feared that the three networks were gaining too much power over their remaining competitors, and they passed the Fin-Syn Rules in 1970 to correct this trend. The primary purpose of the Fin-Syn Rules was to break up the perceived monopoly of the major networks by limiting the networks' financial control over their programming.

Syndication, generally speaking, refers to the process of producing and selling programming. Networks can purchase programs from independent production companies or commission programs from network-owned companies. Prior to Fin-Syn, ABC, NBC, and CBS were all moving toward a vertically integrated syndication system where they produced and broadcast a great deal of their own programming. However, the newly enacted Fin-Syn Rules limited the amount of broadcasted programming the major networks could hold the financial rights to. In combination with the Prime Time Access Rule, which reduced the amount of network-produced programming the three could broadcast between 7 and 11 p.m., the Fin-Syn Rules forced the major networks to purchase syndicated programming from other, smaller production companies. In addition, the rules prohibited the networks from retaining financial rights to off-network syndicated shows (original network programming rerun on non-network stations).

With the rise of the Fox network and the growing popularity of cable throughout the 1980s, the networks slowly began losing their perceived stranglehold on the American media market. Subscribing to cable services and their diverse array of specialty channels was now a viable option for many Americans. The FCC responded to this shifting social trend by relaxing the Fin-Syn Rules in 1993 to allow networks to hold the financial rights to half of their prime-time broadcast line-up. In 1995 the FCC abolished them all together, which (understandably) resulted in a system where the networks produced or co-produced much of their prime-time line-ups.[8] As a historical example of government regulation, the Fin-Syn Rules represented an attempt to halt a network programming monopoly to promote the growth of independent stations and production companies as a source of media competition.

The repealing of the Fin-Syn Rules was one example of a larger trend toward federal deregulation (and increased media self-regulation) that characterized the 1980s and 1990s. The most salient example of this deregulation related to media monopoly is the Telecommunications Act of 1996. The Act shifted the regulations on ownership patterns in broadcast, telephone, and cable industries. For example, prior to 1996, the FCC capped the amount of stations an individual could own at seven television channels and 14 radio stations (seven each of AM and FM, and only one per market area at that). The new language in the Act abandoned this strict formula and bases current ownership rules on relative audience size. Though there is no specific limit on the number of television and radio stations a single broadcaster may own, ownership is restricted to no more than 35 percent of the national audience for television and varies according to market size for radio. The Act also allowed companies to purchase and control multiple mediums in an unprecedented way. This resulted in increased cross ownership of television and radio stations in the same market, and it allowed cable companies to expand their offerings to telephone services (and vice versa).

The deregulatory spirit of the Act may seem counter-productive for a government hoping to combat media monopolies. However, legislators believed that decreasing ownership barriers would in fact spur competition, increase content quality, and lower prices for consumers. The Act continued to operate within the historical public-interest paradigm because it "equated the public interest with a competitive economic environment . . . in which consumer and producer desires and needs can be matched efficiently in the marketplace, not structured by regulators."[9] The logic here is that fewer restrictions on ownership result in more possibilities for more people, thereby increasing the potential for competition across all media markets. The Act safeguards against monopoly by instilling a traditional economic system of supply and demand that encourages the media to monitor itself. As we will see, this "free-market" approach to the media is often used to justify acts of deregulation in the American context.

From a Pragmatic perspective, the Fin-Syn Rules and the Telecommunications Act of 1996 invite a mixed judgment. Most media critics of the 1996 Act agree that its free-market logic failed to inspire competition; contemporary media industries are marked by an increase of corporate mergers and conglomerations that resemble monopolies (see Chapter 2). However, the Act was a genuine attempt to respond to the economic, political, and social climate of the 1990s. The Fin-Syn Rules, on the other hand, did not clearly consider multiple contingencies (aiding smaller production companies to the obvious detriment of the networks), but they did result in a diversity of programming options for the American public. These examples reveal that the Pragmatic evaluation of regulation is not often a clear process of sorting regulations into "good" and "bad" categories, but rather a nuanced assessment of the factors that inform the creation and effect of a regulation.

Protecting intellectual property

Regulations concerning intellectual property in the media industry deal with legally protecting the creative work of artists. Policies and technologies in this area establish clear parameters regarding what work can be protected, how it should be protected, and any limits placed on that protection. In addition, these regulations also stipulate the ways in which creative work can be legally disseminated and used in the media.

The most familiar form of intellectual property protection is **copyright**, or the granting of exclusive control of a creative work to that work's creator. Although the practical purpose of copyright is to legally award a creator power over the use of his/her work, its theoretical purpose is to ensure that individuals will continue to generate innovative products. After all, if there were no way for creators to make money off of their work, much less stop others from using their works toward financial interests other than their own, why would anyone choose to become a creator? This aspect of copyright is especially important to media industries because they are in the business of marketing and selling innovation. Without new television shows or broadcast technology, the media industry would cease to exist.

The notion of owning one's own creative work is actually spelled out in Article 1 of the US Constitution, but the various resulting copyright laws could not keep up with increasing changes in technology and the media. Congress passed the Copyright Law of 1978 in order to correct many of the problems with earlier laws. As a result of the 1978 Law (and certain Acts in 1998), we now have a flexible system of copyright that is able to keep up with most forms of technological innovation. Contemporary copyright protection gives a work's author/creator the exclusive control over the reproduction, dissemination, and sale of the work. A work retains this protection for the lifetime of its creator plus 70 years, upon which the holder of the copyright can renew it. Moreover, a work is protected the second an author creates it in a physical medium (such as a computer or film strip). This means that authors enjoy the benefits of copyright protection even if they have not officially registered their work. Most importantly, copyright is limited in certain ways: small portions of a work can be copied under the notion of *fair use* (in scholarly contexts, for example), and copyright can only cover the *material expression* of an idea, not the idea itself. You could not copyright your personal interpretation of the events of September 11, 2001, for example, but you could copyright a particular song or screenplay that expresses those views.

The legal system of copyright also stipulates rules regarding the distribution of creative works, and these systems have given rise to additional regulatory agencies in the media industries. Because it would be virtually impossible for musicians to keep track of all of the film directors and television producers who use their copyrighted songs, licensing companies like Broadcast Music Inc. (BMI) and the Recording Industry Association of America manage the collection and distribution of musicians' royalty fees. BMI is even responsible for licensing music for use in nightclubs, hotels, and restaurants.[10] The Motion Picture Association of America performs a similar function in the film industry, gathering royalty fees from the use of films (for example, in the popular DVD board game *Scene It!*). These companies implement copyright law and represent one of the various ways copyright is actually enforced in the media industries.

A more recent form of intellectual property protection closely related to copyright is industry-based **digital rights management** (DRM for short). DRM refers to any number of different software programs that media industries employ to control the distribution and use of digital intellectual property. It attempts to duplicate for the online/digital world the types of protection granted by copyright and medium in the real world.[11] Digital versions of intellectual property, such as music or movie computer files, are by nature much easier to copy and pirate than their real-world counterparts (CDs and DVDs), so DRM represents an extra level of security attached to these digital versions. This security takes many forms. One of the most familiar to college students is the type of DRM embedded in products purchased from Apple's iTunes store. iTunes limits users from playing purchased songs or movies on more than five Apple devices at any one time, and users can only burn a playlist of songs up to seven times. Users are not allowed to burn movies.[12] Apple began selling DRM-free versions of favorites by the likes of the Rolling Stones and Frank Sinatra in May of 2007,[13] and has since made its entire music library DRM-free.

In theory, both copyright and DRM seem to represent attempts by the government and the media industry to protect the intellectual property of individuals. However, critics of these systems claim that they actually protect private corporate interests. Some agree that the American system of copyright provides a fairly good way to ensure people are paid for their creative work, but they point out that contemporary copyright law often goes beyond its original, historical intention to unnecessarily hamper creativity and protect businesses.[14] Others claim that the rise of DRM signals a shift away from legal regulatory standards that historically work in the public interest to industry-based technological guards that privilege the rights of owners over customers.[15] Pragmatically speaking, both copyright and DRM work toward correcting issues related to information piracy, but both fall short of ably balancing issues of free speech and the public interest. While copyright at least attempts to preserve public interest through the doctrine of fair use, DRM is almost entirely economic in nature. Thus, they are both somewhat flawed forms of regulation, with DRM being the more significantly problematic of the two.

Maintaining national interest

Media regulations with the goal of maintaining national interest are concerned primarily with American domestic infrastructure and global image. Often most apparent in times of war, these regulations ensure that media technology and practices do not compromise national security and the government's ability to protect the public. Their association with issues of federal privilege and restricted information often makes them quite controversial.

A notable historical example of this type of regulation is President Clinton's Escrow Encryption Standard of 1994. **Encryption** is the process of scrambling important digital messages by software so only those who possess a complementary decoding program can read them. As encryption technology increased in complexity throughout the 1980s and 1990s, government officials worried that such systems would hamper the government's ability to intercept communications that undermined national security. The federal government had restricted the export of powerful encryption software to other countries according to the Export Administration Act, but these restrictions had grown increasingly lax since the end of the Cold War.[16] As a result, the Clinton administration enacted the Escrow Encryption Standard to provide the federal government with a way of gaining access to encrypted messages sent over telephone wires that they felt posed a national threat.

The Standard outlined a system where the government authorized certain companies to manufacture encryption chips (called Clippers) that would then be installed in communications devices like fax machines and computers. An independent executive agency would collect the decoding keys, split them in half and distribute them between two separate facilities. This was primarily a security measure; any half key would be useless without accessing its complementary half in the other facility. The government could appeal to the agency for the two halves of the necessary decoding key only when it had reasonable cause to suspect that a message endangered national security. In many ways, the Escrow Encryption Standard worked as a trade-off. It offered the public access to powerful encryption software, but it also provided a back door for government officials to decode and read encrypted messages. It was also a way for them to strike a balance "between a person's right to privacy and the government's ability to monitor hostile foreign governments, terrorists and criminals."[17] However, lukewarm reception by technology industries and public backlash over privacy invasion forced the government to abandon the Standard only a few years after its inception.

The Escrow Encryption Standard was one way the federal government has tried to regulate media in relation to foreign threats. During times of actual war, the government also invokes a number of other regulations on the media, and we can see many examples of these policies in the media coverage of the war in Iraq. For example, embedded journalists are often censored in what information they are allowed to broadcast. Award-winning reporters Peter Arnett and Geraldo Rivera were both removed from Iraq on the same day in 2003 for infractions of "too much information." While Rivera mistakenly revealed on national television the location of the 101st Airborne Division he was stationed with, Arnett consented to an interview on Iraqi TV where he spoke critically of the American war effort.[18] Arnett's dismissal echoes of the silent regulatory pressure placed on the media overall to keep dissenting opinions on war quiet.[19] Another restriction on the media during the Iraq war is the Bush administration's now famous refusal to publish pictures of coffins containing the bodies of American soldiers. Although the administration officially claimed that they halted publication of the photos to maintain the privacy of the soldiers' families, many speculated that it was really an attempt to block negative images of the war from the public eye. The ensuing debate over the pictures between proponents of national interest and freedom of information[20] reflects the greater problem of how to best manage the particular demands of war without sacrificing peacetime standards.

Evaluating the Escrow Encryption Standard and various wartime policies from a Pragmatic perspective yields fairly negative judgments. The Encryption Standard was a Pragmatic failure because it simply did not make much of an impact at all. Additionally, it failed to gain public support because it neglected to adequately address the contingency of the American right to privacy. Similarly, while some of the wartime policies are pragmatically functional (limiting Rivera's free speech regarding troop location to protect American forces), others are rather questionable (limiting Arnett's free speech or the publication of coffin photos because they tarnish the national image of the war). Regulations in the service of national interest by their nature champion the public interest over free speech, but better ones carefully consider the ways to manage both.

Promoting diversity

Regulations with the end goal of promoting diversity in media industries have attempted in some way to establish a sense of equality in media content. Because wealthy, privileged social groups usually have the most access to media outlets (and very often own them), these regulations are motivated by the desire to ensure that minority viewpoints and perspectives find a place on television and radio as well.

One of the clearest examples of this type of regulation is the Fairness Doctrine established in 1949. The Fairness Doctrine was an FCC policy that urged broadcasting stations to air programming on controversial issues and fairly represent both sides of the issues to viewers. Its supporters justified the Doctrine by claiming that it was in the public interest to hear both sides of an issue. This might sound like a good way to promote diversity, but most scholars agree that it actually decreased the amount of controversial material on air. Rather than give up precious airtime to both sides of a given issue, many television and radio stations avoided covering such costly issues all together. Many stations also complained that the Doctrine violated their First Amendment rights by dictating what material they had to cover. Moreover, the rule resulted in the impression that all ideas and perspectives on an issue are equally good, something not always true in the real world. The FCC voluntarily rescinded the policy in 1987 as a consequence of "free-market" logic and deregulation, but we still find glimmers of its underlying ideology today. When we see a news program invite both a supporter of evolution and a supporter of intelligent design to comment on the origin of humanity, we are looking at vestiges of the Fairness Doctrine. However, the demise of the Doctrine has also led to the creation of new television and radio programs that communicate a single point of view, like *Fox News* or *Democracy Now!*.

Another example of regulation intended to promote diversity is the equal time rule, which is still in place today. The rule clearly outlines how stations must handle the broadcast of political advertisements for primary or general elections. Television and radio stations cannot refuse airtime to paying political candidates and must charge candidates the lowest rate they would charge other advertisers. Stations must charge all candidates equally. If the station chooses to give free advertising to a particular candidate, it must offer all other candidates an equal amount of free time with a roughly equal audience size (audience size is determined by a number of factors, including time of broadcast or day of the week). As a whole the equal time rule addresses a very narrow part of the industry, but at times it has led to some interesting situations within broadcast media. For example, after actor Arnold Schwarzenegger officially announced his candidacy during the 2003 race for the California governor's office, broadcast television stations were prohibited from airing any of his films under the equal time rule.[21] If they did air a film, they risked having to give time to the other 134 candidates equivalent to the film's length.

Comparing the Fairness Doctrine and the equal time rule from a Pragmatic perspective yields judgments similar to the public perception of these regulations. The Fairness Doctrine had clear negative consequences in that it reduced the amount of controversial issues on air, and it trampled over the regular contingency of free speech by stipulating content. In this sense, the Doctrine was probably not one of the better examples of diversity regulation. However, the equal time rule promoted diversity in a Pragmatically responsible way. The rule results in equal access to the media for all public candidates, and it is built upon contingencies (current rates for advertising, rules that only apply when a station gives away free advertising, etc.). Rather than enforcing a blanket understanding of diversity like the Fairness Doctrine, the equal time rule presents a flexible system of encouraging equality without specifying or restricting content.

Managing morality

Regulations concentrated on the management of morality in media content and programming are one of the more controversial areas in media industry law. Because one cannot truly "legislate" morality without endangering free speech, the types of regulations in this tradition often (1) offer general guidelines rather than definite understandings of issues related to morality and (2) restrict access and consumption of questionable texts rather than their production. The three key types of regulated media content are obscenity, profanity, and indecency.

Obscenity has been a historically difficult term to define, but most obscene media content is sexually explicit in nature. Obscene material is not protected by the freedom of speech. Although this standard has, on occasion, been applied to non-broadcast material, it is overwhelmingly used in the evaluation of broadcast content. The 1973 court case *Miller vs. California* famously defined obscene content according to a three-pronged test. Content is considered obscene when it meets all of the following standards:

1 the average person, applying contemporary community standards, would find that the work, taken as a whole, appeals to prurient interest;
2 the work depicts or describes, in a patently offensive way, sexual conduct specifically defined by applicable state law; and
3 the work, taken as a whole, lacks serious literary, artistic, political, or scientific value.

The regulation of obscene content is straightforward: it is illegal. However, images or words are not obscene until someone challenges them as such in a court of law. In this way, the legal definition of obscenity acts as an informal regulation by shaping the decisions made about content so that it cannot be declared obscene. Remember, if the content does not meet all three of the *Miller* definitions, then it is not obscene.

Profanity is often equated with comedian George Carlin's act about the seven "filthy" words banned from public broadcast: shit, piss, fuck, cunt, cocksucker, motherfucker, and tits. Although speech outside of these seven words can be considered profane, the seven have become the standard for FCC regulation. Generally, the regulation of profanity falls under the greater regulation of indecency. **Indecency** refers to any material that is morally unfit for general distribution or broadcast, and indecent material most often depicts sexual or excremental activities. Unlike obscenity, indecent content is not illegal, but it is regulated in a number of ways. For example, radio and television stations may broadcast indecent programming only between the "safe harbor" hours of 10 p.m. and 6 a.m. when it is unlikely that any children are watching/listening. Media outlets that do not observe these kinds of rules are subject to FCC fines, loss of broadcasting license, and more. Radio shock jock Howard Stern set records for FCC indecency fines throughout the early 1990s and eventually racked up fines of $1.7 million for his distributor, Infinity Broadcasting.[22]

The management of indecent content is a historically important area of media self-regulation. One of the earliest forms of industry-based content restriction is the Hollywood production code of the 1930s, which was primarily "written by a Jesuit priest and a Catholic layman."[23] It outlined what could and could not be depicted in Hollywood films, and movies that ignored these restrictions could not earn the approval of the Motion Picture Producers and Distributors Association necessary for widespread distribution. Along with the eradication of images of violence and sex, the production code also prohibited the depiction of homosexuality, interracial relationships, and the benefits of illegal activity in films. While prudish and discriminatory by today's standards, the code was an attempt by Hollywood to halt what they perceived to be invasive federal intervention in the movie industry. If industry officials could prove to the government that they could sufficiently

Table 4.1   Breakdown of television ratings in the USA

Rating	(V) Violence	(L) Language	(S) Sexual situations	Example
TV-Y	***	***	***	*Rugrats*
TV-Y7	Mild	Mild	***	*SpongeBob Squarepants*
TV-G	***	***	***	*Pokemon*
TV-PG	Moderate	Mild	Mild	*Seinfeld*
TV-14	Strong	Moderate	Moderate	*Family Guy*
TV-MA	Extreme	Strong	Strong	*South Park*

*** means none.

regulate themselves, then the government would have less of a presence in the business overall. This, to many film makers, was an attractive trade-off.

Industry-based standards like the production code are still the primary form of moral regulation in Hollywood today, with a few significant changes. Most notably, the burden of managing indecent or questionable material has transferred from film makers to audiences. Access to indecent or violent content is now based on audience age, a decision that recalls the *safe harbor* rule. Instead of maintaining a production code that severely censors the content of films, the Motion Picture Association of America has developed a ratings system (G, PG, PG-13, R, NC-17) that restricts viewers instead. The ratings system maintains freedom of speech for film makers while simultaneously enforcing content standards. Television, music, and video game industries have all followed suit in the last 20 years by developing their own ratings systems in relation to questionable content (see Table 4.1 for a breakdown of television ratings). In theory, young children cannot purchase tickets to R-rated films, CDs stamped with a "Parental Advisory" notice, or video games marked T (for Teen) or M (for Mature). However, according to a Federal Trade Commission study on media violence released in September 2000, media industries regularly market these products to minors and young people routinely have access to them.[24] Studies like this one question the effectiveness of industry-based media regulation related to indecent or violent content.

From a Pragmatic perspective, the regulation of morality through obscenity, profanity, and indecency is more contingent on socio-historical factors than almost any other form of regulation. However, we can make some initial judgments based on our discussion thus far. The federal regulations of obscenity and indecency are both largely effective because they yield practical results in relation to questionable content while balancing factors like social norms, free speech, and public interest. The general definition of obscenity importantly hinges on whether or not the particular community in which the content is consumed would find the material objectionable, which often binds particular definitions of obscenity to specific geographical locations in the USA. The regulation reduces obscene content overall without applying a blanket standard. Similarly, the restriction of indecent material to particular hours of broadcast limits access to questionable material in the public interest while maintaining notions of free speech. In the end, these regulations are very much in line with the Pragmatic tenets of consequences and contingencies because they control the access of audiences to questionable material while remaining relatively open to contextual, cultural factors.

We cannot say the same for the systems of media self-regulation discussed here. The production code of the 1930s was clearly a negative form of regulation because it was not sensitive to the varied social and historical factors of the time period. Instead of attempting to balance multiple perspectives, the code imposed a very narrow and somewhat religious conception of morality on film makers. In a Pragmatic sense, the code appealed to a constant and predetermined definition of morality rather than a flexible, contingent one, and this definition in turn supported notions of the public interest while greatly restricting free speech. Current ratings standards, on the other hand, champion free speech but do not actually solve the problem of minors' access to indecent and violent material. In Pragmatic terminology, current media ratings systems are ill-conceived forms of regulation because they do not practically address the social problems they are intended to solve. The aforementioned Federal Trade Commission report clearly outlines how to fix this problem: "Self-regulatory programs can work only if the concerned industry associations actively monitor compliance and ensure that violations have consequences."[25] Only with increased vigilance can ratings systems actually result in effective regulatory consequences.

Ensuring accuracy

Regulations aimed at ensuring accuracy primarily deal with the news broadcast and print industries. Equally balanced between government and industry-based standards, these regulations attempt to prevent the dissemination of false (and possibly damaging) information and provide systems of legal correction if such information does become public. In short, these regulations concentrate on ensuring that journalists and news reporters use media forums to responsibly report the truth to the American public.

The two most important forms of government regulation aimed at ensuring accuracy are the twin legal concepts of slander and libel. **Slander** refers to publicly spoken, untrue, and defamatory statements, while **libel** refers to false printed statements that similarly damage a person's character. Neither is protected under the freedom of speech. While the line between slander and libel was originally very easily understood, the rise of broadcast media has blurred it significantly. After all, news broadcasting relies primarily on the spoken word, but the preparation of news for broadcast resembles the same procedures as print media. Slander and libel laws together force reporters and broadcasters to double check their stories for accuracy. Legal definitions of slander and libel are like definitions of obscenity in that they regulate primarily by guiding the informal decisions made about news content: industry workers avoid disseminating content that is slanderous or libelous. However, these laws also provide a means of legal recourse for defamed individuals who are the victim of slander and libel. If a media outlet is found guilty of slander or libel in a court of law, they often must pay hefty sums in monetary compensation.

Although slander and libel laws represent a significant factor that journalists and newscasters must consider in reporting, there are defenses against them. The most important of these is truth. If a statement is true, no matter how damaging it is to the character of an individual, then it is not subject to slander or libel laws. Similarly, the media is allowed to comment on public figures and their actions under the doctrine of *fair comment*. Because the press is often responsible for acting as a check to governmental powers, they have the right to report and editorialize on aspects of a public figure that may be defamatory as a result. This notion of fair comment also covers the news media's right to judge and critique the products of public institutions (like restaurants) without committing libel.

However, even with fairly clear definitions and defenses against slander and libel, those within the media industry still find themselves in other binds related to accuracy. Should a journalist publish crucial material if the source of that material wishes to remain anonymous? How soon after a terrible accident should a reporter attempt to interview a victim's family? There are no clear or definite answers to these kinds of questions, and issues like the ones above have given rise to industry-based codes of ethics. A **code of ethics** is a self-imposed set of rules that outlines the ethical strivings of a particular media outlet (goals which typically revolve around notions of truth and fairness), and they often stipulate the particular ways that those within the organization should handle conflicts of interest, ethical dilemmas, and other problem areas. By adhering to a code of ethics, news media outlets ensure that they consistently address issues accurately and fairly for the parties involved.

Within a Pragmatic lens, regulations directed toward ensuring accuracy in the media are relatively effective ones. Slander and libel laws halt potential abuse of the individual and help contain the power of the media in shaping public perception. The heavy penalties that result from slander and libel legal cases push media outlets to remain ever vigilant about the facts that they report. While there has been some slippage between the terms as a result of technological development, the laws still strike a nice balance between maintaining freedom of the press and protecting the public. Similarly, codes of ethics provide reporters and broadcasters with general guidelines for resolving specific issues particular to the news industry. Because it is ultimately the individual who makes the call after consulting the code, these rules are practical without being rigid. Sometimes these codes fail to provide good answers, just as media outlets occasionally commit libel or slander, but in general these regulations give flexible structure to the ways in which the industry approaches notions of truth and accuracy.

Violence in the Media: a Closer Look at Pragmatic Regulation

Many of the regulations we have discussed thus far do not occupy a significant place in the public consciousness. Issues like syndication rights, political advertisements, and libel laws often fail to attract the attention of the typical American media consumer. But the same cannot be said for violence. In fact, one would be hard pressed to point to a media issue that garners more public concern than violence in film, television, music, and video games. Because the *perceived* effects of media violence (especially on children) are so great, concerned parents, special-interest groups, and politicians often respond with extreme, reactionary proposals that border on outright censorship. Soon-to-be Republican Presidential nominee Bob Dole, for instance, made headlines in 1995 when (on a campaign stop in Los Angeles) he condemned the entertainment industry for cultivating moral depravity, deviancy, and cultural contamination. In this section, we advocate a more measured approach that attempts to balance the complex interplay of contingencies and consequences related to media violence. In doing so, we hope to illustrate that a Pragmatic perspective is uniquely suited for discussing and appraising media regulations, be they government- or industry-based.

Violence in the media is often treated in a unified, monolithic way. But representations of violence vary greatly in both form and function, and thus it is vital that the Pragmatist distinguish among the different forms of media violence. A useful starting point in this regard is Henry A. Giroux's differentiation between reflective, gore, and stylized violence.[26] According to Giroux, reflective or **historical violence** "probes the complex contradictions that shape human agency, the limits of rationality, and the existential issues that tie us to other human beings and the broader social world."[27] This type of violence typically accompanies the portrayal of actual historical events and can be seen in films such as *Platoon* (1986), *Schindler's List* (1993), and *Amistad* (1997). The visual and narrative framing of historical violence invites audiences to contemplate the horrors of war or the historical atrocities perpetrated against particular social groups; it encourages audiences to think critically about the way violence is connected to hatred and social injustice. Historical violence, then, can be said to heighten social consciousness by imparting larger philosophical messages about humanity and its struggles.

Whereas historical violence engenders thoughtful reflection, gore or **ritualistic violence** generates mostly emotional excitement because, in Giroux's words, it is "pure spectacle in form and superficial in content."[28] Depictions of ritualistic violence are typically fast-paced, adrenaline-pumping, sensationalistic, and hyper-masculine. This form of violence is common to both horror (slasher) and action genres, and is exemplified in films like *Rambo: First Blood* (1982), *True Lies* (1994), and the *Rush Hour* trilogy (1998, 2001, 2007). Rather than imparting social messages, ritualistic violence serves primarily to stimulate and entertain. Consequently, audiences tend to respond to ritualistic violence on a visceral (rather than rational) level. Anyone who has screamed during a gruesome horror scene or clutched his or her seat while viewing an explosive action sequence can attest to the capacity of ritualistic violence to move us at a bodily level.

Giroux's third category of media violence, stylized or **hyper-real violence**, is the most challenging to define. The difficulty arises, at least in part, because it blurs the boundaries between historical and ritualistic violence. To borrow a phrase from the Police song, "Murder by Numbers," hyper-real violence turns "murder into art."[29] Elaborating on the character of hyper-real violence, Giroux explains that it is "marked by technological over-stimulation, gritty dialogue, dramatic storytelling, parody, and an appeal to gutsy realism."[30] Like historical violence, hyper-real violence is extremely realistic and believable. But like ritualistic violence, it is visceral and entertaining (not to mention graphic and shocking). Put another way, hyper-real violence combines the *look* of historical violence with the *feel* of ritualistic violence. A few films that typify this form of media violence include *Reservoir Dogs* (1992), *Pulp Fiction* (1994), and *Sin City* (2005). Since hyper-real violence lacks the reflective dimension of historical violence, it is unlikely to induce audiences to think critically.

Though not every instance of violence in the media fits neatly into one of Giroux's three categories, his typology nevertheless offers a helpful way to begin sorting through the diverse effects of media violence. Research on media violence suggests that it has four primary effects: the aggressor, victim, bystander, and catharsis effects. Before discussing each of these effects, however, we wish to stress that the relations between media violence and audience actions are complex and indirect, not simple and causal. Moreover, social-environmental factors such as family and viewing contexts as well as individual characteristics like gender, age, and academic achievement influence and mitigate the effects of media violence.[31]

Perhaps the most studied consequence of media violence is the **aggressor effect**, which suggests that exposure to media violence triggers arousal and promotes aggressive behavior. Accounts of this effect typically involve one of three theories: disinhibition, enculturation, or imitation. The theory of *disinhibition* posits that the consumption of media violence undermines the social norms and sanctions against violence that individuals would otherwise abide by. While disinhibition hypothesizes that media violence undercuts the social norms against violence, *enculturation* theory speculates that long-term exposure to media violence constructs violence as the norm and thereby encourages aggressive behavior (through social scripts). In other words, violence begets violence by suggesting it is an appropriate and acceptable response to certain life situations. Finally, the theory of *imitation* maintains that some audiences (most often young viewers who do not fully understand violent displays) will mimic the aggressive behavior they observe in media. Despite decades of study, however, findings related to the aggressor effect are, at best, inconsistent.[32] Part of the problem may be that much of the research does not distinguish among different forms of media violence: an important contingency. Imitation, for instance, seems most probable when children consume ritualistic violence, as it is often enacted by the (super)hero and thus positively coded. Meanwhile, disinhibition and enculturation are more likely to result from hyper-real violence, which is morally ambiguous.

Research also suggests that media violence can produce a **victim effect** in which people develop and experience a heightened fearfulness of violence. The victim effect can be explained through George Gerbner's empirical work on television and media cultivation.[33] Gerbner argues that individuals who consume heavy amounts of television undergo a process of *mainstreaming* in which they begin to view mediated images as accurate representations of reality. In this theory, repeated exposure to media violence leads to an exaggerated sense of danger or mistrust about the world. Regular viewers of crime dramas like *24, Law and Order*, and *CSI*, for example, may develop an unrealistic perception of crime in the USA and subsequently an irrational fear of being the victim of crime themselves. In short, heavy viewing of media violence leads people to see themselves as likely victims in a cruel and scary world. Unlike the aggressor effect, which appears to be connected to specific forms of media violence, the victim effect is probably a consequence of the sum of all violent images circulating in society.

A third major strain of research into media violence concerns the **bystander effect**, which holds that media violence fosters increased callousness about or insensitivity toward violence directed at others. The bystander effect is rooted in the theory of *desensitization* or the idea that repeated viewing of media violence leads to a reduction in emotional responses to violence and thus an increased acceptance of violence in real life. The basic premise of the bystander effect is that we consume so much violence in the media that we no longer regard it as shocking or abhorrent when we witness it in real life; we are essentially unfazed by it. The potential danger of desensitization and the bystander effect is that people "are less likely to intervene when they witness aggression [and] less likely to take action to prevent aggression"[34] in their everyday lives. Since historical violence promotes social consciousness and ritualistic violence is perceived by most viewers as unrealistic, the bystander effect is almost certainly associated most closely with hyper-real violence.

Finally, some research indicates that media violence can actually have a **catharsis effect**, meaning that it can reduce and alleviate feelings of aggression. Unlike the three previous effects, the catharsis effect is regarded as a pro-social outcome, for it leads to a reduction in real-world violence. Most of the research on the catharsis effect concerns the way that consuming media violence relieves individuals of their own violent urges by allowing them to live vicariously through the actors on screen. But we would like to suggest that catharsis need not be limited to vicarious release. If catharsis is understood in the more general sense of renewal, then it might help to explain how audiences generally respond to historical violence. In contrast to hyper-real violence, which may result in increased aggression, historical violence is likely to reduce aggressive feelings and tendencies by inviting audiences to reflect on the negative social consequences of violence.

What this brief overview highlights is that any attempt to regulate media violence must carefully balance the consequences (aggressor, victim, bystander, and catharsis effects) with the relevant contingencies (various forms of mediated violence such as historical, ritualistic, and hyper-real). This means that both media producers and consumers need to stop treating all instances of media violence as identical. The pitfalls of doing so are evidenced by the failure of the television ratings system and the development of the v-chip.

Historically, the US government has taken a largely "hands-off" approach when it comes to violence on television. Not wanting break with that tradition or curtail the freedom of speech, but under mounting pressure from lobbyist groups, Congress signaled its desire for the television industry to develop industry-based ratings standards in 1990,[35] and later enforced the adoption of these standards with the Telecommunications Act of 1996. The implementation of a television ratings system was designed to help parents identify what programming was appropriate for their children. In connection with v-chip technology, which allows select programs to be blocked on individual television sets based on the industry ratings, the system promised to protect children from inappropriate content. In 1999, the FCC required all manufacturers to begin including v-chip technology in US televisions. By 2001, however, only 7% of parents in the country were actually using the chip to screen content for their children.[36]

One problem with the newly instituted television ratings system and subsequent v-chip technology was that it could not distinguish between reflective violence, which might serve educational purposes, and ritualistic and hyper-real violence, which offered little more than shock and titillation. In the end, using v-chip technology to screen violent content was akin to conducting brain surgery with a chain saw. The results were unlikely to satisfy. The chip has been so ineffective that the FCC has recently begun to look into regulating violence in the same way that it regulates indecent content.[37] Had policy-makers adopted a Pragmatist approach and more carefully taken into account the relevant contingencies (i.e. various forms of media violence), the FCC might not be currently looking into ways to increase the federal government's role in regulating violent content.

Conclusion

In this chapter we have looked at many different regulations from a Pragmatic perspective, and those regulations have taken a number of different forms: laws, policies, standards, technologies, etc. While some of the regulations have been clearly beneficial or disastrous, many more fall somewhere in between. The relatively ambiguous nature of most media regulation is indicative of the many factors that legislators and industry representatives must take into account when trying to craft quality guidelines. On top of social and technological issues related to the historical moment, these individuals must also pay special attention to issues of free speech, the public interest, and the ratio between federal and industry-based regulation. The philosophy of Pragmatism helps us to bring order to these various issues, and it provides a good foundation for making evaluations of resulting regulations. In addition, the special emphasis that Pragmatism places on contingencies helps us deconstruct the various factors that inform some of the most pressing regulatory issues facing us today. The regulation of the media is as old as the media itself, but a Pragmatic approach is a relatively new way of understanding the relationship between the two. In short, it helps us make some sense of the historically varied and sometimes confusing terrain of American media regulation.

MEDIA LAB 3: DOING PRAGMATIC ANALYSIS

OBJECTIVE

The aim of this lab is to use the tenets of Pragmatism to understand the regulation of American media. Specifically, students will be generating Pragmatic, original regulations for contemporary problems within American media.

ACTIVITY

- Divide the class into small groups of 4–5 students each.
- Have each group identify a social problem within contemporary American media that affects them. Potential problems include traditional issues like violence in the media or youth access to indecent material, but students should feel free to choose less common problems as well (volume settings on iPods, for example).
- Have each group generate an original regulation to address the problem in 3–4 paragraphs. Students need not address every detail of the regulation, but basic points should be clear. In crafting their regulation, each group should attend to the following.
  1 What are the perceived consequences of your regulation? How are these beneficial? How might they be detrimental?
  2 What historical contingencies does your regulation take into account? In other words, what contemporary political, social, or cultural issues does your regulation attempt to integrate and satisfy?
  3 How does your regulation balance issues of free speech against the public interest? Does it support one more than the other?
  4 Does your regulation rely on federal enforcement, industry enforcement, or both? How?

SUGGESTED READING

Aufderheide, P. *Communications Policy and the Public Interest: The Telecommunications Act of 1996.* New York: The Guilford Press, 1999.

Bandura, A., Ross, D., and Ross, S.A. Transmission of Aggression Through Imitation of Aggressive Models. *Journal of Abnormal and Social Psychology* 1961; 63: 575–82.

Dewey, J. *The Quest For Certainty: a Study of the Relation of Knowledge and Action.* New York: Minton, Balch & Co., 1929.

Dewey, J. The Need for a Recovery of Philosophy. In *Creative Intelligence*, pp. 3–69. New York: Octagon Books, 1970.

Diffie, W. and Landau, S. *Privacy on the Line: The Politics of Wiretapping and Encryption.* Cambridge, MA: The MIT Press, 2007.

Dubow, E.F. and Miller, L.S. Television Violence Viewing and Aggressive Behavior. In *Tuning in to Young Viewers: Social Perspectives on Television*, MacBeth, T.M. (ed.), pp. 117–47. Thousand Oaks, CA: Sage Publications, 1996.

Freedman, D. Dynamics of Power in Contemporary Media Policy-Making. *Media, Culture & Society* 2006; 28: 907–23.

Gillespie, T. *Wired Shut: Copyright and the Shape of Digital Culture*. Cambridge, MA: The MIT Press, 2007.

Giroux, H.A. Racism and the Aesthetic of Hyper-Real. In *Fugitive Cultures: Race, Violence and Youth*, pp. 55–88. New York: Routledge, 1996.

Herman, B.D. Breaking and Entering My Own Computer: The Contest of Copyright Metaphors. *Communication Law & Policy* 2008; 13: 231–74.

Hindman, E.B. When is the Truth not the Truth? Truth Telling and Libel by Implication. *Communication Law & Policy* 2007; 12: 341–67.

James, W. *Pragmatism: A New Name for Some Old Ways of Thinking*. London: Longmans, Green and Co., 1908.

James, W. *Pragmatism and the Meaning of Truth*. Cambridge, MA: Boston University Press, 1978.

Keith, S., Schwalbe, C.B., and Silcock, W.B. Images in Ethics Codes in an Era of Violence and Tragedy. *Journal of Mass Media Ethics* 2006; 21: 245–64.

Leone, R. and Houle, N. 21st Century Ratings Creep: PG-13 and R. *Communication Research Reports* 2006; 23: 53–61.

Lessig, L. *Free Culture: How Big Media Uses Technology and the Law to Lock Down Culture and Control Creativity*. New York: The Penguin Press, 2004.

Postigo, H. Capturing Fair Use for the YouTube Generation: The Digital Rights Movement, the Electronic Frontier Foundation, and the User-Centered Framing of Fair Use. *Information, Communication & Society* 2008; 11: 1008–27.

Rorty, R. *Contingency, Irony, and Solidarity*. New York: Cambridge University Press, 1989.

Rorty, R. Pragmatism, Relativism, and Irrationalism. In *Consequences of Pragmatism (Essays: 1972–1980)*, pp. 160–75. Minneapolis: University of Minnesota Press, 1982.

Russill, C. Through a Public Darkly: Reconstructing Pragmatist Perspectives in Communication Theory. *Communication Theory* 2008; 18: 478–504.

Samoriski, J.H., Huffman, J.L., and Trauth, D.M. The V-Chip and Cybercops: Technology vs. Regulation. *Communication Law & Policy* 1997; 2: 143–64.

Timmer, J. The Seven Dirty Words You Can Say on Cable and DBS: Extending Broadcast Indecency Regulation and the First Amendment. *Communication Law & Policy* 2005; 10: 179–215.

West, C. *The American Evasion of Philosophy*. Madison, WI: University of Wisconsin Press, 1989.

NOTES

1. W. James, *Pragmatism and the Meaning of Truth* (Cambridge, MA: Boston University Press: 1978), 30.

2. C. West, *The American Evasion of Philosophy* (Madison, WI: University of Wisconsin Press, 1989), 60.

3. J. Dewey, The Need for a Recovery of Philosophy, in *Creative Intelligence* (New York: Octagon Books, 1970), 14.

4. R. Rorty, Pragmatism, Relativism, and Irrationalism, in *Consequences of Pragmatism (Essays: 1972–1980)* (Minneapolis: University of Minnesota Press, 1982), 164.

5. Rorty, 168.

6. J. Dewey, Reconstruction in Philosophy, in *The Middle Works of John Dewey, Volume 12, 1899–1924: 1920, Reconstruction in Philosophy and Essays*, J.A. Boydston (ed.) (Carbondale, IL: Southern Illinois University Press, 1988), 181–2.

7. S.J. Baran and D.K. Davis, *Mass Communication Theory: Foundations, Ferment, and Future*, 2nd edn. (Belmont, CA: Wadsworth Publishing, 1999), 97.

8. R.E. Caves, *Switching Channels: Organization and Change in TV Broadcasting* (Cambridge, MA: Harvard University Press, 2005).

9. P. Aufderheide, *Communications Policy and the Public Interest: The Telecommunications Act of 1996* (New York: The Guilford Press, 1999), 61.

10. BMI 101, *Broadcast Music Incorporated*, www.bmi.com/about (accessed June 18, 2008).

11. B. Rosenblatt, B. Trippe, and S. Mooney, *Digital Rights Management: Business and Technology* (New York: M&T Books, 2002).

12. iTunes Store Terms of Service, *Apple*, www.apple.com/legal/itunes/us/service.html (accessed June 20, 2008).

13. Apple Launches iTunes Plus: Higher Quality DRM-Free Tracks Now Available on the iTunes Store Worldwide, *Apple*, www.apple.com/pr/library/2007/05/30itunesplus.html (accessed June 20, 2008).

14. L. Lessig, *Free Culture: How Big Media Uses Technology and the Law to Lock Down Culture and Control Creativity* (New York: The Penguin Press, 2004).

15. T. Gillespie, *Wired Shut: Copyright and the Shape of Digital Culture* (Cambridge, MA: The MIT Press, 2007).

16. W. Diffie and S. Landau, *Privacy on the Line: The Politics of Wiretapping and Encryption* (Cambridge, MA: The MIT Press, 2007).

17. D. Abrahms, Lawmakers Seek to Ensure Electronic Privacy, *The Washington Times*, March 5, 1996, final edition, B6.

18. P. Johnson and D. Leinwand, TV Networks Pull Arnett, Rivera, *USA Today*, April 1, 2003, first edition, 1A.

19. D. Dadge, *The War in Iraq and Why the Media Failed Us* (Westport, CT: Praeger Publications, 2006).

20. T. Shanker and B. Carter, Photos of Soldiers' Coffins Spark a Debate Over Access, *New York Times*, April 24, 2004, late edition, A14.

21. S. Zeidler, Arnold's Films Sidelined During Governor's Bid: Considered TV Air Time: 'It May Beg a Competitor to File a Complaint', *National Post (Canada)*, August 14, 2003, national edition, A15.

22. A. Trebbe, Indecency Fine Ripples Stern's Shock Waves, *USA Today*, October 29, 1992, final edition, 1D; D. Wharton, Infinity Hit With 600G Stern Fine, *Daily Variety*, December 21, 1992, 3; FCC Drops Old Stern Fines, *Daily News*, February 7, 2001, 71.

23. H.M. Benshoff and S. Griffin, *America on Film: Representing Race, Class, Gender and Sexuality at the Movies* (Malden, MA: Blackwell, 2004), 39.

24. Marketing Violent Entertainment to Children: a Review of Self Regulation and Industry Practices in the Motion Picture, Music Recording & Electronic Game Industries, *Federal Trade Commission*, www.ftc.gov/reports/violence/070412MarketingViolentEChildren.pdf (accessed June 19, 2008).

25. Marketing Violent Entertainment to Children, vi.

26. H.A. Giroux, Racism and the Aesthetic of Hyper-Real, in *Fugitive Cultures: Race, Violence and Youth* (New York: Routledge, 1996), 55–88.

27. Giroux, 63.

28. Giroux, 61.

29. Sting and A. Summers, "Murder By Numbers," *Synchronicity*, A&M (CD release date October 25, 1990).

30. Giroux, 64.

31. E.F. Dubow and L.S. Miller, Television Violence Viewing and Aggressive Behavior, in *Tuning in to Young Viewers: Social Perspectives on Television*, T.M. MacBeth (ed.) (Thousand Oaks, CA: Sage Publishing, 1996), 117–47.

32. J. Staiger, *Media Reception Studies* (New York: New York University Press, 2005), 167.

33. G. Gerbner, Cultivation Analysis: an Overview, *Mass Communication and Society* 1, no. 3/4, 1998, 175–94.

34. J.L. Freedman, *Media Violence and its Effect on Aggression: Assessing the Scientific Evidence* (Toronto: University of Toronto Press, 2002), 177.

35. D.E. Newton, *Violence and the Media: A Reference Handbook* (Denver, CO: ABC-CLIO, 1996).

36. J. Rutenburg, Survey Shows Few Parents Use TV V-Chip to Limit Children's Viewing, *New York Times*, July 25, 2001, late edition, E1.

37. S. Labaton, F.C.C. Moves to Restrict TV Violence, *New York Times*, April 26, 2007, late edition, C1.

Part II

Media Messages: Rhetorical, Cultural, Psychoanalytic, Feminist, and Queer Perspectives

5 Rhetorical Analysis

KEY CONCEPTS

AESTHETICS AFFECTS CLUSTER CONNOTATION DENOTATION FORM GENRE ICONIC SIGNS INDEXICAL SIGNS NARRATIVE RHETORIC SEMIOLOGY SEMIOTIC SIGN SIGNIFIED SIGNIFIER SIGNIFYING SYSTEM STRUCTURALISM SYMBOLS TEXTS

James McTeigue's 2005 film *V for Vendetta*, which is based on Alan Moore and David Lloyd's graphic novel of the same name, tells the fictional story of a British totalitarian state in the year 2020. The story concerns a vigilante by the name of V – played masterfully by Hugo Weaving – who seeks to blow up the Houses of Parliament to inspire the country's citizens to stand up to their repressive government. *V for Vendetta* is an engaging and entertaining film. But it is also an allegory: an extended metaphor for life in George W. Bush's America. And in that sense, the film functions as rhetoric, as an attempt to shape and influence its viewers' attitudes. *V for Vendetta* stages its critique of the Bush administration on a number of levels. At a narrational level, for instance, visual and verbal accounts of the British government's actions closely parallel Bush administration policies on "surveillance, torture, fear-mongering, and media manipulation [through] . . . vivid allusions to Abu Ghraib and references to Iraq, Afghanistan and Syria."[1] The film's explicit references to living in a repressive state are viscerally reinforced by the film's camera work; extreme close-ups of V's co-conspirator Evey Hammond (Natalie Portman) create a feeling of captivity, while low-angle shots of government officials evoke fear and anxiety. In short, *V for Vendetta* urges audiences to condemn the Bush administration and its practices in the "war on terror." The attempt to move audiences is by no means unique to this film, however. As this chapter demonstrates, our whole media landscape is rhetorical.

Rhetorical scholars of the media (sometimes referred to as Rhetorical critics) analyze texts for the ways they encourage audiences to inhabit certain moods, believe certain ideas, or undertake certain actions. These scholars view texts as complex webs of interrelated parts that work together to influence consumers in particular ways. We begin this chapter with an introduction to the concept of rhetoric, emphasizing its inherently suasory character. Then, we illustrate how signs – the basic building blocks of language and most other forms of rhetoric – create meaning by examining the work of three important philosophers of signs. Next, we consider how signs in complex combination form media texts, whose various structures invite and elicit particular responses from audiences. Finally, we conclude by examining how the aesthetic elements of media such as sound and color move audiences at a bodily level.

Rhetoric: an Overview

The tendency to view popular media products like the film *Anchorman*, or the television show *So You Think You Can Dance*, or the Kid Rock song "All Summer Long," or the video game Guitar Hero as *mere* (which implies only) entertainment obscures the fact that media messages inevitably persuade as well as entertain us. Media messages cannot help but convey meanings, and meanings are never neutral or objective. Consequently, films, television shows, songs, video games, etc. are constantly inviting us to adopt certain attitudes, values, and beliefs, while simultaneously encouraging us to overlook and discount others. This is because all media products are rhetorical.[2] **Rhetoric** refers to the ancient art of oratory, or as Aristotle famously defined it, "an ability, in each particular case, to see the available means of persuasion."[3] The art of rhetoric as practiced by Greek politicians in the fifth century BC may seem distant and unrelated to the art of rhetoric as utilized in the spectacular images of *Lord of the Rings* (2001). But both instances of rhetoric rely on symbols to influence what (and how) audiences think and feel. Indeed, were we to update Aristotle's definition, we might simply define rhetoric as the use of symbols by humans to influence and move other humans.[4]

If what is meant by the idea that media products are rhetorical is still not entirely clear, then consider Michael Moore's controversial 2004 film *Fahrenheit 9/11*. The film takes a highly critical look at the role played by big money, oil, and the Bush administration leading up to and following the tragic events of September 11, 2001. Like Moore's previous artistic endeavors (*Roger and Me* and *Bowling for Columbine*), *Fahrenheit 9/11* is a documentary. But many critics, and especially those on the political right, responded to the film with vitriol and venom because of its biased, one-sided presentation of events: an offense that was only further heightened by the film maker's insistence that it was a documentary. The outrage of critics stemmed, at least in part, from the "perception" that documentaries ought to be objective. But as we have already noted, all symbols are value-laden and thus all messages, as symbolic creations, are necessarily biased.[5] As Kenneth Burke explains, "Even if any given terminology is a *reflection* of reality, by its very nature as a terminology it must be a *selection* of reality; and to this extent it must function also as a *deflection* of reality."[6] Thus, it is naïve to think that discourse in any form, be it a documentary film or scientific monograph, can be anything other than biased and suasory.[7]

Theories of the Sign

In 1993, the Sweden-based pop group Ace of Base released their smash hit "The Sign," which spent six weeks atop the Billboard Hot 100 chart in the USA. Although the song owes its success to its infectious dance beat, our interest is in the song's mind-numbing lyrics and popular refrain, "I saw the sign and it opened up my eyes. I saw the sign." As cheesy and cliché as these lines may be, they succinctly describe the basic operation of signs. A **sign** is something that invites someone to think of something other than itself, such as the way an image of a person invites one to think of that person or the way the unique letter combination d/o/g invites one to think of a four-legged canine. Since nearly everything has that potential, virtually anything can function as a sign. When multiple people agree on what a sign refers to, we say that it has shared meaning. Shared meaning is, of course, what makes human communication possible. Without it, no social structures or institutions could exist. Moreover, since no sign (no matter how clear it may seem) can guarantee that everyone will interpret it the same way (i.e. understand it to be referring to the same thing), communication is an extremely fragile thing. Think of all the times in your life you have said something to someone that was intended to be innocent, but that was (mis)interpreted as an offense. Signs are significant, then, because they are the fundamental building blocks of meaning and hence communication. In this section, we consider how three prominent scholars have theorized the sign: Ferdinand de Saussure, Charles Sanders Peirce, and Roland Barthes.

Ferdinand de Saussure (1857–1913)

The Swiss linguist Ferdinand de Saussure is generally regarded as "the founder of modern linguistics,"[8] a title he earned by shifting the study of language away from the historical roots (philology) and changing meaning of specific words (semantics) to the study of language as a structured system. Although Saussure never wrote a book, his lectures on linguistics at the University of Geneva were compiled and published posthumously in 1915 under the title of *Course in General Linguistics*. Saussure called his unique approach to linguistics **semiology**, which he defined as, "a science which studies the role of signs as part of social life. . . . It [semiology] would investigate the nature of signs and the laws governing them."[9] Since Saussure understood language as a system of signs, he began by asking what is a sign and what rules does it obey. All linguistic signs, he argued, were a combination of signifier (*signifiant*) and signified (*signifié*). The **signifier**, or sound-image, refers to the material form of a sign as perceived by the senses, such as the word "dog" as heard by a listener. The **signified**, or mental concept, is the idea evoked by the signifier; in this case, the idea of "dogness." Note that an actual dog is not part of this equation. Together, the signifier and signified constitute a sign, which Saussure designated in the manner shown in the diagram.

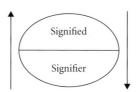

For Saussure, the linguistic sign has two defining traits. First, signs are *arbitrary*,[10] meaning there is no natural correspondence, no necessary relationship, between signifier and signified. It is precisely because there is no inevitable or inherent link between signifiers and signifieds that the idea of "dogness" can be conveyed by different signifiers: dog (English), *perro* (Spanish), *chien* (French), *cane* (Italian), *Hund* (German), 狗 (Chinese). We could even invent our own word for "dogness," such as *plink*, and if we agreed that *plink* meant "dogness," then we would have a new signifier. It is this principle of arbitrariness that allows Trekers (fanatical fans of *Star Trek*) to invent entire alien languages (Klingon, for instance) that can be spoken and understood by other "Klingons." The constant creation and addition of new words, like "Truthiness," and the changing meaning of existing words, like "hot" (which went from meaning "extremely warm" to also meaning "cool," "sexy," and "hip" thanks in large part to Paris Hilton), highlight the arbitrariness of signs. "The fact that the relation between signifier and signified is arbitrary means, then," elaborates Culler, "that since there are no fixed universal concepts or fixed universal signifiers, the signified itself is arbitrary."[11] This is to say that while the terms *dog* and *perro* may both evoke the mental idea of "dogness," "dogness" is itself understood differently in different cultures.

The second key trait of the linguistic sign is *linearity*. Since the signifier, being auditory, is unfolded solely in time, it is impossible to utter two distinct linguistic signs simultaneously. Saussure recognized that this trait did not hold true for visual signs, which can, in fact, "exploit more than one dimension simultaneously."[12] Saussure regarded the principle of linearity to be a significant one because it means that signifiers operate in a temporal chain, which if reordered, changes the meaning of what is being said.

Having identified the basic character of signs, let us turn now to Saussure's methods for investigating the rules that govern signs. To understand and appreciate his perspective, we need to introduce three additional ideas: *langue* versus *parole*, synchronic versus diachronic, and difference. For Saussure, it is important to distinguish between *langue*, the linguistic system, and *parole*, individual speech acts or utterances (i.e. actual manifestations of the sign system). To study *langue* is to study the rules and conventions that organize the system, while to study *parole* is to study specific uses or performances of language. Saussure was a strong proponent of the former, which he believed to be the proper goal of linguistics. Another distinction of significance to Saussure was that between synchronic and diachronic analysis. *Synchronic analysis*, which was de Saussure's principal commitment, concerns the state of language in general: the linguistic system in a static state. It aims to illuminate the conditions for the existence of any language by examining the rules of combination and substitutability within a system. *Diachronic analysis* or evolutionary linguistics, by contrast, concerns the origins of languages and changes in sound or pronunciation over time (phonology). Since such changes are found in *parole*, Saussure did not see diachronic analysis as a suitable method for investigating *langue*.

The final concept of great import to de Saussure's science of signs is difference. Saussure astutely recognized that signs signify by virtue of their difference (i.e. distinctiveness) from other signs. The word "dog" can signify because it sounds different than "cat," "horse," or "mouse." Though this may seem like an elementary observation, its implications are profound. On a basic level, it simply means that if we cannot distinguish one word from another, then we cannot communicate. This is what occurs when someone is speaking too softly; though we can still hear sounds, we can no longer distinguish among the sounds. But on a second level, it suggests that the specific "relations of difference" matter. "Dog" sounds different than "red." But "red" is not meaningful (at least not primarily) because it differs from "dog;" it is meaningful because it differs from "blue," "green," "yellow," etc. Our ability to notice different colors in the world depends upon distinguishing between them. Without specific relations of difference, there can be no meaning. The differences do not have to be universal, just socially agreed upon. It matters not what the bishop looks like in chess, only that the bishop follows certain rules and looks different from the other pieces. If one of the bishops were lost, the game could continue using a bottle cap or checker so long as both players agreed the object represented the bishop and therefore was limited to a certain kinds of movement.

Charles Sanders Peirce (1839–1914)

At about the same time de Saussure was putting forward his theory of signs in Europe, a Harvard-trained American philosopher by the name of Charles Sanders Peirce was developing his own theory. Peirce called his program **semiotic** (semiotike), which he defined as "the quasi-necessary, or formal, doctrine of signs."[13] Unlike Saussure's theory of signs, which was conveniently compiled into one book, Peirce's work on signs spans across his writings and intersects with a diverse array of topics. His notion of semiotic has been distilled from the eight-volume *Collected*

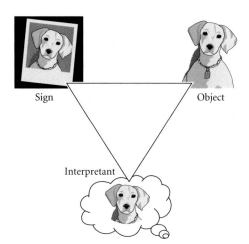

Sign

Object

Interpretant

Figure 5.1
C.S. Peirce's semiotic
theory.

Papers of Charles Sanders Peirce, the first two volumes of which appeared in 1932. Peirce's semiotic differs greatly from Saussure's semiology because it both repudiates the principle of arbitrariness and expands the category of signs to include all modes of human communication (not just language). Peirce's semiotic is based upon the triadic relation between sign, object, and interpretant.

"A sign, or *representamen*," as Peirce called it, "is something which stands to somebody for something in some respect or capacity."[14] The "equivalent sign" it creates in a person's mind is the known as the *interpretant*, and the something that the sign stands for is its *object*. In this scheme, the representamen (sign) loosely corresponds to Saussure's idea of the signifier and the interpretant to his notion of the signified. For Peirce, the image or picture of a dog functions as a sign that refers to an object, a real dog, and creates an interpretant, or mental interpretation of the dog (Figure 5.1).

Peirce classified signs into three categories: icons, indices, and symbols. **Iconic signs** operate according to the logic of similarity or likeness; icons are representamens that structurally resemble the objects they stand for. Examples include diagrams, maps, photographs, and other types of image. **Indexical signs** are linked by cause or association to the objects they represent. Since smoke indicates fire, it functions as an indexical sign for fire. Peirce noted that, "anything which focuses the attention is an index," citing the example of a "rap on the door" because it draws our attention to someone's arrival.[15] **Symbols**, the third category of signs, are linked to their corresponding objects purely by social convention or agreement; symbolic signs are learned rather than intuited. As this is how language works, Peirce argued that "All words, sentences, books, and other conventional signs are Symbols."[16] It should be noted that Peirce did not regard these three categories as mutually exclusive, believing instead that certain signs could function in more than one way.

Roland Barthes (1915–1980)

Roland Barthes has been described as "the most important French thinker to emerge from the post-war period."[17] Despite this ringing endorsement, Barthes was famous not so much for proposing intellectually revolutionary ideas, but for refining and expanding upon the ideas of others. As we will see, Barthes's theory of signs, which we term the **signifying system** to distinguish it from semiology and semiotics, draws heavily upon the work of both Saussure and Peirce. The signifying system grew out of Barthes's fascination with how "cultural" practices and beliefs are "naturalized" (i.e. made to appear natural), an idea he first began to explore in his writings on myth (see especially *Mythologies*). Over time, Barthes increasingly began to view myth through the lens of signification, and in particular through Saussure's conception of signs as signifier and signified.

To demonstrate the relation of myth to Saussure's scheme, Barthes famously introduced the distinction between denotation and connotation in *Elements of Semiology* (1964). **Denotation** describes first-order signification or what Barthes called the first "plane of expression."[18] The denotative plane involves the literal or explicit meanings of words and other phenomena. At a purely denotative level, for instance, the word "lion" (signifier) evokes the mental image of a large cat (signified). But Barthes recognized that meaning does not end there, that the signifying system is characterized by process not product.[19] When one hears the word "lion," he or she may briefly form the mental image of a large cat, but that mental image (as a signifier itself) will evoke still other associations (new signifieds) such as "courage" and "pride." This second plane of expression is what Barthes called connotation. **Connotation** is second-order signification and operates at the level of ideology and myth. While "dog" and "perro" may evoke similar mental images (i.e. denotative meaning), the connotative meaning of dog can vary greatly from culture to culture (everything from "companion" or "family member" to "pest" or "food"). Figure 5.2 visually depicts the relation of denotation to connotation.

The advantage of Barthes's signifying system over Saussure's semiology is not that it illustrates meaning as always cultural (Saussure was well aware of this fact), but that it emphasizes meaning is never final or closed.

Like Peirce, Barthes recognized that signs need not be linguistic. Moreover, he agreed that the relationship between the signifier and the signified is not really arbitrary so much as it is *unmotivated*.[20] But even in the case of image-based signifying practices such as photography and cinema or object-based signifying practices

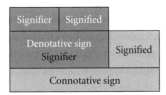

Figure 5.2
The relation of a denotative sign to a connotative sign.

Figure 5.3   Panzani
advertisement.

such as clothing and food, Barthes found value in the signifier/signified binary. Thus, when studying images, Barthes would isolate the signifiers and signifieds operating on both the denotative and connotative planes of expression. One of Barthes's most well-known analyses is of an advertisement for Panzani products that appeared in a French magazine (see Figure 5.3).

Barthes argued that the Panzani advertisement comprised three messages (codes): a linguistic message (printed text), a denoted image (non-coded iconic message), and a connoted image (coded iconic message). The linguistic message in adverts performs the function of anchorage according to Barthes. *Anchorage* limits the (potentially infinite) meanings an image can have by "directing" the reader through the visual signifieds.[21] In other image-based forms such as cinema or comic strips, the linguistic message can also perform a *relay* function, in which the words complement and reinforce the images. For Barthes, the denoted image is analogical in nature, the visual signifier "tomato" referring to the mental idea of "tomato-ness," the visual signifier "net" referring to mental idea of "net-ness," and so forth. Perhaps less obviously is the meaning of the connoted image, which evokes the ideas of freshness or return from market, Italianicity, total culinary service, and "still life." Just as the elements in this image derive their meaning in relation to one another, Barthes believed that each element within a signifying system was dependent upon every other element in that system for its meaning. In other words, not only are the individual signs in a message key to its meaning, but so too are their arrangement in particular texts and rhetorical structures.

Texts and Rhetorical Structures

Signs, of course, rarely exist or function in isolation. Rather, they are combined with other signs to form media products or **texts**. "A text," according to Barry Brummett, "is a set of signs related to each other insofar as their meanings all contribute to the same set of effects or functions."[22] The Panzani advertisement discussed in the previous section, as well as songs, internet sites, video games, television shows, and movies can all be thought of as media texts because the individual signs that comprise them are strategically structured to elicit particular responses from listeners and viewers. Though the organizational pattern of signs that can exist in a text is potentially infinite, there are some general rhetorical structures shared by many, if not all, texts. This section of the chapter focuses on four rhetorical structures in particular: clusters, form, genre, and narrative.

Clusters

Perhaps the most basic rhetorical structure in texts is the **cluster**, or the way individual signs are associated with and dissociated from one another. Expounding on this idea, Kenneth Burke writes, "Now, the work [text] of every writer [or media producer] contains a set of implicit equations. He uses 'associational clusters.' And you [the critic] may, by examining his work [text], find 'what goes with what' in these clusters: what kinds of acts and images and personalities and situations go with his notions of heroism, villainy, consolation, despair, etc."[23] To understand how the clusters in a text are working rhetorically, the critic should begin by identifying the key signs within the text: those signs that are privileged through repetition, intensity, or prominence. In the Candie's Fragrances advertisement (Figure 5.4), for instance, the critic would classify the two perfume bottles as key signs because they are bright, prominently placed in the center of the advert, and the focus of the model's attention, a technique designed to focus our attention on them as well. The critic would then ask, what other signs are associated with (i.e. cluster around) these key signs? This would likely lead one to note that the two perfume bottles are swimming in an ocean of condoms. The implicit suggestion, of course, is that wearing Candie's Fragrances will lead to sex . . . lots and lots of sex! The absence of certain signs or clusters in a text may also be central to its appeal. Notice in the Candie's ad that there is nothing in the medicine cabinet besides condoms and perfume.

Figure 5.4
Candie's Fragrances
advertisement.

Other objects (i.e. visual signs) that one might expect to find in a medicine cabinet such as creams, deodorants, and aspirin are all conspicuously missing. These absences are not accidental. Rather they are strategic, as the advertiser does not want to risk consumers associating Candie's Fragrances with rashes, body odor, headaches, and upset stomachs. Finally, the critic explores whether the particular clustering of signs in a text fosters a positive, negative, or ambivalent valence toward the key signs. In the case of the Candie's Fragrances ad, the association of the product with condoms, a half-naked Alyssa Milano, and a pristine, white bathroom all work to make the product more desirable by associating it with a series of positive signifiers.

Form

A second prominent rhetorical structure in texts is form. **Form**, explains Burke, is "an arousing and fulfillment of desires. A work has form in so far as one part of it leads a reader to anticipate another part, [and] to be gratified by the sequence."[24] Simply stated, form is the creation and satisfaction of desire. When a gun is drawn by a character in a film, for instance, it fosters a desire for violence. Although the violence may not occur immediately, which further heightens our desire for it (by withholding or prolonging fulfillment), it must occur eventually; otherwise our desire goes unfulfilled (this is known as "bad form"). If you have ever had a friend break a promise to you, then you know just how frustrating and disappointing bad form can be. Form is at play in virtually all messages. Consider the opening sentence of this paragraph: "A second prominent rhetorical structure in texts is form." This sentence generates a desire to know what "form" is, which the next sentence graciously affords by providing a definition. Similarly, the sentence that immediately precedes the one you are currently reading fulfills the desire to know the significance of the first sentence in this paragraph: a desire created by the phrase, "Consider the opening sentence of this paragraph."

Form comes in a variety of, for lack of a better word, forms. Burke proposes that there are four general varieties of form: progressive form, repetitive form, conventional form, and minor or incidental forms. Progressive form describes the way a story advances step by step, each step following logically from the previous step. "The arrows of our desires," Burke writes, "are turned in a certain direction, and the plot follows the direction of the arrows."[25] Progressive form is particularly evident in television crime dramas such as *CSI*. Each episode begins with a homicide, which (necessarily) leads to the search for a killer. As clues are gathered and analyzed over the episode, suspects are slowly eliminated until the culprit is finally revealed and confronted. Though there may be brief "misdirection" along the way, ultimately the clues will point to the guilt of one individual. The second major type of form, repetitive form "is the consistent maintaining of a principle under new guises. It is the restatement of the same thing in different ways."[26] Repetitive form can be seen in the actions of most characters on television; they are recognizable to us as "characters" precisely because they repeat the same behaviors over and over again. Though the context changes, Quagmire repeatedly makes sexual advances on *Family Guy*, Phoebe repeatedly behaves eccentrically on *Friends*, and Dr House repeatedly treats others callously on *House*. Each time we witness these behaviors, it heightens our appetite to see them repeated in a new context. That they are repeated is extremely rewarding because it satiates an appetite created by repetition.

Conventional form, the third major variety of form, is not so much an appeal *within* the text (as progressive and repetitive forms are) as it is an appeal *of* the text. When two friends are trying to decide what movie to go see and one of them says, "I'm in the mood for a romantic comedy," she is articulating a preference based on conventional form. One way of classifying media texts is according to the structural and aesthetic conventions they share. Horror films are scary, action films are thrilling, and romantic comedies are funny, or at least we "expect" them to be. We often select the media texts we do because we desire a particular set of conventions at a particular moment in time. When someone is depressed and chooses to listen to a sad, sappy love song, it is because that *type* of song fulfills the desire to wallow in self-pity. The fourth and final variety, minor or incidental forms, is sort of a catch-all category. It includes the brief, frequently literary devices that may appear within a text such as metaphor, paradox, reversal, contraction, expansion, etc. Minor forms are what allow us to take pleasure in segments, sections, or pieces of larger texts. One may delight, for example, in a particular scene from a film independent from the whole because it creates and fulfills a desire all its own.

Genre

Another way to investigate what media texts mean and how they move us is from the perspective of genre. Genre is based upon the idea that individual media messages can usefully and meaningfully be categorized (i.e. organized) into discernible groups according to their structural elements. A **genre** is a type, kind, or class of messages that share distinctive and identifiable aesthetic, stylistic, substantive, and/or ideological conventions. Genres typically originate or emerge in one of two ways: historically or theoretically. Historical genres are those constructed by media producers to meet common social needs or situational demands, and are generally recognizable to the culture they serve, namely consumers. Popular TV genres such as soap operas, talk shows, crime, medical, or legal dramas, situation comedies, reality TV shows, quiz and game shows, and entertainment variety programs are all examples of historical genres. Theoretical genres, by contrast, are those identified and defined by critics and scholars for the purpose of explaining large-scale, often unconscious, social phenomena. Let us look at some examples of both in greater depth.

The daytime talk show comes in two major types: "tabloid" talk shows such as *Ricki Lake*, *The Jerry Springer Show*, and *The Jenny Jones Show*, and "confessional" talk shows such as *The Oprah Winfrey Show*, *Ellen*, and *The View*. Though similar in some respects, the tabloid and confessional talk show are distinct historical genres typified by the conventions in Table 5.1. The differences (in conventions) between these two types of television programming are obvious to most people, which is precisely what makes them recognizable historical genres. Because tabloid and confessional talk shows repeatedly rehearse their distinctive conventions, they not only generate easy recognition but also produce particular audience expectations. The central appeal of genre works in virtually the same manner as does Burke's

Table 5.1   Comparison of tabloid and confessional talk shows

Tabloid talk show	Confessional talk show
Host as (circus) ring leader	Host as (personal) therapist
Outrageous people with *bizarre* (sensational, salacious, and socially taboo) problems	*Ordinary* people with *everyday* (personal, financial, and familial) problems
Personal experience of guests is combined with confrontational comments or behaviors from other (frequently surprise) guests	Personal experience of guests is combined with advice and counseling from *experts*
Young studio audience that hoots, shouts, and chants	Middle-aged studio audience that asks questions and shares experiences
Contentious, carnivalesque culture	Feel-good, celebrity-friendly gossip culture

notion of conventional form. Viewers come to tabloid and confessional talk shows expecting certain things to happen and to the extent that those things do happen, the shows are formally rewarding. Moreover, audiences are drawn to certain genres because the rhetorical tropes of those genres fulfill their particular needs and desires. From this perspective, we can conclude that one reason tabloid talk shows are appealing is because – by creating an escapist atmosphere of spectacle – they provide temporary refuge from the restrictive rules and regulations that daily discipline us. Alternatively, confessional talk shows are appealing because they comfort and reassure us with the knowledge that other people share in our daily struggles.

Though not all genres are widely recognized by audiences, they are no less important in terms of their symbolic inducements. The most sustained study of television from the perspective of theoretical genre is Brian Ott's *The Small Screen*. In that work, he contends that US prime-time television programming in the 1990s can usefully be categorized according to ways in which it assists viewers in negotiating the transition from the Industrial Age to the Information Age. Using that standard, Ott's groups shows into the genres of hyperconscious and nostalgia television, arguing that the former is defined by the stylistic conventions of eclecticism, intertextuality, and self-reflexivity, and the latter by the conventions of purity, unity, and security. Ott then conducts an in-depth Rhetorical analysis of an archetypical example from each genre – *The Simpsons* for hyperconscious television and *Dr. Quinn, Medicine Woman* for escapist television – to illustrate the very different sets of symbolic resources these genres afforded viewers for confronting the social anxieties (e.g. information overload, identify drift, acceleration, not knowing much, and fragmentation) associated with the rise of the Information Age. The value of genre analysis (be it historical or theoretical), then, is that it illuminates how the rhetorical patterns that extend *across* media texts as well as within them influence and appeal to us.

Narrative

A fourth rhetorical structure common to media texts is narrative. **Narrative** describes a series of events, real or fictitious, that occur in (often chronological) succession. For narrative theorist Gérard Genette, narrative can be divided into three levels: story (*histoire*), discourse (*récit*), and narrating (*narration*). To appreciate the rhetorical complexity of narrative, it is worth looking at each of the three levels in greater detail. *Story* refers to what happens to whom in a narrative. It is comprised of events and existents. The particular events that occur within a story are further divided according to the function they perform: kernels (or nuclei) are the key nodes or hinges that actively contribute to a story's progression and satellites (or catalyzers) are the more minor plot events that fill in the narrative. The distinction between kernals and satellites becomes evident when a story is condensed into its simplest form. Take the following story as example.

> Boy meets girl. Girl is endangered. Boy rescues girl from danger. Girl falls in love with boy. Boy and girl get married and live happily ever after.

This is what a story might look like if it were totally stripped of all satellites. Each of these events functions as kernels because they formally necessitate subsequent cardinal events. The endless array of minor events that connect these kernals will likely be satellites. After meeting girl, for instance, boy may drive home (satellite), tell friend about girl (satellite), and call and ask girl to go on a date (satellite). These events are satellites because they can be substituted with other events or even deleted without altering the basic story. Stories are also made of existents, which include characters (actants) and indices (informants and setting). Characters are often classified with respect to the actions they perform within a story. In his study of Russian fairy tales, Vladimir Propp identifies seven typical characters: hero (seeker or victim), villain, donor (provider), helper, princess (sought-after person), dispatcher, and false hero. This list was later streamlined by A.J. Greimas into three pairs (subject/object, sender/receiver, helper/opponent), which he argued accounted not just for the characters in fairy tales, but for those in stories in general. What audiences know about characters – specific details such as their age, hair color, and favorite food – are known as informants, while the location and overall atmosphere in which characters find themselves is called the setting.

The second level of narrative according to Genette is discourse. *Discourse* describes the actual words, written or spoken, used to tell a story. Since the narratives in contemporary media are increasingly visual, we would add images or pictures along with words to Genette's category of discourse. As is evidenced by the silent film era, words are not a requirement for storytelling. Because signs (i.e. words and images) are never neutral, the specific discourse of a narrative is central to its meaning. The meaning of the event, "boy meets girl," is significantly altered if, in the telling, the narrator says, "a seedy-looking man wearing a dark overcoat confronts Gillian in a dimly lit alley" rather than, "a businessman approaches Gillian at the bar and politely offers to buy her a drink." When analyzing how a narrative functions rhetorically, a critic ought to attend not just to what happens and to whom (i.e. story), but also to the precise language used to tell the story (i.e. discourse).

For Genette, the third level at which we can approach narrative is narrating. *Narrating* refers to the actual act of recounting (the situation *within* which discourse is uttered). It involves questions such as who is speaking, from what perspective or point of view, and in what relation to the listener/audience. To address these questions, Genette proposed analyzing narration along three axes: tense, mood, and voice. Drawing upon the work of Russian narratologist Tzvetan Todorov, Genette understood tense to refer to narrative temporality. The temporal relations of the narrative (tense) can further be divided into the categories of order, duration (speed), and frequency. The category or order has to do with how time unfolds for the narrator, who may or may not also be a character in the story. Narrators can transport audiences to the past through flashbacks (analepses) or into the future through flash forwards (prolepses), or they can create anticipation for future events through character premonition. The concept of reach refers to how far back or ahead the events that the narrator recalls or anticipates lie. The second category of narrative temporality is duration or speed, and it involves the relation between the period of time described (story-time) and the period of time required for the telling (discourse-time). According to Sarah Kozloff, there are five possible relations between story-time and discourse-time:

- scene: discourse-time and story-time are roughly equal (such as the technique utilized during the first season of the television series *24*).
- summary: discourse-time is shorter than story-time (such as the way a week can pass in an hour-long program).
- ellipsis: discourse-time is zero (such as the way two or three weeks can pass with a simple cut in film of television).
- stretch: discourse-time is longer than story-time (slow motion).
- pause: discourse-time is longer than story-time, which is zero (freeze-frame).

Frequency, the final category of temporal relations, refers to the number of times a single event or incident is recounted by the narrator. Genette noted four potential expressions of frequency: narrating once what happened once (e.g. "Yesterday, I went to bed early."), narrating *n* times what happened *n* times (e.g. Monday, I went to bed early. Tuesday, I went to bed early. Wednesday, I went to bed early."), narrating *n* times what happened once (e.g. "Yesterday I went to bed early, yesterday I went to bed early, yesterday I went to bed early."), and narrating one time (or rather, at one time) what happened *n* times (e.g. "I went to bed early every day of the week.").

Whereas tense (i.e. order, duration, and frequency) describes narrative temporality, Genette employs the term mood to describe the "*regulation of narrative information*,"[27] such as how much or how little is told (distance) and through what channel (perspective). Distance involves the words and thoughts of a character, while perspective or point of view describes who sees in the narrative and his or her capacities of knowledge. Perspective varies greatly, as a story can be told from (focalized through) or about (focalized on) a specific character. In the television series *Sex and the City*, for instance, the story is told from the perspective of Carrie Bradshaw, who frequently shares her personal thoughts. Consequently, viewers are invited to identify with Carrie and to see the world through her eyes. Genette's final category, voice, entails the position, type, and relation of the narrator. Questions of voice include: Is the narrator a character in the story (homodiegetic) or is she or he outside the story-world (heterodiegetic)? What is the narrator's degree of omniscience? Is the narrator reliable? Is the story told in first or third person? Genette regarded the distinction between voice and mood to be an important one because narrative voice frames how audiences understand and relate to narrative mood. While a character in a story may have a particularly optimistic outlook about the future (mood), the audience may know that such optimism is unwarranted because the character is about to experience bad fortune (voice). This is precisely the situation in horror films when the audience is shown (afforded special knowledge by the narrator) that there is a killer hiding under the bed that a character is unwittingly having sex on. Having more knowledge than the character in this case heightens the audience's fear by creating the expectation of violence. As is likely evident by this point, narratives are complex rhetorical structures involving many variables. Thus, we have included Figure 5.5 to clarify how those variables relate to one another.

<u>Elements of narrative</u>

   I. Story (content plane): the totality of narrated events
      A. <u>Events</u>:
         1. kernals (nuclei)
         2. satellites (catalyzers)
      B. <u>Existents</u>:
         1. characters (actants)
         2. indices:
            a. informants
            b. setting (motif)
   I. Discourse (expression plane): the actual written or spoken words
  II. Narration: the very act (recounting) that produces the discourse
      A. <u>Tense</u> (temporal relations)
         1. order
         2. duration (speed)
         3. frequency
      B. <u>Mood</u>
         1. distance: quantitative modulation
         2. perspective: qualitative modulation
      C. <u>Voice</u> (narrator)

Figure 5.5
The elements of
narrative.

Affect and Aesthetics

Up to this point, our discussion of a Rhetorical approach to media has focused on how signs or sets of signs working together create meaning and move audiences. We have, in keeping with a rather traditional Rhetorical perspective, concentrated on how texts move and influence audiences at a purely symbolic, cognitive level. But more recently, Rhetorical scholars have begun to ask how rhetoric moves us at a material, bodily level. Music scholars, for instance, are quick to point out that melody, harmony, and rhythm do not function in the same manner that linguistic and visual signs do, for they do not represent (i.e. stand in, for) anything else.[28] Yet, these non-symbolic elements of music exert an influence on us. Our bodies can literally feel the rhythm of a song, which may, in turn, prompt us to tap our feet. Similarly, the sound or grain (the material message) of someone's voice can – independent of what one is saying (the symbolic message) – sway us depending upon whether it is pleasing or displeasing. Thus, as Rhetorical scholars continue to investigate how messages move audiences, they are increasingly attending to the material as well as the symbolic dimensions of media.

The historical bias in favor of symbolicity, over and at the expense of materiality, is a consequence of two closely related, but mistaken philosophical assumptions: (1) that the mind and body are separate, independent structures, and (2) that meaning belongs primarily to the purview of the former. Today, most scholars reject the mind/body dualism that originated with the French philosopher René Descartes in the seventeenth century, and recognize that:

> A person is not a mind *and* a body. There are not two "things" somehow mysteriously yoked together. What we call a "person" is a certain kind of bodily organism that has a brain operating within its body, a body that is continually interacting with aspects of its environments (material and social) in an ever-changing process of experience.... In short, "mind" and "body" are merely abstracted aspects of the flow of organism-environment interactions that constitutes what we call experience.[29]

In addition to rejecting the Cartesian mind/body dichotomy, scholars increasingly understand that "*Meaning is grounded in our bodily experiences*,"[30] and that one must study our visceral and corporeal connections to the world to apprehend human meaning-making.

How, then, does one interpret or "read" bodily experiences? As bodies interact with their material surroundings, a process known as organism–environmental coupling,[31] they experience various energies, intensities, pulsations, and rhythms through sense data (sights, sounds, tastes, smells, and tactile sensations) that, in turn, produce affects. Charles Altieri defines affects as "immediate modes of sensual responsiveness to the world characterized by an accompanying imaginative dimension."[32] **Affects**, which can be divided into the basic categories of feelings, moods, emotions, and passions, shape the way we process sensory data, and, therefore, serve as the basis of human meaning-making. Our affective responses to the world are far from random and arbitrary. Similar sensorimotor experiences of space and time, or "recurring pattern[s] of organism-environment interactions"[33] tend to illicit similar affective responses. In the context of media, these recurring patterns manifest themselves as aesthetic experiences.

Traditionally, aesthetics has referred to the beauty of art and the sensual enjoyment it engenders. But understood a bit more broadly, **aesthetics** can be defined as the meaningfulness of art (and life) as apprehended through the senses. Aesthetic experience arises out of textual properties such as "consonance, dissonance, harmonies of tone, light, colour, sound and rhythm."[34] Although media aesthetics is frequently ignored by Rhetorical scholars because it is seen as involving purely subjective judgments and tastes,[35] it is vital to the way media texts function to produce meaning. As Arthur Asa Berger explains, "The way a scene is shot – the cutting, the editing, the use of music and sound effects, the lighting, the camera work – conveys a great deal of information and gives a sense of the importance of what we are seeing relative to other images and events in the text."[36] It is useful, therefore, to highlight a few important aspects of media aesthetics.

1 *Color.* Though color can be symbolic, such as the use of red to mean hot and blue to mean cold, color also has an immediate "emotional quality, which derives partly from personal associations; partly from experience in nature."[37] The ability of color to impact our mood and emotions is well established in both psychological and media scholarship.[38] Indeed, with regard to film, Barbara Kennedy argues that, "Colour functions as the main modulator of sensation."[39] So, for instance, while red stimulates excitement, blue and pink have a calming effect.[40]

2 *Lighting.* Like color, light (or its absence) has a strong symbolic dimension. While light signifies good, virtue, and salvation, darkness signifies evil, sin, and doom.[41] But light also operates on a material level and "can have profound effects on emotional states."[42] The intensity, focus, and shape of light can be used to guide or direct attention, to create depth and perspective, and to establish or enhance a particular mood. Since darkness can induce fear, horror films use dimly lit images to reinforce feelings of dread and fright. Meanwhile, films such as *Batman Begins* (2005) and *The Dark Knight* (2008) employ darkness to create a general sense of malaise

3 *Editing.* Editing describes the sequencing and length of individual shots within film and television, as well as the type (cuts, fades, dissolves, wipes, etc.) and frequency of transitions or shifts between shots. The way moving images are edited can have a profound influence on how an audience feels during a scene. Berger notes, for instance, that "Quick cutting between shots creates a sense of excitement in viewers; they work in a way opposite to that of lingering shots,

which slow things down."[43] Identifiable editing practices often emerge in relation to specific media forms, and thus influence the way audiences respond to that form. So, unlike Hollywood's classical narratives, whose editing functions to locate one in time and space, music videos rely on montage, a rapid editing style more likely to generate a feeling of discontinuity.[44]

4   *Movement and framing.* Camera movement (i.e. panning, dollying, and tracking) along with framing techniques, like angle of elevation, can powerfully shape the way audiences feel about a person or event they see on screen. As Ann Marie Seward Barry observes:

> The language of camera angles is . . . highly manipulative emotionally. . . . If the angle is extreme, the attitude becomes emphatic. Low angles (shot from beneath with the camera looking up at a subject) give the subject a sense of importance, power, and respect. . . . In contrast, when a film is shot from a high place looking down on the figure (that is, high angle), the reverse effect is achieved, and the figure looks small, helpless, and insignificant.[45]

Since camera angles are only one of the many techniques involved in image framing, the critic who wishes to understand the emotional valence created by the camera will need to attend to viewpoint, field of view, and picture composition as well.

5   *Sound.* In media such as television and film, sound is omnipresent; while noises (i.e. sound effects) such as a ringing phone or car engine generate a sense of verisimilitude by actualizing time and space, music plays a central role in establishing mood.[46] In a study of the mode, texture, and temperature of music, for instance, Gregory Webster and Catherine Weir found that major keys, non-harmonized melodies, and faster tempos were more likely to result in happier responses, while minor keys, harmonized melodies, and slower tempos were more likely to evoke sadness.[47] Similarly, Kevin Donnelly has demonstrated how the ephemeral character of film music manipulates audiences' emotions.[48]

The five aspects of media aesthetics discussed here do not constitute a comprehensive list, especially since different media have different aesthetics. When evaluating painting, posters, or photography, for instance, a critic would want to consider balance, shape, and form in place of editing, camera movement, and sound. The study of stationary images and other visual artifacts such as public memorials, buildings, and fashion has become so popular in recent years that it has produced its own rich body of literature known as visual rhetoric.[49] In many ways, the scholarship on specifically visual rhetorics, which typically excludes moving images such as film, video, and television[50] in addition to music, mirrors the basic trajectory of the Rhetorical study of media generally. It began with an almost exclusive focus on the symbolic dimensions of visuality (a bias that is still widely evident), but has slowly begun to recognize the importance of visual imagery's fully embodied, material dimensions. As the Rhetorical approach to the study of media continues to develop, it will need to more fully theorize and appraise the relation between the symbolic and the material.

Conclusion

In this chapter, we have considered what it means to approach media from a Rhetorical perspective by discussing what signs are, how they create meaning, how they combine to form texts, and how texts are structured to appeal to audiences. In the final section, we considered the affective dimensions of aesthetic experience, of how media move us materially and sway us somatically, and contribute to human meaning-making as a fully embodied experience. The Rhetorical approach, as we have described it thus far, reflects a rather structuralist perspective. **Structuralism** is the idea, largely popularized by the anthropologist Claude Lévi-Strauss, that each element in a cultural system derives its meaning in relation to other elements in that system;[51] moreover, it tends to regard such systems (language, food, fashion, kinship, etc.) as relatively closed and independent. This latter assumption has come under some critique from poststructuralists, who tend to view systems as interlocking and structures themselves as more open.

We wish to be careful of drawing too sharp a distinction between structuralism and poststructuralism, however, as most theorists agree that the seeds of poststructuralism are already present in structuralism. Perhaps the most important distinction is in how they conceptualize "texts." In structuralism, the meaning of a text derives from "internal" or immanent structures. The producer and receiver of a text (and to some extent even other texts) are seen as having very little to do with a text's meaning. Poststructuralism, by contrast, sees meaning as a complex interaction among texts (intertextuality) as well as between audiences and texts. The practical consequence of this distinction is that structuralism treats texts as more closed (possessing singular meanings) and poststructuralism treats texts as more open (inviting multiple meanings). The implications of this shift in perspective are more fully explored in Chapter 10 on Reception theory, which considers the centrality of audiences in meaning-making.

MEDIA LAB 4: DOING RHETORICAL ANALYSIS

OBJECTIVE

The aim of this lab is to critically assess a media text from a Rhetorical perspective. Attending to the rhetoric structures (clusters, forms, genre, and narrative) of a text, students will identify the text's central modes of appeal and influence.

ACTIVITY

- Divide class into small groups of 4–5 students each.
- Show students a recruiting video for one of the armed services (i.e. Army, Navy, Air Force, Marines).
- Ask students to record their answers to the following questions.
    1 What are the key signs? What other signs cluster around them? What associations and dissociations are invited by the clustering of signs? What is strategically absent from the text?
    2 What formal appetites does the text create? How are they resolved?
    3 Identify three other messages that share at least some structural similarities with the video. What are the similarities? What expectations do they foster?
    4 What is the story being told in the video? What are its main characters and events? What do you notice about the specific discourse being used in the video? What are the characteristics of the narration?

SUGGESTED READING

Altieri, C. *The Particulars of Rapture: an Aesthetics of Affect*. Ithaca, NY: Cornell University Press, 2003.

Barry, A.M.S. *Visual Intelligence: Perception, Image, and Manipulation in Visual Communication*. Albany, NY: State University of New York Press, 1997.

Barthes, R. *Elements of Semiology*. Translated by A. Lavers and C. Smith. New York: Hill and Wang, 1967.

Barthes, R. *Image, Music, Text*. Translated by S. Heath. New York: Hill and Wang, 1988.

Bordwell, D. *Making Meaning: Inference and Rhetoric in the Interpretation of Cinema*. Cambridge, MA: Harvard University Press, 1989.

Brummett, B. *Rhetoric in Popular Culture*, 2nd edn. Thousand Oaks, CA: Sage Publications, 2006.

Burke, K. *Counter-Statement*. Los Altos, CA: Hermes Publications, 1931.

Burke, K. *The Philosophy of Literary Form: Studies in Symbolic Action*. Baton Rouge, LA: Louisiana State University Press, 1941.

Campbell, K.K. and Jamieson, K.H. *Form and Genre: Shaping Rhetorical Action*. Falls Church, VA: Speech Communication Association, 1976.

Chandler, D. *Semiotics: the Basics*. New York: Routledge, 2002.

Chatman, S. *Story and Discourse: Narrative Structure in Fiction and Film*. Ithaca, NY: Cornell University Press, 1978.

Clarke, Jr, D.S. *Sources of Semiotic: Readings with Commentary from Antiquity to the Present*. Carbondale, IL: Southern Illinois University Press, 1990.

Culler, J. *Ferdinand de Saussure*, revised edn. Ithaca, NY: Cornell University Press, 1986.

Deming, C. Hill Street Blues as Narrative. In *Critical Perspectives on Media and Society*, R. Avery and D. Eason (eds), pp. 240–64. New York: Guilford, 1991.

de Saussure, F. *Course in General Linguistics*. Translated by R. Harris. Chicago, IL: Open Court, 1986.

Feuer, J. Genre Study and Television. In *Channels of Discourse, Reassembled: Television and Contemporary Criticism*, R.C. Allen (ed.), pp. 138–60. Chapel Hill, NC: University of North Carolina Press, 1992.

Fry, N. *Anatomy of Criticism: Four Essays*. Princeton, NJ: Princeton University Press, 1957.

Genette, G. *Narrative Discourse: an Essay in Method*. Translated by J.E. Lewin. Ithaca, NY: Cornell University Press, 1980.

Grant, B.K. *Film Genre Reader II*. Austin, TX: University of Texas Press, 1995.

Hoopes, J. (ed.) *Peirce on Signs: Writings on Semiotics by Charles Sanders Peirce*. Chapel Hill, NC: University of North Carolina Press, 1991.

Johnson, M. *The Meaning of the Body: Aesthetics and Human Understanding*. Chicago, IL: University of Chicago Press, 2007.

Kennedy, B.M. *Deleuze and Cinema: The Aesthetics of Sensation*. Edinburgh: Edinburgh University Press, 2000.

Kozloff, S. Narrative Theory and Television. In *Channels of Discourse, Reassembled: Television and Contemporary Criticism*, R.C. Allen (ed.), pp. 67–100. Chapel Hill, NC: University of North Carolina Press, 1992.

Massumi, B. *Parables for the Virtual: Movement, Affect, Sensation*. Durham, NC: Duke University Press, 2002.

Metz, C. *Film Language: a Semiotics of Cinema*. Chicago, IL: University of Chicago Press, 1974.

Olson, L.C., Finnegan, C.A., and Hope, D.S. (eds) *Visual Rhetoric: a Reader in Contemporary Communication and American Culture*. Los Angeles, CA: Sage Publications, 2008.

Ott, B.L. *The Small Screen: How Television Equips Us to Live in the Information Age*. Malden, MA: Blackwell Publishing, 2007.

Scholes, R., Phelan, J., and Kellogg, R. *The Nature of Narrative*. 40th anniversary edn. Oxford: Oxford University Press, 2006.

Seiter, E. Semiotics, Structuralism, and Television. In *Channels of Discourse, Reassembled: Television and Contemporary Criticism*, R.C. Allen (ed.), pp. 31–66. Chapel Hill, NC: University of North Carolina Press, 1992.

Smith, K., Moriarty, S., Barbatsis, G., and Kenney, K. (eds) *Handbook of Visual Communication: Theory, Methods, and Media*. Mahwah, NJ: Lawrence Erlbaum Associates Publishers, 2005.

Wallace, M. *Recent Theories of Narrative*. Ithaca, NY: Cornell University Press, 1986.

Wright, W. *Six Guns & Society: a Structural Study of the Western*. Berkeley, CA: University of California Press, 1975.

NOTES

1. C. Chocano, It's All a Little Murky under the Mask. *Los Angeles Times*, March 17, 2006, E-1, http://articles.latimes.com/2006/mar/17/entertainment/et-vendetta17 (accessed December 11, 2008).

2. The claim that all media are rhetorical should not be taken to mean that media are nothing but rhetorical. On this distinction, see M.J. Medhurst and T.W. Benson, *Rhetorical Dimen-*

sions in Media: A Critical Casebook, 2nd edn (Dubuque, IA: Kendall/Hunt Publishing Company, 1991), xix.

3. Aristotle, *On Rhetoric*, trans. G.A. Kennedy (New York: Oxford University Press, 1991), 14.

4. This definition closely mirrors Kenneth Burke's view of rhetoric as, "The use of symbols to induce action in beings that normally communicate by symbols" [K. Burke, *A Rhetoric of Motives* (Berkeley, CA: University of California Press, 1950), 162].

5. "[S]peech in its essence is not neutral. Far from suspended judgment, the . . . speech of people is loaded with judgments. It is intensely moral—its names for objects contain the emotional overtones which give us cues as to how we should act toward these objects. Even a word like 'automobile' will usually contain a concealed choice (it designates not merely an *object*, but a *desirable object*). Spontaneous speech is not a naming at all, but a system of attitudes, of implicit exortations. . . . speech is profoundly *partisan*" [K. Burke, *Permanence and Change: an Anatomy of Purpose*, revised edn (Los Altos, CA: Hermes Publications, 1954), 176–7].

6. K. Burke, *Language as Symbolic Action* (Berkeley, CA: University of California Press, 1968), 45.

7. The authors of this book reject the idea that invitational rhetoric, which is believed by a small group of scholars to be an alternative to persuasive discourse, is somehow not suasory. Continuing to promote invitational rhetoric as such dangerously obfuscates the ways in which it, like any other form of discourse, necessarily entails and promotes particular biases.

8. J. Culler, *Ferdinand de Saussure* (Ithaca, NY: Cornell University Press, 1986), 15.

9. F. de Saussure, *Course in General Linguistics*, trans. R. Harris (Chicago, IL: Open Court, 1986), 15.

10. Saussure, 67.
11. Culler, 33.
12. Saussure, 70.
13. Quoted in D.S. Clarke, Jr, *Sources of Semiotic: Readings with Commentary from Antiquity to the Present* (Carbondale, IL: Southern Illinois University Press, 1990), 58.

14. Quoted in Clarke, 59.
15. Quoted in Clarke, 71.
16. Quoted in Clarke, 74.
17. M. Ribière, *Barthes: A Beginner's Guide* (London: Hodder & Stoughton, 2002), 1.
18. R. Barthes, *Elements of Semiology*, trans. A. Lavers and C. Smith (New York: Hill and Wang, 1967), 89.
19. One can never, as Barthes would say, arrive at a final signified.
20. Barthes, *Elements*, 50.
21. R. Barthes, *Image, Music, Text*, trans. S. Heath (New York: Hill and Wang, 1988), 40.
22. B. Brummett, *Rhetoric in Popular Culture* (Thousand Oaks, CA: Sage Publications, 2006), 34.
23. K. Burke, *The Philosophy of Literary Form: Studies in Symbolic Action* (Baton Rouge, LA; Louisiana State University Press, 1941), 20.
24. K. Burke, *Counter-Statement* (Los Altos, CA: Hermes Publications, 1931), 124.
25. Burke, *Counter*, 124.
26. Burke, *Counter*, 125.
27. G. Genette, *Narrative Discourse: an Essay in Method*, trans. J.E. Lewin (Ithaca, NY: Cornell University Press, 1980), 162.
28. M. Johnson, *The Meaning of the Body: Aesthetics and Human Understanding* (Chicago, IL: University of Chicago Press, 2007), 238.
29. Johnson, 11–12.
30. Johnson, 12.
31. Johnson, 50–1, 123–4.
32. C. Altieri, *The Particulars of Rapture: an Aesthetics of Affect* (Ithaca, NY: Cornell University Press, 2003), 2.
33. Johnson, 136.
34. B.M. Kennedy, *Deleuze and Cinema: the Aesthetics of Sensation* (Edinburgh: Edinburgh University Press, 2000), 114.
35. This bias against aesthetic experience is largely inherited from Immanuel Kant. See Johnson, 211–18.
36. A.A. Berger, *Essentials of Mass Communication Theory* (Thousand Oaks, CA: Sage Publications, 1995), 81.
37. A.M.S. Barry, *Visual Intelligence: Perception, Image, and Manipulation in Visual Communication*

(Albany: State University of New York Press, 1997), 130.

38. In psychology, see M. Hemphill, A Note on Adult's Color-Emotion Associations, *The Journal of Genetic Psychology* 157, 1996, 275–80, and K.W. Jacobs and J.F. Suess, Effects of Four Psychological Primary Colours on Anxiety State, *Perceptual and Motor Skills* 41, 1975, 207–10. In media studies, see B.H. Detenber, R.F. Simons, and J.E. Reiss, The Emotional Significance of Color in Television Presentations, *Media Psychology* 2, 2000, 331–55, M.-C. Lichtlé, The Effect of an Advertisement's Colour on Emotions Evoked by an Ad and Attitude Towards the Ad, *International Journal of Advertising* 26, 2007, 37–62, and P. Valdez and A. Mehrabian, Effects of Color on Emotions, *Journal of Broadcasting & Electronic Media* 42, 1994, 113–27.

39. Kennedy, 115.

40. R. Arnheim, *Art and Visual Perception: a Psychology of the Creative Eye*, The New Version (Berkeley: University of California Press, 1954), 368; see also Barry, 132.

41. Arnheim, 324.

42. Barry, 134.

43. Berger, 83.

44. C. Vernallis, *Experiencing the Music Video: Aesthetics and Cultural Context* (New York: Columbia University Press, 2004), 37.

45. Barry, 135–6.

46. J. Monaco, *How to Read a Film: the Art, Technology, Language, History, and Theory of Film and Media*, revised edn (New York: Oxford University Press, 1981), 179.

47. G.D. Webster and C.G. Weir, Emotional Responses to Music: Interactive Effects of Mode, Texture, and Tempo, *Motivation and Emotion* 29, 2005, 19–39.

48. K. Donnelly, *The Spectre of Sound: Music in Film and Television* (London: British Film Institute, 2005).

49. For an overview of this literature, see B.L. Ott and G. Dickinson, Visual Rhetoric as/and Critical Pedagogy, in *The SAGE Handbook of Rhetorical Studies*, A. Lunsford (ed.), pp. 391–405 (Los Angeles, CA: Sage, 2009).

50. Visual rhetoric scholars are beginning to consider media that include moving images, but historically the focus has been on stationary imagery and artifacts.

51. C. Lévi-Strauss, *Structural Anthropology*, trans. C. Jacobson and B. Grundfest Schopf (New York: Basic Books, 1963), 33.

6 Cultural Analysis

KEY CONCEPTS

AMERICAN DREAM
ASSIMILATION
CONSPICUOUS CONSUMPTION
CULTURAL STUDIES
CULTURE
DIFFERENCE
DOXA
EXCLUSION
EXOTICISM

HEGEMONY
IDEOLOGY
INTERPELLATION
MYTH
OTHERING
STEREOTYPING
STRUCTURE OF FEELING
TOKEN

Consider the following scenario: a father and son are driving home from a hockey game across town. They are arguing about the various strengths and weaknesses of the players during the game when a drunk driver smashes into the driver's side of their car. The father is killed instantly in the collision, but the son lives through the ordeal, although with serious injuries. Paramedics who arrive on the scene realize that the boy will die without immediate medical attention, and they rush him to the hospital in an ambulance. At the hospital, the boy is laid out on the operating table so that a jagged piece of the car's interior can be removed from his ribcage. The surgeon arrives in the emergency room accompanied by a group of nurses, only to pull back in utter horror at the sight of the boy on the table.

"I can't operate on this boy," the surgeon says. "This boy is my son!"[1]

When you read the story above for the first time, did the surgeon's revelation confuse you? Did it take you a few moments to realize that the surgeon is the boy's *mother*? If it did, what caused you to assume that the surgeon was a man in the first place (thereby creating the confusing paradox of the dead father)? It's true that in contemporary American culture the image of the medical surgeon is often the image of a male doctor, but where does that gendered association come from? Moments like the one captured in the story of the surgeon force us to question how we think about the world around us and where those ideas originate. These issues are especially important to consider when attempting to understand the approach to media studies based on issues of culture and ideology. Scholars in this strand of media studies seek to understand how media texts shape the way we think about the world as cultural, political, and social beings. Currently described by the scholarly umbrella term Cultural studies, cultural and ideological critics claim that media texts like television shows or newspapers, far from merely reflecting the world around us, actually represent a skewed version of society in relation to class, race, gender, sexuality, age, disability, and a host of other social constructs. In essence, media texts represent particular perspectives on the world and society at the cost of excluding other views, and the resulting worldviews represented in the media are often those of socially powerful or privileged groups.

This chapter begins with a discussion over theories of culture and ideology, concentrating on how the ideologies of any given culture work to normalize and privilege certain perspectives on reality. We then briefly outline the historical development of the British Cultural studies tradition as a way of understanding the political underpinnings of Cultural studies scholarship. Finally, we consider how ideologies influence the construction of media texts in relation to two historically relevant social issues in the Cultural studies tradition: class and race.

Cultural Theory: an Overview

As a way of understanding social organization, **culture** can be a problematic term. Scholars disagree over the best way to conceptualize or understand the issue of culture. In mulling over the idea of culture, sociologist Michael Richardson provides this possible definition: "Culture is simply what human beings produce and the means by which we preserve what we have produced."[2] This definition provides a good foundation for understanding culture: that it is constructed, multi-faceted, and uniquely human. However, it is helpful in formulating a specific definition of culture to consider the key ingredients or aspects that make a culture known. The "building blocks" of culture fall into roughly three forms.

The first form of culture is physical. Picture a society thousands of years in the future attempting to study and gain knowledge about our current culture. How might they understand us better? The most obvious way would be through the physical objects that we leave behind for them to find, called artifacts. Artifacts are any of the material aspects of daily life that possess widely shared meanings and manifest group (national, social, political) identification to us. Artifacts include clothing, music, television shows, automobiles, computers, comic books, billboards, carnival rides, space shuttles, and more; virtually any manufactured item that you can point to (including this textbook) is an example of an artifact. An artifact is a physical symbol that represents who we are as a culture.

The next form of culture is social. After collecting and analyzing our artifacts, the futuristic society studying us will attempt to decipher the social codes and rules that governed the creation of those artifacts. They will attempt to reconstruct the practices or customs of our daily lives, the habitual performances of our particular social conventions. If they found this textbook, for example, they might assume that reading, learning, and critiquing were all social practices of ancient American culture. Similarly, they might formulate some ideas about our hygienic customs if they were to discover any one of the wide assortment of tools related to personal upkeep: toothbrushes, blow dryers, contact lens cases, etc. If artifacts are the products of our shared lives, then customs are our shared, lived experiences: eating, working, dancing, mourning, sex, exercise regimens, driving laws, power hours, etc.

The final form of culture is attitudinal. Our customs, laws, and traditions reflect particular ways of understanding the world. To continue with our futuristic society example, scholars of the next millennium might piece together enough artifacts to find that we as Americans tended to support the notion of free speech or the concepts of individualism and personal responsibility. They might discover documents with the acronym PLUR, describing the beliefs and attitudes expressed by members of modern rave culture: Peace, Love, Unity, and Respect. In essence, attitudes display the overarching ways a particular culture makes sense of the world and itself, including values, tastes, concepts of right and wrong, religious systems, economic beliefs, or political philosophies.

Now that we have some understanding regarding what constitutes culture, we can begin to pick out some of the common qualities that define culture. First, culture is *collective*. While individuals may be a part of a particular culture, they can never inhabit a culture on their own. Culture must be shared among a group of people. However, it is important to remember that a cultural group in itself may be as large as a nation or as small as a fandom of a syndicated television show. Computer hackers constitute a distinct cultural group; only individuals who participate in hacking know about the artifacts, practices, and attitudes that make up the distinct culture of hackers. Therefore, while culture must be shared among a group of people, it also by definition does not include everyone. Society is always a collection of cultures and co- or subcultures (cultural groups that exist within larger cultural groups), and all individuals will be members of multiple cultural groups at one time.

Second, culture is *rhetorical*. Culture functions symbolically. Possessing culture is not natural or inherent to our biology as human beings, but rather a result of our shared symbol systems that allow us to communicate meaning to one another. This means that a culture is sustained and transmitted exclusively through the words and images that carry significance for members of the culture. The artifacts of a particular culture only have significance because members of the culture can *name* them, and the customs or attitudes of a cultural group can only be meaningful because that can be *described* as such. For instance, the report card is a powerful artifact in the culture of American education, but its power only comes from the rhetorical, symbolic aspect of our national culture. There is nothing intrinsically powerful or threatening about a piece of paper with markings on it, and there is nothing that requires an A to mean "outstanding" and an F to mean "failure." Instead, we as a culture have symbolically and rhetorically agreed upon the meaning of the report card.

Third, culture is *historical*. It changes, evolves, mutates, fades, and even disappears over time. Like everything else, culture is subject to the whims and shifts of history. Some cultures have existed for millennia in different forms (Greco–Roman culture, Jewish culture, etc.), and some appear and vanish in a matter of years. A good example of this type of sudden cultural ascent and decline is the Club Kids phenomenon of the 1980s and 1990s. The Club Kids were a subculture within the New York party and nightlife scene of the time. The group dressed in wildly outrageous and androgynous costumes, experimented with a number of drugs, and promoted hedonistic philosophies of life. Although at times club owners paid the group to show up and promote specific venues, they were really a culture unto themselves, oftentimes throwing spontaneous parties in public places throughout New York. The Club Kids culture began to decline in the 1990s, and they are all but non-existent today. They stand as a stark example of how cultures can suddenly form and dissipate depending on the historical moment.

Finally, and perhaps most important to our present discussion, culture is *ideological*. The cultures we inhabit teach us to see the world in some ways and not in others. The attitudes, practices, and artifacts of our everyday lives encourage us as individuals to interpret the world according to certain frameworks of culturally based knowledge. French discourse scholar Michel Foucault provides a stark example of how culture functions to direct our attention in his work on madness.[3] The majority of cultures in Renaissance Europe did not perceive madness as problematic. It existed as a constant in daily life, a factor as unpreventable and prevalent as death. Foucault cites various historical examples and texts, including celebratory "Feasts of Fools" and the works of Shakespeare, to show how madness was intrinsically tied into the cultural fabric of the time. However, the seventeenth century saw the rise of sanitariums and other confinement houses in Europe, and these institutions were responsible for removing undesirable individuals from everyday life: the poor, the indecent, and the mad. The common denominator among all of these groups was their inability to contribute to the newly emerging process of economic production and consumption that marked Europe during the time. Thus, the widespread "lock up" of these individuals "concerns not the relations between madness and illness, but the relations between society and itself, between society and what it recognized and did not recognize in the behavior of individuals."[4] We can see from Foucault's example that the structure of a culture directs its inhabitants to perceive the world in a given way. Although there is always room for individual interpretation, ideology is a powerful and distinct force of interpretation in every culture.

Overall, culture can be described as the collection of artifacts, practices, and beliefs of a particular group of people at a particular historical moment, supported by symbolic systems and directed by ideology. This understanding of culture in general, and ideology in particular, is important for media scholars who see mass media texts like magazines or news programs as a central component in the dissemination of a given culture's ideologies. These scholars analyze media texts to better understand the ideologies that inform their creation, and they hope to better conceptualize how the attitudes and beliefs of a culture find their way into the media we consume every day. However, before turning our attention to the specific work of ideological media analysis, it is important that we have a better understanding about the role and scope of ideology in contemporary society.

The Functions of Ideology

We already know that cultures give rise to ideologies and that ideologies influence how individual members of the culture see the world, but we still need to understand the subtle ways that ideology accomplishes this directed attention. Remember, an **ideology** is a system of ideas that unconsciously shapes and constrains both our beliefs and behaviors. The way that we unconsciously define the world around us, the explanations about the world that we take for granted, and the unquestioned beliefs that we hold are all the result in some way of our cultural ideologies. The four ways that ideology structures our social world are through limitation, normalization, privileging, and interpellation.

First, a given ideology *limits* the range of acceptable ideas that a person may consider within a particular cultural context. It promotes and legitimates certain perspectives and values while obscuring or devaluing others. Some ideologies are easy to spot because the interpretations they promote are obviously one-sided, but other types of ideology are much more difficult to identify. For example, Republicans and Democrats both posses highly visible political ideologies. Each party functions as a culture with particular artifacts, customs, and attitudes, and each party provides its members with an ideology that limits interpretation and helps those individuals distinguish between right and wrong, true and false, good and bad. However, some ideologies define our world in a more unconscious fashion, and we enact or support them often without realizing it. These are ideologies that have become so ingrained in our minds and everyday lived experiences that we fail to notice their influence as ideological.

A good example of this kind of unconscious ideology concerns biological sex in contemporary American society. In American culture we tend to understand the concept of sex according to one of two groups: male or female. The reality, of course, is that the human form can often display physical characteristics of both sexes, leading to a condition known as intersexuality (a term that has replaced the more archaic hermaphrodite). Intersexuality is more common than most people realize. Approximately one in every 2,000 children is born with sexually ambiguous genitalia,[5] compared to only one in 17,000 born with albinism.[6] However, despite the relatively common occurrence of the condition, sexual ideologies in our culture and media erase the presence of intersexuality from everyday thought in many ways. Public restrooms are assigned according to male and female sexes, as are clothing departments in retail stores. It would be a difficult to pick out even one major intersexed character in the history of American television. The two-sex system becomes even more visibly constructed when compared to the complex fabric of Indian society, where the culture recognizes a valid third sex called the Hijra. The Hijra are an assembly of eunuchs, intersexuals, transsexuals, and others that the society understands as neither male nor female. With this knowledge, we can see how ideology subtlety directs our attention toward perceiving sexuality and biology in America from a certain perspective. Just like gender in the story of the surgeon, we only think about intersexuality and sexual ideologies when we are consciously confronted with the ideas. It is this unconscious form of ideology and the ways it structures our perception that will be the primary focus of the rest of this chapter.

By limiting the possible perceptions or interpretations of the world, ideology also *normalizes* certain aspects of it. This process of defining normalcy is especially important in the realm of social relations. Ideology often makes social relations and arrangements between individuals seem normal, and it makes established relationships of power appear to be the natural order of things. For example, you are probably reading this chapter right now because your instructor assigned it as homework. Your resulting responsibility as a student is to read the chapter and absorb the information for class discussion or tests. However, have you ever stopped to question where this student/teacher relationship comes from? Why does the teacher have more authority than you do in your own education? The social roles that we occupy throughout our lifetime, like *child*, *student*, or *employee*, inscribe us into relationships of unequal power as a result of ideological value hierarchies. All social relations are inherently relations of power because all social relations exist in a web of ideologies which award power to certain roles. Your instructor has power, or "the ability to control events and meanings,"[7] only because American cultural ideology often awards authority to highly educated experts in a given field.

The distribution of power according to ideology extends well beyond the college classroom. For example, the ideology of American capitalism ensures that employers have power over their employees, and this relationship between owner and worker seems to be a natural part of everyday life instead of a culturally constructed system. In some cultures older people wield a great deal of power as revered elders, but in American society elderly individuals are often treated as helpless, feeble, or "a drain on the system." As we can see, power is inextricably tied up with the ideological constructs of a particular culture. At times relationships of power can be beneficial (after all, you *are* receiving an education even if your instructor has the power), but they are never *natural*. Ideology normalizes these relationships of power and their control over individuals.

This unequal distribution of power between social actors explains one of the most important aspects of ideology: ideology *privileges* some interests over others. In the process of normalizing relations of power, it also informally confirms that the perspectives, qualities, or needs of socially powerful groups are more important or valid than those of socially dominated groups. The capitalist economic and ideological structure of American business culture is full of examples of this distinction. Although employees tend to do much of the actual work in a capitalist business, it is the more socially powerful management and owners that reap the most profits generated from the work. Likewise, most businesses in America favor managerial styles that emphasize masculine qualities like assertiveness, independence, or competitiveness, a fact that helps men move up through a company and often creates difficult situations for women seeking promotion. Outside of business culture, a hotly debated example of power and privilege now is the issue of marriage. As a result of American religious and political ideologies, the institution of marriage as of this writing generally reflects the needs and interests of (socially powerful) heterosexual couples to the detriment of (socially powerless) homosexual couples.

It may seem at this point that ideology permeates every aspect of a culture, fashioning the limits of knowledge and influencing power structures at every level of social organization. This seemingly overarching quality of ideology is central to Louis Althusser's concept of *interpellation*, the fourth function of ideology. Althusser was an Algerian Marxist interested in the ways that ideology controls individuals. He claims that ideology is so infused into the social structure that it actually serves as the force to interpellate us, or the force that calls us into existence as social subjects.[8] Individuals, far from being unique or original, are actually a collection of different ideological systems fused into one identity through the process of "hailing." Hailing occurs when individuals recognize and respond to an encountered ideology and allow it to represent them. Althusser also posits that because culture and ideology necessarily predate the individual, individuals are "always already interpellated."

In order to make the process of interpellation clearer, consider the following questions: At what age do you remember recognizing your particular gender identity? Chances are that before you even consciously took up that identity, your parents had already given you toys, surrounded you with colors, or played with you in ways that communicated the norms or limits of that identity to you. Each of these moments constituted a hailing, or a moment of exchange where you recognized the existence of a way of understanding yourself and responded to it, allowing it to define or constitute you in the process. The process of forming identity is a process of ideological recognition. For Althusser, ideologies exhibit the range of possible identity expressions, and individuals are a collection of the ideologies to which they consciously or unconsciously ascribe. Ideological discourse not only speaks to us, it creates the *us*.

Althusser's assertion that individuals are caught in a web of ideologies from which they draw their individual identities is an interesting perspective on the role of ideology in society, but it also importantly confirms the existence of multiple ideologies circulating throughout a culture. Remember, ideology is an aspect of every culture, and even relatively small subcultures can have powerful ideologies (one only needs to look at historical cults like Heaven's Gate or Jonestown to confirm this point). However, it is also clear that not all ideologies carry the same weight on a widespread scale, and we can see that some are more present than others in the minds of most people. The aforementioned concepts of social power and privilege hint at the reason for this imbalance, but something else explains the supremacy of certain ideologies in American culture. It is to these ideas that we turn our attention now.

Ideological Processes: Myth, Doxa, and Hegemony

A number of theories explain how ideologies within a culture become widespread, common, or dominant. This section will focus on three interrelated concepts: Roland Barthes's *myth*, Pierre Bourdieu's *doxa*, and Antonio Gramsci's *hegemony*. Although myth and doxa both shed light on how ideology works, hegemony has gained a certain theoretical dominance within the field of ideological analysis. As a result, the majority of this section will focus on ideas surrounding hegemony, and hegemony will be a central theme throughout the rest of the chapter.

In his book *Mythologies*, Barthes outlines a theory of ideological dominance based on the notion of myth. A **myth** is a sacred story or "type of speech"[9] that reaffirms and reproduces ideology in relation to an object. *Mythologies* itself is a collection of essays in which Barthes identifies a variety of cultural objects (children's toys, soap advertisements, etc.) and investigates them for their mythological components. Myth operates as the "higher" level of meaning of a particular object. For example, all objects relay a basic meaning. At some level, the video game *Super Mario Brothers* literally means "a video game named *Super Mario Brothers*." However, most objects also relay larger, culturally connotative meanings: the realm of myth. For instance, in addition to signifying "video game," *Super Mario Brothers* also relates a classic story of a hero undertaking a voyage to rescue a princess from an evil captor. In this way, the mythological or "higher-level" meaning of the game connotes ideas of bravery, heroism, and masculinity that are central to American ideological formations. The game reinforces certain ideologies above others by making their mythological content seem innocent, everyday, or "natural." Barthes claims that cultural myths normalize the ideologies of the ruling or socially privileged groups and reinforce power differentials between classes.

Bourdieu provides similar ideas related to ideology in his concept of doxa. **Doxa** represents knowledge "which is beyond question and which each agent tacitly accords by the mere fact of acting in accord with social convention."[10] In other words, doxa refers to the constructed aspects of a culture that its members do not really challenge or critically reflect upon. A good synonym for doxa is "common sense." Like myth, doxa supports certain ideologies over others by making them seem natural or simply as "they way things are." Bourdieu, like Barthes, views doxa as intrinsically tied to the ideologies of socially dominant groups. Those with social power wish to preserve the cultural doxa, while those without power seek to resist or alter it.

It is important to realize that expressing a minority opinion is not the same as resisting the "common-sense" ideologies present in doxa. Consider the process of watching a popular movie at a theater with your friends. The members of your group may disagree over the relative merit of the film, but none of you would be likely to question why you had to pay to see the film in the first place. The discussion between your friends over their opinion of the film represents what Bourdieu calls "the universe of discourse," made up of issues that can be discussed and debated. The process of handing your money over to the theatre to gain admittance represents "the universe of doxa," made up of social rules and processes that go unquestioned. In turn, paying to see the film supports capitalist ideology and reaffirms its validity in our cultural context.

Although myth and doxa both lend valuable insight into why certain ideologies are more widespread than others, the concept of hegemony is especially important because it accounts for the *evolution* of dominant ideologies. First proposed by Italian Marxist Antonio Gramsci in the 1920s and 1930s, the concept of hegemony is key in understanding the ascension and persistence of dominant ideologies. **Hegemony** is the process by which one ideology subverts other competing ideologies and gains cultural dominance. Gramsci developed his theory of hegemony to address some of the shortcomings of Marxism. Recall the basic structure of Marxist theory from Chapter 2. Marx believed that ideology was a byproduct of the economic system in any culture, and at most it was a reflection of industry owners' interests used to fool the working class into a false consciousness. He asserted that in time the large working class would recognize this systemic oppression and overthrow the relatively small owning class. This revolution never occurred, and Gramsci proposed his theory of hegemony as an explanation for its absence.

Hegemony is the process of convincing people to support the continued existence of a social system that does not support them in return. Gramsci characterizes hegemony as "'spontaneous' consent."[11] In other words, the working class (or any socially marginalized group) does not revolt because they actually consent to being dominated by the ideologies of privileged groups. Dominant (or hegemonic) ideologies still reflect the desires and interests of socially powerful groups, but these ideologies also come with the added promise that it is in the best interest of dominated individuals for them to accept these *particular* values and beliefs. In other words, socially powerful groups seek to have their worldview accepted by members of society as the universal way of thinking, and individuals within the culture accept the hegemonic ideologies because these systems of interpretation seem to benefit them in some way.

The best way to understand the hegemonic winning of consent is through an example. Paying for one's own college education is a hegemonic ideology in American society. It is a constructed system normalized through practice. We consent to the hegemonic belief that we should pay for a college education because supporting the system seems to benefit us. By securing a college degree, we gain additional knowledge about the world and a probable increase our future paychecks. However, by consenting to this system, we also support ideologies of American capitalism that award power to economic producers over consumers. Although these systems ultimately harm us as consumers, we willingly consent to systems of ideological domination because of the perceived benefits. This type of economic hegemony is most evident in the notion of the American Dream, discussed later in the chapter.

The concept of hegemony also helps explain how dominant ideologies persist through a process of flexible appropriation. Hegemonic systems never go away; they simply change form. When consent fails and socially marginalized ideologies gain significant visibility in a culture, these resistant ideologies represent a challenge to that society's overarching hegemonic ideologies. In such a situation, it is likely that the hegemonic ideological structures will absorb the marginalized ideologies and integrate them into the privileged ideological matrix. A number of classic studies in the field provide examples of this process. For instance, in *Subculture: The Meaning of Style*, Dick Hebdige looks at the subculture of British punks in the 1980s to understand hegemonic appropriation.[12] The British punk movement's emphasis on anarchy and gratification represented a challenge to the hegemonic British ideologies of governance and order. As the punk movement increased in popularity and visibility, they became more of a threat to the traditional, ideological British "way of life." In order to circumvent this threat, hegemonic ideological institutions in Britain began to absorb punk life. Retail shops began to sell punk clothing, and newspapers began running stories on punks and their families. By integrating the punk movement into dominant economic and cultural systems, the British hegemonic structures sanitized the punk movement and greatly diminished its resistive potential. In a sense, "punk" was absorbed and put in the service of hegemonic ideologies.

We can see from this example that hegemonic ideologies survive by validating or normalizing the ideologies of marginalized groups without actually altering the larger, dominant ways of understanding the culture. This process is one of constant give and take. John Fiske's discussion of jeans is a good example of the back and forth struggle that characterizes hegemony.[13] Wearing blue jeans in the 1960s was a sign of opposition to the dominant American culture. However, as the popularity of such resistance began to take hold, retailers responded by creating an elaborate system of different mass-produced styles and labels for jeans. Jeans became "popular" and normal. In response, many individuals began to intentionally rip and disfigure their new jeans in an attempt to distinguish themselves from the newly established normalcy. However, retailers in turn began to fade and destroy their jeans on a large scale. Thus, hegemonic ideological structures maintain control through a never-ending process of integration and appropriation of marginalized ideologies.

Overall, concepts of myth, doxa, and hegemony explain a great deal about the ideologies and power structures of a given culture. Myth is the preservation of ideology through the active retelling of dominant cultural stories. Doxa is the preservation of ideology through silence and maintaining the distinction between what should and should not be debated. Hegemony is the preservation of ideology through won consent and flexible adaptation toward resistance. For media scholars interested in issues of culture, the concept of ideology helps to explain the structures and themes of a culture's media texts, and the concept of hegemony helps to explain the presence of certain ideologies over others. Scholars do this type of media analysis under the academic banner of **Cultural studies**, an umbrella term for a wide variety of scholarship concerned with culture, ideology, privilege, and oppression. The Cultural studies tradition is relatively new in comparison to other media studies approaches, and it represents an important area in the contemporary discipline of media studies.

Cultural Studies: History, Theory, and Methodology

In a sense, the academic discipline of Cultural studies has two histories. The actual or literal discipline can be traced to 1964 with the founding of the Centre for Contemporary Cultural Studies at the University of Birmingham in Britain. However, the theoretical or conceptual history of Cultural studies actually begins in the early twentieth century. The formation of Cultural studies as a scholarly perspective was in many ways a response to previous conceptions of "culture" as the exclusive realm of the upper class. Based on the works of literary/cultural critics like Matthew Arnold and F.R. Leavis, many academics in Britain at this time limited the definition of "culture" to the best aesthetic products and traditions of contemporary society. In essence, artistic products like operas, high art, and literary classics could be considered culture within this framework. Horse races, quilted blankets and cartoons could not.

Leavis endorsed literature as an especially important aspect of culture because he believed that great literary works preserved essential moral qualities of a bygone era in British history. Popular fiction, as his wife and fellow scholar Q.D. Leavis characterized it, was "not only formed to convey merely crude states of mind but it [was] destructive of any fineness."[14] From the Leavises' perspective, it was the duty of intellectuals and academics to uphold the legacy of "cultured" literature in order to maintain moral standards in an increasingly industrialized, mediated society like Britain in the 1920s and 1930s. Thus, we can see that defining culture was more than just an arbitrary distinction of aesthetics for these thinkers. Limiting the academic definition of culture was also a political attempt to combat the perceived ills of increased exposure to a popular mediated system that engaged "the unruly desires and immorality of the masses."[15]

Reflecting on this academic movement (widely referred to as Leavisism), we can see that it clearly drew elitist distinctions between culture and mass society along class lines. "Culture" here referred exclusively to the aesthetic forms most accessible to educated or wealthy individuals in society, and "mass society" referred to the activities and products of the lower or working classes. This distinction held academic sway until the publication of Richard Hoggart's *The Uses of Literacy* in 1958, which blurred the link between the notion of "culture" and upper-class pursuits.[16] Drawing on his personal experiences as a youth in the British working class, Hoggart outlines a detailed account of working-class culture and its norms in relation to family relationships, neighborhood structures, religious belief, and more. In this way, *Uses* departs from Leavisism by making a claim for the importance of working-class cultural norms, pointing out that issues of morality are not exclusive to the upper class. However, the second half of the book engages in a decidedly Leavisist criticism of mass culture like popular music and "sex-and-violence novels," which Hoggart sees as a threat to the working class way of life. In retrospect, although Hoggart's work importantly expanded ideas of morality to working-class culture, it also continued the Leavisist tradition by affirming the perceived dangers of popular culture.

While Hoggart began to break the notion of culture free from its Leavisist roots, the most important scholar in laying the theoretical groundwork for the distinct discipline of Cultural studies is Raymond Williams. The publication of his book *The Long Revolution* in 1961 marked an important turn in the understanding of culture. In it, Williams recognizes the importance of viewing culture from ideal (Leavisist) and documentary (anthropological) standpoints, but he also proposes a third, social definition: "Culture is a description of a particular way of life, which expresses certain meanings and values not only in art and learning but also in institutions and ordinary behavior."[17] For Williams, no analysis of culture is complete without looking at all three of these dimensions. Moreover, this newly proposed social definition extends the idea of culture to include virtually all aspects of contemporary society, considering both high art *and* pop art, literature *and* comics to be important expressions of a particular culture at a particular moment in history. Williams also claims that every culture is governed by a structure of feeling. A **structure of feeling** is the sum of the subtle and nuanced aspects of a historical culture, those aspects not obviously or completely captured in the artifacts of a society. Williams claims that the contours of this structure become most apparent in intergenerational social exchanges or discussions about one's own culture with members of another culture. In many ways, the structure of feeling is intimately related to the aforementioned concepts of myth, doxa, and hegemony.

In expanding the notion of culture to include aspects of everyday pursuits, Williams importantly opened the door for the academic study of mass culture products and institutions. A few years after the publication of *The Long Revolution*, a collective of British academics established the Centre for Contemporary Cultural Studies to study popular culture with special focus on ideological components of the mass media. Stuart Hall, who served as the head of the Centre from 1969 to 1979, wrote an essay entitled "Cultural Studies: Two Paradigms" in 1980 that many consider to be a crucial outlining of the institutionalized Cultural studies approach.[18] The two paradigms indicated in his title are culturalism (work in the tradition of Hoggart and Williams which scrutinizes particular beliefs and activities of individuals in a given culture) and structuralism (work derived from Marx and anthropologist Claude Lévi-Strauss which looks at how social systems limit the activities of individuals through ideology). Hall claims that contemporary Cultural studies brings together the best aspects of each tradition, and that the traditions "pose, together, the problems consequent on trying to think both the specificity of different practices and the forms of the articulated unity they represent."[19]

However, while Hall appears to give a balanced approach to both paradigms on the surface of the essay, some scholars point out that his true scholarly commitments lie more closely with the structuralist focus on ideology.[20] Thus, although the culturalist focus on the meanings made by particular individuals within a culture importantly paved the way for Cultural studies' attention to popular texts, the structuralist concepts of ideology, power, privilege, and oppression have become the primary theoretical hallmarks of the contemporary Cultural studies approach. The culturalist focus has been largely absorbed into an approach based on the ethnographic study of audiences, addressed in Chapter 10 of this book.

This structuralist lens has shaped the Cultural studies discipline across five methodological motifs. First, Cultural studies is *interdisciplinary*. As a method of textual criticism, Cultural studies appropriates and combines theoretical tools from many different fields to assemble a new approach specifically designed to address the text in question. Second, Cultural studies is *pragmatic*. The ideal criticism of texts from a Cultural studies perspective should be practical in nature, toward a specific end, and understandable to a wide variety of people. This practicality is closely related to the third aspect of Cultural studies: it is *political*. Cultural studies scholarship seeks not only to identify particular ideologies, but also to challenge and alter their effects on systems of social (in)equality. Fourth, Cultural studies is *self-reflexive*. Cultural studies scholars adopt a critical awareness of their own social locations and the implications of that positioning. In other words, work within Cultural studies is often hyper-aware if its own socio-political biases, and scholars often acknowledge these limitations within their writing. Finally, Cultural studies is culturally and historically *contingent*. Textual criticism from this perspective is always tied to particular social systems at particular moments in time. Jenkins, McPherson, and Shattuc refer to this dual quality as Cultural studies' commitment to "contextualism" and "situationalism," respectively.[21]

With these five themes as a guiding framework, the remainder of this chapter will look at ideologies of class and race in American media to provide an in-depth understanding of the type of work that constitutes a Cultural studies approach. This decision is purposeful. Issues of class were intimately involved in the historical evolution of British Cultural studies (both in the gradual displacement of "culture" from the upper class and in the Marxist underpinnings of structuralism), and notions of race provided an early and important historical focus to the budding discipline. However, it is important to keep in mind that issues of ideology and power are applicable to the investigation of any social construct in a text: class, race, gender, age, sexuality, disability, etc. To extend the same amount of attention to each of these is beyond the scope of an introductory chapter to Cultural studies, but we encourage you to independently pursue the important work done in each of these areas.

Ideology and Media Representations of Class

Cultural studies scholars interested in ideological issues of class look at the ways in which popular media texts communicate, justify, and maintain disproportionate socio-economic status divisions. At the same time, they look to notions of class to understand the particular structures and effects of media texts. Overall, these scholars analyze the interplay between popular media texts and hegemonic ideologies of class that convince individuals that capitalism and class immobility are "natural" forms of social existence.

Basically, social class refers to the division of society into "haves" and the "have-nots." You may already be familiar with many of the more specific ways to discuss class, including the divisions of upper, middle, and lower class, hybrids like upper middle class, and even phrases like "working class" or "working poor." Marx, the preeminent theorist on social class, originally divided capitalist society into three major classes: the *bourgeoisie*, or large-business owners who control the means of production; the *proletariat*, or blue-collar workers who sell their labor to the owners; and the *petite bourgeoisie*, or small-business owners and white-collar professionals (doctors, lawyers, etc.) who represent a minority middle class. However, he also envisioned that capitalist societies evolve according to changing social relations. As such, what we have in contemporary American capitalist society is a class system reminiscent of Marx's original divisions with two important differences.

The first difference is in the size of the petite bourgeoisie. Unlike in Marx's time, where the petite bourgeoisie or middle class encompassed a relatively small number of professionals, the middle class now represents the largest class division in American society. This growth of the middle class (and relative shrinking of the upper bourgeoisie and lower proletariat classes) is intrinsically tied to the second important deviation from Marx: the rise of information- and media-based occupations in the twentieth century. As computers and technology industries have increased in scope and popularity in the last 50 years, the demand for knowledge-based positions like technicians and programmers has increased as well. This signifies a shift away from a Marxist economy focused on material production toward one focused on mediated information dissemination. Such a shift influenced class distinctions in a number of ways. Newly created white-collar jobs increased the size of the middle class, and patterns of ownership became increasingly focused on the *cultural* production of lifestyles and leisure. As you may have already guessed from the ideas discussed thus far in this chapter, the production of culture in these media industries also means the production and reification of ideologies.

Thus, the rise of the media is important for multiple reasons in attempting to understand ideologies of class in America. Media outlets like television, film, and newspapers play an interesting dual role when it comes to messages about class. On one hand, the American public is bombarded with images that communicate clear class distinctions. MTV broadcasts many different programs, including *The Fabulous Life of...* and *Cribs*, that depict the elaborate wealth and decadence of popular music, sports, and film stars. These shows reveal to younger, largely middle- to lower-class audiences that a clear disparity exists between their own lives and the lives of the famous and wealthy. They communicate that, through hard work and determination, anyone can overcome economic disparity and succeed in America. Films like *Pretty Woman* (1990) and *Forrest Gump* (1994), for instance, champion the idea that success is available to all those who work for it. So, though the messages of "class distinction" and "anyone can be economically successful" may at first seem contradictory, they are, in fact, both bound up in the complex system of class ideologies disseminated by the American media. In essence, they work together to hegemonically preserve the status quo and make permanent the current economic power discrepancies of our nation.

Two concepts help us understand how class ideologies function in American media. The first is the **American Dream**, or the aforementioned idea that a person's level of success is directly related to the amount of effort or drive they put forth in attaining that goal. The American Dream is one of the most prevalent hegemonic ideologies in American media texts. There is large-scale consent to the American Dream because in return it provides people with a definite avenue toward success and happiness. It boils down all of the complications of modern life into a simple equation (hard work=success), and it symbolically erases real issues of social inequality, class struggle, profit motive, and others that may provide barriers toward success. In reality, adhering to the American Dream probably does more to transform individuals into compliant workers for capitalist owners than it does to actually elevate their personal socio-economic statuses, but this fact is difficult to see because of hegemonic qualities which veil the interests of the upper class inherent to the ideology. In addition, the repetition of the American Dream over and over in media images like *Pretty Woman* and *Forrest Gump* helps to solidify the Dream as truth in the popular consciousness.

One of the more celebrated media images in the ideological web of the American Dream is the token. A **token** is an exception to a social rule that affirms the correctness of an ideology. In this case, a token is an individual who has actually fulfilled the promise of the Dream and broken through to the upper class based on personal initiative. Although they are exceptions rather than the norm, tokens often gain high visibility within the media. Oprah Winfrey and Bill Gates are good examples of tokens often cited in the media; both built vast empires from fairly meager economic beginnings. A token lends a sense of legitimacy to the American Dream ideology: if these people can succeed, then anyone can. Of course, media outlets do not also address the millions of other individuals who do not ever transcend their class despite their personal effort and hard work. In this way, highly visible media tokens symbolically erase the presence of systemic ideological systems based on class.

However, it should be obvious that the American Dream is not beyond reproach. Even within the media we have films like *Born on the Fourth of July* (1989) that scathingly critique the ideology. Therefore, there must be other ideologies of class that function to hegemonically maintain the status quo. The second important concept to understand in relation to class ideologies is Thorstein Veblen's idea of conspicuous consumption.[22] **Conspicuous consumption** is the belief that one can attain the kind of happiness or completeness often conceived of as upper class through the purchase of material goods and services. When people refer to houses as status symbols or express a need to "keep up with the Joneses," they are hinting at this belief. People often consent to the doctrine of conspicuous consumption because it allows them to feel as if they have succeeded in life as a result of owning nice things. In truth, individuals who believe they have "made it" because of their consumption often move only slightly up the scale of the large American middle class. In fact, many of the stars featured in *The Fabulous Life of . . .* and *Cribs* are often members of the upper middle class themselves. As such, the ideology of conspicuous consumption works hegemonically to blind the majority of Americans from realizing what true upper-class wealth actually looks like. This in turn works to solidify class distinctions.

Media advertising thrives on the notion of conspicuous consumption and is a primary support system for this ideology. In her book *Born to Buy*, Juliet B. Schor claims that Americans are becoming the target of advertising at increasingly younger ages. "Children," she writes, "have become conduits from the consumer marketplace into the household, the link between advertisers and the family purse."[23] Advertising literally does the work of conspicuous consumption. Its duty is to manufacture desires for products and services within the general public under the guise of consumer choice. As a result of multi-billion dollar advertising companies, ideas of conspicuous consumption are deeply ingrained into the American public from birth and appear to be the natural or normal consequence of competition and taste.

In sum, the dual ideologies of the American Dream and conspicuous consumption work via media texts to solidify current class divisions in America even while such boundaries appear to be outdated or permeable. In 2004, the top 10 percent of US households held 80.9 percent of all financial assets (i.e. houses, boats, stocks, bonds, etc.), while the households that made up the remaining 90 percent possessed only 19.1 percent of net financial assets.[24] That same year, the wealthiest 1 percent of US households controlled a larger share of national wealth (an average of nearly $15 million per household) than the entire bottom 90 percent (see Figure 6.1).[25] Such disparity points to the fact that class clearly continues to matter in America. However, class is not the only issue of privilege that continues to operate in this way. Another hotly contested area that often appears to be a non-issue as a result of ideological intervention is race.

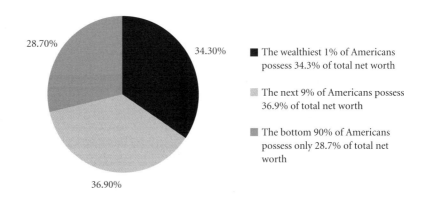

Figure 6.1   US wealth distribution (in terms of net worth), 2004. Source: L. Mishel, J. Bernstein, and H. Shierholz, *The State of Working America 2008/2009* (Washington, DC: Economic Policy Institute), 249.

28.70%   34.30%

36.90%

■ The wealthiest 1% of Americans possess 34.3% of total net worth

▨ The next 9% of Americans possess 36.9% of total net worth

■ The bottom 90% of Americans possess only 28.7% of total net worth

Media, Ideology, and Representations of Race and Ethnicity

Cultural studies scholars interested in media representations of race investigate how a culture's racial ideologies help determine the structures of popular media texts like television shows, films, music, and periodicals. They analyze these texts to better understand how the media reinforce cultural and ideological power hierarchies, systems that usually award privilege and power to white individuals at the expense of non-white individuals. These scholars are especially interested in how media texts reflect hegemonic racial ideologies, concentrating on the ways these texts invite consumers to accept whiteness as the norm in relation to issues of race.

Thomas K. Nakayama and Robert L. Krizek refer to discourses of whiteness in America as "strategic rhetoric."[26] In essence, the images and words most commonly used to discuss whiteness reinforce its privileged place at the center of our understanding of race. Through media representations, social organizations, and even everyday objects, "white" becomes an overarching norm, a privileged non-race against which all other races are measured and compared. Peggy McIntosh outlines a variety of ways this privilege manifests in her own life as a white individual in America: "I can turn on the television or open to the front page of the paper and see people of my race widely represented. . . . When I am told about our national heritage or about 'civilization,' I am shown that people of my color made it what it is. . . . I can choose blemish cover or bandages in 'flesh' color and have them more or less match my skin."[27]

Scholarship regarding the media representation of race is vast, but work within this area can be summarized into a group of key concepts that explain how media texts operate across ideological lines within the context of American culture. These concepts are exclusion, stereotyping, assimilation, and othering.

Exclusion

Ironically, a prevalent representation of race in American media is actually better characterized as an *absence* of representation. **Exclusion** is the process by which various cultural groups are symbolically annihilated, or "written out of history," through under-representation in the media. If the media were an actual reflection of race in American culture, then one would expect to see a clear ratio between the size of a racial population in real life and its visible population in television or films. However, research in this area points out that the relationship between population and mainstream media visibility is highly skewed. In other words, racial minorities simply do not "exist" in much of the media that we consume every day, and this absence reinforces ideological power structures by over-representing the dominant white group in media texts.

We can clearly see the process of racial exclusion if we look at the Latino population in America and compare it to Latino representation in mainstream American media. Latinos are the fastest-growing minority population in the USA, numbering about 35.3 million in 2000, or 13 percent of the total US population.[28] To get an idea about how large this number really is, consider the fact that there are more Hispanics in the USA than there are Canadians in Canada. If you were to take the entire US Hispanic population and transform it into a Latin American country, it would have the fourth largest population by comparison. And yet, despite the obviously large numbers of Hispanic or Latino individuals living in America, images of the lives and issues of Latin American people are largely absent from mainstream American media. The next time you turn on your television, try and find a sitcom that centers on a Latin American family or social group. You might stumble across syndicated episodes of *The George Lopez Show* or catch the latest installment of *Ugly Betty*, but there is a stronger possibility that you will discover a litany of shows depicting white American culture like *Friends*, *Seinfeld*, or *Everybody Loves Raymond*. Likewise, many of the more popular or critically recognized films about Latinos since 2000, such as *All the Pretty Horses* (2000), *Y Tu Mamá También* (2001), *Frida* (2002), *The Motorcycle Diaries* (2004), *Maria Full of Grace* (2004), and *Volver* (2006), are either produced by foreign film companies or largely focused on the lives of Latino and Hispanic individuals *outside* of the USA.

Overall, systems of symbolic exclusion do not completely remove a Latino presence from American media (as many television shows or films feature Latinos as friends, neighbors, co-workers, or other minor characters), but they do manage to partially erase the perspectives, interests, and needs of the significant US Latino population from the everyday American conscious. Naturally, this process of symbolic annihilation extends to other racial groups beyond Latinos, and excluding images of minorities in the media in turn reinforces ideological systems of white privilege by constructing whiteness as prevalent, multifaceted, and normal.

Stereotyping

When people of color *do* appear in the media, they often fall victim to the second major form of racial representation. **Stereotyping** is the process of constructing misleading and reductionist representations of a minority racial group, often wholly defining members of the group by a small number of characteristics. Media stereotypes by definition make value judgments about the worth, taste, and morality of another culture, and in doing so they can influence our attitudes, behaviors, and actions toward members of that culture. Racial stereotypes are not always a negative reflection of a culture (the stereotype of the "smart Asian" is a good example of a positive stereotype), but all stereotypes overlook the inherent complexity of a racial group and present media consumers with simplified and flawed representations. These simplified racial caricatures enable systems of white privilege by presenting consumers with a world where the majority of complex, interesting, and realistic characters are white.

One example of a long-standing racial stereotype in America media is that of people of Middle Eastern descent as violent or barbaric terrorists. Even before September 11, 2001, the image of the "Arab terrorist" was prevalent in American films like *Back to the Future* (1985), *True Lies* (1994), *The Siege* (1998), and *Rules of Engagement* (2000). Films about the terrorist bombing of the World Trade Center like *United 93* (2006) naturally resonate with this stereotype, and it continues to endure in films like *American Dreamz* (2006) and Fox's hit television show *24*. When the media aren't depicting Middle Easterners as terrorists, other common stereotypes include shady, big-nosed, and often irate individuals who wear turbans and ride camels (*Aladdin*, 1992), drive taxis (*Quick Change*, 1990), or own convenience stores (*The Simpsons*). The repetition and combination of these stereotypical images over time reduces the infinite variability of Middle Eastern peoples to a few exaggerated, stock representations. Like the process of exclusion, stereotyping establishes the hegemonic norm of whiteness by largely reducing realistic or affirming images of racial minorities, thereby erasing an accurate presence of them from the minds of many consumers.

The matter of racial stereotyping in the media is a sensitive and delicate one because it raises questions of both perception and intent. Consider, for example, the April 2008 cover of *Vogue* magazine, which features an image of NBA sensation LeBron James clutching Brazilian supermodel Gisele Bündchen. The cover – the first to feature an African American man in the magazine's history – quickly ignited a critical firestorm in the blogosphere.[29] For many, the *Vogue* cover, which was shot by renowned photographer Annie Leibovitz, resembled images of "King Kong," casting James as the dangerous (black) gorilla and Bündchen as the helpless (white) damsel.[30] This interpretation was dismissed by *Vogue* spokesperson Patrick O'Connell, who claimed the image simply "sought to celebrate two superstars at the top of their game[s]."[31] Though the magazine's editors almost certainly did not perceive (let alone intend) the image to be racially insensitive, it nevertheless elicited strong condemnation from those who believed it tapped (even if only unconsciously) into decades-old, racial stereotypes of the "black brute" and "white damsel." In support of this claim, the image is frequently juxtaposed with the World War I recruiting poster shown in Figure 6.2. What we hope this example illustrates is that media executives and editors, even those who have the best of intentions, must be vigilantly on guard against the reproduction of racial stereotypes.

Assimilation

The comparatively small number of media texts that do focus on the lives or experiences of people of color often display the third type of racial representation. **Assimilation** is the process by which media texts represent minority groups in a positive light while simultaneously dehistoricizing or stripping them of their cultural identities. Minority groups are often shown to possess equal or better socioeconomic standings than their white counterparts, but issues of past or continued political struggle for that equality are virtually absent. Instead, racial minorities become

Figure 6.2   World War I US Army recruiting poster.

Figure 6.3
Motorola RAZR
advertisement.

assimilated into a middle or upper class that largely reflects the perspectives of white individuals. Except for the possibility of "very special episode" about racism here or there, most of the problems that concern assimilated individuals involve family problems, occupational issues, or romantic pursuits, not issues of social power and oppression that often inform the lives of racial minorities in the real world. In this way, structures of inequality are hidden behind an apparent "face" of diversity in these texts.

The quintessential example of a racially assimilating media text is *The Cosby Show*. The Emmy-Award-winning show follows the antics and trials of the Huxtables, an African American, upper-middle-class family led by parents Cliff (Bill Cosby) and Clair (Phylicia Rashad). Cliff is an obstetrician and Clair is a successful attorney, and the family overall represents middle-class achievement and the possibilities of social mobility for racial minorities. In line with the American Dream, *The Cosby Show* suggests that success is open to all those who are talented and hard working if only they educate and apply themselves. Consequently, the show's viewers may come to think that widespread African American poverty is a result of individual weakness or cultural deficiency instead of systemic and ideological oppression. Shows like *Cosby* and *The Jeffersons* paved the way for other successful African American television shows that displayed tendencies toward assimilation, including *Family Matters* and *The Fresh Prince of Bel-Air*. Compared to the popular 1970s show *Good Times*, which chronicled the life of an African American family in the face of poverty, unemployment, and other social troubles often tied to racial power, these later shows virtually ignored issues of political struggle and "whitewashed" their African American characters.

Similar to the aforementioned discussion of the American Dream, issues of racial assimilation are closely tied to issues of tokenism. A token here is a character or personality of color whose presence in the media supposedly proves that systemic racism and white privilege no longer exist. The logic is that consciously injecting a single racial minority into an otherwise dominant or "white" program means that the program is fairly and realistically representing that minority perspective. In reality, tokens are a surface-level conceit to diversity because the token often displays qualities of hegemonic assimilation. Lisa Turtle, a character on the popular television show *Saved by the Bell*, is a good example of a media token. Not only is she the solitary African American character on the program, but she also fits comfortably into white suburbia with wealthy surgeon parents and an endless string of fashionable, expensive outfits. Media tokenism is present outside of sitcoms as well, especially in local news teams often made up of one reporter from each major ethnic group that predominates in the area. In a satirical jab at this system, *South Park* creators Matt Stone and Trey Parker have named the only African American child in their titular Colorado town "Token Black."

Assimilation and tokenism support ideological systems of white privilege by constructing middle-class life and norms as implicitly white. Characters and personalities of color assimilated into the white, middle-class media landscape seem to testify to the non-existence of racial ideological power, obscuring real issues of racial dominance and privilege by presenting consumers with images of false diversity. This functions as a tool of hegemony, convincing people to believe in mainstream media representations because they seem to present a racially equitable world even as the images reinforce current racial power relations.

Othering

The final type of media representation builds from this relationship between "normal" and "white." **Othering** is the process of marginalizing minorities by defining them in relationship to the (white) majority, which is assumed to be the norm or the natural order. The understanding of "white" as a non-race addressed at the beginning of this section is both the cause and consequence of othering practices. Examples of othering within the media are often difficult to identify because they rely on the unquestioned ideological assumptions about race and culture that we use to make sense of the world. Harry M. Benshoff and Sean Griffin point out that othering was evident in the predominant practice in early Hollywood to have actors of color play a variety of ethnic characters. "African Americans and Latinos were often hired to play Native American characters, and Hispanic, Italian and Jewish actors played everything from Eskimos to Swedes."[32] This process drew clear distinctions between white and non-white actors, privileging the unique qualities of the former and erasing the individuality of the latter. Instances of othering still exist today. For example, it is common to run across descriptions of Eddie Murphy or Chris Rock that characterize them as "black comedians." However, it is unlikely that one would ever encounter material describing Jeff Foxworthy as a "white comedian." A generic "comedian" is assumed to be white unless he/she is specified otherwise.

The notion of othering greatly influences the ways media texts function in America. One of the most prevalent is the ideology of **difference**, or the depiction of subordinate and racialized "others" as a source of pleasure for US American tourists and consumers. Consider, for instance, the depiction of race in Figure 6.3. hooks refers to engaging examples of difference this way as a process of "eating the other," where white individuals literally "consume" images and representations of racialized others in order to feel pleasure. She claims that within this ideological structure, privileged white individuals act "on the assumption that the exploration into the world of difference, into the body of the Other, will provide a greater, more intense pleasure than any that exists in the ordinary world of one's familiar racial group."[33]

A common example of difference in the media today surrounds the rap music industry. Although popular rap musicians are overwhelmingly African American, and the genre is often characterized in the public consciousness as "African American" in style, many rap consumers are young, white, middle-class individuals. Ideologies of difference help explain the draw of white suburbanites to this quintessentially African American form: to consume rap is to dabble in the other, to transgress racial norms in a self-gratifying manner. This notion of gratification is paramount to understanding difference. While it may seem that actions based in difference reject racial norms in a progressively political light, in reality these moves reduce aspects of minority culture to mere products for privileged white individuals to consume toward their own ends.

The other way that othering often manifests itself in media is through a process of exoticism. **Exoticism** refers to the ideological circulation and consumption of images of foreign lands that romanticize or mystify other cultures. Exoticizing a racial group often strips them of contemporary political agency by constructing them as primitive, unintelligent, or animalistic. Virtually any issue of *National Geographic* participates in this form of othering. One usually encounters images of scantily clad "tribal groups" while flipping through the pages of the magazine, and these societies seem largely exotic and bestial in the context of the magazine's stories on foreign lands and unusual animals. While the magazine covers a variety of racial groups in this way, none of them are ever white. In this way, exoticism positions non-white groups as socially and cognitively inferior to white, "civilized" society.

Thus, while difference represents actively seeking out aspects of non-white cultures as a source of pleasure, exoticism represents a mental distancing and superiority of white culture over others. Together they represent the most prevalent forms of othering in American media. Othering, difference, and exoticism all ideologically reinforce white privilege by making whiteness the invisible and central concept in American race relations. These ideologies equate whiteness with normalcy, and white stands as the unspoken norm around which all other races revolve.

Conclusion

This chapter has looked at how television shows, films, songs, news outlets, and other popular media forms support certain perspectives on social reality over others as a function of ideology. Operating under the ambiguous and flexible label of Cultural studies, scholars in this research vein seek to understand the ways in which the worldviews of socially privileged groups (men, whites, the wealthy, heterosexuals, adults, middle-aged individuals, etc.) are over-represented in the media to the detriment of socially marginalized groups (women, non-whites, the poor, homosexuals, children, the elderly, etc.). They regularly critique media texts for their role in structuring hegemonic and ideological systems of power. Cultural studies is unabashedly political in relation to this goal, and the approach has turned out some of the more radical and interesting research in contemporary media studies. The real strength of Cultural studies is its concentration on the ever-changing dynamic between media texts and the social systems that create them. As American society continues to evolve in relation to media images and technology, the Cultural studies approach will continue to provide perspective on how ideology informs these changes.

MEDIA LAB 5: DOING CULTURAL/IDEOLOGICAL ANALYSIS

OBJECTIVE

The aim of this lab is to utilize concepts of representation to analyze media texts. Specifically, students will investigate how issues of social power and ideology help structure the representation of particular social groups in the contemporary media landscape.

ACTIVITY

- Divide the class into small groups of 4–5 students each.
- Have each group select a cultural group. Students may choose their own groups or they may select a group from the following list: children, elderly, rich, poor, women, men, blacks, whites, Asians, Hispanics, gays, heterosexuals, persons with disabilities.
- Ask students to record their answers to the following prompts.
  1 Based on your experiences with the media, with what frequency is your group represented? Do you think this group is over- or under-represented? Why?
  2 What associations (stereotypes) are frequently made with this group? List at least ten. Are these associations generally positive, negative, or both?
  3 Provide examples of specific media texts that either reinforce or challenge the associations you listed in question 2. Which column is longer? Why?

SUGGESTED READING

Althusser, L. Ideology and Ideological State Apparatuses (Notes Toward an Investigation). In *Lenin and Philosophy and Other Essays*, translated by B. Brewster, pp. 85–126. New York: Monthly Review Press, 2001.

Aronowitz, S. *How Class Works: Power and Social Movement*. New Haven, CT: Yale University Press, 2003.

Barthes, R. *Mythologies*. Translated by A. Lavers. New York: Hill and Wang, 1972.

Bell-Jordan, K.E. *Black. White.* and a *Survivor* of *The Real World*: Constructions of Race on Reality TV. *Critical Studies in Media Communication* 25, 2008, 353–72.

Bourdieu, P. *Outline of a Theory of Practice*. Translated by R. Nice. Cambridge: Cambridge University Press, 1977.

Eagleton, T. *Ideology: an Introduction*. London: Verso, 1991.

Fiske, J. The Jeaning of America. In *Understanding Popular Culture*, pp. 1–21. Boston, MA: Unwin Hyman, 1989.

Gramsci, A. *Selections from the Prison Notebooks*. Translated by Q. Hoare and G. Nowell Smith. New York: International Publishers, 2003.

Hall, S. Cultural Studies: Two Paradigms. In *Media Culture & Society: a Critical Reader*, R. Collins, J. Curran, N. Garnham, P. Scannell, P. Schesinger, and C. Sparks (eds), pp. 33–48. Beverly Hills, CA: Sage, 1986.

Hall, S. *Representation: Cultural Representations and Signifying Practices*. Thousand Oaks, CA: Sage Publications, 1997.

Hebdige, D. *Subculture: the Meaning of Style*. New York: Routledge, 1979.

hooks, b. *Black Looks: Race and Representation*. Boston, MA: South End Press, 1992.

hooks, b. *Where We Stand: Class Matters*. New York: Routledge, 2000.

Johnson, A.G. *Privilege, Power and Difference*. New York: McGraw-Hill, 2001.

Kendell, D. *Framing Class: Media Representations of Wealth and Poverty in America*. New York: Rowman & Littlefield, 2005.

Larson, S.G. *Media & Minorities: The Politics of Race in News and Entertainment*. Lanham, MD: Rowman & Littlefield, 2005.

Mason, R. Conspicuous Consumption: a Literature Review. *European Journal of Marketing* 18, 1984, 26–39.

McIntosh, P. White Privilege: Unpacking the Invisible Knapsack. *Peace and Freedom* July/August, 1989, 10–12.

Nakayama, T.K. and Krizek, R.L. Whiteness: a Critical Rhetoric. *Quarterly Journal of Speech* 81, 1995, 291–309.

Peterson, R.T. Consumer Magazine Advertisement Portrayal of Models by Race in the U.S.: an Assessment. *Journal of Marketing Communications* 13, 2007, 199–211.

Rogers, R.A. Pleasure, Power and Consent: The Interplay of Race and Gender in *New Jack City*. *Women's Studies and Communication* 16, 1993, 62–85.

Shugart, H.A. Sumptuous Texts: Consuming "Otherness" in the Food Film Genre. *Critical Studies in Media Communication* 25, 2008, 68–90.

Torck, D. Voices of Homeless People in Street Newspapers: a Cross-Cultural Exploration. *Discourse & Society* 12, 2001, 371–92.

Torgovnik, M. *Gone Primitive: Savage Intellects, Modern Lives*. Chicago, IL: University of Chicago Press, 1991.

Veblen, T. *The Theory of the Leisure Class*. New York: The Macmillan Company, 1899.

NOTES

1. The story of the surgeon is commonly circulated as a mental puzzle in American culture, and its origins are unknown. Some variations reverse the role of the parents, recounting the death of the *mother* in the accident and a refusal by a *nurse* (who is the father) to give aid to the son. Some position the car as stalled on railroad tracks instead of in a traffic accident. The version here is an original adaptation. For another, see H. Stoeger, A. Ziegler, and H. David, What is a Specialist? Effects of the Male Concept of a Successful Academic Person on Performance in a Thinking Task, *Psychology Science* 46, no. 4, 2004, 514–30.

2. M. Richardson, *The Experience of Culture* (Thousand Oaks, CA: Sage Publications, 2001), 2.

3. M. Foucault, *Mental Illness and Psychology*, trans. unknown (New York: Harper & Row Publishers, 1976).

4. Foucault, 68.

5. How Common is Intersex?, *Intersex Society of North America*, www.isna.org/faq/frequency (accessed January 5, 2007).

6. What is Albinism?, *The National Organization for Albinism and Hypopigmentation*, www.albinism.org/publications/what_is_albinism.html (accessed January 5, 2007).

7. B. Brummett, *Rhetoric in Popular Culture*, 2nd edn (Thousand Oaks, CA: Sage Publications, 2006), 5.

8. L. Althusser, Ideology and Ideological State Apparatuses (Notes Toward an Investigation), in *Lenin and Philosophy and Other Essays*, trans. B. Brewster (New York: Monthly Review Press, 2001), 85–126.

9. Roland Barthes, *Mythologies*, trans. A. Lavers (New York: Hill and Wang, 1972), 109.

10. P. Bourdieu, *Outline of a Theory of Practice*, trans. R. Nice (Cambridge: Cambridge University Press, 1977), 169.

11. A. Gramsci, *Selections from the Prison Notebooks*, ed. and trans. Q. Hoare and G.N. Smith (New York: International Publishers, 2003), 12.

12. D. Hebdige, *Subculture: the Meaning of Style* (New York: Routledge, 1979).

13. J. Fiske, The Jeaning of America, in *Understanding Popular Culture* (Boston, MA: Unwin Hyman, 1989), 1–21.

14. Q.D. Leavis, *Fiction and the Reading Public* (New York: Russell & Russell, 1965), 211.

15. J.P. Surber, *Culture and Critique: an Introduction to the Critical Discourses of Cultural Studies* (Boulder, CO: Westview Press, 1998), 236.

16. R. Hoggart, *The Uses of Literacy: Changing Patterns in English Mass Culture* (Fair Lawn, NJ: Essential Books, 1957).

17. R. Williams, *The Long Revolution* (New York: Columbia University Press, 1961), 41.

18. Surber, *Culture and Critique*.

19. S. Hall, Cultural Studies: Two Paradigms, in *Media Culture & Society: a Critical Reader*, R. Collins, J. Curran, N. Garnham, P. Scannell, P. Schlesinger, and C. Sparks (eds) (Beverly Hills, CA: Sage Publications, 1986), 33–48.

20. A. Milner and J. Browitt, *Contemporary Cultural Theory: an Introduction*, 3rd edn (New York: Routledge, 2002).

21. H. Jenkins, T. McPherson, and J. Shattuc, The Culture That Sticks to Your Skin: a Manifesto for a New Cultural Studies, in *Hop on Pop: The Politics and Pleasures of Popular Culture*, H. Jenkins, T. McPherson, and J. Shattuc (eds) (Durham, NC: Duke University Press, 2002), 3–42.

22. T. Veblen, *The Theory of the Leisure Class* (New York: The Macmillan Company, 1899).

23. J.B. Schor, *Born to Buy: the Commercialized Child and the New Consumer Culture* (New York: Scribner, 2004), 11.

24. L. Mishel, J. Bernstein, and H. Shierholz, *The State of Working America 2008/2009* (Washington, DC: Economic Policy Institute), 249.

25. Mishel *et al.*, 10.

26. T.K. Nakayama and R.L. Krizek, Whiteness: a Critical Rhetoric, *Quarterly Journal of Speech* 81, 1995, 291–309.

27. P. McIntosh, White Privilege: Unpacking the Invisible Knapsack, *Peace and Freedom* July/August, 1989, 10, 11.

28. E.M. Grieco and R.C. Cassidy, *Overview of Race and Hispanic Origin, Census 2000 Brief* (Washington, DC: U.S. Census Bureau, 2001), 1, www.census.gov/prod/2001pubs/c2kbr01-1.pdf (accessed December 11, 2008).

29. W. Morris, Monkey Business: So is That *Vogue* Cover Racist Or Not?, *Slate*, posted March 31, 2008, www.slate.com/id/2187797/ (accessed April 23, 2009).

30. J. Hill, LeBron Should be More Careful with his Image, *ESPN.com*, p. 2, updated March 21, 2008, http://sports.espn.go.com/espn/page2/story?page=hill/080320 (accessed April 23, 2009).

31. Vogue Cover with Lebron stirs up Controversy, *NBCSports.com*, http://nbcsports.msnbc.com/id/23795226/ (accessed April 23, 2009).

32. H.M. Benshoff and S. Griffin, *America on Film: Representing Race, Class, Gender and Sexuality at the Movies* (Malden, MA: Blackwell, 2004), 56.

33. b. hooks, Eating the Other: Desire and Resistance, in *Black Looks: Race and Representation* (Boston, MA: South End Press, 1992), 24.

7 Psychoanalytic Analysis

Cameron Crowe's 1996 film *Jerry Maguire* is certainly one of the more touching American romantic comedies in recent memory. Even a decade after its release, some of the film's lines continue to circulate throughout American culture. Perhaps the most often quoted exchange occurs near the end of the film, when sports agent Jerry (Tom Cruise) finally confesses his romantic feelings for accountant Dorothy (Renee Zellweger):

JERRY: "I love you. You . . . you complete me. And I just—"
DOROTHY: "Shut up, just shut up. You had me at 'hello'. . . ."

In September 1999, Australian pop duo Savage Garden released their smash single "I Knew I Loved You" onto American airwaves. The latest in a string of emotive, romantic hits by the group, the song quickly became popular with American audiences and spent a record-breaking 124 weeks on the Billboard Adult Contemporary Airplay charts. Throughout the tune, breathy vocalist Darren Hayes serenades listeners with lyrics of personal elation: "And in your eyes I see the missing pieces / I'm searching for . . ."; "A thousand angels dance around you / I am complete now that I've found you. . . ."

Though these two texts may seem unrelated at first glance, they both express the basic human desire for emotional wholeness. This raises an interesting question: why do we as a culture tend to describe ideas of love and emotional satisfaction in terms of *completion*? How might we understand the association between our desires and feelings of personal wholeness? These questions underlie a Psychoanalytic approach to media studies, a perspective originally proposed by Austrian psychiatrist

Sigmund Freud that attempts to understand the psychic structure of the mind. Psychoanalytic scholars explore how media texts reflect human mental drives toward unity, pleasure, and desire. Although the body of knowledge in this tradition has changed considerably over time, one could say that the approach is generally grounded in the genesis of individual psychology, the psychology of the media text, and the ways in which the two interact in the process of media consumption.

The first half of this chapter outlines the major tenets of Psychoanalytic theory as well as the two major strands of psychoanalysis that have heavily influenced media studies (Freudian and Lacanian). The latter half of this chapter traces the historical inception and evolution of Psychoanalytic theory in the realm of film studies. For reasons that will become apparent, the vast majority of Psychoanalytic work in media studies has concentrated on film. However, we conclude this chapter by considering more recent Psychoanalytic work that at times extends this branch of theory beyond the cinema.

Psychoanalytic Theory: an Overview

For Sigmund Freud notions of individual subjectivity, identity, and consciousness are born out of an essential opposition between what he called the pleasure principle and the reality principle. The **pleasure principle** is the uncontrollable human drive to satisfy **desire**, or an appetite for something that promises enjoyment, satisfaction, and pleasure in its attainment. Commonly recognized desires include yearnings for sex, power, or food. Likewise, we often desire and find pleasure in the aesthetics of fine art or architecture. However, many Psychoanalytic scholars point out that we can also desire and experience pleasure through other processes like urination, horror, or shock. If you stop to consider your own life, you'll realize that pleasure comes from many things we might not otherwise associate with it. For example, we often gain pleasure from purposefully breaking rules and laws (when we surpass the speed limit) or putting ourselves in situations that feel life-threatening (when we hit the top of a rollercoaster). We can even gain pleasure from observing appalling or gruesome spectacles (which is one reason why people so often slow down to look at terrible car accidents).

In light of these examples, it is apparent that pleasure does not refer only to aspects of life which we associate with comfort or joy. Instead, Psychoanalytic scholars roughly understand pleasure as that which momentarily allows us to transcend everyday existence and reality. The original definition of the word *ecstasy* carries connotations of literally being beside oneself with powerful emotion. Pleasure, then, is that which seems to take us outside of ourselves. Freud associates the pleasure principle with the *id*, or the inherited, instinctual part of the psyche, because "the one and only urge of these instincts is towards satisfaction."[1] The human mind can desire and experience pleasure in many different ways, and the pleasure principle pushes individuals toward the unrestricted satisfaction of every possible desire.

However, because some of these desires are socially unacceptable or unhealthy, the reality principle intercedes and regulates the individual's experience of pleasure. The **reality principle** represents the constant curbing of desire according to possibility, law, or social convention. As infants we are driven by the pure, uncontrolled gratification of desire, but we learn to control that drive as we grow older and integrate into society (we will address this process again later in the chapter). If the reality principle were to suddenly disappear, individuals would do nothing but unabashedly pursue their desires without regard to the well being of themselves or others. Society as we know it would dissolve. To keep social chaos at bay, the reality principle constantly keeps the pleasure principle in check. For example, instead of gorging ourselves on delicious food all of the time because the process is pleasurable, American social custom dictates that we break up our eating schedule into breakfast, lunch, and dinner. Instead of urinating whenever and wherever we feel, we "hold it" until we can find a proper bathroom to relieve ourselves. In this way, reality and society constantly place constraints on when and how individual members may experience desire and pleasure in their lives. Freud associates the reality principle with the *ego*, or the regulatory part of the conscious mind that "comes to a decision on whether the attempt to obtain satisfaction is to be carried out or postponed or whether it may not be necessary for the demand by the instinct to be suppressed altogether as being dangerous."[2] The control of the ego is the reason why we may find pleasure in shocking, thrilling, or upsetting aspects of life. In the process of viewing disturbing art or engaging in sexual taboos, we seem to temporarily loosen the constraints of the reality principle and allow the pleasure principle a bit more reign.

Psychoanalytic theory posits that the human psyche is born out of the tense relationship between the pleasure and reality principles. There are two major ways to consider the nature of this relationship: repression and lack. **Repression**, proposed by Freud, is the process of mentally containing our desires below conscious recognition or expression. The fact that the reality principle forbids certain desires and pleasures does not purge them from our minds, so individuals repress those desires into the unconscious in order to manage the tension between the principles. The **unconscious** for Freud is the part of the mind that acts as a reservoir for desire, and it always attempts to make repressed desires felt again by interjecting them into conscious life. When people describe misspeaking as a "Freudian slip," they are recognizing a moment where their repressed desires broke through their conscious ones.

The second explanation, **lack**, is based on the theories of French psychoanalyst Jacques Lacan. In this perspective, there is not so much a struggle between pleasure and reality as there is a gap that separates them. We still desire and wish for pleasure, but we are trapped in a reality whose social order and language keep us from knowing or expressing pleasure fully (this will become more clear in the section on Lacanian psychoanalysis). We experience a feeling of lack because we are consciously divided from the pleasures that cannot be captured or expressed in the symbol systems of our everyday reality. For Lacan, then, the unconscious is the shared realm of pleasures and desires that remain beyond our access because of the insufficiency of language in knowing those pleasures. The idea of traversing the gap and reuniting with those lost pleasures motivates many of our actions throughout life.

For media theorists, understanding both repression and lack in relation to issues of desire and pleasure is very important. They assert that repressed or lost desires influence the creation of media texts and explain the mental drives activated by those texts. Because psychoanalytic theory roughly constructs all individuals as mentally similar, it is important to note that psychoanalysis as an approach to media studies has been more fruitful in explaining the structures of media texts than it has in describing the processes of audience consumption of those texts. Cultural theorists like David Morley have critiqued psychoanalysis for considering the audience as one homogeneous group,[3] but the approach still provides an interesting perspective regarding the implicit psychological appeal of media texts.

Before moving any further into the specific work of Psychoanalytic media scholars, we need to answer a basic question: When and how does this relationship between pleasure and reality crystallize to form subjectivity in individuals? Both Freud and Lacan agree that events surrounding the human infant's initial experiences with its parents are responsible for this formation, but they disagree on the specific aspects of the process. Because the work of Lacan is in many ways a direct answer to that of Freud, we will begin with Freudian psychoanalysis before turning our attention to its Lacanian counterpart.

Freudian Psychoanalysis

Sigmund Freud, the founder of modern Psychoanalytic theory, was an Austrian psychiatrist interested in psychosis and the ways that sexual experiences and drives direct human action. He claims that an individual's identity, far from being inherent or preordained, was actually the result of outside forces encountered early in life. According to Freud, infants are born "polymorphously perverse," or with the ability to experience pleasure in an infinite number of ways, because they have no self-control and are uninhibited by social conventions. Newborn infants are also unaware of their individual nature, and they understand the world they inhabit only as an extension of themselves. Therefore, infants in the earliest stages of life experience everything as both pleasurable and a result of their own doing, an alignment that establishes the pleasure principle within the individual. As Freudian scholar Pamela Thurschwell explains, "the youngest babies make no distinction between having a desire and fulfilling it – this sort of distinction is something that must be learned."[4]

For Freud, the process of learning this distinction and forming a conscious self is intrinsically tied up with the notions of developing sexuality. The origins of sexual pleasure are found in the "oral stage," or the union between mother and child in the act of breastfeeding. The mouth is the first erotogenic zone in the developing human, and "all psychical activity is concentrated on providing satisfaction for the needs of that zone."[5] Although the purpose of breastfeeding is primarily one of nourishment, "the baby's obstinate persistence in sucking gives evidence at an early age of a need for satisfaction which . . . strives to obtain pleasure independently of nourishment and for that reason may and should be termed *sexual*."[6] In other words, although the child initially breastfeeds only for sustenance, it begins to derive other pleasures from the breast that are exclusively libidinal or sexual.

Eventually the child will progress through the other two stages of sexual development: the anal and phallic stages. Pleasure in the anal stage comes from the retention and expulsion of waste, and pleasure in the phallic stage involves shifting libidinal concentration to the genitals. Psychoanalytic scholar Anthony Elliot points out that each stage is accompanied by specific fantasies integral to the developing sexual identity: the oral stage features comforting fantasies, the anal stage hosts sadistic fantasies, and the phallic stage involves fantasies of control and self-sufficiency.[7] He claims that through the sexual pleasures and fantasies of these stages, "the child creatively and imaginatively establishes an emotional relation to its own body, to other people and the wider world."[8] Although at this point the child still exists in an undifferentiated state of pleasurable connection to the mother, the developing ability to fantasize about the self importantly lays the foundation for notions of identification with the outside world.

This identification primarily occurs when the father, representing the Freudian reality principle, intercedes on the mother/child union and dissolves the infant's intensely pleasurable and sexual desire for the mother. Freud refers to this moment as the **Oedipus complex** (named for the mythic Greek king who unknowingly killed his father and married his mother). In the Oedipus complex, the child undergoes a mental structuring that takes the raw libidinal materials of the oral, anal, and phallic stages and splits them into conscious and unconscious desires. Although Freud claims that young boys and girls undergo different experiences at this point, in both cases successfully navigating the process gives rise to human sexual subjectivity.

In the case of young boys, the arrival of the father in the family unit signals a threat to the sexual and pleasurable union between child and mother. The boy, realizing that his father's phallus has more sexual power over the mother than his own, represses his desires for the mother into the newly formed unconscious at the threat of "castration" from the father figure. This initial sexual repression becomes a template for all other socially "perverse" desires, and the young child funnels these additional desires into the unconscious throughout development. The newly formed conscious becomes the vessel for all remaining socially acceptable modes of pleasure, forming the basis of "normal" human subjectivity. For the young girl, the Oedipus complex becomes a process of recognition and lacking. The presence of the father and his powerful phallus forces the young girl to recognize she is without one (leading to the widely known phrase "penis envy"). The knowledge that she lacks a penis causes the young girl to reject the penis-less, powerless mother and sexually desire the powerful father and the idea of bearing him children. However, because the young girl does not experience the powerful threat of castration (but rather understands herself as already castrated), "the girl's Oedipal stage is understood to be relatively unstable, forever shifting between maternal and paternal identifications, and thereby always incomplete."[9]

Obviously, Freudian Psychoanalytic theory can be critiqued on a number of fronts for its sexual reductionism and ignorance of gender constructs. Feminists especially have critiqued the approach for its construction of female sexuality and subjectivity as a reverse or after-effect of male sexuality. However, his theory was the first to begin to explore the nature of the human mind in relation to concepts of pleasure and repression, and it provides an initial foray into explaining the formation of mental structures. Although contemporary scholars have rejected many of the more intricate details of Freud's theory, his overriding claims that *our subjectivity is the result of identification with outside forces* and *contact with those outside forces results in the formation of the conscious/unconscious divide* forms the basis of the majority of modern Psychoanalytic theory.

Lacanian Psychoanalysis

As discussed in the introduction to this chapter, one theorist who importantly extends Freud's work is the French psychoanalyst Jacques Lacan. Like Freud, Lacan was interested in the causes of mental disorders and psychosis. However, he was also fascinated with the ways that the individual mind interacted with the culture at large. Lacan agrees with Freud in the belief that the mind fractures into conscious and unconscious aspects upon the infant's realization of reality, but he claims that the process is more a result of the individual's induction into systems of language than a process of strictly sexual development. Lacanian psychoanalysis recognizes three separate orders, or realms, of human existence: the Real, the Imaginary, and the Symbolic. The Real is beyond signification. It is made up of things in the world that cannot be consciously known or put into words. The remaining realms of the Imaginary and the Symbolic represent the path a newborn individual travels in the process of developing a "normal" psychical structure.

The realm of the **Imaginary** is similar to the Freudian pre-Oedipal, pleasurable stage where the infant feels whole and connected to everything via the bond to the mother. While it is somewhat synonymous with the Freudian pleasure principle, it is also the site of an important development Lacan refers to as the "mirror stage." Here the child catches its reflection in a mirror and misrecognizes itself as an autonomous and total whole. The "mirror" can also be interpreted metaphorically as the confirming gaze of another individual, such as another infant or the mother. By identifying with the reflected image, the child begins to conceive of its own distinctness as a complete identity and takes the first steps toward ego formation (although he/she is still somewhat beheld by the Imaginary and the pleasures it affords). Lacan claims that this stage importantly lays the foundation for subjectivity in that it functions as "a drama whose internal pressure pushes precipitously from insufficiency to anticipation."[10] Overall, the mirror stage recalls Freud's own theories about identification because it is the first time that the child recognizes a connection between objects in the outside world and itself, thereby establishing a link between outside images and individual subjectivity.

Such ego/consciousness construction is complete when the subject acquires the use of language and enters the **Symbolic** realm, or the cultural plane of social meanings and relationships. The Symbolic is analogous to the reality principle in Lacanian psychoanalysis, specifically in the ways that language structures, orders, and constrains the impulse for the Imaginary desire that continues to exist in the individual. Lacan keeps Freud's basic Oedipal assumptions about the father/mother/child triad intact here. However, the father's phallus is not a sign of personal male sexual power, but rather represents what Lacan refers to as "the Law of the Father." Lacan departs from Freud in claiming that the father, far from threatening the child sexually, actually functions to usher in knowledge of social convention and taboo for the child (who rejects the now incestuous feelings for mother as a result). Broken from the Imaginary through the introduction of language and social norms, the child is forced to construct a personal identity with its newly acquired language.

For Lacan, then, the idea of subjectivity or consciousness is entirely a fiction, one born out of misrecognition of individual wholeness (in the mirror stage) and solidified in a symbolic system of language where subjects can only ever *attempt* to represent themselves. Scholars in this tradition strongly assert that individual subjectivity or consciousness is actually an effect of language and symbols because we are forced to use them to articulate a consciousness or identity. There simply are no other tools we can use. However, we cannot fully articulate all of our desires and pleasures using language or symbols because many of these desires and pleasures are rooted in the Imaginary, experienced before language and beyond linguistic expression. Therefore, the unconscious in Lacanian psychoanalysis is not a personal quality we as individuals carry with us, but a shared sense of the unnamable (and therefore lost) desires of the Imaginary we desperately yearn to experience again. This yearning for absent pleasures becomes a sense of lack, and Lacanian psychoanalysts claim that the lack dominates the ways that we understand life and the decisions we make.

Interestingly, the plot of the 1999 family comedy film *Baby Geniuses* provides an accessible parallel to the major concepts of Lacanian psychoanalysis. The film centers on two crooked scientists (Kathleen Turner and Christopher Lloyd) attempting to crack the secret language of infants in order to increase profits for the baby products company they work for. Far from being mere babble, baby talk is constructed in the film as a highly evolved form of communication that all infants and toddlers share. As viewers watch a number of clever children outwit the bumbling adult scientists, they also learn that the babies are young enough to remember the mystical secrets surrounding the purpose of life. However, the sacred knowledge is contingent on the linguistic development of the child. At the end of the film, the pint-sized protagonist Sly unexpectedly and spontaneously acquires his first English words, promptly forgetting the secrets to life he knew moments before.

Although widely panned by critics and audiences alike, the film is a helpful allegory for the path that children take between the Imaginary and Symbolic orders. The secrets to life alluded to throughout the film are akin to the pleasures of the Imaginary realm; they both represent a pre-conscious understanding of existence as complete, unified, and perfect. In both instances, the acquisition of language and knowledge of social-symbolic reality strips the child of that understanding. Language gives rise to the conscious, banishing whatever cannot be expressed in symbols into the unconscious. In the same way that the babies in the film will likely grow up and want to know the secret of life again, we as subjects spend the rest of our lives looking for a way to fill the lack created by the lost pleasures.

Clearly, Lacanian psychoanalysis is very different from its Freudian counterpart in the way it uses language instead of sex to explain the infantile break from wholeness and subsequent mental structures of individuals. His emphasis on the power of language and communication in the formation of the unconscious make Lacan very popular among Psychoanalytic media scholars interested in the ways that media symbols and images engage our minds. Although they conceive of the conscious/unconscious divide quite differently (see Table 7.1), both strands of Psychoanalytic theory offer important insights into the ways that the unconscious influences human behavior.

Table 7.1 Comparing Freud and Lacan

	Freud	Lacan
Pre-Oedipal stage	Polymorphous perversity gives rise to the pleasure principle. Pleasurable union with mother; perceived connection to everything. Sexual pleasure experienced in *oral*, *anal*, and *phallic* stages.	*The Imaginary*: pre-linguistic order. Pleasurable union with mother; perceived connection to everything. *Mirror stage*: child misrecognizes self as complete and in control; lays basis for eventual ego formation.
Post-Oedipal stage	Subjectivity based on constant curbing of pleasure principle according to reality principle.	*The Symbolic*: linguistic order. Subjectivity arises from attempts to represent self in language.
Desire explained according to . . .	*Repression*: socially unacceptable desires suppressed from consciousness but retain influence.	*Lack*: desires are unknown to our conscious self because they remain beyond linguistic expression.
Definition of the unconscious	Personal psychical reservoir that retains repressed desires and attempts to make them known/felt.	Shared sense of loss between linguistically constructed individuals in relation to Imaginary pleasures.
The phallus	Actual: the father's penis that represents sexual power and masculine presence to the child.	Symbolic: the "Law of the Father;" social convention and norms that represent patriarchal power to child.

Now that we have a basic understanding of psychoanalysis, you may be wondering what concepts like *repression*, *penis envy*, or the *mirror stage* have to do with the media that we consume every day. To better understand the connection, consider the following questions: Why do people continue to attend movie theaters when they can just rent films or receive them through the mail at a fraction of the cost? Why do some people watch the same movie over and over again, year after year? Why do we see new movies when we recognize that the vast majority of them rely on the same conventions or plotlines of those we have seen before? Potential answers to these questions can be found in psychoanalysis. Generally speaking, film scholars have used psychoanalytic concepts to explain the structure and appeal of films according to the unconscious desires discussed in the works of Freud and Lacan. They claim that there is something unique about the movie theater venue, the edited shot sequence of film, and the bond between the spectator and filmic narrative that is wholly psychological. They believe that the relationship between the pleasure and reality principles inherent in each of us plays out on American movie screens every day, and we watch movies to mitigate this tension in our daily lives. In order to understand how this process takes place, we will now turn our attention to some general assertions of Psychoanalytic media studies and the ways that these translate into specific theories.

Psychoanalytic Studies of Media

Scholars in this tradition draw on a number of different theoretical foundations when attempting to understand films, but most agree on a few overriding principles. First, films are structured in such a way that they activate the desires of the unconscious. When we watch a movie, we do so because it allows us to experience the parts of ourselves that are there but not consciously known. In Freudian terms, this means that films are constructed in such a way to allow us to indulge in unconscious, repressed, or socially prohibited pleasures. From a Lacanian perspective, this means that the structure of films allows us to traverse the lack and access the Imaginary pleasures which language divides from our conscious mind. Perhaps it is helpful overall to consider films as a way to temporarily undermine the hold of the reality principle and allow the pleasure principle a bit more free reign over our psyche.

Second, many scholars also agree that psychoanalytic concepts in some way explain the widespread phallocentrism in American culture and films. **Phallocentrism** is a social condition where images or representations of the penis carry connotations of power and dominance. Both Freud and Lacan point to the male phallus as a symbol of power in the creation of the human psyche (although Lacan claims it is more of a symbolic power than does Freud). In both strands of psychoanalysis, the powerful father figure is defined by presence of the phallus, while the rejected mother is defined by the absence of one. Navigating the Oedipus complex and entering the Symbolic realm of language becomes intertwined with the notion that men are powerful and women are powerless in society, and as a result this erroneous concept finds its way into the culture through patriarchal systems of power. To understand the prevalence of the link between power and maleness in our culture, one need only to consider how many tools and structures made to signal awe and power are shaped like a phallus: rifles, rockets, skyscrapers, the Washington Monument, etc.

Issues of gender and power are central in much of the canonical work in Psychoanalytic media studies, and much of this work deals with the ways that films reflect and influence the ways that gender plays upon our minds. Although many Feminist scholars initially rejected psychoanalytic theory for its reduction of female sexuality, some have attempted to reread the theory as a powerful indictment of contemporary gender inequality. Scholars such as Juliet Mitchell[11] claim that the work of Freud and Lacan, far from being an *a priori* account of why male domination "naturally exists," actually addresses how the social systems we encounter at an early age infuse our developing minds with constructed notions of gendered power and inequality. In this way, some Feminist scholars see psychoanalysis as a potential field of resistance because it displays how social constructions of power come to be naturalized within a culture.

The three areas of Psychoanalytic film studies discussed here are apparatus theory, the male gaze, and fantasy. There are many divergent strands of psychoanalytic theory and equally divergent forms of textual criticism that accompany them, but these three represent a somewhat clear trajectory of theoretical development appropriate to an introductory chapter on psychoanalysis. Consider how each theory critiques, responds to, and builds upon the one preceding it. After establishing this baseline, the chapter will conclude with a brief discussion regarding other significant developments within Psychoanalytic media studies.

Apparatus theory

First proposed by scholar Jean-Louis Baudry, **apparatus theory** is the earliest psychoanalytical approach to film. This approach claims that the actual environment and machinery of the cinema activates a number of psychoanalytic desires within spectators. In his analysis of Plato's cave allegory, Baudry points out that "the text of the cave may well express a desire inherent to a participatory effect deliberately produced, sought for, and expressed by cinema."[12] The same unconscious desires present in Plato's writings may have also inspired the creation of the modern movie theater and the genesis of film itself. Here Baudry is suggesting that all human beings throughout time have experienced the repression or loss of desires as a result of psychic development, and film is simply the contemporary means by which we access them again.

The mechanics of cinema allow for this access in a number of ways. According to Baudry, the actual context of viewing a movie in a theater "reconstructs the situation necessary to the release of the 'mirror stage' discovered by Lacan."[13] In other words, the theater environment plays upon the process of image identification first enacted in the Lacanian mirror stage. Lacan points out that the child approaching its mirror image lacks significant motor control and relies mostly on vision to understand the world. The mirror stage is pleasant and confirming for the child precisely because it displays a false sense of wholeness and control to make up for this lack. Baudry explains that the conventions of the theater (giant images on the screen, a passive, seated audience) also create a sense of visual dominance and restricted movement, causing viewers to again unconsciously rejoice in mirror stage feelings of wholeness, mastery, and control while watching the film.

For Baudry, then, the narrative or content of the film is not as appealing as the actual process of viewing because "the spectator identifies less with what it represented, the spectacle itself, than what stages the spectacle, makes it seen, obliging him [sic] to see what it sees."[14] He also draws connections between the movie theater and the womb, claiming that the context of watching a movie in a theater causes viewers to unconsciously regress back to the Imaginary and pleasurable experience of a connection to the mother (and therefore everything). This assertion may seem odd until we consider the manner in which theater audiences actually watch films. The darkness of the theater and the relative immobility of spectators both suggest aspects that break us from our daily routine and recall womb-like qualities.

Christian Metz, another scholar interested in the psychoanalytic aspects of film, agrees with Baudry's basic understanding the cinematic apparatus and extends it in important ways. Metz recognizes that identification is an important component of the apparatus, but he claims that it also taps into the Freudian drives of voyeurism and fetishism. The three concepts of identification, voyeurism, and fetishism provide a foundation for a great deal of Psychoanalytic work to follow Metz, and it is important to understand how each of these notions informs the spectator/film relationship.

Like Baudry, Metz asserts that identification with the screen occurs by re-enacting the confirming mirror stage for viewers, but he points out that it can never actually function as a mirror. Because the film can never reflect back the actual image of the viewer, the relationship between the viewer and the screen/mirror is primarily one of identification with *the actual ability to perceive* first encountered in the mirror stage. In his book *The Imaginary Signifier: Psychoanalysis and the Cinema*, Metz characterizes the viewer's mental process thus:

> I know that I am perceiving something imaginary . . . and I know that it is I who am perceiving it. This second knowledge divides in turn: I know that I am really perceiving, that my sense organs are physically affected, that I am not phantasizing, that the fourth wall of the auditorium (the screen) is really different from the other three. . . . In other words, the spectator *identifies with himself* [sic], with himself as a pure act of perception (as wakefulness, as alertness).[15]

In this way, instead of merely regressing back to the context of the mirror stage as Baudry claims, spectators experience the mirror stage's process of perception by establishing a primary identification with the camera's field of vision as it captures the events in the film. This in turn leads to a secondary identification with the looks of characters in the film whose points of view are captured in film shot and editing techniques. In essence, Metz claims that viewers know that they are not seeing themselves in the screen/mirror, but they do resonate with the actual mirror-stage processes of perceiving and identifying with objects outside of themselves through aligning themselves with the scope of the camera and the looks of the characters.

After establishing these primary and secondary identifications with the apparatus, Metz claims that viewers then participate in what he calls "the passion for perceiving," or scopohilia. **Scopophilia** refers to the pleasure that comes from the process of looking, and Freud identifies it as one of the primary sexual pleasures. In his 1905 article "Three Essays on Sexuality," Freud claims that "visual impressions remain the most frequent pathway along which libidinal excitation is aroused."[16] Simply focusing our attention upon a thing, consuming it visually and binding it to our gaze activates unconscious desire and gives us pleasure. For Metz, derivatives of the scopophilic drive like voyeurism and fetishism help explain the draw of the movie theater and the fascination with film.

Voyeurism, or the process of experiencing pleasure by watching a desired object or person from a distance, is a powerful concept at work in the movie theater. Maintaining distance between looker and object is key to the pleasure of voyeurism, and Metz sees this distinction as a result of the very nature of desire and the Lacanian notion of lack. To reach something desired destroys the feeling of desire for it (when we have it, we no longer desire it as intensely), so the possibility of experiencing desire and pleasure is only possible as long as we cannot reach the object. The lack (or distance) of the object keeps our desire alive. Metz recognizes that many arts rely upon activating the voyeuristic drives inherent in viewers, but film is an especially potent realm of this type of scopophilic pleasure. Like the theatrical performance of plays, cinema screenings place viewers at a distance from the object watched. However, unlike live drama, the objects and characters of a film are not actually present in the movie theater. There is no true exhibitionist complement to the cinematic voyeur, no actual object or person to be watched beyond the flat, projected image. This absence increases the perception of distance and lack between voyeur and object, thereby increasing the possibility of scopophilic pleasure.

Fetishism, or the psychic structuring of an object or person as a source of sexual pleasure, is another Freudian concept bound to the notion of looking that helps explain the draw of the cinematic apparatus. For Freud, the process of fetishizing is an important part of navigating the Oedipus complex and castration anxiety. In recognizing that the mother lacks the phallus, the developing male child is forced to hold two contradictory thoughts: (1) all people are born with the phallus (an initial belief) and (2) some people don't have the phallus (discovered in the mother). In paraphrasing Freud, Metz claims that the child will "retain its former belief *beneath* the new one, but it will also hold to its new perceptual observation while disavowing it on another level."[17] The newly discovered absence of the phallus also terrifies the male child, who now understands that he can be similarly "castrated" like the mother. The anxiety and fear of castration is so great that the child will fixate on a nearby object, transforming it into a fetish that denies the absence of the phallus and becomes a source of desire and pleasure in itself. In this way, the fetish "puts a 'fullness' in place of a lack, but in doing so it also affirms that lack. It resumes within itself the structure of disavowal and multiple belief."[18] In essence, fetishism is a way for the child to overcome the contradictions and fears inherent in the Oedipal stage.

Metz sees fetishism operating in the cinematic apparatus through the process of disavowal inherent to the watching process. On one hand, viewers understand that the objects, characters, and events unfolding in the film before them are not real. On the other hand, quality films will attempt to mimic real life as much as possible and instill within viewers a sense of realism. Viewers, wrestling with the tension between consciously disavowing the film as false and unconsciously believing the story as true, turn their attention to a fetish to relieve this discomfort. For Metz, the diversionary cinematic fetish is the machinery of the film itself, the director's techniques that help frame and progress the film. "The cinema fetishist," Metz writes, "is the person who is enchanted at what the machine is capable of."[19] Thus, the apparatus is the site where viewers relive Oedipal conflict and anxiety, and they negotiate these negative feelings again through the process of fetishism.

Apparatus theory (and especially the work of Metz) provides an important foundation for the field of Psychoanalytic media studies, but one would be hard pressed to find a contemporary Psychoanalytic scholar who wholly supported this viewpoint. In many ways apparatus theory is considered a historical moment rather than a vibrant area of research today. Critics of apparatus theory claim that it is a naïve approach to film that ignores a number of cinematic qualities (sound, historical context, etc), and Feminists critique the approach for its relative silence toward issues of gender inequality and representation in film. In fact, this critique represents the next significant application of psychoanalytic theory in film scholarship, a body of work centered on how psychoanalysis influences the depiction and reception of gender in film.

The male gaze

With the publication of Laura Mulvey's landmark piece "Visual Pleasure and Narrative Cinema" in 1975, some Psychoanalytic media scholars began shifting their attention away from the context of the cinema and focused more on the actual form and narrative of the films involved. This opened up a field of study on what has become known as the **male gaze**. In her article, Mulvey contends that the film viewer is not merely called upon to participate in unconscious desire via the apparatus theories of Baudry and Metz, but that the cinema itself uses psychoanalytical concepts of desire, identification, voyeurism, and fetishism to frame the narrative across gendered, ideological lines.[20] It is no accident that the protagonists of many film narratives are male, and Mulvey asserts that the matrix of identification and scopophila proposed by Metz actually operates within a powerful phallocentric frame of reference.

Remember that within a phallocentric frame, men are defined by presence of the phallus, and masculinity and male sexuality are defined by favorable concepts of action, power, and primacy. Women are defined by an absence of the phallus, and therefore femininity and female sexuality are associated with passiveness and powerlessness. In considering this perspective, Mulvey writes:

> There is an obvious interest in this analysis for feminists. . . . It gets us nearer to the roots of our oppression, it brings an articulation of the problem closer, it faces us with the ultimate challenge: how to fight the unconscious structured like a language (formed critically at the moment of arrival of language) while still caught within the language of the patriarchy. There is no way in which we can produce an alternative out of the blue, but we can begin to make a break by examining patriarchy with the tools it provides, of which psychoanalysis is not the only but an important one.[21]

Accordingly, Mulvey turns to psychoanalysis to propose a theory of the cinema that associates desire and looking with gendered power. She melds concepts of identification and scopophilia with the male-presence and female-absence thesis of phallocentrism to arrive at a structure for filmic narrative: male/subject/looker and female/object/looked at. Within classic film narrative, Mulvey claims that male characters are active subjects who look upon female characters as passive objects. Likewise, the look of the camera, the way that the shot decisions of the director frame the narrative, is also inherently male and places the female body on display for audiences. Taken together, these two concepts form Mulvey's notion of the male gaze. In accessing a film through this male gaze, film spectators experience unconscious, scopophilic pleasure in two ways: (1) by identifying with the male gaze of the camera as it concentrates on female characters and (2) by identifying with the male characters who gaze at female characters within the film itself.

The original purpose of Mulvey's article was to attack the gendered conventions of classic Hollywood cinema via psychoanalysis. However, one can still find examples of the male gaze in fairly recent films. The 1997 science fiction blockbuster *The Fifth Element* is a good example.[22] The film follows Korbin Dallas (Bruce Willis) as he teams up with a ragtag group of individuals to assemble an elemental weapon that will save the world from impending destruction at the hands of evil Zorg (Gary Oldman). Besides the blatant objectification of the young and sexy "fifth element" Leeloo (Milla Jovovich) throughout the film, the film's opera scene on the pleasure ship *Fhlostan Paradise* is a particularly striking example of how the male gaze has an enduring presence in contemporary film.

Dallas is invited to the show in order to receive parts of the weapon from opera diva Plavalaguna. Although on a strict military mission to save the world, Dallas finds himself enraptured during the diva's performance. She is not a human female, but the character exudes femininity through her voice, actions, and physical appearance (including the features of her chest which suggest human breasts). Throughout the scene, the camera sweeps around the diva and positions her as an object to be consumed visually by audiences both inside and outside of the actual film. As such, the film's audience can gain scopophilic pleasure by looking at the diva on screen *and* by identifying with the audience watching the diva in the film. This identification is driven home by the camera work that establishes a visual connection between the diva and Dallas during the show. At times the camera is focused solely on the diva, and the audience understands that they are looking from Dallas's perspective. However, in the return shot where one would expect to see Dallas in a similar way through the diva's eyes, instead the camera hovers just to the side of her head (which viewers can see on the screen). In this way, the film invites viewers to identify with Dallas looking at the diva but not with the diva looking at Dallas. Here again, the man is the subject looking and the woman is the object looked at.

Concepts of the male gaze do not end here. Mulvey asserts that all female objects in the film will eventually create anxiety for viewers/subjects because their very existence as woman references the lacking phallus, sexual difference, and Oedipal castration. In order to contain the threat of castration, Mulvey claims that female characters in film are neutralized through notions of voyeurism or fetishism. In voyeurism, viewers and lookers experience a "preoccupation with the re-enactment of the original trauma (investigating the woman, demystifying her mystery), counterbalanced by the devaluation, punishment or saving of the guilty object."[23] Mulvey associates voyeurism with sadism, claiming that this avenue of neutralization visually consumes and controls the female object by subjecting her to physical punishment. In fetishism, viewers and subjects simply disavow castration anxiety by transforming the female object (or parts of her body) into a source of sexual beauty and pleasure.

Sometimes the female object within the narrative experiences both voyeuristic punishment and fetishism, as is the case with the diva in *The Fifth Element*. Moments after she finishes her performance, a group of alien bounty hunters break into the opera house and brutally gun down the singer in front of the entire audience. Dallas, rushing to her aid, finds her in her last breaths explaining that the weapon pieces he is looking for are actually inside of her body. After a moment's hesitation, he slowly reaches into her gunshot wounds and removes the pieces as she dies in his arms. In this way, the female diva as threatening object is punished with a violent death and fetishized when the film reduces her to nothing more than a supple chest cavity containing the weapon.

It is important to pause here and note an important distinction. The fact that the gaze of the camera is inherently male (and heterosexual, for that matter) does not preclude other social groups from gaining scopophilic pleasure from film. It would be ridiculous to say that only men gain pleasure from watching movies (the sheer popularity of the institution in America speaks against the fact). Instead, research on the gaze points to the ways that film taps into our psychoanalytic structures and orients us to receiving unconscious pleasure across gendered, ideological lines.

All spectators can experience the pleasure of looking in a film, but they are asked to do so by identifying with a masculine perspective (as Mulvey later asserted in a 1981 article[24]). For Mulvey, that process of identification decreases the possibility of subjugated groups forming their own viewing positions and continues systems of social inequity.

However, the very fact that social groups other than heterosexual men regularly watch films prompted a number of theorists to question Mulvey's theory of the male gaze. They rejected the notion that women and non-heterosexual men must identify with the heterosexual male gaze in order to gain pleasure. These theorists assert that Mulvey's distinction between male subject and female object is not nearly as clear or explanatory as it may originally appear, and the process of identification with film look or narrative is actually far more complicated than she claims. One of the most prominent areas of study that reflects this destabilization of the subject/object relationship is fantasy theory.

Fantasy

In her 1984 article "Fantasia," Elizabeth Cowie draws upon the work of Freudian scholars Jean Laplanche and Jean-Bertrand Pontalis to explain how concepts of psychoanalysis may allow for a more fluid or mobile processes of identification in films than proposed by Mulvey.[25] A **fantasy** is a mental representation of conscious or unconscious wish fulfillment, and (following Freud) Laplanche and Pontalis see it as a primary function intrinsically tied to issues of desire and pleasure in the infant psyche. Fantasy is born in the moment that the suckling child begins to gain sexual satisfaction from the mother's breast; it desires and fantasizes about being with the breast when the mother is absent. The work of Laplanche and Pontalis gives rise to two very important concepts about fantasy. First, *desiring creates fantasy*, and we fantasize only because we desire. Second, fantasy is a *scene* of desire. It is not desire in itself, but rather a mental structure that contains the manifestation and achievement of desire.

Fantasy also importantly allows us to assume multiple perspectives. For Freud and Laplanche, this ability to identify with multiple perspectives in the fantasy scene is intrinsically tied to primal or original fantasies about the (literally) seminal events that created us. It is natural to wonder about who we are and where we came from, and we entertain these thoughts by picturing our beginnings through fantasy. Conscious or unconscious fantasies about the Oedipal complex and sexual differentiation involve multiple parties, and in considering the perspectives of those parties we establish a template for all future fantasies. A child might fantasize about watching the father and mother engaging in the sexual union that created the child, and within the fantasy that child might identify with the father, the mother, its own watching self, another person watching, etc. In this light, we can see that desire, the pleasure principle, and fantasy all come from the same psychoanalytic origins of the individual. However, just as many of our desires remain beyond our conscious recognition, much of the fantasy we experience as individuals also manifests on the unconscious level as well.

It is this type of unconscious fantasy that primarily informs the work of media scholars in this theoretical tradition. They claim that films engage us like a fantasy, inviting us to unconsciously identify with multiple parties in the narrative in order to work through and satisfy our desires. Because we can identify with multiple perspectives in the filmic/fantasy scene, these scholars question Mulvey's notion that audiences gain pleasure from only identifying with the watching male subject on screen. Instead, the film operates as an imaginary space where spectators can identify with the camera's gaze, same-sex characters, opposite-sex characters, objects, and virtually any other aspect of the narrative. Pleasure comes not from visually consuming the female objects in the film through the male gaze (as Mulvey claims), but rather in identifying with characters involved in overcoming lack and satisfying their desires on screen. Instead of identifying solely with the male protagonist as he searches to fill his lack in the narrative, audiences in fantasy are free to identify with any aspect of the quest (or with multiple aspects at different times during the film).

Much like Metz's earlier claims about voyeurism in film, Cowie asserts that pleasure in the filmic fantasy comes from the endless deferment of desire within the narrative. Remember that desire is predicated on the subject always being removed from the desired object; to overcome the Lacanian lack and reach the object dissolves the intense desire for it. So, spectators identifying with characters in the film gain pleasure in the narrative moments that defer and prolong desire, not in the moments where characters actually achieve their desires. As Cowie puts it, although narratives almost always come to closure by the end,

> inevitably the story will fall prey to diverse diversions, delays, obstacles and other means of postponing the ending. For though we all want the couple to be united, and the obstacles heroically overcome, we don't want the story to end. . . . The pleasure is in how to *bring about* the consummation, is in the happening and continuing to happen; is how it will come about, and not in the moment of *having happened*.[26]

Hopefully the mechanics of psychoanalytic fantasy and film are coming more into focus now. In this tradition, we engage films because they represent public fantasies that allow us to work through unconscious issues of desire and pleasure. We identify with a range of subject positions within the overarching narrative of the film, a narrative that metaphorically represents the quest and desire to fill the lack and establish wholeness. However, pleasure in watching comes from the moments in the film when the process of filling the lack is prolonged or stunted, such as the introduction of the antagonist or other obstacles that keep the protagonist from reaching his/her goal.

The 2003 film *Girl With a Pearl Earring* provides an excellent example of the fantasy approach discussed thus far. The film is a fictitious account of how the famous Johannes Vermeer painting of the same name came to be. It follows the painfully slow seduction of house servant Griet (Scarlett Johansson) by the tortured artist (Colin Firth) and his decision to secretly paint her as his masterpiece. The minimal dialogue in the film, coupled with its dreamlike reliance on color and ambient sound, makes it an especially ample fantasy environment for spectators.

A forbidden mutual attraction is present from the first contact between Griet and Vermeer, she for his artistic brilliance and he for her inspiring beauty. Their "courtship" is achingly drawn out and deferred countless times, and it perfectly embodies the fantasy construct of unattainable desire. Spectators who engage the film as fantasy can identify with either or both characters as they yearn for each other throughout the film, and the postponed consummation of their relationship provides the environment where desire continues to thrive. The film is peppered with moments where the two are just barely kept apart. At one point, while teaching Griet to mix and produce paint, Vermeer allows his hand to casually fall near her own at the work table. He pauses before barely inching his hand toward the servant's. Startled, she looks at it, but the two are interrupted before she can accept his tender offering. In these moments, where outside influences continually divide the characters, viewers can experience the play of their own unfulfilled, unconscious desires.

The ending of the film is equally (un)satisfying. Shortly after Vermeer paints her into his masterpiece, Griet is banished from the home by his envious wife Catherina. However, the final scene shows another servant arriving at Griet's new residence with a package from Vermeer: inside are Catherina's pearl earrings that the artist asked Griet to wear while posing for the painting. Again, their attraction is endlessly deferred in this open-ended conclusion, which stands in stark contrast to the typical Hollywood romantic ending where the couple in question is finally united. Spectators are left pondering the future of the couple, playing out infinite unfulfilled instances of possible desire between the two while unconsciously activating personal issues of lack, desire, and pleasure.

Fantasy theory based around concepts of cinematic narrative and fluid identification represents only one answer to the perceived limitations of apparatus theory and ideas regarding the male gaze. The publication of Mulvey's article incited a great deal of Psychoanalytic scholarship that sought to understand the complex ways in which film texts appealed to audiences. The rest of this chapter will concentrate on a number of these areas, including female spectatorship, male objectification, and queer viewing, to investigate how issues of psychoanalytic subjectivity may function outside of the traditional male gaze perspective.

Contemporary Scholarship in Psychoanalytic Analysis

Female spectatorship

It was only a matter of time after the publication of Mulvey's article that scholars would begin to question the place of female spectatorship or the "female gaze." If the cinema is constructed as a place for male spectators only, they ask, then what explains the innumerable female audiences that regularly attend films? Major work in this area divides roughly into two camps: a more traditional Psychoanalytic approach based on concepts of identification and desire, and a more ethnographic approach (see Chapter 10) based on interviews with actual female spectators.

Psychoanalytic approaches to female spectatorship largely focus on how women can find a subjectivity "between the lines" of the institutional male gaze. For example, in a follow-up article to "Visual Pleasure and the Narrative Cinema," Mulvey asserts that female subjectivity is possible only because femininity is a psychoanalytically incomplete construct according to Freud.[27] Because the repressed masculine remains present in female viewers throughout their lives, they can temporarily slip into this "transvestite" masculine subjectivity in order to gain pleasure through the male gaze. Similarly, Mary Ann Doane suggests that while the male spectator gains pleasure from the Metzian voyeuristic distance of the cinema, the female has no comparable lack between herself and the image: she is over-represented in the image as an object.[28] Doane claims that pleasurable lack and female subjectivity can come from the concept of "gender masquerade," where the female spectator recognizes the falsity of gender norms and invents a distance between herself and the constructs of femininity represented on screen. Finally, Teresa De Lauretis identifies a female subjectivity resulting from the similarity between the Oedipus complex and film narrative.[29] Because the Oedipus complex primarily focuses on the male's sexuality and constructs the female's sexuality as an inverse, the overarching masculine position is the "subject" (aligned with the narrative hero) and the overarching feminine position is the "context" (the obstacle in or environment of the narrative). Female spectatorship, then, could operate outside of the male gaze where female spectators are able to identify directly with the actual movement and progression of the filmic narrative.

The other important vein of research in the area of female spectatorship concerns itself with the impressions and feelings of actual female viewers. Scholars here claim that complicated Psychoanalytic theories of the female gaze are not nearly as explanatory as the actual experiences of women who attend and consume films. This work departs from the textual focus of most traditional Psychoanalytic theory in favor of a more audience-based approach, but the conclusions drawn are still helpful in understanding the relationship between women and the cinema. Miriam Hansen's piece on the films of Rudolph Valentino is a good example of this trend.[30] Valentino popularized the famous "Latin Lover" image in films of the 1920s, and Hansen sees his collection of films as a significant realm of female spectatorship. Although she addresses Psychoanalytic concepts of identification, the gaze and erotic looking, she expands her analysis by including discussion on the popular female reception of Valentino and the relationship of his star image to changing notions about female sexuality. Likewise, one of the more important pieces in the area of reception-based female spectatorship is Jackie Stacey's project regarding British women's impressions of female stars of the 1940s and 1950s.[31] Through an extensive collection of questionnaires, Stacey provides a multi-faceted account of female viewing governed by notions of escapism and identification with stars. Like Hansen, Stacey both utilizes and challenges Psychoanalytic concepts in explaining the specific experiences of her sample group.

Male objectification

Another area of scholarship to come out of the responses to Mulvey's male gaze thesis is the notion of the male object. Within a complementary Psychoanalytic framework, the possibility of a female subject necessarily points to an eroticized male object. However, unlike the various conclusions about the female object discussed thus far, much of the work within this area points to a social trend of refusing to recognize the male as passive, sexual object. For example, in his analysis of the male pin-up in popular magazines, Richard Dyer claims that the erotic image of the male always contains "instabilities."[32] Though objectified, the male model denies the look of the spectator by looking away from the camera or positioning his body in ways to connote ideas of power and independence. Male objects tend to be more active than their female counterparts, and the "natural" link between muscles and the male object also works to break the image free of passive connotations. Thus, while instances of male objectification do occur, they carry connotations of power and activity that are absent in representations of female objects. In a sense, the image of the male disavows its role as an object.

This disavowal of the male as object carries over in other ways as well. Steve Neale claims that though the male body does work as a spectacle in older films like *Spartacus* and *Ben Hur*, those images come to audiences primarily through the looks of other characters who fear or hate the characters objectified (thereby dampening the possibility of erotic desire).[33] Male bodies that *do* carry an air of erotic appeal are also subsequently feminized (such as the body of Rock Hudson in the melodramas of Douglas Sirk). Similarly, Kenneth MacKinnon asserts that the male object in society is always assumed to be a source of pleasure for some other social group.[34] To illustrate this point, he discusses the reaction of students in a film seminar after viewing music videos that prominently objectify and sexualize the male body.

> An older woman thought that it was surely meant for teenaged girls; a younger woman was sure that it was meant for gay males; and a remarkably "out" male who should, by the latter's logic, have recognized his centrality in the audience for those videos claimed with certainty that they were not for "the likes of" him.[35]

MacKinnon goes on to theorize a female spectator that exists on a mostly theoretical level, a cultural invention necessary to deny the potential homoeroticism a male erotic object creates. Overall, scholarship on the male object tends to reinforce Mulvey's original thesis that "the male figure cannot bear the burden of sexual objectification."[36] Scholars largely conclude that the cultural overlays and technological qualities of film and other media reinforce the male gaze by denying the image of the male any significant object status.

Queer spectatorship

Finally, an important and recent trend in relation to Psychoanalytic concepts of the gaze comes from the growing academic discipline of queer theory (see Chapter 9). Queer theorists question the usefulness of gender and sexual divisions in relation to the gaze, asserting that such divisions are entirely constructed and essentialist. Queer theory troubles the very foundation of much Psychoanalytic film theory by calling attention to the fluid nature of sexual drives and identities. For example, Steven Drukman theorizes a "gay gaze" implicitly tied up in notions of performance and camp.[37] Through an analysis of music videos on MTV, he proposes that gay viewing involves recognizing and deconstructing images as an unstable composite of appearance and reality. These ideas are mirrored in Caroline Evans and Lorraine Gamman's article on the nature of queer viewing.[38] They claim that Mulvey and other Psychoanalytic theorists who base their work on the notion of a stable sexual identity cannot fully capture the spectator/screen relationship. Instead, they see value in a perspective that recognizes the link as ambiguous, containing spectator "identifications which are multiple, contradictory, shifting, oscillating, inconsistent and fluid."[39] In general, queer approaches to Psychoanalytic theory seek to destabilize most of the foundational concepts regarding sexuality set out by Freud and Lacan, replacing them instead with questions of social construction, artifice, and sexual possibility.

In many ways, the issues brought up by queer theorists pose a fitting challenge to the discipline of psychoanalysis, a field that has always been marked by contradiction and varied interpretation throughout its history. Beyond questioning or expanding canonical Psychoanalytic media studies, the scholarship on female subjectivity, male objectification, and queer viewing presented in this final section signals an important trend toward moving psychoanalysis outside of the theater. Scholars are now using concepts of the male gaze and fetishism to understand the non-filmic media texts like music videos and magazine advertisements. Although some scholars believe that Psychoanalytic theory has run its academic course in relation to media studies, we can clearly see that it continues to offer us intriguing ways of understanding the structure and role of media texts in our lives.

Conclusion

This chapter has looked at how Psychoanalytic concepts of desire help explain the structure of media texts, with film as the historically predominant area of analysis.

Psychoanalytic theorists Sigmund Freud and Jacques Lacan provide a somewhat overlapping understanding of the formative process that results in an individual's psychical structure, and their respective theories of repression and lack each help shed light on why films appeal to audiences based on this mental formation. The three approaches to film outlined in this chapter (apparatus theory, theories of the male gaze, and fantasy theory) all attempt to explain how the early structuring of the human mind results in the particular management of film in society: filmic evolution, screenings, shot sequences, characterization, narratives, etc. Contemporary scholars have extended these approaches by questioning their assumptions about the nature of gender, sexuality and desire, resulting in a vibrant (and complex) field of Psychoanalytic research today. Although Psychoanalytic approaches to media texts are not as popular as they were in the 1970s and 1980s, Psychoanalytic scholars continue to present the field of media studies with a fascinating synthesis of psychology and image. If nothing else, psychoanalysis provides us with a multifaceted interpretation of the psyche, an important perspective on contemporary media, and a language to articulate the inexplicable attraction of the cinematic image to the human soul.

MEDIA LAB 6: DOING PSYCHOANALYTIC ANALYSIS

OBJECTIVE

The aim of this lab is to utilize Psychoanalytic concepts to analyze media texts. Specifically, students will investigate how notions of the male gaze work to structure the "look of" and "look within" magazine advertisements.

ACTIVITY

- Divide the class into small groups of 4–5 students each.
- Display the advertisements for Candie's Fragrances and Absolut vodka shown in Figures 7.1 and 7.2.
- Ask students to record their answers to the following questions.
  1 How, if at all, is the concept of the male gaze reflected in these advertisements? Discuss both the frame of the ads and the looks of the male characters within them. Where/what is the phallus in each ad?
  2 How do these advertisements construct a female object? Is there evidence of voyeuristic punishment or fetishization present in the image? If yes, how so?
  3 Attempt to locate an example of a male object in the advertisements. How, if at all, is that character negating object status and asserting subject status? (Looking away? Activity? Muscles?)

Figure 7.1
Candie's Fragrances
advertisement.
COURTESY OF ICONIX
BRAND/CANDIE'S
FRAGRANCES.

Figure 7.2   Absolut vodka advertisement.
ADVERTISING ARCHIVES.

SUGGESTED READING

Baudry, J.-L. Ideological Effects of the Basic Cinematographic Apparatus. In *Film Theory and Criticism: Introductory Readings*, 5th edn, L. Braudry and M. Cohen (eds), pp. 345–55. New York: Oxford University Press, 1999.

Cooper, B. "Chick Flicks" as Feminist Texts: the Appropriation of the Male Gaze in *Thelma & Louise*. *Women's Studies in Communication* 23, 2000, 277–306.

Cowie, E. *Representing the Woman: Cinema and Psychoanalysis*. Minneapolis, MN: University of Minnesota Press, 1997.

de Lauretis, T. *Alice Doesn't*. Bloomington, IN: Indiana University Press, 1984.

Elliot, A. *Psychoanalytic Theory: an Introduction*, 2nd edn. Durham, NC: Duke University Press, 2002.

Freud, S. *An Outline of Psycho-Analysis*. Translated by J. Strachey. New York: W.W. Norton & Company, 1970.

Gallop, J. *Reading Lacan*. New York: Cornell University Press, 1985.

Kaplan, E.A. (ed.) *Feminism and Film*. New York: Oxford University Press, 2000.

Lacan, J. *Ecrits: a Selection*. Translated by B. Fink. New York: W.W. Norton & Company, 2002.

MacKinnon, K. After Mulvey: Male Erotic Objectification. In *The Body's Perilous Pleasures: Dangerous Desires and Contemporary Culture*, M. Aaron (ed.), pp. 13–29. Edinburgh: Edinburgh University Press, 1999.

Manlove, C.T. Visual "Drive" and Cinematic Narrative: Reading Gaze Theory in Lacan, Hitchcock and Mulvey. *Cinema Journal* 46, 2007, 83–104.

McGowan, T. *The Real Gaze: Film Theory After Lacan*. Albany: New York: State University of New York Press, 2007.

Metz, C. *The Imaginary Signifier: Psychoanalysis and the Cinema*. Translated by C. Britton, A. Williams, B. Brewster, and A. Guzzetti. Bloomington, IN: Indiana University Press, 1982.

Mitchell, J. *Psychoanalysis and Feminism*. London: Penguin, 1974.

Mulvey, L. Visual Pleasure and Narrative Cinema. In *Media and Cultural Studies: Keyworks*, M.G. Durham and D.M. Kellner (ed.), pp. 342–52. Malden, MA: Blackwell, 2006.

Oates, T.P. The Erotic Gaze in the NFL Draft. *Communication and Critical/Cultural Studies* 4, 2007, 74–90.

Ragland-Sullivan, E. *Jacques Lacan and the Philosophy of Psychoanalysis*. Chicago, IL: University of Illinois Press, 1986.

Recuber, T. Immersion Cinema: the Rationalization and Reenchantment of Cinematic Space. *Space and Culture* 10, 2007, 315–30.

Rushing, J.H. and Frentz, T.S. *Projecting the Shadow: The Cyborg Hero in American Film*. Chicago, IL: University of Chicago Press, 1995.

Sherwin, M. Deconstructing the Male: Masochism, Female Spectatorship, and the Femme Fatale in *Fatal Attraction*, *Body of Evidence* and *Basic Instinct*. *Journal of Popular Film and Television* 35, 2008, 174–82.

Singer, L. Eye/Mind/Screen: Toward a Phenomenology of Cinematic Scopophilia. *Quarterly Review of Film & Video* 12, 1990, 51–67.

NOTES

1. S. Freud, *An Outline of Psycho-Analysis*, trans. J. Strachey (New York: W.W. Norton & Company, 1970), 55.
2. Freud, *Outline*, 56.
3. D. Morley, *Television, Audiences, and Cultural Studies* (New York: Routledge, 1992).
4. P. Turschwell, *Sigmund Freud* (New York: Routledge, 2000), 44.
5. Freud, *Outline*, 10–11.
6. Freud, *Outline*, 11.
7. A. Elliot, *Psychoanalytic Theory: an Introduction*, 2nd edn (Durham, NC: Duke University Press, 2002).
8. Elliot, 19.
9. Elliot, 24.
10. J. Lacan, The Mirror Stage as Formative of the *I* Function, in *Ecrits: a Selection*, trans. B. Fink (New York: W.W. Norton & Company, 2002), 6.
11. J. Mitchell, *Psychoanalysis and Feminism* (London: Penguin, 1974).
12. J.-L. Baudry, The Apparatus: Metaphysical Approaches to the Impression of Reality in Cinema, in *Film Theory and Criticism: Introductory Readings*, L. Braudy and M. Cohen (eds), 5th edn (New York: Oxford University Press, 1999), 767.
13. J.-L. Baudry, Ideological Effects of the Basic Cinematic Apparatus, in *Film Theory and Criticism: Introductory Readings*, L. Braudy and M. Cohen (eds), 5th edn (New York: Oxford University Press, 1999), 353.
14. Baudry, Ideological Effects, 354.
15. C. Metz, *The Imaginary Signifier: Psychoanalysis and the Cinema*, trans. C. Britton, A. Williams, B. Brewster, and A. Guzzetti (Bloomington, IN: Indiana University Press, 1982), 48–9.
16. S. Freud, Three Essays on the Theory of Sexuality, in *The Standard Edition of the Complete Psychological Works of Sigmund Freud*, vol. 7, ed. and trans. J. Strachey (London: Hogarth Press, 1962), 156.
17. Metz, 70.
18. Metz, 71.
19. Metz, 74.
20. L. Mulvey, Visual Pleasure and Narrative Cinema, in *Media and Cultural Studies: Keywords*, M.G. Durham and D.M. Kellner (eds) (Malden, MA: Blackwell, 2006), 342–52.
21. Mulvey, Visual Pleasure, 343.
22. B. Ott and E. Aoki, Counter-Imagination as Interpretive Practice: Futuristic Fantasy and *The Fifth Element*, *Women's Studies and Communication* 27, no. 2, 2004, 149–76.
23. Mulvey, Visual Pleasure, 348.
24. L. Mulvey, Afterthoughts on "Visual Pleasure and Narrative Cinema" Inspired by King Vidor's *Duel in the Sun*, in *Feminist Film Theory: A Reader*, S. Thornham (ed.) (New York: New York University Press, 1999), 122–30.
25. E. Cowie, Fantasia, in *Representing the Woman: Cinema and Psychoanalysis* (Minneapolis, MN: University of Minnesota Press, 1997), 123–65.
26. Cowie, 133.
27. Mulvey, Afterthoughts.
28. M.A. Doane, Film and the Masquerade: Theorizing the Female Spectator, in *Feminist Film Theory: a Reader*, S. Thornham (ed.) (New York: New York University Press, 1999), 131–45.
29. T. De Lauretis, *Alice Doesn't* (Bloomington, IN: Indiana University Press, 1984).
30. M. Hansen, Pleasure, Ambivalence, Identification: Valentino and Female Spectatorship, in *Feminism and Film*, E.A. Kaplan (ed.) (New York: Oxford University Press, 2000), 226–52.
31. J. Stacey, *Star Gazing: Hollywood Cinema and Female Spectatorship* (New York: Routledge, 1994).
32. R. Dyer, *Only Entertainment* (New York: Routledge, 1992).
33. S. Neale, Masculinity as Spectacle: Reflections on Men in Mainstream Cinema, in *Feminism and Film*, E.A. Kaplan (ed.) (New York: Oxford University Press, 2000), 253–64.
34. K. MacKinnon, After Mulvey: Male Erotic Objectification, in *The Body's Perilous Pleasures: Dangerous Desires and Contemporary Culture*, M. Aaron (ed.) (Edinburgh: Edinburgh University Press, 1999), 13–29.
35. MacKinnon, 18.

36. Mulvey, Visual Pleasure, 347.

37. S. Drukman, The Gay Gaze, or Why I Want My MTV, in *A Queer Romance: Lesbians, Gay Men and Popular Culture*, P. Burston and C. Richardson (ed.) (New York: Routledge, 1995), 81–95.

38. C. Evans and L. Gamman, The Gaze Revisited, or Reviewing Queer Viewing, in *A Queer Romance: Lesbians, Gay Men and Popular Culture*, P. Burston and C. Richardson (ed.) (New York: Routledge, 1995), 13–56.

39. Evans and Gamman, 45.

8 Feminist Analysis

When R&B singer India Arie proclaimed "I am not my hair" on her 2006 album *Testimony: Vol. One, Life & Relationship*, she was drawing attention to an interesting aspect of contemporary American culture. Hair is an important way we express who we are in our society. In particular, it is a key way we mark gender norms. Scores of products and procedures exist for women to remove "unsightly" hair from their legs, face, underarms, and bikini area. *Newsweek* magazine even caught flack in October 2008 when it featured Republican Vice Presidential candidate Sarah Palin on a cover but failed to airbrush out the hair on her upper lip. At the same time, hair-coloring kits marketed toward men emphasize masking gray hair in order to shake off the image of old age. Even more "unmanly" than grey hair for men is baldness, and a variety of shampoos and medications exist to help men continue to look virile with a full mane of hair. In each of these examples, the biological quality of hair becomes a way that we understand the cultural rules surrounding what it means to be masculine or feminine.

The kinds of associations and meanings made between biology and culture exemplified by hair are at the heart of Feminist analysis. Feminist scholars concentrate on how biological categories like male and female become conflated with cultural gender expectations, resulting in discriminatory social systems that privilege men over women. Feminist media scholars, in particular, concentrate on revealing the limiting nature of mass media texts that reinforce dominant social understandings of sex and gender. As a result, feminism, like Cultural studies (see Chapter 6), is also marked by a political commitment to deconstruct these oppressive systems in order to transform society into a fairer, more equitable place for diverse peoples.

This chapter focuses on the place of feminism in understanding media texts. We begin with an introduction to feminism, paying particular attention to the ways in which it concentrates on issues of gender as a whole (and not, as is often portrayed in the mass media, the needs of women alone). After briefly considering the roles and functions of stereotypes, we spend the bulk of this chapter deconstructing common stereotypes of masculinity and femininity in the media and considering the impact of the "postfeminist" sensibility on the project of Feminist media studies.

Before we continue, though, we feel it is necessary to first address a pressing issue. In truth, "feminism" represents a fairly broad theoretical approach to media texts. There are many different kinds of feminism that each stress particular aspects of social power and difference over others. In order to present an introduction to feminism without sacrificing its essential spirit, this chapter will concentrate on the main theoretical impulse(s) behind the tradition before considering representations of gender and sex in the media. If you find this theoretical introduction compelling, we encourage you to explore the diverse body of feminist scholarship at your leisure. See the Suggested Reading section at the end of this chapter for suggestions.

Feminism: an Overview

Feminism, broadly, is a political project that explores the diverse ways men and women are socially empowered or disempowered. It is often a highly charged word that requires some explanation to fully understand. Contrary to popular belief, contemporary feminism is not anti-male. As cultural critic bell hooks defines it in *Feminism is for Everybody*, "feminism is a movement to end sexism, sexist exploitation, and oppression."[1] **Sexism** is discrimination based upon a person's sex. Instead of targeting individual men or even men as a social group, feminism seeks to reveal and eradicate socially ingrained *systems* of sexism that harm *all* individuals in some way. In short, feminism is a political project focused on deconstructing sexist oppression present in our everyday norms and experiences.

A number of interlocking factors contribute to the creation of a sexist social system. The first is the confusion between sex and gender.[2] **Sex** refers to the innate, biological differentiation between men and women: anatomy, reproduction, hormones, etc. **Gender**, on the other hand, refers to the culturally constructed differences between men and women: tastes, roles, activities, etc. It is a biological fact that only women can give birth to children, but the tendency to view women as nurturing and mothering is a gendered quality. A good way to distinguish between sex and gender is to look at the respective categories they govern. Sex refers to the categories male and female, while gender refers to the categories masculine and feminine. A Y chromosome is a male trait, whereas aggressiveness is a masculine one. Trouble arises when societies such as ours confuse gendered qualities with sexual ones, understanding culturally constructed norms as innate biological traits. For example, the common belief in American society that women are naturally more emotional then men is a result of this confusion. The belief that gender distinctions are innate and natural is called **essentialism**.

Another factor intrinsic to our sexist social system is patriarchy. **Patriarchy** is a system of power relations in which women's interests are subordinated to those of men. Essentializing a group is one way of defining them and marking their worth, and patriarchy essentializes women in a way that devalues them while predominantly serving the interests of men. We can see patriarchal logic especially in relation to economics in America. If we believe that women are innately more nurturing then men, then it "makes sense" for women to stay home with newborn children while men continue to work, earn money, and contribute to their skills sets or resumés. If we believe that women are biologically predetermined to fail at math and science, then it "makes sense" that the majority of workers in high-paying engineering and medical occupations are men. Patriarchal systems empower men and disempower women by making constructed, gendered power imbalances seem natural and innate. The often tangible benefits that men reap from this system make them less likely to challenge patriarchy than women.

Does the fact that men benefit from patriarchy mean that all men are sexist? Yes and no. To understand the difference between individuals and social systems, we turn to an analogy adapted from Allen G. Johnson's *Privilege, Power and Difference*.[3] Do you consider yourself an excessively greedy person in your everyday life? Probably not. Most of us think of greed as a negative character trait. However, would you say that you have expressed greedy traits while playing the game *Monopoly* at some point in your life? Probably so. Most of us have spent a rainy afternoon buying up properties on the *Monopoly* board and showing little financial mercy when our siblings, parents, or friends land on them. We may not consider ourselves greedy individuals, but we exhibit extremely greedy traits when playing *Monopoly*. The same can be said about how we act in sexist social systems. We may not consider ourselves sexist in the sense that we do not consciously discriminate against people in our everyday life, but when we play the "game" of sexism – when we go out into the world and take part in social systems that are inherently sexist – we, in a sense, are sexist as well. Social systems cannot happen without people, just as *Monopoly* cannot play itself, but we enact social systems and board games according to rules determined before we as individuals joined. So, to answer the question posed at the beginning of the paragraph, yes, all men are sexist. But so are all women, because we are all playing by the rules of the game when we unconsciously enact sexist social conventions. At the same time, many women and some men have attempted to reject the rules as much as possible in their individual lives. These are feminists.

Understanding that we are all subject to sexist social rules opens up additional understanding about feminism. Feminism does attempt to recognize and disable patriarchal social systems that disempower individual women, but recent feminist scholarship has also begun looking at the ways in which patriarchy harms individual men. The gendered expectations that patriarchy places on women also exert pressure on men, often demanding that men show little emotion, avoid certain occupations, or act as the breadwinner for their families. This fact underscores the wide scope of the feminist project. Everyone is harmed by sexist social systems, although patriarchal power relations increase the harm they do to women. Both men and women enact these systems, and both women and men can be feminists in their attempts to resist them.

Feminist media scholars understand media texts as products of sexist social systems, and they look especially at the ways in which patriarchal systems of power inform the creation of media texts. Scholars in this tradition analyze television programs, films, magazines, radio programs, and internet sites to understand how these texts reflect, support, and create systems of unequal gendered power. Although contemporary feminist scholarship is complex in its analysis of the media, the issue of gendered representation and stereotypes is a historically primary focus that still has relevance for today. The remainder of our discussion on feminism will concentrate on media representations of gender and how particular media texts express stereotypes. First, however, it is important to fully understand the social role of stereotyping.

Stereotyping in American Media

A **stereotype** is a misleading and simplified representation of a particular social group. You are probably familiar with many stereotypes already: The elderly drive badly, fraternity members are only in college to party, and Southerners are not very smart. Stereotypes are damaging because they gloss over the complex characteristics that actually define a social group and reduce its members to a few (usually unfavorable) traits. When these stereotypical representations become commonly accepted in the media, the result is often the social oppression and disempowerment of individuals within the stereotyped group. Many people have had experiences with stereotypes. And yet, if the vast majority of people know that stereotypes are false and socially damaging, why do they persist in life and the media? There are a few different answers to this question.

A conventional (and nonetheless accurate) critical explanation for the presence of stereotypes in the media is something akin to the following: socially powerful groups like men have greater access to media outlets as a function of their privilege, and this access allows them to represent their particular perspectives on other social groups to the widest audiences. These perspectives are often stereotypically reductionist, but they become the most widely known and accepted representations of these groups. However, while the repetition of stereotypes is certainly a powerful force in securing their place in the American context, it is important to consider how other qualities of stereotypes contribute to their presence in the media.

First, everyone stereotypes. Stereotyping helps individuals make sense of an increasingly complex contemporary society. As social creatures we absorb and reflect upon the experiences we have with others, and we use past experiences to make sense of present and future interactions. Stereotypes, or mental categories of people we carry with us, allow us to quickly process incoming information about strangers by greatly reducing the amount of information we have to take in. If we actually took the time to notice the subtle nuances of every individual we encounter on a daily basis, then we would spend much more time in our lives discussing social issues with every street petitioner and the pros and cons of long-distance service with every telemarketer. Stereotypes, however inaccurate, form mental shortcuts that allow us to quickly make snap judgments about individuals and move on.

Moreover, for such simplistic reductions of character, widespread social stereotypes are actually rather intricate in their construction. You may have heard the saying that there is a "kernel of truth" to every stereotype. This is true to the extent that stereotypes often blend realistic aspects of life, material conditions, and social roles into inaccurate assumptions and false traits. The continuing power and "strength of stereotypes lies in this combination of validity and distortion."[4] Stereotypes persist in the media because they have enough truth to *sound* plausible without much critical thought. To complicate the matter even more, sometimes members of socially oppressed groups will believe the stereotypes they see in the media to be true and emulate them.[5] Here stereotypes mimic reality by actually creating it. Thus, stereotypes often persist because it is difficult to distinguish their truth from falsity.

The fact that everyone stereotypes to some degree, and that aspects of stereotypes often ring true, helps explain a rather unique function of stereotypes in the media. The stereotypes we see in the media often lend their texts a certain sense of credibility with audiences.[6] When we see a sitcom with a foreign exchange student speaking in broken English, or watch a movie that features a group of black gang members, these representations unfortunately "ring true" with the stereotypical knowledge we already have as members of society. In other words, media images that feature stereotypes gain an informal credibility because they match some of the common stereotypes people use every day to reduce information processing. Media producers who present representations that challenge social stereotypes risk losing this informal credibility. While the media create and reinforce stereotypes just as much as they use them to attract audiences, the issues of stereotyping and credibility remains a powerful influence.

In discussing these issues, we do not wish to give the impression that the media use of stereotypes is permissible because stereotyping is a human tendency, a quasi-reflection of reality, or an effective way to appeal to audiences. We also do not excuse individuals who ignorantly hold racial, gendered, sexual, or other stereotypes. Stereotypes are harmful by nature, and we should work to eradicate them as much as possible. In this section we simply hope to situate our discussion of gendered stereotypes within a larger framework of the complex ways that stereotyping operates in the media and society. It deepens our understanding of the power and place of the various mediated stereotypes we will look at. As we address these in detail in the next section, keep these various aspects of stereotypes in mind. Consider how issues like human tendency, reflections of reality, or audience adaptation methods inform the creation of these stereotypes.

Gendered Stereotypes in American Media

Exceptions exist for every rule. Recognizing exceptions is the mark of quality scholarship and true understanding. With that in mind, the stereotypical images of gender we discuss in this section signify some of the general, overarching, historical trends within media representation most apparent in Feminist criticism. They are by no means absolute truths: the contemporary American media landscape is far too diverse to fit only within the narrow range of these stereotypes. However, as archaic as they may sound, these classic stereotypes continue to thrive in today's media, and concentrating on these particular stereotypes will provide a useful initial glimpse into the process of Feminist analysis.

The constructed opposition of masculinity and femininity provides a binary understanding of gender in American society, so it is understandable that many gendered stereotypes in the media also function as complementary inverses of each other. In general, stereotypes of masculinity are defined by power, significance, agency, and social influence. Stereotypes of femininity are defined by powerlessness, insignificance, passiveness, and limited control. Although these trends construct narrow gender norms for individual members of both sexes, they reinforce patriarchal systems of power by supporting the domination of men over women. The four interrelated, stereotypical binaries we focus on in this section are active/passive, public/private, logical/emotional, and sexual subject/sexual object.

Active/passive

Mainstream media representations of men and masculinity are often marked by strength and activity. Advertisements tend to depict men engaging in sports, working with tools, or driving powerful vehicles, and the models in these advertisements are often full of vitality or in clear physical shape. Images of women, on the other hand, tend to emphasize passiveness and weakness. Female models often simply sit or stand beautifully to advertise their product, and many of them possess dangerously underweight figures.[7] This general contrast between men and women in advertising is striking, and the repetition of this motif across many different kinds of ads makes the distinction seem normal. Notions of power and physical prowess begin to define masculinity and "being a man" in American society, while femininity and "being a woman" are tied to passive acceptance and helplessness.

Consider the difference in gendered representation between two "Got Milk?" advertisements (Figures 8.1 and 8.2). The advertisement with Jackie Chan exudes masculinity. The daring aerial escape from a burning car constructs Chan as physically strong and in control of his situation, so much so that he can kick a milk bottle with precision despite a rather threatening environment. While there is a great deal of activity in the scene itself (an ascending helicopter and raging flames, for example), the focus here is on Chan's agency. In fact, Chan is so sure of his abilities in

Figure 8.1 Milk advertisement with Jackie Chan. ADVERTISING ARCHIVES.

Figure 8.2 Milk advertisement with Kate Moss. ADVERTISING ARCHIVES.

this situation that we see him literally laughing in the face of danger and taking time to educate readers on the importance of drinking milk. The cityscape that fills the background of the advertisement reminds us that action always requires a context; a subject's actions make no sense unless we understand what prompts them. Additionally, this advertisement conjures many images of Chan's film career, where the actor often portrays a powerful martial artist. Even if one has never seen a Jackie Chan film before encountering this advertisement, the image reflects the "action hero" trope popular in mainstream Hollywood films.[8] Overall, the Chan advertisement taps into many different American cultural codes in order to present an image of masculinity marked by power and strength. In some ways it is easy to forget that this is an advertisement for milk.

The advertisement with model Kate Moss provides a marked contrast to that of Chan. Glancing back over her shoulder, her arm shielding her breasts from the curious eye of the camera/viewer, Moss's pose is innocent and inviting. She is naked and therefore completely vulnerable, and her body is certainly on display for the viewer in a way that Chan's is not. The text, which references Moss's famous facial bone structure, draws additional attention to her physical beauty rather than her abilities or talents. A recognizable background would at least allow readers to imagine Moss reacting to her environment, but the lack of any context here signals that Moss is merely to be visually consumed like a piece of art. The image of Moss also invokes the cultural notion of the pretty, demure model, an individual whose entire career involves constantly being directed by others. Through these various visual cues and references, the advertisement presents an image of femininity defined by passivity and vulnerability. Whereas the Chan ad implies that drinking milk will make readers active and strong, the Moss ad suggests that drinking milk will leave one passive and exposed.

Public/private

The binary of active man/passive woman helps shed light on other, related gendered stereotypes. Popular American television shows often draw sharp distinctions between men and women in relation to public and private spheres. Because men are represented as active and strong, they also tend to fulfill the role of "family provider" in media texts. Audiences often encounter scenes in which men are working on the job as the breadwinner for their families. Women, in contrast, are coded as passive and weak, and media texts tend to represent women as the "family nurturer" as a result. The common media sitcom image of the housewife is the most obvious expression of this domestic stereotype. Here the woman's responsibility is to nurture the family by cleaning the house, taking care of children, and fixing meals. Older television couples, such as Fred and Wilma Flintstone or Ward and June Cleaver (of *Leave it to Beaver*), perfectly embody these binary stereotypes.

Contemporary audiences may consider the provider/nurturer stereotype to be a gross oversimplification, and it is true that some media texts portray heterosexual couples with a much more fluid understanding of family roles. However, despite examples of progressive programs, these gender stereotypes continue to endure in popular American television programming. *The Simpsons* is an excellent example of this type of representation. Homer Simpson may be inept in his job at the Springfield Nuclear Power Plant, but he is still the sole source of income for the cartoon family. Throughout the run of the show, audiences have laughed at Homer's various misguided but heartfelt attempts to provide for his family. For example, in the first full-length episode of the series, Homer fails to get a Christmas raise and takes a job as a mall Santa to earn the money necessary for Christmas presents. Although he loses the Santa job and gambles away his meager paycheck at the Springfield dog track as a last option, he ends up securing a "Christmas" puppy for the family in the process. At various other times throughout the series, Homer works as a monorail conductor, a snowplow operator and a manager for a country singer in order to be an effective breadwinner for the Simpson family.

In contrast, Homer's wife Marge spends most of her days as the doting house-wife taking care of the Simpson family. Many episodes reinforce Marge's centrality to the Simpson home. In one episode Marge cracks under the pressure of her domestic responsibilities and leaves the family for a relaxing vacation, upon which the household promptly falls apart. Homer is at a loss without Marge's nurturing skills and ends up "misplacing" their youngest daughter Maggie. When Marge eventu-ally returns, the family begs her to never leave them again. We see this theme again in a later episode where Marge is injured at a ski resort and leaves her domestic responsibilities to her daughter Lisa. The home devolves into a complete mess in only a few days. Apparently, the Simpson home cannot survive without Marge as its domestic nucleus. Additionally, even though Marge takes on various jobs throughout the series (including as an actress, an artist, and a pretzel-maker), these never last longer than an episode. When Homer fails at his second jobs, he can always return to the power plant. Marge simply returns home.

Logical/emotional

The association of the public, working sphere with men and the private, domestic sphere with women feeds into a third related gender binary: logic/emotion. Tradi-tionally, media texts construct logic as a masculine trait and emotion as a feminine one. The masculine public sphere is related to politics and decision-making, so mas-culinity is marked in turn by the kinds of rational thinking associated with these processes. The private sphere is concerned with family and nurturance, and femin-inity is defined by irrational or emotional impulses as a result. A classic form of this stereotypical dualism is the association of men with mental processes and women with bodily ones, and the effect on our perceptions of gender is very much the same.

A striking example of the logical/emotional binary can be found on the popular syndicated television series *Star Trek: The Next Generation*. The characters of Data and Deanna Troi are clear manifestations of these gender stereotypes. Data (Brett

Spiner), the starship's lieutenant commander, is an android: a "mechanical man" made completely of circuitry and wires. His technology is sophisticated enough that the crew considers him an individual, but Data lacks the ability to feel emotion. He approaches problems throughout the series with a cool logic and clear predilection for reasoned decision-making. Although he experiments with humor and special devices that give him the ability to emote in the series, Data never really achieves his desire to be a "fully-feeling" human. Deanna Troi (Marina Sirtis) is the exact opposite of Data. As the ship's psychological counselor, she is responsible for listening to crewmembers' problems and helping them through their emotional issues. Deanna is also part Betazoid, an alien race in the *Trek* universe who can psychically sense what others are feeling. This factor heightens her counseling abilities and often positions her as the ship's moral conscious or emotional expert. However, Deanna's empathic abilities backfire at certain times when she cannot stop the flood of others' emotions from overtaking her, actually becoming a psychological "dumping ground" for an evil alien in one episode.

Data and Deanna are nearly perfect examples of the logical/emotional gender binary. Despite their best efforts to resist, each character is dominated by a stereotypically gendered way of understanding the world around them. While (masculine) Data cannot experience emotion, (feminine) Deanna sometimes cannot stop experiencing emotion. This duality is especially interesting in light of the original character sketches producers used while casting actors for the series. While Data should be "in perfect physical condition and . . . appear very intelligent," Deanna need only be "tall (5′8–6′) and slender, about 30 years old and quite beautiful."[9] Such a distinction begins to illustrate the subtle connections between stereotypes. Beauty and emotion (and femininity) are stereotypically bound together in a single character in this text.

Sexual subject/sexual object

The final gendered binary is related very strongly to the first three. Masculine stereotypes of strength, ability, and intelligence often translate into media images of sexual subjectivity. In other words, media texts tend to identify men as sexually powerful and pursuant. To be masculine is to be "in charge" of the sexual encounter, to direct its progress and "make it happen." On the other hand, feminine stereotypes of weakness and emotion give rise to the sexual objectification of women. Media representations of women construct them as sexual conquests to be pursued and lusted after. To be feminine is to be available, responsive, and open to male sexual advances. The famous French feminist Simone de Beauvoir captures the sexual subject/object binary poetically in her treatise on the oppression of women, *The Second Sex*:

> For him she is sex—absolute sex, no less. She is defined and differentiated with reference to man and not he with reference to her; she is the incidental, the

inessential as opposed to the essential. He is the Subject, he is the Absolute—she is the Other.[10]

Journalist Naomi Wolf echoes de Beauvoir in her conception of the beauty myth, or the cultural beauty standards that continue to control women in an apparently progressive society. For Wolf, "the beauty myth tells a story: The quality called 'beauty' objectively and universally exists. Women must want to embody it and men must want to possess women who embody it."[11]

Examples of the sexual subject/object binary cut across media texts, ranging from relatively innocent representations to vaguely pornographic ones. The Disney film *Sleeping Beauty* (1959) is a good example of a children's media text that hinges on this binary. Princess Aurora falls into a deep slumber after pricking her finger on a spinning wheel spindle cursed by the evil fairy Maleficent. The only thing that can break the curse and wake the Princess is a kiss from her true love, Prince Philip, who spends the second half of the film attempting to break free of Maleficent's clutches in order to reach Aurora. The entire narrative resolution rests on Philip's pursuit of kissing Aurora, who passively awaits her prince while sleeping atop a high castle tower (very much on sexual display in a beautiful bed). In this text, Philip is clearly the active, pursuant sexual subject, and Aurora is the passive, waiting sexual object he seeks. The film itself is not highly or explicitly sexual, but it does feed into this stereotypical binary.

Of course, this binary is even more present when the sexual content of the text is more explicit. The number of films that portray horny young men pursuing women only as sexual conquests is almost too large to count: the *American Pie* series (1999–2007), the *Porky's* series (1982–1985), *Animal House* (1978), *Old School* (2003), etc. However, the subject/object distinction differs from the others we have discussed thus far because it often functions as the basis for a relationship between media text and media consumer. In other words, many media texts feature women as sexual objects with the (supposedly male) consumer of the text as a complementary sexual subject (see Chapter 7 on Psychoanalytic analysis for an in-depth discussion of this relationship). A clear example of this type of representation is the popular men's magazine *Stuff*. The magazine addresses a variety of "stuff" supposedly pertinent to the contemporary man's life: technology, movies, music, and women. In fact, virtually every cover of the magazine features a young, scantily clad woman in a sexually provocative pose. By constructing women as mere "stuff" for men's enjoyment, on the same level as golf clubs or video games, the magazine reinforces the traditional sexual subject/object distinction between men and women.

Overall, gendered stereotypes of masculinity and femininity tend to structure the possible roles that men and women can fulfill in society. Although by no means do these images dictate or control how men and women should act, they are powerfully persuasive in constructing the social rules we tend unconsciously to live by. When we belittle sexual harassment policies or dissuade young girls from playing football, or when we raise our eyebrows at the mention of a "stay-at-home" dad or encourage young boys to look tough and hold back tears, we are enacting the social rules regarding gender disseminated by the media. It is in these moments that supposedly "outdated" gender stereotypes continue to manifest as very real influences on our lived experience. Although patriarchal systems of power ensure that media stereotypes tend to affect women more than men, in truth all individuals are harmed by these limiting images.

Postfeminism and Media Representation

Although difficult to clearly define, **postfeminism** broadly refers to a conceptual shift within the popular understanding of feminism: an evolution in feminist emphasis from the systemic oppression of all women to the empowerment of individual women. It is important to look at the history of feminism to fully understand the role of postfeminism. The term first-wave feminism refers to nineteenth- and early twentieth-century activists like Elizabeth Cady Stanton and Susan B. Anthony who primarily fought for women's right to vote. Second-wave feminism refers to activists in the 1970s like Gloria Steinem and Betty Friedan who fought for women's workplace and reproductive rights. The real progress made by second-wave feminists in relation to women's occupational and sexual roles throughout the 1970s prompted some people to wonder if the feminist goal of sexual equality and freedom had been achieved. Those who claimed that feminism had, indeed, "worked" were labeled postfeminists. The postfeminist logic was simple: since prior incarnations of feminism had given women an "equal" place in society, any remaining feminist project should now concentrate on women's "individualism, sophistication and choice."[12] Additionally, postfeminists critiqued second-wave feminists for what they saw as an overly negative view of the traditional family structure. Women, according to postfeminists, could have both a career and a family, be both empowered and nurturing. Quite simply, women could be whatever they wanted to be.

However, beyond this historical positioning, it is difficult to pin down a clear definition of what, exactly, it means to be a postfeminist. Rosalind Gill, responding to this relative lack of understanding, frames postfeminism as an emerging "sensibility" made up of a number of interrelated aspects: (1) a melding of femininity, female sexuality, and the body as a response to an increasingly sexualized culture, (2) the dominance of philosophies of individual choice and responsibility, with a concurrent focus on self-discipline and surveillance, (3) the support of theories of irrevocable sexual difference between men and women, and (4) a reliance on irony and "knowingness" as a means of navigating cultural messages.[13] Gill points to a number of media texts as evidence of these qualities, including women's magazines and popular "make-over" television shows, in order to show how the qualities like sex differentiation and self-surveillance manifest in diverse media outlets. However, her identification of these qualities does not signal her embrace of them. In fact, she remains rather suspicious of the supposed empowerment that postfeminist doctrines of individualism, sexuality, and choice offer to women. For example, in reflecting on postfeminism's philosophy of choice and women's claim to acting sexy "for themselves," she points out that

> it presents women as entirely free agents and cannot explain why—if women are just pleasing themselves and following their own autonomously generated desires— the resulting valued 'look' is so similar—hairless body, slim waist, firm buttocks, etc. . . . It simply avoids all the interesting and important questions about the relationship between representations and subjectivity, the difficult but crucial questions about how socially-constructed, mass-mediated ideals of beauty are internalized and made our own.[14]

This suspicion is indicative of many Feminist media scholars' perspective on the postfeminist sensibility, and it gets at the heart of the current debate over postfeminism, especially in relation to media studies. On one hand, the rise of postfeminist discourses helps explain the presence of some media representations of gender that apparently challenge classic stereotypes. Scholars disagree over when postfeminist ideals of women's empowerment and agency really took hold in the media,[15] but since the 1980s media representations of women have increasingly depicted them as able, intelligent individuals. Media texts like *Bridget Jones's Diary* (2001) and *Sex and the City* feature strong, independent heroines who mostly have the ability to satisfy their own economic, sexual, and emotional needs. These images are a far cry from the images of the doting housewife, the emotional wreck, or the passive sexual object that dominated earlier media representations of women. On the other hand, as we have pointed out in this chapter, those traditional gendered stereotypes continue to pervade the media. Echoing Gill's sentiments, Angela McRobbie suggests that postfeminist claims regarding the inapplicability of earlier feminist politics are ill-founded and ignore the fact that real, systemic, gendered inequity continues to inform the lives of many women.[16] Patriarchal power structures may have loosened their hold on women, but they are far from gone.

An excellent example of media textual analysis that looks at the interplay between the postfeminist sensibility and continuing issues of women's oppression is Karen C. Pitcher's analysis of the popular *Girls Gone Wild* video/DVD series.[17] The series, which captures young, often inebriated women stripping at hedonistic gatherings like spring break celebrations or Mardi Gras, in some ways exemplifies the doctrines of choice and personal sexual agency that postfeminists espouse. Pitcher even quotes some women who star in the videos as saying that they consciously participate in the taping as a display of sexual freedom. However, the larger context of the series production effectively strips the interaction of any significant, widespread emancipatory potential. Women's agency, Pitcher contends, is largely constructed or staged within the filming context, resulting in a system of economic exploitation. The company that produces the series always includes footage of women giving their consent to be filmed, a move curiously absent in the series' mirror project, *Guys Gone Wild* (where men of similar age and state of drunkenness strip). Pitcher sees this absence as tantamount to the ways the videos function in a patriarchal system:

For these men, consent and agency is an unproblematic given, so much so it need not be included in the footage. Thus, even in a complete gender-role reversal format, *Guys Gone Wild* reinforces the ways in which voluntarily disrobing on camera entails little from men but requires an elaborate staging of agency for women. While *Guys Gone Wild* may be framed as the "mirror image" of *GGW*, its erasure of the consent and reward scenes ultimately highlights the distorted representation of agency that *GGW* fosters.[18]

In the end, postfeminist themes of choice become a means toward economic domination as *Girls Gone Wild* producers commandeer agency as a way of popularizing the series. Clearly, merely asserting that patriarchy is gone does not make it so.

The tension between feminism and postfeminism exists even in far more "innocuous" texts than the *Girls Gone Wild* series. For example, in the popular American television series *Buffy the Vampire Slayer*, the main character of Buffy Summers in many ways flies in the face of traditional gendered representation. As the inheritor of the "Slayer" role (a single female in every generation who is endowed with mystical abilities to be used in humanity's war against vampires), Buffy is supernaturally strong, agile, and brave. Throughout the seven-season series, viewers watch as she holds her own in physical fights against male vampires. Buffy also acts as the (somewhat masculine) assertive head of the Scooby Gang, the group of individuals dedicated to helping her fight vampires. Additionally, the show features a number of other strong female characters, including Willow (a powerful witch and Buffy's best friend) and Kendra and Faith (alternate, rogue Slayers who show up at different points in the series).

Despite these positive images, however, Buffy and friends are not completely free of traditional gender stereotypes. When she is not saving the world from (largely male) vampires, Buffy is often found in bed with them. Much of the early series deals with her on-again-off-again relationship with the vampire Angel, and later seasons address the palpable sexual tension between Buffy and the vampire Spike.

Understandably, these romantic attractions to vampires often lead her into dangerous situations. Buffy is also not wholly autonomous in her slaying, and she only comes into her empowered role after continual training at the hands of the intelligent and wise "Watcher" Giles (and Wesley later in the series). While slight, these aspects of the show certainly echo classic feminine and masculine stereotypes: Buffy is often irrationally led by her emotions into sleeping with the enemy, and the most intelligent or knowledgeable figures on the show are often men. Even the underlying messages of female empowerment are questionable as we watch assertive women die (Jenny Carpenter, Kendra, Dr Walsh), work for evil (Faith, Anya), or go insane (Willow) throughout the series. When Buffy must take on a traditional "mothering" role to kid sister Dawn upon the death of their mother in season five, the ideal of female individualism and choice becomes even more suspect.

It is probably safe to say that *Buffy* is representative of the general impulse within contemporary American media in relation to issues of gender. The program is certainly progressive when compared to older television shows with clear gender stereotypes, but it is also problematic in continuing certain stereotypical themes (and perhaps even more damaging by concealing them within overarching messages of gender equality). In analyzing *Buffy*, we can see that neither the extreme postfeminist nor traditional second-wave assessments of media representation of gender are wholly correct. In truth, many media texts today are complex images that require careful deconstruction across many layers of meaning, and Feminist media scholarship is constantly examining and assessing the complexity of these texts.

Consequences of Sexist Media Representation

Media texts influence people. The television shows we watch, the albums we listen to, and the websites we visit give us an impression about the world and how we should live in it. We have probably all been moved to tears by a particular film or convinced to purchase a product by a clever advertisement, so when media texts present us with skewed images of gender and sexuality, it is understandable some people will take those stereotypes as "the truth" and act upon them. In this section we wish to outline some of the major, real-world consequences of sexist stereotypes in the media. Far from existing as mere entertainment, these images are crucial in constructing the social world of American culture.

One of the most prevalent material effects of mediated gender stereotypes is the proliferation of eating disorders. Stereotypes that construct women as passive or sexually attractive also tend to emphasize the absolute necessity of a slender figure. American daytime and prime-time television shows routinely portray female characters as skinnier than their male counterparts, while the remaining "over-weight" characters are less likely to be portrayed in a romantic light.[19] Dieting advertisements which once focused on overall weight now regularly talk about zapping problem areas that are "soft, loose or 'wiggly'" in an effort to rid the body of any sign of fat.[20] Ironically, advertisements for food continually encourage Americans to indulge in excess even as we learn that "fat is bad." Advertising analyst Jean Kilbourne views eating disorders as one of the primary ways that "women cope with the difficulties in their lives and with the cultural contradictions involving food and eating."[21] Stereotypical images of "passive femininity" present women with an unhealthy, underweight, and virtually impossible body image that many internalize and destructively pursue.

Although eating disorders are certainly a significant problem for many women, recent research suggests that many men also suffer from body dysmorphia as a result of mediated, sexist stereotypes. In 2000, Pope, Phillips, and Olivardia published *The Adonis Complex: The Secret Crisis of Male Body Obsession*, bringing popular attention to male eating disorders for the first time.[22] Though not an officially accepted medical term, the so-called Adonis Complex is a catch-all condition that refers to "an array of usually secret, but surprisingly common, body image concerns of boys and men."[23] These concerns include dissatisfaction with one's musculature, body-fat ratio, and size, issues that often result in steroid use, unhealthy weightlifting practices, and eating disorders like anorexia and bulimia. The authors cite the increasing images of "perfect" men in the media as a significant cause of the Complex; showing, for example, how sexually risqué images of men have steadily risen to be just as common as images of women in popular women's magazines. These representations of men, usually shown with slender waists, rock-hard abs and/or huge biceps, place pressure on individual men to live up to nearly impossible standards of masculinity. *The Adonis Complex* revealed that eating disorders resulting from media representations of gender are not just a woman's problem. The active/passive gender binary gives rise to a culture of the figure where being "too big" is as deadly as being "too thin."

The role of media texts in exposing consumers to impossible or unhealthy body types is certainly an important one to examine, especially when those images result in harmful personal choices, but it is also necessary to understand how these texts influence the make-up of social institutions. Media representations are the result of cultural attitudes toward sex and sexuality, but stereotypes also reinforce those attitudes and help shape them through workplace and government policies. One of the most apparent areas of the institutionalized discrepancy between the sexes is the issue of pay. Women as a whole earned only 77 cents for every dollar that men did in 2006.[24] The National Committee on Pay Equity at the time cited women's career choices as a primary cause for the pay gap. In other words, gender expectations (including the association between women and domesticity, and the supposed masculine acumen for math and science) cause fewer women to pursue higher-paying jobs. Women who *do* attempt to enter the upper echelons of the working world by pursuing management positions often come up against the **glass ceiling**, or informal, gendered workplace policies that allow women to progress only so far in promotion. The logic is that women often lack the (traditionally masculine) qualities of assertiveness and rational thinking that management positions require. Thus, media representations of femininity that position women as meek, subservient, or overly emotional contribute to a culture where it is permissible for women to earn less and have fewer occupational opportunities.

Conclusion

Throughout this chapter we have looked at how media representations of sex and sexuality contribute to social systems of unequal power distribution. Although contemporary feminist analysis is a highly complex and varied critical tradition, we have addressed some of the major issues regarding representation that this approaches contributes to the field of media studies. Media representations of men tend to define masculinity according to power, agency, rationality, and sexual prowess, while images of women mark femininity according to passiveness, domesticity, emotion, and beauty. It is the goal of Feminist analysis to deconstruct popular media texts to reveal these false binaries and the systems of inequity that they support. At the same time, feminists remain weary of postfeminist sensibilities that too quickly proclaim the end of patriarchy and the primacy of female individualism and choice. These competing interpretations of gender in contemporary society give rise to confusing, often contradictory messages about the various roles of men and women. Feminist analysis, then, is also a way of beginning to untangle these texts and tease out their social, cultural, and political implications.

Because feminism has often unfairly garnered the reputation of being anti-male, we wish to conclude this chapter by again reiterating that stereotypes of femininity and masculinity are both damaging to individual media consumers in everyday life. Everyone suffers when skewed media stereotypes become the basis for social interaction. Although patriarchal systems of power ensure that representations of women are more restricted and harmful, even representations of men encourage limited modes of action and identification for those individuals. Thus, it is in everyone's interest to participate in the types of analyses outlined by Feminist scholars. It is only by interrogating *all* constructed representations of gender and sexuality that we can move beyond the harmful social structures that characterize contemporary life.

MEDIA LAB 7: DOING FEMINIST ANALYSIS

OBJECTIVE

The aim of this lab is to utilize concepts of Feminist theory to analyze media texts. Specifically, students will investigate how stereotypes of gender and sexuality function as a convention of American television.

ACTIVITY

- Divide the class into small groups of 4–5 students each.
- Show a short clip (5–6 minutes) of a contemporary, mainstream American situation comedy. We suggest programs like *The King of Queens, Everybody Loves Raymond*, or *Family Guy*. Older sitcoms, such as *Home Improvement*, may also be used as a point of comparison if time permits.
- Have students record answers to the following questions.
  1 What gender stereotypes discussed in this chapter (active/passive, public/private, logical/emotional, sexual subject/sexual object) do you see present in the text?
  2 What additional gender stereotypes not addressed in this chapter can you identify? How might they be related to the four listed above?
  3 Are there any examples of gender reversals in the text? (For example, men acting emotionally, or women in the workplace.)

SUGGESTED READING

Banet-Weiser, S. Girls Rule!: Gender, Feminism, and Nickelodeon. *Critical Studies in Media Communication* 21, 2004, 119–39.

Bordo, S. *Unbearable Weight: Feminism, Western Culture, and The Body.* Berkeley, CA: University of California Press, 1993.

Butler, J. *Gender Trouble: Feminism and the Subversion of Identity*. 10th anniversary edn. New York: Routledge, 1999.

Connell, R.W. *Masculinities*. Berkeley, CA: University of California Press, 1995.

D'Acci, J. *Defining Women: Television and the Case of* Cagney & Lacey. Chapel Hill, NC: University of North Carolina Press.

de Beauvoir, S. *The Second Sex*. Translated by H.M. Parshley. New York: Alfred A Knopf, 1952.

Dow, B. *Prime-Time Feminism: Television, Media Culture, and the Women's Movement Since the 1970's*. Philadelphia, PA: University of Pennsylvania Press, 1996.

Dow, B. and Condit, C. The State of the Art in Feminist Scholarship in Communication. *Journal of Communication* 55, 2005, 448–78.

Gill, R. Postfeminist Media Culture: Elements of a Sensibility. *European Journal of Cultural Studies* 10, 2007, 147–66.

Haraway, D.J. *Simians, Cyborgs, and Women: The Reinvention of Nature*. New York: Routledge, 1991.

Hernandez, D. and Rehman, B. (eds) *Colonize This! Young Women of Color on Today's Feminism*. New York: Seal Press, 2002.

Holland, S.L. The Dangers of Playing Dress-Up: Popular Representations of Jessica Lynch and the Controversy Regarding Women in Combat. *Quarterly Journal of Speech* 92, 2006, 27–50.

hooks, b. *Feminism is for Everybody: Passionate Politics*. Cambridge, MA: South End Press, 2000.

Hylmo, A. Girls on Film: An Examination of Gendered Vocational Socialization Messages Found in Motion Pictures Targeting Teenage Girls. *Western Journal of Communication* 70, 2006, 167–85.

Jansen, S.C. Media in Crisis: Gender and Terror, September 2001. *Feminist Media Studies* 2, 2002, 139–41.

Johnson, A.G. *Privilege, Power and Difference*. New York: McGraw Hill, 2001.

Johnson, D. and Swanson, D.H. Undermining Mothers: a Content Analysis of the Representation of Mothers in Magazines. *Mass Communication & Society* 6, 2003, 243–65.

Kaplan, E.A. Feminist Criticism and Television. In *Channels of Discourse, Reassembled: Television and Contemporary Criticism*, R.C. Allen (ed.), pp. 247–83. Chapel Hill, NC: University of North Carolina Press, 1992.

Katz, J. *The Macho Paradox: Why Some Men Hurt Women and How All Men Can Help*. Naperville, IL: Sourcebooks, 2006.

Lind, R.A. and Salo, C. The Framing of Feminists and Feminism in News and Public Affairs Programs in U.S. Electronic Media. *Journal of Communication* 52, 2002, 211–28.

Moraga, C. and Anzaldua, G. (eds) *This Bridge Called My Back: Writings by Radical Women of Color*. New York: Kitchen Table: Women of Color Press, 1984.

Pitcher, K.C. The Staging of Agency in *Girls Gone Wild*. *Critical Studies in Media Communication* 23, 2006, 200–18.

Rodgers, S., Kenix, L.J., and Thorson, E. Stereotypical Portrayals of Emotionality in News Photos. *Mass Communication & Society* 10, 2007, 119–38.

Shugart, H.A., Wagoner, C.E., and O'Brien Hallstein, D.L. Mediating Third-Wave Feminism: Appropriation as Postmodern Media Practice. *Critical Studies in Media Communication* 18, 2001, 194–210.

Vavrus, M.D. Domesticating Patriarchy: Hegemonic Masculinity and Television's 'Mr. Mom'. *Critical Studies in Media Communication* 19, 2002, 352–75.

White, S.E., Brown, N.J., and Ginsberg, S.L. Diversity of Body Types in Network Television Programming: a Content Analysis. *Communication Research Reports* 16, 1999, 386–92.

Wolf, N. *The Beauty Myth: How Images of Beauty are Used Against Women.* New York: William Morrow and Company, 1991.

NOTES

1. b. hooks, *Feminism is for Everybody: Passionate Politics* (Cambridge, MA: South End Press, 2000).

2. Understanding socially constructed qualities of gender as biological constants does contribute to systems of patriarchal power. However, contemporary queer feminist scholarship has also productively challenged this classic distinction between gender and sex. See J. Butler, *Gender Trouble, Feminism and the Subversion of Identity*, 10th anniversary edn (New York, Routledge, 1999). This is also heavily discussed in Chapter 9.

3. A.G. Johnson, *Privilege, Power and Difference* (New York: McGraw Hill, 2001).

4. T.E. Perkins, Rethinking Stereotypes, in *Turning it On: a Reader in Women & Media*, H. Baehr and A. Gray (eds) (New York: Arnold, 1996), 21.

5. R. Dyer, Stereotyping, in *Media and Cultural Studies: Keyworks*, revised edn, M.G. Durham and D.M. Kellner (eds) (Malden, MA: Blackwell, 2006).

6. T. Linn, Media Methods That Lead to Stereotypes, in *Images That Injure: Pictorial Stereotypes in the Media*, 2nd edn, P.M. Lester and S.D. Ross (eds) (Westport, CT: Praeger, 2003), 23–7.

7. K. Walsh-Childers, Women as Sex Partners, in *Images That Injure: Pictorial Stereotypes in the Media*, 2nd edn, P.M. Lester and S.D. Ross (eds) (Westport, CTL Praeger, 2003), 141–8.

8. S. Bordo, *The Male Body: a New Look at Men in Public and Private* (New York: Farrar, Straus, and Giroux, 1999).

9. L. Nemecek, *The Star Trek: The Next Generation Companion* (New York: Pocket Books, 1992), 13.

10. S. de Beauvoir, *The Second Sex*, trans. H.M. Parshley (New York: Alfred A. Knopf, 1952), xix.

11. N. Wolf, *The Beauty Myth* (New York: William Morrow and Company, 1991), 12.

12. S. Thornham, *Women, Feminism and Media* (Edinburgh: Edinburgh University Press, 2007), 16.

13. R. Gill, Postfeminist Media Culture: Elements of a Sensibility, *European Journal of Cultural Studies* 10, no. 2, 2007, 147–66.

14. Gill, 154.

15. See B. Dow, *Prime-Time Feminism: Television, Media Culture, and the Women's Movement Since the 1970's* (Philadelphia, PA: University of Pennsylvania Press, 1996); A. McRobbie, Post-Feminism and Popular Culture, *Feminist Media Studies* 4, no. 3, 2004, 255–64.

16. McRobbie, Post-Feminism.

17. K.C. Pitcher, The Staging of Agency in *Girls Gone Wild*, *Critical Studies in Media Communication* 23, no. 3, 2006, 200–18.

18. Pitcher, 215.

19. S.E. White, N.J. Brown, and S.L. Ginsberg, Diversity of Body Types in Network Television Programming: a Content Analysis, *Communication Research Reports* 16, no. 4, 1999, 386–92.

20. S. Bordo, *Unbearable Weight: Feminism, Western Culture, and the Body* (Berkeley, CA: University of California Press, 1993), 190.

21. J. Kilbourne, *Deadly Persuasion: Why Women and Girls Must Fight the Addictive Power of Advertising* (New York: The Free Press, 1999), 116.

22. H.G. Pope, Jr, K.A. Phillips, and R. Olivardia, *The Adonis Complex: The Secret Crisis of Male Body Obsession* (New York: The Free Press, 2000).

23. Pope *et al.*, 6–7.

24. Why Women Earn Less, *USA Today*, June 6, 2008, final edition, 14A.

9 Queer Analysis

Unless you lacked a reliable internet connection in September 2007, you were probably one of the millions of people who watched Chris Crocker's impassioned video defense of pop singer Britney Spears's widely maligned performance at the MTV Music Video Awards. His "Leave Britney Alone!" video, where the MySpace celebrity howled, gnashed his teeth, and generally blubbered on for over 2 minutes about why we should appreciate Spears's "talent," quickly rocketed to the seventh most popular video on YouTube at the time, with over 92,000 comments.[1] As of this writing, the original video has been viewed over 23.5 million times.[2] For those who didn't catch the original YouTube broadcast or its simultaneous showing on Crocker's MySpace account, the mass media quickly picked up the video and featured it on pop culture round-up programs like VH1's *Best Week Ever*. The short even inspired a variety of parodies, including some by "bonafide" celebrities like actor Seth Green, that also circulated online.

More significant than the content of the video, at least for the purposes of this chapter, is the resulting visibility and public recognition of Crocker himself. Many viewers who further investigated Crocker's other online videos were puzzled by his playful take on gender and sexuality. Crocker regularly appears to his fans in shocking blonde hair extensions and dark mascara around his eyes, and the star's MySpace account features a series of glamour shots with Crocker sporting wigs, dresses, and wedge platform heels. This refusal of traditional gender norms, coupled with the star's open discussions of his homosexuality, has understandably accrued equal amounts of adoration and admonition from viewers. However, whether one praises Crocker's originality or finds his performance morally reprehensible, he is undoubtedly one of the most recent and widespread sites of ambiguity and "queerness" in the media.

This chapter looks at the interplay between media texts and the notion of queerness, or purposeful ambiguity surrounding gendered and sexual norms. We place this chapter at the end of the section on media texts because in many ways it is the most difficult to conceive of as a textual approach. The perspective of Queer theory, discussed at length below, does not lend itself to easy definition as an analytical perspective. Rather than a perceived weakness, though, this lack of coherence is Queer theory's contribution to critical media studies. Generally speaking, Queer media scholars attempt to understand how media texts, as significant outlets of cultural discourse, contribute to the ordering of human understanding surrounding gender, sex, and sexuality. The specific notion of queerness in this perspective – of ambiguity, performance and play – becomes a powerful way to refuse this structured understanding. This refusal in turn challenges prevailing cultural norms and the power relations that they reinforce.

This chapter is roughly divided into three major thematic sections, which we label "visibility I", "visibility II," and "invisibility." The first, visibility, takes up the project set forth in Chapter 8 (Feminist Analysis) by looking at traditional sexual stereotypes in the media. Here we consider how images and representations of heterosexuality and homosexuality, replicated across media and throughout time, create a binary understanding of sexuality that privileges heterosexuality and marginalizes homosexuality. The third section, invisibility, is our term for considering the work of two pioneering Queer theorists, Michel Foucault and Judith Butler, and the influence their research has had on understanding how the very *idea* of a thing called "sexuality" functions to inscribe people into relations of power. In this section we consider how the disruptive perspective of queerness laid out in these works can be used to analyze media texts for the ways that they naturalize or make invisible the highly constructed links between gender, sex, sexuality, and the family. However, before we consider Queer analysis of the media, it is important to have a general understanding of Queer theory. We lay out the major tenets of this perspective below.

Queer Theory: an Overview

Queer theory is an interdisciplinary perspective that seeks to disrupt socially constructed systems of meaning surrounding human sexuality. **Sexuality** is an enduring emotional, romantic, or sexual attraction toward others based upon their gender or sex. Americans traditionally interpret sexuality according to the heterosexuality/homosexuality binary; the fact that even "alternate" forms like bisexuality are understood in reference to this binary speaks to its primacy. Queer theorists assert that this traditional understanding misrepresents the full spectrum of human sexuality. Individual sexuality is fluid and difficult to categorize, and as a result the rather simple categories we use to name sexuality can never fully represent an individual's actual, varied sexual drives. Queer theorists work to expose the shortcomings of these labels and show how they work to support systems of social power and privilege.

Let us pause here and consider the full meaning of the above paragraph. A woman who prefers to have sex with men is not inherently heterosexual: she is simply a woman who has sex with men. Growing up in American society, this woman likely took part in the institutions and stories circulating throughout the culture that taught her such attractions and behaviors are properly called "heterosexual." Unconsciously, she probably adopted that word, "heterosexual," in order to identify herself. *But there is no actual connection between that word and her individual sexual drives and practices.* Instead, heterosexuality (and homosexuality, for that matter) is a cultural construction that functions as a heuristic, a mental shortcut, which people draw upon to describe their sexual drives. While *sexuality* is particular to each individual, the social constructions of *heterosexuality* and *homosexuality* are cultural categories humans use to make sense of their sexuality. Key to our discussion of the media is how these categories function in society: just as mistaking gender expectations for inherent biology gives rise to sexist social systems (as we discussed in Chapter 8), assuming that the heterosexuality/homosexuality binary represents human sexuality results in the unequal distribution of social power. Put another way, *heterosexuality* and *homosexuality* are cultural constructions like *masculine* and *feminine*. They allow for the social classification, essentializing, and (dis)empowerment of the groups that identify with them.

The system of inequity derived from the heterosexual/homosexual binary is called **heteronormativity** (or heterosexism). It refers to a diverse set of social practices that function to perpetuate the heterosexual/homosexual binary and privilege heterosexuality. Heteronormative social practices maintain the distinction between heterosexuality and homosexuality out of necessity. Remember that sexism rests upon the visible differences between men and women, and systems of sexist power seem to have some biological or physical component to support them. When talking about the social roles or powers of men and women, we can (for the most part) easily point to individuals that fill the categories of *men* and *women*. However, an individual's sexuality is largely a psychic or internal component, and clear outer manifestations tend to occur behind closed doors. As a result, heteronormative social practices must convince people that the distinct categories of heterosexuality and homosexuality do exist even if they are not as easily demarcated as biological sex. Furthermore, feminist scholar Adrianne Rich refers to the constructed institution of heterosexuality as "compulsive," in the sense that people (and women in particular) are coerced into identifying with the social definitions and norms of heterosexuality from birth.[3] Heteronormative practices encourage individuals to identify with heterosexuality from an early age and regularly re-convince people that it is mutually exclusive of homosexuality.

This binary must exist if heterosexuality is to be considered normal or desirable, the second function of heteronormative social practices. Homosexuality provides an opposite and a point of contrast to heterosexuality. As Queer theorist Eve Kosofsky Sedgwick pointedly puts it, "The gay closet is not a feature only of the lives of gay people."[4] In the same way that our understanding of "night" could not exist without "day," the norm of heterosexuality could not exist as a coherent category without homosexuality as its "abnormal" opposite. The process of stigmatizing homosexuality (or really any non-heterosexual practice) as abnormal to privilege heterosexuality is called **sexual othering**. We can see examples of heteronormativity and sexual othering widely in American culture. When people are asked to consider what the ideal nuclear American family looks like, they will often default to a picture of a husband and wife with two or three children. There are variations on this theme (the addition of a grandparent or pet, or increasingly a single parent), but the core image is almost always exclusively heterosexual. Here homosexual couples represent the abnormal, the other, and the non-ideal. Moreover, identifying as heterosexual in American society grants individuals easy access to a variety of social practices denied to others, including marriage, military service, insurance benefits, medical visitation rights, and more. Even the American-English language reveals the inequity. There are countless derogatory terms one can use to degrade a non-heterosexual person, and many of these words (like *gay*, *faggot*, or *dyke*) have become epithets that can broadly refer to anyone in a negative fashion. However, outside of select terms used at times by members of the GLBTQQIA (Gay, Lesbian, Bisexual, Transgendered, Queer, Questioning, Intersexed, and Allies) community (like *breeder*), there are no widely accepted words to ridicule heterosexuals on the basis of their sexuality.

The fact that Queer theorists attempt to destabilize the sexual binary and reveal heterosexual privilege does not mean that Queer theory is opposed to individual sexual practices or feelings that we would label heterosexual. Instead, as Michael Warner puts it in his introduction to *Fear of a Queer Planet*, the word "'queer' gets a critical edge by defining itself against the normal instead of the heterosexual."[5] In the same way that feminists work against sexist *systems* and not individual men (as we discussed in Chapter 8), Queer theorists work against the systemic normalization of heterosexuality and not individual heterosexuals. Originally a derogatory word, "queer" is often used now as an umbrella term to refer to any and all people whose individual sexualities do not fit into the traditional understanding of heterosexuality. "Queer" has also come to symbolize a rejection of clear sexual definitions in one's scholarship, interaction, and daily life.

In the research tradition that forms the basis of the following section on queer visibility and media representation, Queer theorists look at the ways in which popular media texts promote heterosexuality as normal and other forms of sexuality as deviant, abnormal, or "other." They are interested in understanding and critiquing the ways that media texts paint a picture of the world where sexuality fits conveniently into particular categories according to conventional meanings. Like feminists, they are politically committed to educating individuals about the falsity of sexual binaries and reforming the American media system. Although the focus on upsetting constants makes the perspective a difficult one to pin down, the section on visibility will look at some of the important issues Queer theory has brought to light in relation to media representations of sexuality.

Queerness and Visibility I: Sexual Stereotypes in American Media

In maintaining a clear binary conception of sexuality, heteronormative systems persuade us to sort sexual practices and messages into one of two categories. This establishes a cultural understanding of sexuality where being "heterosexual" means displaying characteristics differently from those who are "homosexual." This binary understanding, in turn, leads to media stereotypes that exist in opposition to one another. We outline a number of these stereotypes below. It may seem strange to you that images of heterosexuality can also be stereotypes, since the word is commonly used to refer to images of marginalized social groups. However, this is exactly the point of Queer theory: any conception of sexuality is culturally constructed and distorting. That fact that heterosexual stereotypes don't appear to be constructions speaks to the power of heteronormative systems.

Natural/deviant

We have already discussed the normalization of heterosexuality and the stigmatization of homosexuality in this chapter, but it is important to understand how these meanings influence the content of popular media texts. The actual number of heterosexual and homosexual characters and personalities in American media is wildly disproportionate. Heterosexuality becomes natural simply by functioning as the overwhelmingly present type of sexual identity in popular media texts. In order to mark its 1,000th publication, the pop culture magazine *Entertainment Weekly* dedicated an entire issue in 2008 to the "new classics" in American media, a collection of the best films, television shows, albums, and books in the last 25 years.[6] Out of the top 50 best television shows, a surprising number (20) contain non-heterosexual characters or personalities. However, many of these programs feature these individuals in secondary roles (*The Simpsons, Roseanne, Friends*), only in select seasons (*Survivor, The Real World*), or only occasionally (*Seinfeld, thirtysomething, NYPD Blue*). Other programs portray gay or lesbian characters in a stereotypical fashion (*South Park*), and many programs had limited reach on the cable network HBO (*Sex and the City, The Sopranos, The Wire*). Of the top 50 television shows in the last 25 years, only a handful could legitimately claim to regularly feature non-heterosexual characters in primary roles (*Buffy the Vampire Slayer, ER*), and only two focus extensively on the lives of homosexual characters (*Six Feet Under, My So-Called Life*). NBC's *Will and Grace*, perhaps one of the most popular television shows featuring queer characters, came in at number 53. With such slight representation of non-heterosexual characters, it is clear that heterosexuality continues to remain the norm in American broadcasting.

Outside of frequency of representation, Hollywood has historically used homosexuality as a marker for deviance or criminality. Older films often link homosexuality to abnormal or antisocial behavior, in the process affirming heterosexuality as normal. For example, the shifty Joel Cairo (Peter Lorre) in the noir thriller *The Maltese Falcon* (1941) is coded as homosexual with effeminate voice, mannerisms, and impeccable dress. The sexual dimension of the character is unimportant to the plotline except to signal to audiences that the character is homosexual, abnormal, and therefore untrustworthy or dangerous (which, in the course of the film, turns out to be true). Similarly, Alfred Hitchcock's *Rope* (1948) tells the story of two young men (played by John Dall and Farley Granger) who strangle a former classmate in an attempt to prove that they can get away with murder. They go so far as to lock the body into a chest, transform it into a table, and invite guests over to have dinner, including the boy's mother and a beloved former teacher (Jimmy Stewart). Although the murderers' homosexuality is never explicitly expressed in the film, the dialogue between the two was enough to catch the attention of censors and audiences alike at the time.[7] The connection between "deviant" homosexual feelings and murder crops up in other Hitchcock films as well, including his much-lauded *Strangers on a Train* (1951).

Although the tendency to associate homosexuality with deviance and criminality is largely a thing of the past, we still see vestiges of this formula in contemporary films. The evil character Scar in *The Lion King* (1994) is a good example of this marking.[8] Compared to the masculine and brave king of the pride Mufasa, Scar is skinny and rather effeminate with a sculpted mane, limp paws, and "a feminine swish in his walk."[9] His eyelashes are long and sit atop rather colorful eyes, which are reminiscent of cooing Hollywood starlets of the 1930s. In the film Scar ruthlessly kills Mufasa and drives young prince Simba away from the pride in order to secure his place as ruler of the African savannah. Again, it would be a stretch to say that Scar is homosexual, but his character certainly echoes some of the earlier Hollywood visual cues that link homosexuality to evil. Other contemporary films that more explicitly link queerness to deviance and abnormal behavior include *The Silence of the Lambs* (1991), *Basic Instinct* (1992), and *The Shawshank Redemption* (1994).

Monogamous/promiscuous

On top of drawing clear distinctions between heterosexuality and homosexuality, the American media also tend to characterize the very nature of these categories by linking heterosexuality to monogamy and homosexuality to promiscuity. Think quickly: how many popular romantic comedies in the last decade can you name? Now, how many of those movies ended with two main heterosexual characters entering a monogamous relationship by the end of the film? Give yourself bonus points if you can think of films where the relationship was monogamous *but not* one of marriage. In truth, the entire genre of the mainstream American romantic comedy relies on the eventual, monogamous coupling of heterosexual characters, and the genre supports the long-standing stereotype that associates heterosexuality with monogamy.

This is not to say that heterosexuals in the media are always monogamous. MTV's *The Real World* would be far less interesting if that were the case. However, it is important to take frequency into account when looking at this stereotypical binary. Media images of promiscuous heterosexuals certainly exist, but they represent one of the many varied ways of "being" heterosexual in the American media. Homosexual characters show up less often in American films and television shows, but when they do they often exhibit a "hyper-sexual" drive that encourages coupling with multiple partners. The lower frequency of homosexual characters in the media coupled with their often inflated sexual appetites results in particularly damaging, stereotypical images.

An example of this hyper-sexuality is the short-cartoon series *The Ambiguously Gay Duo*, which ran intermittently on *The Dana Carvey Show* and *Saturday Night Live* between 1996 and 2007. Although clearly poking fun at other male/male superhero duos like Batman and Robin, *The Ambiguously Gay Duo* nevertheless taps into cultural stereotypes that link queerness to an insatiable, almost perverted sex drive. The cartoon bristles with homosexual innuendo as it follows the adventures of superheroes Ace and Gary. For instance, the duo's super-vehicle is shaped like a giant phallus (complete with laser beam that fires from the faux urethra). When not using the phallus-mobile, the two travel by flying through the air as one in a pose reminiscent of anal intercourse. In different episodes viewers watch as the duo disables a threatening pterodactyl by "deep-throating" its beak, breaks into an evil robot by pushing through its rear end, and celebrates their regular victories with a congratulatory pat on the rump. While the duo may be ambiguously gay, they are clearly hyper-sexual.

The image of promiscuity is the case even in supposedly GLBTQQIA-friendly programming like Showtime's *Queer as Folk* or *The L Word*. Although *Queer as Folk* represents an unprecedented televisual foray into queer representation by focusing on the lives of a number of complex gay and lesbian characters in Pittsburgh, PA, some members of the GLBTQQIA community have criticized the show for its regular depiction of anonymous sex.[10] A disclaimer runs at the beginning of every episode announcing that the show represents only a portion of American gay culture. However, its depiction of racy sex scenes between strangers (and "hook-ups" in public places) certainly feeds popular understandings of hyper-sexuality and promiscuity among homosexuals. *The L Word*, a program that follows the lives of a group of lesbian friends in Los Angeles, reinforces this trend by prominently featuring "The Chart." The Chart is a physical map within the storyline maintained by the character Alice (Leisha Hailey) that depicts the various (and voluminous) interconnected sexual affairs between the characters on the show. Again, although *The L Word* depicts homosexual individuals as nuanced, interesting, and complex people, the regular reference to The Chart as a plot device certainly echoes stereotypes of promiscuity.

Gender clarity/gender ambiguity

Perhaps one of the most glaring stereotypes surrounding sexuality in the media blends the concepts of gender laid out in Chapter 8 with sexual norms. Although there is no absolute association between a person's gender (masculinity/femininity) and sexuality, media texts often portray heterosexuals as having definite gender roles and homosexuals as having unclear ones. Heterosexual male and female characters in the media tend to fulfill clearly masculine and feminine roles. Homosexual characters tend to shift unpredictably between classic and opposite gender roles, or they blend aspects of masculinity and femininity in original ways. While Queer theorists celebrate this sort of gender fluidity as a way to eradicate sexual classification (as we will discuss in the next section), the ambiguity often results in a certain level of discomfort in mass audiences toward gay and lesbian personalities. In other words, gender androgyny tends to result in a threatening, unsettling sense that "things are not quite right" with queer characters and personalities.

There are countless historical instances where mediated gender ambiguity has caused discomfort among American audiences: David Bowie's original stage performances, reaction to Neil Jordan's 1992 film *The Crying Game*, news commentary surrounding Rosie O'Donnell's coming out, etc. However, Bravo's hit television series *Queer Eye for the Straight Guy* is a particularly salient example because it relies on the interaction between clear heterosexual gender roles and ambiguous homosexual ones. Each episode of *Queer Eye* follows the Fab Five (a group of gay men who specialize in refined living) in their attempts to make over a hapless, heterosexual male so that he may in turn impress a doting wife or girlfriend. The show implies that the male subjects of these makeovers are often too masculine to care (or indeed even know) about how to groom themselves, choose fashionable clothing, or comprehend the details of interior design. Their heterosexual female counterparts, the wives and girlfriends on the show, enact complementary feminine gender norms by coaxing their partners into getting a makeover and showering them with praise by the episode's conclusion. In short, "men are men" and "women are women" on *Queer Eye*.

That is, except for the Fab Five. In contrast to the heterosexual couples they transform, the Fab Five form a continuum of gender norms on the show that resists easy classification of masculinity. Media critic David Weiss claims that in the Five we see a multiplicity of gender performances that confound and blend traditional understandings of masculinity and femininity.[11] For example, the flamboyant fashion expert Carson will sometimes refer to himself in feminine terms (comparing himself to famous female stars like Annette Funicello or Ellen Degeneres, for example). The grooming expert Kyan, on the other hand, regularly attempts "manly" bonding with the heterosexual subject through a proliferation of high fives and the use of the word "dude." The various gender performances of the Fab Five give the impression that homosexuals are less clear in their gender orientation, especially in comparison to the relatively straightforward gender roles of the heterosexual couples on the show. While some scholars have claimed that the show escapes stereotyping by presenting viewers with multiple ways of being masculine, it still participates in distinguishing between heterosexual and homosexual individuals according to gender clarity and ambiguity, respectively.

Like images of gender, the various sexual stereotypes we see in the American media contribute to a social system defined by restricted sexual expectations. The oppositional images of natural, monogamous, secure heterosexuals and deviant, oversexed, androgynous homosexuals supports the notion that there are only two ways of being sexual (and that those two ways are nothing alike). These images are detrimental to queer individuals by making them seem bizarre and threatening. However, they also harm heterosexuals by laying out a somewhat limited life script. Heteronormative practices lead to a system where non-heterosexuals overwhelmingly bear the brunt of discrimination and hatred, but they also make it difficult for heterosexuals who may wish to resist the doctrines of marriage, having a family, and leading "the good life" to do so. In this way, stereotypes of sexuality permeate and structure the lives of every individual.

Queerness and Visibility II: the Problems with "Positive" Representation

Thus far we have discussed some of the many sexual stereotypes that characterize heterosexuality and homosexuality in the American media. Deconstructing these stereotypes is an important first step in understanding the representation of sexuality in media. However, another important area of research within queer visibility looks at how increasing numbers of apparently non-stereotypical representations continue to influence heteronormative systems of power. Although there are more media images of queer individuals today than ever before, it is important to understand that **visibility** (the number of queer characters present in the media) and **representation** (the way that those queers act, feel, and engage in storylines) are two different concepts. The reduction of queer stereotypes in the media does not necessarily result in an increase in politically potent images. Instead, these images often enact heteronormative social systems in other, less visible ways.

Kevin G. Barnhurst represents queer visibility in the media as a paradox.[12] In other words, increased visibility of certain non-heterosexual characters, personalities or themes always overlooks others. As certain aspects of queer life become more prominent in the media, others are necessarily ignored. Visibility results in invisibility. The drama of the coming-out story, for example, often dominates many of the media texts that feature homosexual characters. The centrality of coming out to homosexual existence in the popular consciousness (and the accompanying themes of risk, tears, secrecy, etc.) obscures the simple problems that homosexuals and heterosexuals share every day as humans. In a way, coming out as a dramatic moment becomes a new way to "other" homosexuals. The same could be said for what Barnhurst calls "professional queers:" official media liaisons and heads of GLBT organizations, queer journalists, etc. As the American population becomes more accustomed to seeing these "types" of gays and lesbians in the media, it becomes easier to overlook the activities of queer people in their everyday lives. Barnhurst's framework is important to consider because it reminds us that increased visibility is not always diverse visibility. Some aspects are always obscured.

Other scholars have pointed out that particular examples of queer visibility are not always as progressive as they might initially seem. One of the most prominent examples of media visibility in recent memory is the simultaneous coming out of comedian Ellen DeGeneres and her character, Ellen Morgan, on the popular television show *Ellen* in 1997. DeGeneres's decision caused a firestorm of controversy, but media critics also hailed it as a milestone in the representation of sexual minorities in American television. After all, Ellen Morgan was not criminal, oversexed, or terribly masculine: she was simply a funny woman who happened to be attracted to other women. And yet, as scholar Bonnie J. Dow has pointed out, the representation of lesbianism on *Ellen* was still problematic.[13] The show positioned Ellen's newfound sexuality as an issue which heterosexual family members, friends, and co-workers learned to accept (or didn't). In short, it constructed homosexuality as a problem and source of conflict. The show went on to poke fun at Queer politics for being too "radical" and instead focused on homosexuality as an exclusively personal issue (which, in reality, it is not). In portraying lesbianism predominantly through the reactions of straight characters on the show and ignoring the potentially threatening dimension of Queer politics, "*Ellen* was a sitcom about a lesbian that was largely geared toward the comfort of heterosexuals."[14]

We see a similar logic at work in the 1978 French film *La Cage Aux Folles*, which was unexpectedly well received by American audiences and resulted in the release of an American version in 1996 (*The Birdcage*, starring Robin Williams and Nathan Lane). The film tells the story of a young man who invites his future in-laws over to dinner in order to meet his parents (who happen to be a gay couple). Media scholar Larry Gross claims that this "gay" film was popular with heterosexual audiences because it supports heteronormative systems even as it appears to challenge them.[15] Rather than forcing the conservative in-laws to face the truth about their son-in-law's alternative family structure, one of the young man's fathers instead dresses in drag and introduces himself as the man's "mother" at dinner. This reification of heterosexual pairing, coupled with the fact that the gay couple is devoid of physical intimacy in the film, results in a narrative with a homosexual surface and a heteronormative core.

Thus, we can see that the mere presence of positive queer characters or themes does not guarantee the unproblematic representation of sexual minorities in American media. Visibility and representation are not synonymous, and the prominence of queerness does not always guarantee an absence of heteronormativity. Media texts that feature queer characters have grown increasingly complex in the ways they represent sexuality, but many of these contemporary texts are both positive and damaging as Barnhurst's paradox suggests. In attempting to fully understand how these images function in complex ways to both help and hinder Queer politics, it is important to consider the tradition of Queer theory outlined in the next section on queerness and invisibility. Theorists in this vein of scholarship address how any representation of definite sexuality, and indeed the very concept of sexuality at all, is problematic for individuals.

Queerness and Invisibility: the "Deployment of Sexuality" and Gender Performativity

In this section we address the work of two foundational scholars in the realm of Queer theory, Michel Foucault and Judith Butler, as a way of introducing Queer theory's emphasis on destabilizing sexuality. In discussing these theorists, we do not mean to represent their work as exclusively or definitively "Queer theory;" in fact, these ideas only became foundational to Queer theory many years *after* they were published and adopted into the perspective. Instead, we address them here because the works of Foucault and Butler are both important historical contributions to the way we understand sexuality as a social or **discursive construction**. "Invisibility" is our guiding metaphor in this discussion of queerness because it aptly describes the conclusions of both Foucault and Butler, namely that sexuality is a social construction made invisible, natural, normal, and indeed "biological" by its discursive aspects. This conclusion runs counter to the traditional conception of sexuality that we defined at the beginning of this chapter as an innate, personal, internal quality possessed by everyone. However, viewing sexuality from this perspective fundamentally shifts our understanding of how sexuality operates, which in turn opens up new avenues for resistance. It is in the work of Foucault and Butler that the notion of queerness primarily gains its political, disruptive edge.

Michel Foucault and *The History of Sexuality, Volume 1: an Introduction*

Michel Foucault was a twentieth-century French philosopher interested in understanding how discourse, or the collective language and symbol systems employed by a given culture/society, enables certain ways of acting and knowing. His work, including *Madness and Civilization* (1961), *The Birth of the Clinic* (1963), and *Discipline and Punish* (1975), focuses on how specific social arrangements allow for human beings to understand and negotiate systems of knowledge like lunacy, medicine, and imprisonment. In other words, our particular understanding of concepts like "madness," "healing," or "justice" are not simply objective constants that human beings discovered at given moments in history. Instead, constellations of factors at specific moments in history gave rise to discourses of madness, healing, and justice, and these discourses in turn mask their discursive nature to appear normal and reasonable.

One of Foucault's last subjects of investigation is of particular importance here. In *The History of Sexuality, Volume 1: an Introduction*, Foucault lays out a theory of discursive sexuality.[16] Rather than conceive of sexuality as a constant quality of humanity, Foucault proposes a theory of sexuality as a discursive construct that allows people to conceive of a thing called "sexuality" as an innate or biological quality. He begins his inquiry into the history of the idea of sexuality with a simple question: Why, in relation to the subject of sex, do we constantly claim that we are repressed? Foucault admits a personal suspicion of the widely held belief in the "repression thesis," which contends that humanity is still subject to the prudish Victorian decorum of the nineteenth century in relation to sex and sexuality. He claims that it has an erroneous and unchallenged interpretive hold over how we come to think about sexuality and ourselves as sexed beings. In actuality, Foucault claims, at exactly the moment when we began to think of sexuality as a thing improper to discuss openly, there was a concurrent explosion of discourse surrounding sexuality in religion, medicine, and politics. At exactly the moment when sexuality was becoming a private, hidden thing, religious leaders were calling for greater detail in the devouts' confession of sexuality, and doctors were investigating and categorizing sexual behaviors for the first time. Thus, Foucault contends, the repression hypothesis, that widely held explanation for sexuality, is in fact a product of a greater discursive power that "did not exclude sexuality, but included it in the body as a mode of specification of individuals."[17] Particular historical negotiations of power made the very idea of individual sexuality possible and coherent.

Foucault spends much of *The History of Sexuality* tracing the development of sexuality as a coherent discourse, showing how our modern understanding of sexuality is in fact merely the latest iteration in a history of understandings. For example, prior to the advent of detailed religious confession and the rise of medical discourses surrounding sexuality, sexual practices were only coherently recognized in relation to marriage: "the marital obligation, the ability to fulfill it, the manner in which one complied with it . . . the moments when one demanded it[,] . . . its frequency or infrequency, and so on."[18] Of course, people knew of the existence of sexual acts outside of the martial union, and many of these acts were considered amoral or even illegal, but they were only conceived of as a vaguely associated group of individual *acts* in opposition to the specific relations of marriage. This slight distinction leads to some strange interpretations by modern standards. For example, in this prior understanding of sexual practices, one could not "be" a homosexual. A man could certainly have sex with another man, but this was merely an act, an individual instance, and not a quality of identity. However, with the rise of religious, medical, and political discourses surrounding sexuality in the seventeenth century, the notion of homosexuality became a coherent classification of people. As Foucault puts it pointedly: "The sodomite had been a temporary aberration; the homosexual was now a species."[19]

Foucault sees this transition in understanding sexual practices in the light of marital relations to a focus on the individual as a historical conflation of the *deployment of alliance* and the *deployment of sexuality*. The deployment of alliance is the historical tendency in almost every society to understand the social fabric according to relationships, namely "a system of marriage, of fixation and development of kinship ties, [and] of transmission of names and possessions."[20] The deployment of sexuality is the more recent historical tendency to understand individuals as possessing a sexuality, primarily through "the sensations of the body, the quality of the pleasures, and the nature of impressions, however tenuous or imperceptible these may be."[21] Foucault claims that the deployment of sexuality historically became entangled in the deployment of alliance at the site of the family. The family, existing as a result of the deployment of alliance, suddenly became the site of regulation of sexuality through regular interaction with the discourses of sexuality in the fields of religion, medicine, and politics. This makes sense if we consider the fact that the family is the only node or place where all of the major themes of sexual attention/fascination of the last 300 years – the various manifestations of the sexualites of women and children, the interaction of the couple, the existence and source of sexual "perverts" – converge.

But where did the deployment of sexuality originate? Foucault posits that this deployment of (individual) sexuality in circulated and shared discourse, or sexuality as we understand it today, was in fact the result of an act of power by the bourgeoisie or ruling class as a means of distinguishing themselves. "With the investment of its own sex by a technology of power and knowledge which it had itself invested," Foucault writes, "the bourgeoisie underscored the high political price of its body, sensations, and pleasures, its well-being and survival."[22] The concept of sexuality and the protections and attentions it affords were merely the most recent form of class maintenance, a function that notions of bloodlines and titles had supported in prior aristocracies. Only after being firmly instilled as a quality of the upper class did the concept of individual sexuality spread to lower working classes, extending the protection granted by a discourse of sexuality as a way to maintain a healthy, reproducing workforce in a rapidly industrializing world. And, with the spread of sexuality to the working class, the bourgeoisie developed another strategy to differentiate themselves: repression. Suddenly, the ruling class differed from the working class "not by the 'sexual' quality of the body, but by the intensity of its repression."[23] For Foucault, the repression hypothesis is not the explanation of sexuality in its contemporary form; sexuality and the repression hypothesis both spring from a much larger system of discourse and power.

Does Foucault's history of sexuality in/of discourse mean that our own sexual attractions and orientations have no basis in ourselves? Is sexuality a lie? In short, yes and no. These are difficult questions to answer clearly. Foucault believed that discourse ordered all knowledge, especially of ourselves, but discourse would also not exist without individuals to enact it. More productive questions regarding Foucault's history, especially for Queer theory, would be: How does Foucault's unique understanding break the concept of sexuality free of binaries that inscribe people into unequal relations of power? How does Foucault's conception of sexuality as a negotiable discursive construct, rather than internal, constant component, allow for more playful, disruptive understandings of sexuality? One of the most significant developments of Foucault's theory of discursive sexuality in line with these questions is Judith Butler's work on gender performativity.

Judith Butler and *Gender Trouble: Feminism and the Subversion of Identity*

Judith Butler is a Professor of Comparative Literature and Rhetoric at the University of California, Berkeley. Her scholarship broadly addresses questions of discourse and its various intersections with theories of poststructuralism, feminism, gender, queerness, and performance. In such works as *Gender Trouble: Feminism and the Subversion of Identity* (1990), *Bodies That Matter: On the Discursive Limits of "Sex"* (1993), and *Excitable Speech: a Politics of the Performative* (1997), Butler questions both the role of language/discourse in structuring our understanding of identity and how people can artfully engage language/discourse in order to reveal (and possibly resist) the machinery of this structuring. We are most concerned here with the theories she puts forth in *Gender Trouble*, arguably her most famous and important contribution to Queer theory. In it, Butler contends that gender, rather than a coherent component of identity incorporated through socialization, is in fact a bodily performance of discourse that exists only because people believe it is significant. Put differently, in the traditional manner of understanding gender, people behave in certain ways because of a cultural construct called "gender" which they have internalized into their identity. In Butler's view, gender only exists because people *act* as gendered beings. Actions that are supposedly the output or manifestation of an inner quality called "gender" are in fact the only force that constitutes any concept of personal gender in the first place. This is the major premise of Butler's theory of **gender performativity**.

In order to fully unpack Butler's thesis, it is important to situate her argument within the context of feminist theory in the early 1990s. Reflecting later on the reasons she undertook the project of *Gender Trouble*, Butler claims that "I found myself increasingly enraged as a graduate student and young faculty member as countless Feminist frameworks seemed either to elide or pathologize the challenge to gender normativity posed by queer practices."[24] *Gender Trouble* and Butler's theory of gender performativity is a significant Queer critique of mainstream liberal feminism's unconscious tendency to represent a category of people called "women." Upon this foundation feminism has built a theory of power and oppression based on unquestioned norms of gender and the "feminine" as a site of resistance. This concentration, for Butler, mistakenly critiques an effect of discursive power rather than discursive power itself, undercutting any true form of resistance and in effect reifying power relations between people in relation to gender and sexuality. Thus, she concludes, only by understanding gender *as discourse made bodily* can we begin to theorize resistance to power.

Butler begins *Gender Trouble* by outlining these arguments against mainstream feminism. "Feminist critique," she writes, "ought . . . to understand how the category of 'women,' the subject of feminism, is produced and restrained by the very structures of power though which emancipation is sought."[25] In other words, considering women as a coherent category in fact creates women as coherent subjects and places them into a network of power in the first place. Here Butler reverses the traditional distinction between sex and gender (addressed in Chapter 8), understanding sex as a product of gender instead of the other way around. For Butler, the discursive construction of gender in a culture – the ways in which a culture creates value and meaning surrounding gender – in turn establishes how that culture makes sense of sex. This may seem strange until one considers all of the ways that our understanding of gender influences the production of "sex" in our culture. The historical use of gender assignment surgeries for intersexed individuals, as well as the contemporary popularity of breast and penis enlargement procedures, reveals how gender norms in fact direct the sex of our bodies. More fundamentally, Butler asserts that the very understanding of sex as "biologically fixed" is a mythical product of our social construction of gender. Like Foucault, she contends that cultural discourse normalizes the idea of sex as biological in order to serve particular interests of power.

The primary way this normalization supports sexual inequity is the connection of gender and sex to desire through the idea of an individual identity: " 'Intelligible' genders are those which in some sense institute and maintain relations of coherence and continuity among sex, gender, sexual practice, and desire."[26] At the same time, "the internal coherence or unity of either gender, man or woman, . . . requires both a stable and oppositional heterosexuality."[27] In this way the concept of gender identity tacitly reinforces systems of heteronormativity by giving rise to two linear, parallel structures of sex/gender/desire (male/masculine/woman-desiring and female/feminine/man-desiring). It is Butler's aim to trouble the very foundation of gender that these systems of identity and heteronormativity are built upon as a way of throwing off the power relations they encourage. By overturning our understanding of the foundational "gender," Butler seeks to theorize new ways of resistance.

The bulk of *Gender Trouble* takes issue with and "rereads" various theories of gender differentiation and desire in feminist, anthropological, and psychoanalytic scholarship. The details of these original arguments, and Butler's subsequent rebuttals, are beyond the scope of an introduction to her work. However, the important claim put forth in all of these arguments is Butler's contention that the notion of gender functions as a discursive construct, much in the same way that Foucault forwards sexuality as a discursive construct. This notion becomes key in her theory of gender performativity.

As a way of understanding the existence of gender as discursive and the coherent existence of gender as performative, we would first like to consider two examples of the phenomena that Butler provides to approximate this double existence. In the preface to the 1999 edition of *Gender Trouble*, she compares gender performativity to the poststructuralist Jacques Derrida's interpretation of Franz Kafka's short story *Before the Law*:

> There the one who waits for the law, sits before the door of the law, attributes a certain force to the law for which one waits. The anticipation of an authoritative disclosure of meaning is the means by which that authority is attributed and installed: the anticipation conjures its object. I wondered whether we do not labor under a similar expectation concerning gender, that it operates as an interior essence

that might be disclosed, an expectation that ends up producing the very phenomena it anticipates.[28]

At the end of the *Gender Trouble*, Butler provides another example in comparing gender performativity to Foucault's discussion of the human soul in *Discipline and Punish*:

> The figure of the interior soul understood as "within" the body is signified through its inscription *on* the body, even though its primary mode of signification is through its very absence, its potent invisibility. The effect of a structuring inner space is produced through the signification of a body as a vital and sacred enclosure. . . . In this sense, then, the soul is a surface signification that contests and displaces the inner/outer distinction itself, a figure of interior psychic space inscribed *on* the body as a social signification that perpetually renounces itself as such.[29]

In both examples, of the legal subject and the soul-possessing human, abstract concepts of discourse ("law" and "soul") intelligibly exist only *because* people act or embody them. We can only understand ourselves as legal subjects because we *stand* before the law, and we only know of our souls because the body is the important physical *presence* that signifies the soul's intangibility. It is the acting out of the discursive law and the soul *on the body over time* that in effect brings them into existence as aspects of identity and of the self. Butler contends that gender operates in a similar fashion. As a function of discourse, a constellation of meanings in symbols and words, gender is only an intelligible construct of identity *because* people act in gendered ways. There is no internal concept of gender that in turn influences the ways we act; cultural discourse inspires a repetition of actions that in turn give rise to the idea of a personal gender. The expectation of gender identity is the genesis of gender identity.

Does this mean, then, that bodies are merely puppets dangling on the strings of gender discourse? No, according to Butler. Understanding gender as performative introduces potentially new possibilities in combining issues of gender, sex, practice, and desire. Rather than conceptualizing gender identity in traditional formations of male/masculine/woman-desiring and female/femin /man-desiring, individuals can (and do) recombine these factors into original ways. These recombinations in turn disrupt the traditional gender binary and the heteronormative power structure that the binary supports. At the end of *Gender Trouble*, Butler offers the notion of drag as one example of this kind of disruption. Drag performances call attention to the lack of clear association between gender, sex, sexual practice, and desire; they exist despite the fact that they challenge conventional associations between the different nodes of identity. Butler points out that drag also draws attention to the notion of performance itself, revealing the vast continuum of combinations available when gender is performative rather than a constant conception of one's identity. Though drag is not itself resistive, in the sense that it still relies upon coherent categories of gender even in its recombinations, it is a site of conflation and ambiguity from which resistance can be theorized.

This ambiguity is central to Queer theory (or, at least, as central as an amorphous, interdisciplinary, ill-defined theoretical tradition will allow); in fact, this ambiguity is *queerness*. Butler's notion of gender performativity introduces the quality of queerness to traditional understandings of gender. Coupled with Foucault's concurrent notion that individual sexuality is also discursive in nature, beholden to the political and social arrangements of given times and histories, the theory of gender performativity severs the classic links that tenuously hold the aspects of one's identity together. However, the severing of those links, far from defeating or ruining individuals, instead frees them from traditional formations of power and allows for new ways of understanding themselves and their social worlds.

A Queer Analysis of "Invisibility" in Media Texts

An important, concurrent project to the individual hermeneutics discussed above is the analysis of media texts for the ways they normalize concepts of sex, gender, and sexuality. This differs from the analysis of representations of GLBTQQIA individuals because it seeks to unmask the unquestioned, implicit assumptions of a text in relation to sexuality. In other words, merging the frameworks of Foucault and Butler to "queerly" analyze media texts allows scholars to understand how these texts link "individual" discursive concepts like gender, sex, sexual practice, and desire with "cultural" discursive factors like politics, medicine, religion, and the family (we distinguish the individual from the cultural only as an interpretive heuristic; they are actually inexplicably linked as discourse). Queer criticism deconstructs texts for their implicit representations of and claims to truth regarding sexuality, troubling the assumptions of a text in such a way as to reveal how they affirm relations of power.

A particularly rich media text for this kind of analysis is pop artist John Mayer's song "Daughters," on his 2003 album *Heavier Things*. The song, like so many of Mayer's pieces, begins with a discussion over a woman with whom he is infatuated (a woman that puts "the color inside of [his] world"). He describes her as an inaccessible labyrinth, exhibiting a strange coldness that results from her family upbringing. "Boys," he claims, "you can break . . . you find out how much they can take." Girls like his coveted female, conversely, are more fragile and susceptible to their family's opinions, and therefore require extra care to avoid ending up romantically damaged or distant. Mayer offers his personal perspective in the chorus:

> So fathers be good to your daughters,
> Daughters will love like you do.
> Girls become lovers, who turn into mothers,
> So mothers be good to your daughters too.

With its emphasis on gender roles, heterosexuality, and family socialization practices, it would be difficult to find a media text more fruitful for Queer criticism than "Daughters." In blaming Mayer's difficult romantic relationship on the woman's childhood experiences, the song links the development of proper gender roles to healthy heterosexuality (promoting a normalizing conflation of gender and sexuality reminiscent of Butler's critiques against gender identity). Improper socialization results in a woman who can't perform heterosexuality, and the inability to be heterosexual becomes the central "problem" in the text and, truthfully, the entire purpose of the song. Thus the song becomes implicitly heteronormative though the machinery of gender. At the same time, by emphasizing the role of the family in the woman's identity formation, the song naturalizes the very unnatural and discursive links between family and sexuality (akin to Foucault's deployment of alliance and sexuality, respectively). This melding masks the historically new conception of sexuality as an individual trait beneath the relatively long-standing discourses of family and relationship. The song, then, not only privileges and normalizes heterosexuality, but also normalizes the concept of individual, innate sexuality itself. Media texts like "Daughters" affirm the kinds of normalizing discourses that Foucault and Butler dissect, and Queer analysis becomes an important way of revealing the presence of power.

Queer analysis can also be productively applied to analyzing how even apparently progressive texts in fact maintain discourses of (hetero)sexuality and gender. The long-running NBC television show *Will and Grace* is an apt example. The show follows the lives to two roommates living in New York (Will, and openly gay lawyer, and Grace, a straight interior designer) and their various antics with friends (Jack, a perpetually unemployed gay actor, and Karen, a straight, alcoholic divorcee). Though the show is certainly one of the more visible instances of queer characters on recent television programming, it still tends to normalize the discourses of sexuality with which Foucault and Butler take issue.

Will and Grace do not act as a heterosexual couple in the traditional sense, but they live "heterosexually" for all intents and purposes in their mutual exchange of affection and support. Though the characters actually met and dated in college within the diegesis of the show, gender norms become key to their later formation as "heterosexual" roommates. As an interior designer, Grace signifies for viewers the traditionally feminine traits of creativity, artistry, and "right-brain thinking." Will, on the other hand, signifies masculine traits of logic, reason, and argument through his profession at a law firm. This masculine/feminine dichotomy so apparent in their jobs continues in the ways in which the two interact at home. Will tends to support and help Grace through her problems more often than the other way around, conjuring images of the protective male and the vulnerable female. The conflation of conventional gender norms with heterosexuality central to Butler's work applies here, as it provides viewers with familiar codes to interpret the show. This reliance on classic gender norms also introduces a heteronormative veneer onto a supposedly "queer" show.

Moreover, the various sexual relationships that the two engage in over the eight-season span are markedly different. Whereas many of Grace's heterosexual encounters represent drawn-out plotlines, her suitors often portrayed by famous actors (such as Harry Connick Jr, Ed Burns, and Woody Harrelson), Will only has one significant long-term relationship in the entire run of the show (portrayed by relatively unknown actor Bobby Cannavale). In the series finale that jumps years ahead into the lives of the main characters, viewers are confronted with increasing degrees of heteronormativity. Both Will and Grace are happily nestled into their own separate families, the result of a falling out from years before that dissolved their status as roommates. Will and his long-time partner Vince (Cannavale) have a son named Ben, and Grace and her husband Leo (Connick Jr) have a daughter named Lyla. On top of the reinforcement of heterosexual family structures present in these couplings, the actual episode concludes with the marriage of the two children. Thus, although the show features queer characters, heterosexuality is certainly the lens through which we understand the characters' personal sexualities. In normalizing the overlapping deployments of alliance and sexuality identified by Foucault, as well as reinforcing the links between gender and heterosexuality, the show makes natural the aspects of sexuality that Queer scholars seek to challenge.

By looking at "Daughters" and *Will and Grace*, we can see how media texts that reinforce and normalize the discursive connections between gender, sexuality, and desire also function to perpetuate social systems of heteronormative power and domination. Queer criticism of these assumptions is the first step in revealing their discursive nature and troubling the binaries on which they rest. The work of Foucault and Butler reveals a complicated nexus of discourse and power that underpins categories we often take to be "natural," and their scholarship points to potential ways of better understanding and resisting these formations of power. However, until more people are equipped with this rather esoteric theory, the political project of Queer media studies will likely continue to focus on more visible representations of queerness and their social consequences. This consideration is the focus of our final section.

Consequences of Heternormative Media Representations

In Chapter 8 we outlined some of the consequences of sexist media representations on actual women and men in their everyday lives. In this section we continue that project by considering the potential effects of heteronormative media representations on queer and non-queer individuals. At this point, the last chapter in the media texts section of this textbook, you should have a fairly clear idea that media representations have both positive and negative effects on individuals in the real world. People often turn to the media, consciously or unconsciously, in order to form values about the world we live in today, and those values influence the impressions we have of ourselves and society. When we form values and impressions on the basis of heteronormative media representations, we run the risk of continuing current and unequal power relations.

Symbolically, the relative absence of positive queer individuals in the media results in limited models of identification for actual queer populations in the real world. In his account of contemporary gay life, *The Culture of Desire*, journalist Frank Browning recalls the importance of identification in exploring his own sexuality while attending high school:

What all of us were doing was sorting through the rush of sensual responses our bodies were offering up, calling on all the available plots of family, church, television, and paperback novels to enable us to savor some and discard others. . . . By what we said, and by what we contrived to be overheard saying, we learned (or didn't) whether we were exploring the same mysteries, whether we were inhabiting common plots.[30]

Early on Browning discovered that his "story's plot showed no sign of connection to any of the other plots other young men were following."[31] People draw upon the stories in the media to learn more about themselves, and heteronormative systems of power limit the amount of positive images with which members of disempowered groups can identify. Whereas young heterosexuals have a variety of (presumably) heterosexual characters and personalities in the media to emulate, queers have fewer unproblematic images to consider. This requires young queer individuals to be more media literate and vigilant in order to separate useful, positive images from stereotypical, negative ones.

The lack of symbolic resources is an important effect to consider, especially in an increasingly media-saturated, image-based world like our own, but heteronormative representations also reinforce public prejudices and help shape social policies that affect queer individuals in the real world. The fact that the overwhelming majority of characters and personalities in the American media are heterosexual contributes to a social system that often marginalizes the interests and needs of queer people. The Human Rights Campaign website lists a number of legal statutes that solidify heteronormative practices into law. For example, the Family Medical Leave Act of 1993 compels certain employers to give unpaid leave to employees for the care of parents, children, or spouses. A "spouse" according to the law is "a husband or wife as defined or recognized under state law for purposes of marriage in the state where the employee resides."[32] Although certain companies have taken the initiative to offer similar domestic partner benefits to homosexual couples, there is no federal mandate that guarantees this protection. The law, guided and reinforced by the kinds of social prejudices embodied in the media, is clearly in support of heteronormative systems of power. Other policies, including the 1996 Defense of Marriage Act and the "don't ask, don't tell" doctrine of secrecy in the US military, are even clearer examples of this trend.

Conclusion

In this chapter we have considered how media representations of heterosexuality and homosexuality, as well as the unproblematic consideration of sexuality itself as a natural or inherent thing to humanity, contribute to a system of unequal power relations between individuals in society. Queer theorists seek to critique both this sexual visibility and invisibility as a way of deconstructing heteronormativity. Part of this project is the analysis of how mass media portray heterosexuals and homosexuals differently in popular texts. Part is discerning the difference between visibility and representation, understanding that the mere presence of queer characters is not enough to make a text resistive. And part is looking at the deep, unquestioned, underlying logics of a text to understand how the aspects of sexuality that we take for granted, such as its individual or personal nature, in fact support very shared, cultural relations of power. Though Foucault and Butler's work in this final area probably best embody the disruptive, shifting, ambiguous sensibility meant by the term "queer," we can see from this chapter that Queer analysis is a diverse project with many different goals. In a sense, this applicability across many fronts is fitting for a perspective that refuses to be clearly pinned down.

Again, like in Chapter 8 on Feminist analysis, we stress here that Queer analysis as a theoretical perspective on the media is not only appropriate for scholars who may also identify as queer. Stereotypes and unquestioned understandings of sexuality work to place limits on all people in relation to issues of personal identity, practice and desire, regardless of how we conceive of ourselves. While heteronormative social systems place greater limits on individuals who identify as homosexual, resulting in both symbolic and material disadvantages, those who identify as heterosexual are also inscribed into relations of power. Only the vigilant and careful consideration of media representations of sexuality can begin to overcome these systems of unequal relation. From this perspective, only by "queering" everyone can we begin to make the world a more equitable place to live.

MEDIA LAB 8: DOING QUEER ANALYSIS

OBJECTIVE

The aim of this lab is to utilize concepts of Queer theory to analyze media texts. Specifically, students will investigate popular and supposedly "queer" movies for the ways in which they challenge and reinforce understandings of visible and invisible sexuality.

ACTIVITY

- Divide the class into small groups of 4–5 students each.
- Play a short clip (5–6 minutes) of a popular movie widely recognized for its inclusion of queer characters. Potential films include *The Rocky Horror Picture Show*, *The Crying Game*, or *To Wong Foo, Thanks for Everything—Julie Newmar*.
- Have students record their answers to the following questions.
  1 How, if at all, does the representation in the clip reinforce systems of heteronormativity? How do you know?
  2 What stereotypes of heterosexuality and homosexuality are present in the clip?
  3 How does the clip link sexuality and gender? In your opinion, do these associations reinforce or challenge heteronormativity?
  4 How, if at all, does the clip portray sexuality as a permanent, personal, or special quality of identity? After reading this chapter, do you find that portrayal troubling or affirming? Why/why not?

SUGGESTED READING

Berlant, L. *The Queen of America Goes to Washington City: Essays on Sex and Citizenship*. Durham, NC: Duke University Press, 1997.

Bersani, L. *Homos*. Cambridge, MA: Harvard University Press, 1995.

Brookey, R.A. and Weterfelhaus, R. Hiding Homoeroticism in Plain View: The *Fight Club* DVD as Digital Closet. *Critical Studies in Media Communication* 19, 2002, 21–43.

Burston, P. and Richardson, C. (eds) *A Queer Romance: Lesbians, Gay Men, and Popular Culture*. New York: Routledge, 1995.

Butler, J. *Bodies That Matter: On the Discursive Limits of "Sex."* New York: Routledge, 1993.

Butler, J. *Gender Trouble: Feminism and the Subversion of Identity*. 10th anniversary edn. New York: Routledge, 1999.

Cramer, J.M. Discourses of Sexual Morality in *Sex and the City* and *Queer as Folk*. *Journal of Popular Culture* 40, 2007, 409–32.

Dhaenens, F., Van Bauwel, S., and Biltereyst, D. Slashing the Fiction of Queer Theory: Slash Fiction, Queer Reading, and Transgressing the Boundaries of Screen Studies, Representations, and Audiences. *Journal of Communication Inquiry* 32, 2008, 335–47.

Dow, B. *Ellen*, Television, and the Politics of Gay and Lesbian Visibility. *Critical Studies in Media Communication* 18, 2001, 123–40.

Erni, J.N. Queer Figurations in the Media: Critical Reflections on the Michael Jackson Sex Scandal. *Critical Studies in Mass Communication* 15, 1998, 158–80.

Foucault, M. *The History of Sexuality, Volume 1: an Introduction*. Translated by R. Hurley. New York: Vintage Books, 1990.

Gamson, J. *Freaks Talk Back: Tabloid Talk Shows and Sexual Nonconformity*. Chicago, IL: University of Chicago Press, 1999.

Goltz, D.B. Laughing at Absence: *Instinct* Magazine and the Hyper-Masculine Gay Future? *Western Journal of Communication* 71, 2007, 93–113.

Gross, L. *Up From Invisibility: Lesbians, Gay Men, and the Media in America*. New York: Columbia University Press, 2001.

Johnson, A.G. *Privilege, Power and Difference*. New York: McGraw Hill, 2001.

Rich, A. Compulsory Heterosexuality and Lesbian Existence. In *Blood, Bread and Poetry: Selected Prose 1979–1985*, 23–75. New York: W.W. Norton & Company, 1986.

Russell, V. *The Celluloid Closet*, 2nd edn. New York: Harper & Row, 1987.

Sedgwick, E.K. *Epistemology of the Closet*. Berkeley, CA: University of California Press, 1990.

Sloop, J.M. *Disciplining Gender: Rhetorics of Sex Identity in Contemporary U.S. Culture*. Amherst, MA: University of Massachusetts Press, 2004.

Warner, M. (ed.) *Fear of a Queer Planet: Queer Politics and Social Theory*. Minneapolis, MN: University of Minnesota Press, 1993.

Warner, M. *Publics and Counterpublics*. New York: Zone Books, 2002.

Weed, E. and Schor, N. (eds) *Feminism Meets Queer Theory*. Bloomington, IN: Indiana University Press, 1997.

Weiss, D. Constructing the Queer "I": Performativity, Citationality, and Desire in *Queer Eye for the Straight Guy*. *Popular Communication* 3, 2005, 73–95.

NOTES

1. J. Hopkins, J. Graham, and M. Saltzman, Videomaker Shoots to YouTube Fame While Defending Popstar, *USA Today*, September 17, 2007, final edition, 3B.

2. For the most current statistics, see Chris Crocker's YouTube account at www.youtube.com/user/itschriscrocker?ob=4 (accessed April 6, 2009).

3. A. Rich, Compulsory Heterosexuality and Lesbian Existence, in *Blood, Bread and Poetry: Selected Prose 1979–1985*, 23–75 (New York: W.W. Norton & Company, 1986).

4. E. Sedgwick, *The Epistemology of the Closet* (Berkeley, CA: University of California Press, 1990), 68.

5. M. Warner, Introduction, in *Fear of a Queer Planet: Queer Politics and Social Theory*, M. Warner (ed.) (Minneapolis, MN: University of Minnesota Press, 1993), xxvi.

6. The New Classics, *Entertainment Weekly*, June 27 and July 4 (double issue), 2008.

7. V. Russell, *The Celluloid Closet*, 2nd edn (New York: Harper & Row, 1987).

8. H.M. Benshoff and S. Griffin, *America on Film: Representing Race, Class, Gender and Sexuality at the Movies* (Malden, MA: Blackwell, 2004).

9. Benshoff and Griffin, 19.

10. G. Kilday, Is it Good for Gays?, *The Advocate*, June 19, 2001, 66–73.

11. D. Weiss, Constructing the Queer "I": Performativity, Citationality, and Desire in *Queer Eye for the Straight Guy*, *Popular Communication* 3, no. 2, 2005, 73–95.

12. K.G. Barnhurst, Visibility as Paradox: Representation and Simultaneous Contrast, in *Media/Queered: Visibility and its Discontents*, K.G. Barnhurst (ed.) (New York: Peter Lang, 2007), 1–22.

13. B.J. Dow, *Ellen*, Television, and the Politics of Gay and Lesbian Visibility, *Critical Studies in Media Communication* 18, no. 2, 2001, 123–40.

14. Dow, 129.

15. L. Gross, *Up From Invisibility: Lesbians, Gay Men, and the Media in America* (New York: Columbia University Press, 2001).

16. M. Foucault, *The History of Sexuality, Volume 1: an Introduction*, trans. R. Hurley (New York: Vintage Books, 1990).

17. Foucault, 47.

18. Foucault, 37.

19. Foucault, 43.

20. Foucault, 106.

21. Foucault, 106.

22. Foucault, 123.

23. Foucault, 129.

24. J. Butler, Against Proper Objects, in *Feminism Meets Queer Theory*, E. Weed and N. Schor (eds), 1–30 (Bloomington, IN: Indiana University Press, 1997), 2.

25. J. Butler, *Gender Trouble: Feminism and the Subversion of Identity*, 10th anniversary edn (New York: Routledge, 1999), 5.

26. Butler, *Gender Trouble*, 23.

27. Butler, *Gender Trouble*, 30.

28. Butler, *Gender Trouble*, xiv.

29. Butler, *Gender Trouble*, 172.

30. F. Browning, *The Culture of Desire: Paradox and Perversity in Gay Lives Today* (New York: Vintage Books, 1994), 17.

31. Browning, 16.

32. Federal Laws Impacting Domestic Partner Benefits, *Human Rights Campaign*, www.hrc.org/issues/workplace/benefits/4829.htm (accessed July 1, 2008).

Part III

Media Audiences:
Reception, Erotic, and
Ecological Perspectives

10 Reception Analysis

KEY CONCEPTS

CODE
DECODING
ENCODING

ETHNOGRAPHY
HERMENEUTIC DEPTH
INTERPRETIVE COMMUNITIES
POLYSEMY
POLYVALENCE
RECEPTION THEORY
RESISTIVE READING
STRATEGIC AMBIGUITY

There is a feeling that I had Friday night after the homecoming game that I don't know if I will ever be able to describe except to say that it is warm. Sam and Patrick drove me to the party that night, and I sat in the middle of Sam's pickup truck. Sam loves her pickup truck because I think it reminds her of her dad. The feeling I had happened when Sam told Patrick to find a station on the radio. And he kept getting commercials. And commercials. And a really bad song about love that had the word "baby" in it. And then more commercials. And finally he found this really amazing song about this boy, and we all got quiet.

Sam tapped her hand on the steering wheel. Patrick held his hand outside the car and made air waves. And I just sat between them. After the song finished, I said something.

"I feel infinite."

And Sam and Patrick looked at me like I said the greatest thing they ever heard. Because the song was that great and because we all really paid attention to it. Five minutes of a lifetime were truly spent, and we felt young in a good way. I have since bought the record, and I would tell you what it was, but truthfully, it's not the same unless you're driving to your first real party, and you're sitting in the middle seat of a pickup with two nice people when it starts to rain.[1]

If you're anything like Charlie, the narrator in Stephen Chbosky's *The Perks of Being a Wallflower* excerpted above, you can probably think of at least one song that holds a unique significance to you. Perhaps the narrative of the song is related to your life, and maybe even the artist who sings it is important to you, but neither of those aspects fully captures what the song *means*. Perhaps this song is the one that played during the slow dance at your senior prom, the last time you saw a grandparent, or even (like Charlie) on the way to your first real high school party. No matter how many other people you encounter who claim to know and love this song, none of them will have the same meaning for it as you do because none of them were dancing, dealing with loss, or growing up with you.

This chapter asks the question: What is the role of the actual audience in the process of meaning-making in the media? Reception scholars primarily seek to understand the personal meanings that individuals make of mass media texts in relation to their lived social systems and experiences. By often interviewing consumers and observing the environments where they read, watch, and listen, Reception scholars provide the field of media studies with a unique perspective on the power of audiences in shaping the media landscape. Instead of looking at how media content or production practices influence helpless media consumers, Reception analysis supports the notion of an "active" audience constantly reformulating the meanings of a media text across lines of race, class, gender, sexuality, and more. This approach is often grounded in a body of work called **Reception theory** which stresses audience interpretation as the primary site of meaning-making. Meaning is fluid and communication is imperfect within this perspective, and negotiation between media producers and consumers constantly skews the "true" meaning of media texts. Reception scholars admit that media owners might have the economic power to craft media texts with particular messages, but it is audiences who determine what a text ultimately signifies or how it actually functions in their own lives.

This chapter will begin with a brief overview of traditional audience studies before looking at three contemporary Reception theories that shed light on how audiences make original meaning out of media texts. These theories are conceptually distinct but broadly convergent, and it is important to understand how they build upon one another to create an overarching understanding of the active audience. The chapter ends with a discussion of the primary research method for Reception scholars, ethnography, and considers one of the most famous examples of ethnographic media research, David Morley's *Nationwide* audience study.

Classic Audience Studies and Media Effects Research

Traditional approaches to understanding the audience are largely social scientific and concentrate on measuring the effects of media messages on mass consumers. We will only briefly summarize these approaches in order to provide perspective on the more critical (and, we believe, more important) tradition of Reception analysis. The earliest model of media effects research conceived of the audience as mindless vessels ready to receive media messages. Often dubbed the hypodermic needle approach, this research tradition was predominantly interested in outlining how the mass media "injected" particular meanings into consumers. Here researchers assumed that media messages signified only exactly what producers intended them to mean, and audiences were unable to ignore or negotiate them. The weaknesses of this approach should be obvious: messages do not mean the same thing to every person, and the audience does not just passively absorb any and all media messages. As a result, media scholar Paul Lazarsfeld and colleagues proposed the "two-step flow" model as a more nuanced version of the hypodermic needle approach.[2] This model posited that certain individuals in the audience attended more carefully to media than others (opinion leaders). Mass media messages would influence these individuals, who would in turn disseminate the information to secondary audiences. Although the two-step model recognized a bit more activity on the part of the audience, it was still problematic because it supported the notion that the meanings of media messages were clear and definite.

Other empirical media effects research looks at the ways in which media messages could have broad, collective effects on the larger population. One of the most significant that still continues today is cultivation analysis, first proposed by George Gerbner.[3] Gerbner claims that individuals who watch heavy amounts of television are hyperconscious to issues of danger and violence in their everyday lives. His theory claims that heavy-viewing audiences develop a distorted view of reality and believe that violence is more prevalent in society than actual statistics support. This kind of widespread effect is mirrored in the work of Donald Shaw and Maxwell McCombs and their theory of media agenda-setting.[4] Shaw and McCombs claim that popular media outlets like news stations tell the American public what to think about and how to think about it: they set the national agenda and fuel public concern. Cultivation analysis and agenda-setting are both more complex and highly developed approaches than the hypodermic needle or two-step models, but they continue the tradition of positioning the audience as mindless consumers who believe and follow most of what they see in the media.

One early approach to studying the audience that significantly departs from the others mentioned here is uses and gratifications theory.[5] This perspective was the first to begin "thinking of audiences as empowered to select their access to specific media and to use that media within the ranges of possibility."[6] Uses and gratifications theory assumes that individuals consciously consume media texts for their own ends, purposefully reworking textual meaning in order to integrate the text into their daily life. Instead of passively absorbing given meanings, audiences are selective in which media they consume and how they choose to use it. For example, audiences may engage media as a means of escapism, as a source of information, or even as a form of interpersonal relationships. In short, this perspective reverses the classic understanding of audiences by revealing how they use the media (instead of the other way around).

Although uses and gratifications theory is often critiqued for being overly optimistic about the audience, it is important to recognize it as a historical development in Reception analysis. Some of the analytical methods utilized by these researchers helped pave the way for contemporary ethnographic research on audiences. Moreover, the theoretical underpinnings of Reception theory were born out of the criticisms leveled against uses and gratifications theory for assuming *conscious* activity on the part of the audience. Reception theory claims that while consciousness may be a factor for some individual consumers, audience members as a whole can refashion dominant media meanings without being completely cognizant of the process. A fully formulated understanding of this reasoning first crystallized in the encoding/decoding model.

Encoding/Decoding: Stuart Hall

Perhaps the most significant, early conceptual paradigm within Reception theory is Stuart Hall's encoding/decoding model (see Figure 10.1),[7] originally published as a polemic against the classic models of audience effects research. Hall is best known for his ideological critiques within the field of British Cultural studies, and the model's emphasis on the production, negotiation, and reception of ideological messages between classes reflects this background. The model recognizes the role of media institutions and owners in engineering media texts with particular messages, but it also accounts for the various ways in which active audiences of different classes can consume and rework these hegemonic or dominant meanings. In a general sense, it outlines all of the possible ways in which the intended meaning of a text can be potentially reworked in the hands of an active audience.

Hall begins with the basic premise that "there is no intelligible discourse without the operation of a code."[8] A **code** is a set of rules that govern the use of visual and linguistic signs within a culture. Popular codes, like Morse code or so-called Pig Latin, are systems where users can disguise a message by translating it according to particular rules. Hall's notion of code is much broader but relies on the same principle. When you want to communicate something meaningful to a friend, you have to "translate" the thought in your head into a verbal sentence. The English language is the code you use in this instance. You could also use sign language or even paint a picture that expresses this same thought: both of these are alternative

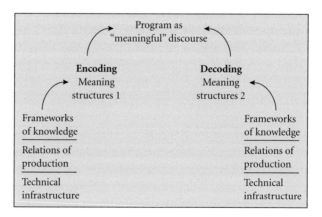

Figure 10.1 Hall's encoding/decoding model.

codes to the English language. Any image or word we can comprehend, for Hall, is the result of a code.

Codes are never neutral in the sense that that they are always *representations* of meaning, not meaning itself, and they reflect the partiality inherent to any representation. Feminist theory is a code that encourages its users to generate and interpret ideas according to issues of gender and power. Christian theology is a code that prompts followers to disseminate and understand messages according to ideas of love and redemption. The codes we use lead to certain ways of seeing the world, and they compel us to interpret the world according to rules of the code. This interpretation occurs in two related moments. **Encoding** is the process of creating a meaningful message according to a particular code, while **decoding** is the process of using a code to decipher a message and formulate meaning. The foundation of Hall's model is the recognition that "the codes of encoding and decoding may not be perfectly symmetrical."[9]

The left-hand "encoding side" of the model is primarily concerned with how dominant ideologies come to exist in mass-mediated texts. The codes that media industries use to create media texts are marked by hegemonic ideologies. For example, some industry codes reflect stereotypical understandings of race and gender (addressed in Chapters 6 and 8). When media producers use these codes to generate media texts (encoding), the ideologies implicit in the code also shape the representations of race and gender in a hegemonic way. The resulting meaning is called the "preferred reading" or desired interpretation of the text: "preferred" in the sense that *this* understanding of race and gender reinforces systems of unequal social power which in turn support media industries. The encoding of preferred meaning in Kelly Clarkson's break-up anthem "Since U Been Gone", for example, would be the encoding of meanings about the wisdom that can result from the dissolution of a heterosexual relationship. Other implicit preferred meanings might be that "true" love is worthy of pursuit, and that being tough after a break-up is an admirable quality. These are all preferred meanings because they are the result of dominant codes that create representations, which reinforce hegemonic ideologies (heteronormativity, individualism, etc.), which in turn benefit the mainstream music industry. A good way to consider the preferred meaning of a media text is to think of what the text apparently "means" on a thematic or cultural level. It is the aspect of the text that draws from and validates dominant cultural ideologies.

Media industries want consumers to interpret texts according to the preferred meaning by employing codes similar to those used in production, but Hall points out that this is not always the case. The right-hand "decoding side" of the model shows how audiences can actually interpret or "read" media texts according to three possible codes or positions: dominant, oppositional, and negotiated. Media audiences operating from a dominant reading position employ a code identical to the industry code and understand the text according to its preferred meaning. These audiences decode the meaning of the text intended by media producers and consciously or unconsciously accept it as true. Communication is "perfectly transparent" here because both parties are using the same code. If the first time you heard

"Since U Been Gone", you thought "Hmm, what a catchy break-up song" and rocked out to it in your car, you probably performed a dominant reading of the song. In other words, you probably accepted the song as meaningful to the extent that it features messages about the necessary trials of heterosexual love and the importance of self-reliance.

However, if upon hearing the song you quickly switched stations and cursed the rise of the pop music love ballad, you probably performed an oppositional reading instead. Oppositional reading is not the same as misunderstanding. For Hall, a media consumer who decodes meaning from the oppositional position "detotalizes the message in the preferred code in order to retotalize the message within some alternative framework of reference."[10] These audiences recognize the preferred reading and dominant code in a text but reject them in favor of a completely different code (and, therefore, a different meaning). For instance, consumers who view the pop music industry as a vapid profit machine might employ a (Marxist) perceptual code that rejects Clarkson's messages of self-sufficiency and empowerment. Instead, the meaning that they decode from the song might recognize "Since U Been Gone" as the latest in a long line of moneymaking schemes by the music industry.

Dominant and oppositional reading strategies represent two of the three possible decoding positions, but in reality they are relatively rare. In truth, it is better to view them as ends on a complex continuum that predominantly features the diverse practices of the third category: negotiated reading. The majority of media consumers interpret media texts from the negotiated position, meaning that they decode part of the text in accordance with the industry code and part of it with an alternative code. These audiences mesh the preferred reading of the text with their personal perspectives and interpretations and produce meaning that is only partially reminiscent of the preferred. Typically, a negotiated reading "acknowledges the legitimacy of the hegemonic definitions to make the grand significations (abstract), while, at a more restricted, situational (situated) level, it makes its own ground rules."[11] It accepts the large-scale meanings while simultaneously assigning personal meanings.

This "hybrid meaning" of negotiated reading can take many forms. For example, some consumers who listen to "Since U Been Gone" might accept its ideologies of heteronormativity and self-reliance, but they might also read the song as an example of female empowerment. Queer individuals who listen to "Since U Been Gone" might reject the implied heterosexual love in the song, but they might accept the messages of personal empowerment in times of emotional crisis. The idea of negotiated readings also helps us understand the various ways that people "use" media texts in their daily lives. When we watch individuals performing "Since U Been Gone" in talent shows, or in their living rooms via YouTube, we are watching a negotiated reading. There is a dimension of meaning for the performer we cannot access by simply looking at the ideologies of the song's lyrics.

Hall views the encoding/decoding process as cyclical. Each exchange of messages between media producers and consumers (every encoding and subsequent decoding) alters the codes and frameworks of knowledge from which both sides operate.

The public reception of "Since U Been Gone" necessarily influenced which song would become Clarkson's follow-up hit. Although the encoding/decoding model was the first of its kind to recognize the roles of media producers and audiences in determining the meaning and influence of media texts, it also has a number of conceptual problems: If the encoding and decoding sides always affect one another, where does a text really "begin" in the model? How is it possible to determine the preferred encoded meaning without engaging in a process of decoding first? These questions and others have led other scholars to look at textual negotiation in a less-structured way through the notion of polysemy.

Polysemy: John Fiske, Celeste Condit, Leah Ceccarelli

The word *polysemy* literally translates to "many meanings." As proposed by television scholar John Fiske, **polysemy** refers to the relative openness of media texts to multiple interpretations. A polysemic text is one that can signify a number of different meanings to many different members of the audience. The medical "dramedy" (dramatic comedy) *Scrubs* is a fairly polysemic text because it blends together divergent television genres, parodies of popular narratives, and diverse intertextual references into a complex piece of television programming. Different audiences will make different meanings of *Scrubs* based on their background and knowledge of American popular culture. Emergency broadcast announcements, on the other hand, have limited polysemic potential. There is only so much a color bar and a loud screeching sound can mean to American audiences. These examples suggest that a text must be polysemic in order to be popular, and the most popular texts are often those most open to audience interpretation (just think of the moral ambiguity at the heart of popular television shows like *Desperate Housewives* or *Grey's Anatomy*).

The notion of popularity becomes an overriding construct that Fiske uses to understand the role of power and the negotiation of meanings in a text. He concedes that all popular texts must have a foundation of dominant social conventions shared by audiences. Quite simply, "a text can appeal to this variety of audiences only if there is a common ideological frame that all recognize and can use, even if many are opposed to it."[12] However, this foundation of dominant understandings cannot fully contain all of the meaning in a media text, a fact that always results in the recognition of what Fiske labels "semiotic excess." This excess is the surplus of signifiers in the text that do not reference clear signifieds, and the degree of polysemy in a text is relative to the text's level of semiotic excess. Polysemy is, therefore, not a quality a text either possesses or lacks, but an ever-present aspect of the text that can be measured in terms of more or less. The greater the semiotic excess and polysemy of a text, the more audiences can negotiate and manage personal meanings. This understanding of texts leads Fiske to view most television programs as "producerly," a term he uses to denote an open, writerly text (see Chapter 11) that is also popular.

A producerly text "relies on discursive competencies that the viewer already possesses, but requires that they are used in a self-interested, productive way."[13]

A clear example of a producerly text that exemplifies the tenets of polysemy is the popular ABC drama *Lost*. The show is a densely packed narrative surrounding a group of individuals whose plane crashes on a mysterious tropical island. On the one hand, *Lost* relies on a number of American ideological assumptions (the importance of love and family, the interplay between faith and science, the re-invention of the self) and televisual conventions (ensemble casts, cliffhangers, flashbacks). These are the aspects of the show that make it popular among American audiences because they are culturally familiar. However, the program is also predicated on the gradual unwinding of secrets that represent free-floating signifiers and semiotic excess. Throughout much of the series, viewers encounter mysteries (strange whispers in the jungle, underground barracks, a group of inhabitants known as "the Others," and more) that do not possess clear meanings within the context of the story. The joy of *Lost* for many of its fans is the speculation that the show generates about its mysteries, and scores of online forums exist where people can share their theories regarding the show. In this way, the program's polysemic ambiguity makes it ripe for multiple readings from different individuals.

Fiske's theory of polysemy re-imagines Hall's encoding/decoding model by aligning Hall's notion of preferred meaning with communal audience decoding practices and his concepts of negotiated or oppositional reading with semiotic excess. Thus the management of meaning from a polysemic perspective is neither linear nor cyclical, and it is best viewed as a ratio between convention and excess on the part of the reading audience. Polysemy is an important contribution to Reception analysis because it recognizes two levels of potential meaning in any given media text, and it allows for scholars to understand the "place" in the text where audience's engage their personal experiences and attitudes. Fiske is one of the strongest proponents of audience power in contemporary media studies, and his theory of polysemy (where meaning can never be fully controlled by producers) reflects that scholarly commitment.

Naturally, such a singular perspective on the audience has its critics. In her essay "The Rhetorical Limits of Polysemy," Celeste Condit outlines a number of issues that Fiske overlooks.[14] The first is a lack of oppositional codes on the part of most audience members. Oppositional codes, such as Marxism or Feminism, are ways of understanding the world that contradict dominant American ideologies. Because most audience members simply do not have access to these codes, it would be difficult to interpret a media text in the truly novel way that the theory of polysemy implies. She also critiques Fiske for ignoring the disproportionate amount of internal work required in generating personal meaning against the dominant meanings in the text. Socially privileged groups whose views resonate most with the conventional level of textual meaning experience pleasure more easily than marginalized groups who must work to pull meaning from the semiotic excess. This leads Condit to question Fiske's assumption that television is a democratic medium, instead asserting that media texts are "compromises that give the relatively well-to-do more of what they want, bringing along as many economically marginal viewers as they comfortably can."[15]

She goes on to point out that even the diversity of programming on television tends to reinforce particular messages about cultural issues, and the historical moment that contextualizes a media program also importantly influences its reception. Both of these factors position television as a more determined medium than Fiske's notion of polysemy allows. In light of the shortcomings of polysemy, Condit proposes the notion of polyvalence as a more applicable term. **Polyvalence** "occurs when audience members share understandings of the denotations of a text but disagree about the valuation of those denotations to such a degree that they produce notably different interpretations."[16] In other words, audiences understand the actual content of media texts in a similar way, but they disagree on the merit or value of that information. One needs to look no further than film critics to see this point. Although most reviewers share common perceptions about how a film's plot develops or the role of characters, their overall assessments of the work can be strikingly diverse. Polyvalence differs from polysemy in that the difference between audience members is one of *connotation*, not of *meaning* as a whole.

Whether viewed as polysemy or polyvalence, the recognition of multiple dimensions of meaning in a text opens up new understanding in media studies and Reception analysis. These approaches shake off the problematic structuring of the encoding/decoding model while still retaining a focus on the interplay between media producers and audiences. However, both Fiske and Condit ironically operate within a textual paradigm even as they concern themselves with methods of reception. They both (unreflectively) consider how polysemic *texts* enable audiences to negotiate meaning. This is somewhat understandable. Prior to the notion of active audiences, many media scholars focused on the kinds of production and textual issues outlined in the first two sections of this textbook. The work of many early Reception theorists (like Fiske and Condit) reflects this tendency to consider the text as central, and it was not until Reception theory developed into a more distinct body of work that scholars began interrogating its internal assumptions.

One of the most significant contributions to the refinement of Reception theory and polysemy is Leah Ceccarelli's 1998 article "Polysemy: Multiple Meanings in Rhetorical Criticism."[17] Until this point, Reception theorists had used the concept of polysemy to explain audience interpretive practices without clearly identifying whether it exists as a quality of the audience, the text, both, or neither. In essence, "the term 'polysemy' is itself polysemous."[18] Ceccarelli is not concerned with pinning down an essential meaning for the term, but she does attempt to understand how it can function through different bodies in different ways toward different ends. Although she is primarily interested in how polysemy functions rhetorically across disciplines, her outline of the three primary "types" of polysemy helps us better understand the process of audience reception in media studies. These three types are resistive reading, strategic ambiguity, and hermeneutic depth.

When scholars view polysemy as a quality of the audience, they are conceptualizing it as a tool of resistive reading. **Resistive reading** is the active, audience-based creation of textual meaning that is contrary to the meaning intended by the text's author, creator, or producer. Here marginalized audiences use the concept of polysemy to distort or transform the messages that reflect the needs and interests of dominant groups. Resistive reading is very close to Hall's notion of oppositional reading in the sense that both rely on audience access to oppositional codes to interpret the message. A Feminist reading of magazine advertisements, for example, is an act of resistive reading. Rather than interpreting the message as an advertisement for a useful product at a good price (which one needs to purchase *right now*), a Feminist resistive reading would understand the advertisement as a text that primarily reinforces the subjugated role of women in society. Polysemy is crucial here because it explains how feminist audiences open up oppositional fields of meaning in a given text.

When scholars view polysemy as a quality of the text and its creator, on the other hand, they are conceptualizing it as an example of strategic ambiguity. **Strategic ambiguity** is the intentional decision to craft a vague, semantically rich text that is purposefully open to multiple interpretations. When textual producers are faced with conflicting demands from different audiences, they may navigate through these expectations by attempting to satisfy all of them with the same text. The use of strategic ambiguity is rhetorical in the sense that it is often tied to a specific situation: particular conflicting audiences at a particular historical moment. The annual State of the Union address is often a good example of a strategically ambiguous text. In the address the president must attempt to satisfy a number of different conflicting audiences across areas like political affiliation, income level, or geographic location. Clear plans are less common than general commitments in the address, which allows these different audiences to interpret plans for the coming year as they see fit. Polysemy allows for ambiguity in this instance.

Finally, when scholars view polysemy as a quality of the critic or analyst, they are conceptualizing it as a dedication to hermeneutic depth. **Hermeneutic depth** refers to the critical recognition of multiple meanings in a text as the source of its overall meaning. When scholars imbue a text with hermeneutic depth, they engage it as a site of academic play and problematize any apparently singular meaning. This process reveals the multiple meanings of the text and encourages the understanding of many, sometimes conflicting interpretations. The textbook you are currently reading is in many ways an extended project in service of hermeneutic depth. We began with the text of "American media" (understandably large and complex) and have run it through eight different perspectives by now. None of these perspectives are wholly correct or incorrect, and true understanding only comes in recognizing the (in)applicability of each one at different times. This lack of clear meaning *is* the meaning. Here polysemy becomes a way of achieving hermeneutic depth, a bridge toward deeper, more complex understandings of texts.

Ceccarelli's landmark essay shed critical light on how different types of polysemy function in different ways toward different ends. Her categorization also better distinguishes between text and audience in the process of audience meaning-making, which is its major strength and weakness for Reception theory. On one hand, by clearly distinguishing between resistive reading, strategic ambiguity, and hermeneutic depth, she reminds Reception theorists to be more conscious in their use of the term and their scholarly worldview. On the other, she implicitly recognizes audience-based and text-based polysemy as equally prevalent and valid. While this may be true, it is not helpful for Reception theorists attempting to understand all of meaning from the audience perspective. Instead, this type of holistic viewpoint forms the central component in the final theoretical section we will consider.

Interpretive Communities: Stanley Fish

Stanley Fish is an important literary critic in the tradition known as reader-centered or reader-response criticism, but his work on textual interpretation is just as applicable to media studies as it is to the analysis of literature. Unlike Hall and Fiske, who recognize some degree of ideological or authorial power in texts as a result of their production, Fish claims that all meaning resides in the readers and audiences of texts. Meaning simply cannot exist outside of audience interpretation. The interpretive strategies we already possess as audience members, he writes,

> are not put into execution after reading (the pure act of perception in which I do not believe); they are the shape of reading, and because they are the shape of reading, they give texts their shape, *making* them rather than, as it is usually assumed, *arising* from them.[19] (emphasis added)

In other words, until audience members engage a media text and begin to read or interpret it, that text literally means nothing. The strategies we use to interpret the text direct us to understand the words and images in a particular way. Only then does the text actually *mean* anything. Although we tend to think that our varied perspectives allow us to access the different kinds of meaning implicit in a text, it is actually the other way around: our ways of understanding create meaning in the text, the only meaning a text can have. Any meaning we generate, anything we notice, "has been *made* noticeable . . . by an interpretive strategy."[20]

This thinking quickly leads to problems. After all, if every individual makes unique and personal meaning out of a text through the process of reading it, then how is it possible that some people tend to read some texts in the roughly same way? If an individual interprets texts according to particular strategies, how can that individual read two similar texts in very different ways? And where do these strategies come from in the first place? Fish's answers to these questions can be found in his notion of **interpretive communities**, or groups who interpret texts similarly because they share similar social positions and experiences. New Yorkers might interpret a film about New York society differently from Arizonans who watch the same film because they share different codes based on geographic location. Naturally, the total meanings that individual audience members generate in each group will vary, but one might expect to see more resemblance between any two New Yorkers than a New Yorker and an Arizonan. At the same time, the Arizonan, who has adored the previous work of the director of the film, might hate this particular film because it disparages Americans. If this were the case, we might reason that the interpretive strategies based on this person's nationality supersede those based on state residency in this instance. Thus, the fact that people can and do belong to many interpretive communities at once explains the similarity and variation in their interpretive strategies.

Meaning ultimately resides in interpretive communities in Fish's paradigm, and that assertion collapses the distinction between producers and audiences that so many other theorists struggle over. Rather than concentrate on whether power over meaning lies in the producer or the audience, Fish claims that interpretive communities give rise to all producers, texts, and audiences in the first place. The communities that an individual belongs to shape how that person will interpret texts, but the communities that an author/producer/creator belongs to also influence how that individual constructs the text initially. Fish points out that all texts carry with them "a projection on the part of a speaker or author of the moves *he* [*sic*] would make if confronted by the sounds or marks he is uttering or setting down."[21] Readers and audiences who belong to the same communities as the author/producer will pick up on these projections as directions for understanding the text; those outside of his/her communities will not. Meaning is not inherent in producers, texts, or audiences, but only in the interpretive communities that constitute each.

One of the most notable historical studies dealing with interpretive communities is Janice Radway's analysis of women and meaning in romance novels.[22] In her study, Radway surveyed and interviewed a sizable group of women in the Midwestern town of Smithson in order to better understand the meanings they attributed to reading romance novels. All of the women in the study were connected to a central respondent named Dot, who worked at a local bookstore and helped women select novels to read. During the course of her study, Radway found that the women did not passively absorb the conventional meanings of romance novels and instead actively used the romances in order to supplement their needs and desires. For example, many of Radway's respondents claimed that they consciously used the novels to escape the emotional demands of their daily life and construct a world of personal meaning and satisfaction. These responses point to the fact that romances do not carry a singular or stable meaning imbued by the novel's author. Meaning comes from interpretation on the part of the audience.

One could speculate that these women belonged to a number of intermingling interpretive communities. Although they differed in their educational levels, family income, and religious conviction, all of the respondents were women, and all lived in the town of Smithson. As a result, Radway discovered that many of the respondents mimicked one another when discussing the meanings of romance novels. Beyond the common theme of escapism, the women in the study also tended to agree on what constitutes a good romance novel.

A romance is, first and foremost, a story about a woman. That woman, however, may not figure in a larger plot simply as a hero's prize. . . . To qualify as a romance, the story must chronicle not merely the events of a courtship but *what it feels like* to be the *object of* one.[23]

This similarity in interpretation speaks to the shared communities of the women in question. Although they disagreed over some aspects of good romances (first-person or third-person narratives, for example), they shared enough reading strategies as women and as romance readers located in Smithson to articulate a common interpretation of quality. The ratio of agreement and disagreement between the women is directly related to the overlapping of interpretive communities between individual women.

Overall, Fish's theory of interpretive communities locates meaning completely in the audience, and it also accounts for similarity and variation among individual audience members. Even textual producers are "audiences" in the sense that they draw from their own experiences and interpretations in creating a text. This is not to say that Fish's approach is the supreme or correct one in relation to media Reception theory, but it is certainly one of the closest to the spirit of ethnographic Reception studies. The best approaches to Reception analysis will consider the work of all of the theorists we have discussed thus far and understand how their various perspectives fit together. Even though Radway's study focused on meaning-making within a particular community, other aspects of the study (such as her discussion of the romance publishing industry) nod to the power relationships found in concepts like encoding/decoding and polysemy. It also provides our first glimpse into the process of ethnographic audience studies in this chapter. The careful designing of surveys, extensive interviewing, and attention to detail we see in Radway's analysis are the hallmarks of the ethnographic process. The remainder of the chapter will further consider the major tenets of this research method.

Ethnographic Research and the *Nationwide* Study

Ethnography is a qualitative research method that focuses on understanding a cultural phenomenon from the perspective of the members of that culture. Ethnographers attempt to immerse themselves in a culture as much as possible through observation, interviews, and participation to gain an insider's knowledge of a cultural phenomenon. In theory, this immersion accomplishes two goals: it (1) minimizes the researcher's cultural biases by displacing the researcher's own culture as the basis for judgment and (2) yields additional understanding about how the phenomenon in question functions within the larger, complex practices of a particular cultural group. Because ethnography has developed predominantly in the fields of anthropology and sociology, many people tend to think of ethnic or national cultures when they think of ethnographic research. In reality, almost any "culture" can be analyzed with this method: workplace culture, videogame culture, fan culture, etc. (see Chapter 6 for an extended discussion of different types of cultures).

Although it is central to the application of Reception theory within media studies, ethnography actually began in the larger field of communication as a tool to better understand the link between language and culture. This early approach, which continues to thrive today, is often called the "ethnography of speaking" or the "ethnography of communication." Here ethnographers approach a culture with two basic questions in mind: what does a speaker need to know to communicate appropriately within a particular speech community, and how does he or she learn to do so?[24] In order to answer these questions, ethnographers of communication look at the interaction patterns, power differentials, and identity performances of a given culture/speech community. Understanding the way members of a culture communicate with one another helps explain particular behaviors and beliefs within that culture.

Perhaps the most famous example of an ethnography of communication is Gerry Philipsen's extended analysis in the 1970s of a blue-collar Chicago neighborhood he dubbed Teamsterville.[25] Philipsen observed and talked to residents of Teamsterville for nearly two and a half years in order to gain a nuanced understanding of the neighborhood's communication patterns. He learned that speaking in Teamsterville was intrinsically tied to concepts of gender, ethnicity, and even physical location. Teamsterville men could talk to other men of similar background and social standing, but for men to talk at length to a person with less social power (a child, for example) was not appropriate. "To speak 'like a man' in Teamsterville," Philipsen elaborates, "required knowing when and under what circumstances to speak at all."[26] Similarly, Philipsen discovered that the front porch of Teamsterville homes functioned as an important place for community socialization. One resident even confessed that a man who had recently moved to the neighborhood could never fully acclimatize because he lacked a porch.[27] By observing and interviewing Teamsterville residents in their own environment, Philipsen was able to assess the subtle communication patterns of the neighborhood culture in a way that would be impossible using other methods.

As we mentioned in Chapter 6, ethnographic research on media audiences grew out of the ideological work of British Cultural studies in the 1970s. Ethnographers interested in media Reception research utilize similar methods as Philipsen to understand how audiences engage media texts. These scholars attempt to immerse themselves in the actual environments of audience media consumption as a way of capturing the intricacies of meaning-making and negotiation. Media ethnographers might, for instance, attend a film society's weekly screenings to discuss what the films mean to the members of the group. By interviewing members of the society and closely monitoring their viewing practices, a media ethnographer would be able to discover the codes, meanings, and complex negotiations that inform how they make sense of the cinema. This method might reveal how the society's conception of "film as art" colors their interpretation of the weekly narratives: a conclusion that would be difficult to fully realize without "knowing" the group first. Other media ethnographers could potentially study the regular patrons of a local music store, the fans of an author, or even the participants in an online role-playing game. In short, these scholars use ethnographic methods of participation, observation, and interviewing to understand how an actual group of people makes sense of specific media texts.

The most significant example of ethnographic analysis in media Reception research is David Morley's *Nationwide* audience study of the 1970s.[28] Morley is a British Cultural studies scholar and was one of the first to break away from traditional conceptions of the "duped" audience. Informed by issues of ideology and Hall's model of dominant, negotiated, and oppositional reading, Morley was interested in investigating the degree to which a person's access to cultural codes influenced their reception of dominant ideologies in media texts. He disagreed with uses and gratifications theories because they often ignored ideology, and he also rejected Hall's focus on class as a determinant for decoding positions. As a result, his *Nationwide* study was an attempt to look at how audiences with different qualities interpreted ideological messages in the British media.

Nationwide was a popular, weekday evening British news program broadcast by the BBC1 network between 1969 and 1983, which at the time placed special emphasis on representing the various parts of Britain in its reporting. Morley (along with colleague Charlotte Brunsdon) had already catalogued the types of dominant ideologies present in the program in a previous study.[29] With "The *Nationwide* Audience: Structure and Decoding," Morley shifted attention to understanding how different members of British society made sense of these ideological messages through the use of dominant, negotiated, and oppositional codes. The study consisted of two phases. In the first, Morley screened a specific episode of the program that "covered a fairly representative sample of *Nationwide*'s characteristic topics"[30] to 18 different small groups. These groups included apprentice engineers, apprentice electricians, black college students, middle school students, teachers in training, and more, all selected on the basis of factors he assumed were related to decoding practices (sex, race, class, union membership, educational level, political affiliation, etc.). In the second phase, Morley screened an episode focused specifically on the economy to 11 different groups like bank managers, sociology students, apprentice printers, shop stewards, etc. In each case Morely gained access to the social groups through courses they were taking together at technical/trade schools and universities. In this way, he attempted to use pre-existing groups that were somewhat cohesive in their shared educational pursuits. After each group viewed the program in the context of their classes, Morley led a focused discussion with the group and recorded their answers on tape.

Morley discovered that the particular combination of social factors in each group led to unique understandings of *Nationwide*. This may not seem like a revolutionary conclusion now, but at the time it represented the first real evidence of an active audience who negotiated or resisted meaning in the media. Certain groups, like the apprentices and bank managers, mostly interpreted the program within the dominant code. Others, like the black college students, felt that "the concerns of *Nationwide* are not the concerns of their world,"[31] as they rejected the very process of interpretation. Most of the groups exhibited different degrees of negotiated reading, either closer to the preferred (teachers) or oppositional (university students) sides of the reading spectrum. Additionally, the study revealed that class was not the determinant factor of reading style as Hall had proposed. The apprentices, shop stewards, and black students all shared a similar class in the study, but they performed widely divergent readings as a result of other social factors like union involvement and racial subcultures.

Morley's landmark study was one of the first to open up room within media scholarship for ethnographic analyses of the actual audience. It reinforced Hall's model by acknowledging the place of both industry ideologies and audience interpretation, but it also dispelled his reliance on class by revealing the multifaceted basis of audience reading strategies. This concentration on audience diversity and variation has become a hallmark of ethnographic analyses ever since.

The *Nationwide* study also provides valuable insight into how media ethnographies can differ significantly from ethnographies of communication. For example, while Morley did attempt to use intact groups in their own educational settings, parts of the study itself resemble more traditional experimental methods. These groups would probably never watch an episode of *Nationwide* in any of their respective classes, much less discuss their personal interpretations of its content. He also spent far less time "in the field" gathering information from audience members. Morley's half-hour interviews with 29 groups hardly compares to Philipsen's two and a half years in Teamsterville. The fact that Morley "set up" the environment and then recorded his findings via interviews seems to downplay the natural qualities of the audience that ethnography seeks to represent. Coupled with a comparatively brief data-collection period, this quasi-experimentation casts doubt on how much the *Nationwide* study could actually be called "ethnography."

However, more recent scholarship in the field of audience studies has argued for a looser definition of ethnography to accommodate the complex process of media reception. Morley's work certainly falls within contemporary standards of media ethnography. Media texts and audiences have become increasingly diverse since *Nationwide*, and some scholars have now recognized that "classic ethnographic fieldwork may not be an appropriate method for studying dispersed media audiences."[32] As a loose methodological movement within audience studies, media ethnography emphasizes certain ethnographic methods over others as a function of the contemporary media landscape. For example, media ethnographers today can attempt to capture the interpretations of a widespread audience, but it has also become permissible to consider smaller groups/cultures (even the reading strategies of a single family). Ethnographic studies of media still focus on the importance of the actual environment in which audiences consume texts, but the amount of time spent observing audiences in these environments is usually far shorter than traditional ethnographic methods require. In this way, media ethnography takes useful aspects of traditional ethnography (a focus on context, allowing people to represent themselves in the research) while discarding parts that often do not fit with the media object of study (lengthy data-gathering periods, extensive immersion into the field). Media ethnography is ethnography in spirit, and "if the means of investigation are not always identical, then the aims of the inquiry can be."[33]

Conclusion

This chapter has looked at the role of Reception theory and ethnography in understanding media from the perspective of the actual audience. Theories of encoding/decoding, polysemy, and interpretive communities allow us to conceive of the audience not as a passive mass ready to absorb singular ideological messages from media texts, but rather as an active group of diverse people who "read" texts according to their social positions and lived experiences. This departure from classic conceptions of the audience shifts the discussion for scholars from media effects to media meanings: Where does meaning in a text come from? How do audiences negotiate meaning? What continues to structure the process of audience meaning-making? Ethnographic research methods are key to answering these questions because they allow scholars to investigate the subtle and otherwise invisible meanings that audiences attribute to the media texts they consume. In many ways ethnography is a complement to the types of industry and textual analyses outlined in the first two sections of this book. By analyzing actual audience media consumption along with the production of media texts, scholars gain a more complete picture of American media today.

MEDIA LAB 9: DOING RECEPTION ANALYSIS

OBJECTIVE

The aim of this lab is to utilize Reception theories of meaning to understand the role of the media audience. Specifically, students will be reacting to and sharing their personal understandings of a media text.

ACTIVITY

- Divide the class into small groups of 4–5.
- Screen a short music video for the groups. We suggest choosing a popular artist with a long-standing career, such as Madonna, in order to maximize possible responses.
- Have each student individually record his/her reactions to the video in a brief paragraph. Possible prompts for this paragraph include: What is this video about? What is the central message of this video? What do you like or dislike about the video?
- Have students convene in their groups, compare reactions, and answer the following questions:
  1 How did the individual responses in your group vary? Which differences are examples of polysemy, and which are examples of polyvalence?
  2 How did the individual responses in your group converge? Identify possible shared interpretive communities that could explain this similarity.
  3 Which group members used dominant codes for interpreting the video? Negotiated codes? Oppositional codes? How do you know?

SUGGESTED READINGS

Acosta-Alzuru, C. Tackling the Issues: Meaning-Making in a Telenovela. *Popular Communication* 1, 2003, 193–215.

Allor, M. Relocating the Site of the Audience. *Critical Studies in Mass Communication* 5, 1998, 217–33.

Bird, S.E. *The Audience in Everyday Life: Living in a Media World*. New York: Routledge, 2003.

Ceccarelli, L. Polysemy: Multiple Meanings in Rhetorical Criticism. *Quarterly Journal of Speech* 84, 1998, 395–415.

Condit, C. The Rhetorical Limits of Polysemy. In *Critical Perspectives on Media and Society*, Avery, R.K. and Eason, D. (eds), pp. 365–86. New York: The Guilford Press, 1991.

Feasey, R. Reading *Heat*: the Meanings and Pleasures of Star Fashions and Celebrity Gossip. *Continuum: Journal of Media & Cultural Studies* 22, 2008, 687–99.

Fish, S. *Is There a Text in This Class? The Authority of Interpretive Communities*. Cambridge, MA: Harvard University Press, 1982.

Fiske, J. Television: Polysemy and Popularity. In *Critical Perspectives on Media and Society*, Avery, R.K. and Eason, D. (eds), pp. 346–64. New York: The Guilford Press, 1991.

Hall, S. Encoding/Decoding. In *Media and Cultural Studies: Keyworks*, M.G. Durham and D.M. Kellner (eds), pp. 163–73. Malden, MA: Blackwell, 2006.

Lowe, M. Colliding Feminisms: Britney Spears, "Tweens," and the Politics of Reception. *Popular Music and Society* 26, 2003, 123–40.

Morley, D. The *Nationwide* Audience: Structure and Decoding. In *The* Nationwide *Television Studies*, D. Morely and C. Brunsdon (eds), pp. 111–288. New York: Routledge, 1999.

Murphy, P.D. Fielding the Study of Reception: Notes on "Negotiation" for Global Media Studies. *Popular Communication* 3, 2005, 167–80.

Press, A. Toward a Qualitative Methodology of Audience Study: Using Ethnography to Study the Popular Culture Audience. In *The Audience and its Landscape*, J. Hay, L. Grossberg, and E. Wartella (eds), pp. 113–30. Boulder, CO: Westview Press, 1996.

Radway, J.A. *Reading the Romance: Women, Patriarchy, and Popular Literature*, 2nd edn. Chapel Hill, NC: University of North Carolina Press, 1991.

Rauch, J. Activists as Interpretive Communities: Rituals of Consumption and Interaction in an Alternative Media Audience. *Media, Culture & Society* 29, 2007, 994–1013.

Schutten, J.K. Invoking *Practical Magic*: New Social Movements, Hidden Populations, and the Public Screen. *Western Journal of Communication* 70, 2006, 331–54.

Staiger, J. *Media Reception Studies*. New York: New York University Press, 2005.

Stout, D.A. Secularization and the Religious Audience: a Study of Mormons and Las Vegas Media. *Mass Communication & Society* 7, 2004, 61–75.

Winocur, R. Radio and Everyday Life: Uses and Meanings in the Domestic Sphere. *Television & New Media* 6, 2005, 319–32.

NOTES

1. S. Chbosky, *The Perks of Being a Wallflower* (New York: Pocket Books, 1999), 32–3.

2. P.F. Lazarsfeld, B. Berelson, and H. Gaudet, *The People's Choice: How the Voter Makes Up His Mind in a Presidential Campaign* (New York: Columbia Press, 1944).

3. For an excellent summary of cultivation analysis, see G. Gerbner, Cultivation Analysis: an

Overview, *Mass Communication and Society* 1, no. 3/4, 1998, 175–94.

4. M.E. McCombs and D.L. Shaw, The Agenda Setting Function of the Mass Media, *Public Opinion Quarterly* 36, no. 2, 1972, 176–87.

5. E. Katz, J.G. Blumler, and M. Gurevitch, Utilization of Mass Communication by the Individual, in *The Uses of Mass Communication: Current Perspectives on Gratification Research* (Beverly Hills, CA: Sage Publications, 1974), 19–32.

6. J. Staiger, *Media Reception Studies* (New York: New York University Press, 2005), 53.

7. S. Hall, Encoding/Decoding, in *Media and Cultural Studies: Keyworks*, M.G. Durham and D.M. Kellner (eds) (Malden, MA: Blackwell, 2006), 163–73.

8. Hall, 167.

9. Hall, 166.

10. Hall, 173.

11. Hall, 172.

12. J. Fiske, Television: Polysemy and Popularity, in *Critical Perspectives on Media and Society*, R.K. Avery and D. Eason (eds) (New York: The Guilford Press, 1991), 359.

13. J. Fiske, *Television Culture* (New York: Methuen, 1987), 95.

14. C. Condit, The Rhetorical Limits of Polysemy, in *Critical Perspectives on Media and Society*, R.K. Avery and D. Eason (eds) (New York: The Guilford Press, 1991), 365–86.

15. Condit, 373.

16. Condit, 369.

17. L. Ceccarelli, Polysemy: Multiple Meanings in Rhetorical Criticism, *Quarterly Journal of Speech* 84, no. 4, 1998, 395–415.

18. Ceccarelli, 396.

19. S. Fish, Interpreting the *Variorum*, in *Is There a Text in This Class? The Authority of Interpretive Communities* (Cambridge, MA: Harvard University Press, 1982), 168.

20. Fish, 166.

21. Fish, 173.

22. J. Radway, *Reading the Romance: Women, Patriarchy, and Popular Literature*, 2nd edn (Chapel Hill, NC: University of North Carolina Press, 1991).

23. Radway, 64.

24. M. Saville-Troike, *The Ethnography of Communication: an Introduction*, 3rd edn (Malden, MA: Blackwell, 2003), 2.

25. G. Philipsen, Speaking "Like a Man" in Teamsterville: Culture Patterns of Role Enactment in an Urban Neighborhood, *Quarterly Journal of Speech* 61, 1975, 13–22; G. Philipsen, Places for Speaking in Teamsterville, *Quarterly Journal of Speech* 62, 1976, 15–25.

26. Philipsen, Speaking "Like a Man" in Teamsterville, 20.

27. Philipsen, Places for Speaking.

28. D. Morely, The *Nationwide* Audience: Structure and Decoding, in *The* Nationwide *Television Studies*, D. Morley and C. Brunsdon (eds) (New York: Routledge, 1999), 111–288.

29. C. Brunsdon and D. Morley, Everyday Television: *Nationwide*, in *The* Nationwide *Television Studies*, D. Morley and C. Brunsdon (eds) (New York: Routledge, 1999), 19–110.

30. Morley, 152.

31. Morley, 257.

32. S.E. Bird, Beyond the Audience: Living in a Media World, in *The Audience in Everyday Life: Living in a Media World* (New York: Routledge, 2003), 7.

33. S. Moores, *Interpreting Audiences: the Ethnography of Media Consumption* (Thousand Oaks, CA: Sage Publications, 1993), 4.

11 Erotic Analysis

KEY CONCEPTS

CLOSED TEXT **JOUISSANCE**
CRUISING **MEDIA EROTICS**
CULTURAL PRODUCTION **OPEN TEXT**
FANDOM **PARTICIPATORY MEDIA**
INTERPRETIVE PLAY **PLAISIR**
RESISTANCE

. . . Spike is coming, spurting onto both their chests, and it's enough to send Xander over the edge, emptying himself into Spike with a gasp of completion. He collapses bonelessly onto the vampire and they['re] still. Lifting his head slowly, Xander blinks, feeling like he has just woken up, but it was no dream, because Spike is still there, smiling tentatively at him, reaching out to brush a sweaty lock of hair out of Xander's eyes. His body shaking only a little, Xander disentangles himself from his vampire lover. With a final, lingering kiss, and a mutual groan of loss as he pulls out of Spike's body, he slumps to the side and they lie, side by side. [He] grins when he realises [*sic*] that he now actually *has* a vampire lover.[1]

For casual viewers of *Buffy the Vampire Slayer*, the preceding story fragment, which recounts a sexual encounter between Spike and Xander – two of the series' popular male characters – probably seems strange and unfamiliar, and perhaps even a little unsettling. But for serious fans of Buffyverse (Josh Whedon's fictional universe about teen vampire slayer Buffy Summers and her friends),[2] it is just one of the hundreds of stories – each written by fans – in which Spike and Xander engage in sexual relations. It typifies a type of fan writing known as slash fiction, which we will discuss in more detail later in this chapter. But what's important to note at this point is that, thanks to the internet, it is just one of the many ways media audiences create and circulate their own media content today. From fan fiction websites like Fanfiction.net, which boasts "more than 87,000 stories about the boy wizard Harry Potter"[3] alone, to the popular image-sharing website, Photobucket, and the exponentially expanding "broadcast yourself" video website, YouTube, media *audiences* are increasingly becoming media *producers*. The decentralizing power of digital technologies has shattered the conventional understanding of media audiences as "inert vessels waiting to be activated by injunctions to . . . consume,"[4] and in the process generated a need for new ways of understanding audiences and their experiences with media. As we will demonstrate in this chapter, the key to understanding contemporary media audiences – audiences who are consumers *and* producers (i.e. prosumers) – is pleasure.

Media Erotics: an Overview

Historically, media scholars have avoided the topic of pleasure, deeming it unworthy of serious attention. On those rare occasions when media scholars have directly addressed it, they have forcefully condemned it. Perhaps the most famous academic assault on pleasure comes from the Frankfurt School scholars Max Horkheimer and Theodor W. Adorno, who in 1972 wrote, "Pleasure always means not to think about anything, to forget suffering even when it is shown. Basically it is helplessness. It is flight; not, as is asserted, flight from a wretched reality, but from the last remaining thought of resistance."[5] Nor were they the last to so vigorously criticize pleasure. Just 3 years later, Feminist film critic Laura Mulvey, in her famous essay titled "Visual Pleasure and Narrative Cinema," set out to "destroy" the pleasure afforded by Hollywood cinema.[6] Initially, then, pleasure – as both an audience experience and an academic pursuit – was ignored or damned.

It was not until the 1980s, when media scholars began to attend carefully to audiences, that pleasure emerged as a subject of sustained inquiry.[7] Challenging the view that pleasure is simple and uncomplicated, media critic Ien Ang argued:

> Both in common sense and in more theoretical ways of thinking, entertainment is usually associated with simple, uncomplicated pleasure – hence the phrase, for example, 'mere entertainment'. This is to evade the obligation to investigate which mechanisms lie at the basis of that pleasure, how that pleasure is produced and how it works – as though that pleasure were something natural and automatic. Nothing is less true, however. Any form of pleasure is constructed and functions in a specific social and historical context.[8]

Though the study of pleasure became increasingly common, pleasure itself continued to be disparaged. The nearly universal condemnation of pleasure was rooted in the widespread belief that "pleasures were 'complicit' with a dominant ideology" and therefore subjugation.[9] More recently, however, scholars have begun to recognize that audience pleasures need not necessarily serve hegemonic interests. This recognition has generated a whole new approach to the study of media that we refer to as Media Erotics. **Media Erotics** explores the array of resistive pleasures that audiences derive from media by examining the various sensuous, creative, and transgressive ways in which persons *use* and *interpret* media.

"Erotics" may seem like a strange descriptor for an approach to studying media, but the meaning and sensibility of the term make it particularly apt. The term *erotic* derives from *Eros*, the Greek god of primordial lust, sublimated impulses, creative urges, and fertility. Like *Eros*, erotics or eroticism has two principle characteristics or dimensions, one involving prohibition, taboo, and transgression (i.e. repressed desire) and the other involving production, expenditure, and dissemination (i.e. seminal fluids).[10] Thus, eroticism is, at once, disruptive (of the status quo or established order) and productive (of something new), which is why *Eros* was also known to the Greeks by the epithet *Eleutherios*, which means "the liberator." But in what way might erotics be said to be liberating: both disruptive and productive? To answer this question, it is worthwhile to consider the difference between animal and human sexual activity. Whereas the sexual behavior of animals is purely instinctual and serves the purpose of procreation, human sexual activity is something more, involving what Georges Bataille calls "an immediate aspect of inner experience."[11] In other words, eroticism concerns the subject and her/his individual desires, and not simply an innate urge to reproduce. Incidentally, it is because eroticism is unique to human sexual activity that they alone can experience shame, not to mention profound enjoyment, in the transgression of taboos.[12] To illuminate how erotics can be utilized to study media, this chapter proceeds in two sections. The first part examines the topic of resistance, identifying its central attributes, while the second part explores the three principal modes of resistive pleasure engaged in by contemporary media audiences.

Cultural Resistance

Ideology and culture notwithstanding, "resistance" is among the most challenging critical concepts to define. The difficulty lies in leaving it open enough to encapsulate the diverse set of practices that function in counter-hegemonic ways without opening it so far that it weakens the force of the concept by casting some practices as universally resistive. For our purposes, Brian Ott and Bill Herman's definition strikes a sufficient balance; they define **resistance** "as those symbolic and material practices that challenge, subvert, or suspend the cultural codes, rules, or norms, which through their everyday operation create, sustain, and naturalize the prevailing social structure in a particular space and time."[13] Building on this definition, we maintain that resistance is governed by five deeply intertwined principles.

1   *Resistance is contextual.* As the last phrase in the definition suggests, the time and place of an act is crucial to its status as resistance. Explains Barker, resistance is not an act with a fixed quality; rather, it is always "specific to particular times, places and social relationships."[14] *Ms.* magazine's "No Comment" section, which reprints ads that are insulting and degrading to women, offers a useful example. In their original contexts (like *Maxim* or *FHM*), such ads function

unreflexively to (re)affirm patriarchy. But when the same ads are reproduced in the "No Comment" section of *Ms.* magazine, they function as resistance by drawing critical attention to the sexist messages that circulate widely in the media.[15]

2   *Resistance is tactical.* For Michel de Certeau, *tactics* (or the art of the weak), which he contrasts with *strategies* (the practices of institutions and structures of power), are maneuvers within the enemy's field of vision. "Maneuvers" is a helpful term because it serves as a reminder that resistance is an action or practice (that occurs temporally), not a product or outcome (that exists spatially). Because resistance always occurs within the dominant social structure, it does not operate from a particular spatial or institutional location, and therefore has no place of its own to stockpile its winning. A tactic seizes propitious moments, turns events into opportunities, and exploits cracks in the system.[16] A tactic is fleeting, disappearing almost as quickly as it appears. If you have ever waited until a teacher turns her or his back to mock that teacher or to send a text message, you have behaved tactically.

3   *Resistance is creative.* Resistance does not eradicate entire social structures, erecting new ones in their place (as revolution does); rather, resistance adjusts and amends the existing social order without overturning it. Consequently, change is personally productive and fulfilling, not emancipatory. Resistance is, in de Certeau's words, about "making do," about turning the rules to one's advantage, and about the diversion of dominant resources for personal benefit (*la perruque*).[17] Resistance does not free one from domination (i.e. social structures and the way they constrain our wants, desires, and behaviors). So, one must settle instead for the way we take advantage of the system for our own ends.

4   *Resistance is cumulative.* Since resistance is tactical, it is reasonable to ask how, if at all, does it foster social change? Treated in isolation, individual acts of resistance rarely constitute a serious threat to the prevailing social structure. But multiple acts of resistance over time have the potential to accumulate. So, while a lone act of resistance may seem innocuous and insignificant, numerous acts can, collectively, bring about more permanent change. Hence, critics should not judge the character (i.e. importance) of a resistive practice according to its immediate effects. One student texting during class does little to undermine the authority of a professor. But many students texting, emailing, sleeping, and doing homework for other classes over the course of a semester may very well begin to undermine the prevailing power structure.

5   *Resistance is incremental.* Because resistance depends upon the cumulative influence of numerous "small wins" to bring about change, it rarely results in rapid or foundational social change. Resistance remakes society gradually and subtly, unlike revolution, which brings about change suddenly and (almost always) violently. Social change fueled by resistance occurs slowly and in increments, as is evidenced by the Gay Rights movement. Although it has won numerous small victories such as partner benefits in the workplace and the right for same-sex partners to legally marry in four states, the overall system remains decidedly heteronormative. The resistive actions of media audiences are almost

always modest and because they are frequently motivated by personal benefits
or desires, they are also often unconscious. Resistance, in other words, does not
require conscious intent.

Resistive Pleasures

Because the approach of this chapter is rooted in Media Erotics, we are specifically
interested in transgressive or counter-hegemonic, as opposed to dominant or hegemonic, pleasures. Audiences, of course, play a central role in the distinction, as hegemonic pleasures arise from the (passive) consumption of media – its messages and
models of identity – by audiences, and resistive pleasures arise from the (active)
production of meaning and modes of being by audiences. Consumption, as we are
using it here, means perceiving (and thus treating) a media text as a finished whole.
When one consumes a media text, they submit to the dominant pleasures it (i.e.
the text) affords; typically such pleasures come in one of three varieties: visual, dramatic, and positional. An example of a hegemonic visual pleasure is scopophilia, which
as we saw in the chapter on Psychoanalysis, involves objectification and voyeuristic desires. Dramatic pleasures, as highlighted in the chapter on Rhetoric, entail those
desires created and satisfied by form, genre, and narrative. A third mode of dominant pleasure derives from identification with a text's preferred subject position.
A *subject position*, explains Brummett, "is not a character in the text itself. Instead,
a subject position is who the text encourages you to be as you, the reader or audience, experience that text."[18] It reflects the perspective or point of view that a text
invites the audience to adopt toward the narrative action. Though hegemonic pleasures are both common and seductive, they do not constitute the full range of pleasures that audiences experience in relation to media.

   Not all audiences (and probably no audience all the time) engage(s) solely in the
passive consumption of media. Increasingly, audiences are, according to Alvin
Toffler, "prosumers,"[19] meaning that they are active in how they both use and interpret media. In altering the prescribed uses and challenging the preferred meanings
of media, prosumptive practices and behaviors have the potential to yield resistive
(i.e. productive) pleasures. In this section, we elaborate upon three major prosumptive
practices: interpretive play, fandom and cultural production, and participatory media.
Although these practices may, at first glance, seem rather disparate, they are united
by their erotic character, by their capacity to privilege abandon, ambiguity, corpor-
eality, creativity, impulsiveness, playfulness, non-conformity, sensuousness, and
visceral experience over the rules of rationality, order, seriousness, and comfort.

Interpretive play

Most media scholars today recognize that the production of meaning involves a
complex interplay between text and audience, and that neither one determines

the other. Critics further recognize that not all texts or audiences are equal. The previous chapter suggested that some texts are more polysemous than others. Rather than viewing polysemy as an either/or question, we propose that the polysemy of a text is relative, ranging on one end of the spectrum from the highly closed text to, on the opposite end of the spectrum, the highly open text. Whereas the **closed text** aims "at eliciting a sort of 'obedient' cooperation," the **open text**, according to Umberto Eco, "not only calls for the cooperation of its own reader, but also wants this reader to make a series of interpretive choices."[20] Applying this framework to film, Steven Spielberg's *Jaws* (1975) provides an example of a relatively closed text, while David Lynch's *Mulholland Dr.* (2001) reflects a more open text. The notion of closed and open texts proposed by Eco closely parallels Roland Barthes's distinction between readerly (*lisible*) and writerly (*scriptible*) texts. Regardless of the particular terminology one prefers, however, the point is that texts vary in the degree to which they constrain or empower audience interpretations.

Similarly, audiences vary in how active they are as interpreters. If we, again, view this question on a continuum, audience activity could be said to range from highly passive (a *vessel* waiting to be filled with meaning) to highly active (a *bricoleur* who invents their own meaning out of the raw semiotic materials found in texts). While one viewer may watch television entirely "in line" with strict programming schedules, another viewer may surf through the channels for an hour or more never settling on one "program." The latter viewer is still having a meaningful and presumably pleasurable experience, but he or she is far more active influencing the shape and texture of that experience. The activity of channel surfing produces its own kind of "text," but it is not one that can be reproduced or experienced by others.

Using the poles from both continua – open/closed texts and active/passive audiences – as boundary markers produces a matrix of the four possible text/audience relations (see Figure 11.1). Each of these relations (i.e. interactions between text and audience) results in a different type of pleasure. But before examining these pleasures, it is helpful to introduce two additional concepts. Unlike English, which has only one word for "pleasure," French has two, *plaisir* and *jouissance*. **Plaisir** describes a comfortable and comforting pleasure: one that conforms to the "dominant ideology and the subjectivity it proposes."[21] **Jouissance**, by contrast, is an ecstatic pleasure that involves disruption of and momentary release from the social order; it is a temporary breakdown of subjectivity and therefore an evasion of ideology.[22] To understand this distinction, consider the difference in pleasure that results from "seeing" a film and "playing" a video game. The pleasure of the former is largely a cognitive one that derives from following the story, identifying with the protagonist, and submitting to the structures of the text. The pleasure of the latter is one of involvement and interactivity, of directing and controlling the action, of "losing oneself" in the game: "the ultimate 'eroticism of the text'."[23]

The quadrants depicted in Figure 11.1 suggest the types of pleasure likely to emerge as a result of various text/audience interactions. Quadrant I, in which a passive audience consumes a closed text, generates strong *plaisir* and functions to reproduce doxa, the prevailing hegemonic order. Quadrant II, in contrast, involving the passive consumption of an open text, results in confusion or boredom associated with

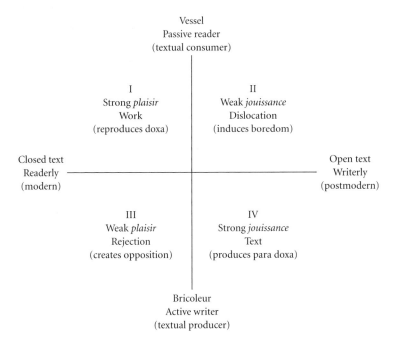

Vessel
Passive reader
(textual consumer)

I
Strong *plaisir*
Work
(reproduces doxa)

II
Weak *jouissance*
Dislocation
(induces boredom)

Closed text
Readerly
(modern)

Open text
Writerly
(postmodern)

III
Weak *plaisir*
Rejection
(creates opposition)

IV
Strong *jouissance*
Text
(produces para doxa)

Bricoleur
Active writer
(textual producer)

Figure 11.1 Ott's pleasure/meaning/identity model.

weak *jouissance*. The pleasure of quadrant II is resistive (*jouissance*) because the confusion (dislocation) or boredom (lack of sustained attention) it evokes disrupts the prevailing order, but is only mildly pleasing (weak) because the audience is not responding to the text's polysemous character. Watching an extremely polysemous film like *What the BLEEP Do We Know!?* (2004) when one is exhausted and unable to engage its complex existential and metaphysical questions could easily produce this effect.

Quadrant III of the model, which involves the active engagement of a closed text, is the most similar to what Stuart Hall had in mind when he proposed the idea of oppositional reading (see Chapter 10). This particular text/audience configuration engenders weak *plaisir*, for even as it recognizes the structured appeals and (dominant) pleasures of the text, it rejects and overturns them. Oppositional reading, while clearly counter-hegemonic, is not very pleasurable, which creates a strong disincentive for audiences to enact it. Quadrant IV couples an open text with an active audience, and it is this text/audience combination that stands the best chance of realizing transgressive pleasure. Strong *jouissance* is a corporeal pleasure that derives from **interpretive play**: an improvisational mode of reading that ignores dominant interpretive codes in favor of pursuing immediate bodily desires. *Jouissance* destabilizes socially produced and controlled subjectivities because it cannot be reproduced, recreated, or shared by others.[24] Bodily pleasure is *always* singular (i.e. fleeting) and individual (i.e. experienced personally). Though multiple bodies can experience pleasure simultaneously (e.g. during sex), the bodies are nevertheless experiencing their *own* pleasures. Barthes refers to the practice of "reading" with one's body as textual **cruising**. Since *jouissance* is a radically personal pleasure, we cannot provide universal examples. So, instead, we describe six *ways* of reading with the body, of cruising, each of which has the "potential" to produce *jouissance*.

1　Abjection. In the *Powers of Horror*, Julia Kristeva defines *abjection* as "what disturbs identity, system, order. What does not respect borders, positions, rules."[25] Abjection arises from the crossing of cultural boundaries and the pollution/defilement of social categories. By dividing the world into internal and external, the body establishes an ideal boundary for staging the abject. Hence, that which is discharged or expelled from the body (i.e. menstrual blood, spittle, sweat, urine, feces, mucus) evokes disgust and revolt. For some, the frequent images of and discourse about excrement on *South Park* may give rise to the abject. The pleasure of abjection lies within its very transgressions, which captivate as well as revolt, attract as well as repel, fascinate as well as disgust. Abjection desires the very things it casts out. Like the compulsion to stare at a horrific traffic accident, the abject registers and appeals at an affective, bodily level.

2　Carnivalesque. The notion of the *carnivalesque* was an idea developed by Mikhail Bakhtin to describe the ritual spectacles, comic verbal compositions, and billingsgate typical of the culture of folk humor seen at popular (as opposed to "official") festivals/feasts in the Middle Ages. Central to carnivalesque's three basic forms is the concept of grotesque realism, which concerns degradation, debasement, or uncrowning: "the lowering of all that is high, spiritual, ideal, abstract."[26] Through grotesque imagery and language (curses, profanities, insults, etc.), lofty things are brought down to a material, earthly level, while lowly or less privileged things are valued and celebrated. Such "social inversion" is another familiar trope or common theme on the television show *South Park*, where adults and celebrities are frequently uncrowned. In the episode, "Stupid Spoiled Whore Video Playset," for instance, Paris Hilton is depicted as an unintelligent, selfish "whore." The pleasure involved in inverting "normal" cultural hierarchies – of bringing adults and celebrities down to earth, and elevating children as superior in insight – is carnivalesque, "for it is the pleasure of the subordinate escaping from the rules and conventions that are the agents of social control."[27]

3　Intertextuality. *Intertextuality* is the idea that texts refer to other texts. In some cases, the gesture to other texts is purposeful: an intentional allusion or reference included by the text's author. This type of intertextuality might be called strategic because it resides in the text itself, and exists for anyone to find. In contrast to the planned and deliberate references typical of strategic intertextuality, tactical intertextuality describes associations to other texts produced by the reader. Tactical intertextuality arises not from the text, but from a reading practice: one in which the audience reads laterally as opposed to linearly. Rather than "following the text" along with its calculated allusions, the text "follows the reader" as she forms connections and makes personal links. Tactical intertextuality is not daydreaming; it does not originate from boredom or a lack of attention to the text (i.e. weak *jouissance*), but from a deep focus on elements within the text. When one reads with this sort of intensity, one does not see associations, one *makes* them. If you have ever been watching a television show and suddenly stopped watching because your mind was now following an association it had made, you were engaged in tactical intertextuality.

4   Irony. *Irony*, as we are using it here, refers more to an attitude or sensibility than to the well-known literary device in which the author means the opposite of what is explicitly said. Nor do we mean irony in the Alanis Morissette "Isn't It Ironic" sense, which (ironically!) has absolutely nothing to do with irony . . . just really bad luck. In philosophy, the ironic sensibility is comic and humble; it does not assess an issue from a particular angle, but adopts a particular issue to assess all angles. The ironic attitude is neutral, though not disinterested; it refuses to take sides because of the "realization that anything can be made to look good or bad by being redescribed."[28] Frequently, though certainly not always, Jon Stewart enacts this perspective on Comedy Central's *The Daily Show*. At his best, Stewart does not advocate a specific view on an issue, but shows his audience the limitations of all (common) views. The pleasure of irony comes from recognition that no view is precisely right or precisely wrong; lacking a definitive position or perspective, the ironist is never fully interpellated by ideology.

5   Liminality. Because *liminality* deals with borders and boundaries, it is often confused with abjection and the carnivalesque. But whereas the abject involves boundary crossing and the carnivalesque entails social inversion, the liminal concerns (occupying, imploding, or dissolving) the boundary itself. "Liminal entities are," writes Victor Turner, "neither here nor there; they are caught betwixt and between the positions assigned and arrayed by law, custom, convention, and ceremonial."[29] Androgyny, a gender identity that combines masculinity and femininity in an ambiguous way, furnishes one example of liminality. But perhaps a more familiar example is the way listening to a favorite song can evoke such strong emotions and memories that one is caught (even if only momentarily) between the past and the present, existing neither fully then nor now. In dissolving institutionalized structures and relationships in favor of indeterminacy, liminality releases instinctual energies (*jouissance*).[30]

6   Depthlessness. The development and spread of the new information technologies has given way to a culture of surface and spectacle. The appeal of media texts in this new culture of *depthlessness* is more about sensuous surfaces and less about underlying structures. As Harms and Dickens note, "images and communications are not rationally interpreted for their meaning, but received somatically as bodily intensities."[31] Depthlessness creates novel opportunities for resistance, as audiences can now "consume images without consuming their meanings, whether referential or ideological."[32] Quotations and characters from films and television programs are endlessly spun into commercial products like t-shirts, which are purchased and worn for pleasure not politics. But it is the apparent apolitical act of wearing a *Family Guy* t-shirt that turns out, in Baudrillard's words, to participate in a resistive politics of "hyperconformity." The consumer's relation to politics, history, and culture today is one of curiosity,

not investment, commitment, or responsibility.[33] Whereas, "in the case of the media," explains Baudrillard, "traditional resistance consists of reinterpreting messages according to the group's own code and for its own ends [i.e. oppositional reading]. The masses, on the contrary accept everything *en bloc* into the spectacular, without requiring a code, without requiring any meaning . . . but making everything slide into an indeterminate sphere . . . [of] fascination."[34]

These six modes of cruising are neither comprehensive nor mutually exclusive. Indeed, they often work in tandem, as the body can have multiple, often competing desires. The common link between them, as well as others we might add to the list, is play. Play, especially as children engage in it, is a highly creative and inventive activity. Objects are utilized for undesignated and illegitimate purposes (e.g. a large box becomes a fort) and rules are created, modified, and often discarded as desire dictates. Impulsive and loosely structured, children's play models what we mean by interpretive play. To approach a media text in this fashion is, paraphrasing de Certeau, to take neither the position of the author nor the author's position, to detach it from its origin, to invent in the text something different than was intended, and to create something unknown from its fragments.[35] Cruising texts may seem like a bizarre and uncommon activity, but it is a regular practice of fans.

Fandom and cultural production

All of us are fans of something: a sports team, an actor or actress, a musical group, or perhaps, like Carrie Bradshaw, Manolo Blahnik shoes. Fans are audiences who possess a special affinity for and loyalty to a particular medium or cultural text; they are, in a word, enthusiasts. One of the authors of this book is a committed fan of Fox's *So You Think You Can Dance*. He views the show religiously, reads online blogs about it, cheers for his favorite dancers, analyzes it (at length) with other friends who are also fans, and occasionally goes to see the live tour. The show is, to say the least, quite meaningful to him. The other author is a diehard fan of the sandwiches made at a little shop in Boulder, Colorado, called Snarf's. He would eat one everyday if he could (but it's a 50-mile drive), and has frequently described the sandwiches as orgasmic. Obviously, they are a source of great pleasure for him! These examples suggest that fans do not merely receive media texts, but also rework them "into an intensely pleasurable, intensely satisfying popular culture."[36] In this section, we will examine the multitude of ways that fans actively make meanings, derive pleasures, and fashion senses of self through media.

The study of **fandom** – organized communities or subcultures comprised of persons who share a special affinity for or attachment to a media text, which they, in turn, express through their participation in communal practices (fan fiction, etc.) and events (conventions) – began in the 1980s. At that time, fans were often derided by the media and non-fans as fanatics, obsessive nut jobs, and just plain weird. The first wave of scholars to study fandom, which included figures such as John Fiske,

Henry Jenkins, Camille Bacon-Smith, and Constance Penley, was very much interested in challenging this stereotype. For them, fandom involved interpretive communities whose creative and productive activities empowered fans and challenged the hegemonic culture. Contemporary fan scholar Jonathan Gray has dubbed this period and type of scholarship, "Fandom is Beautiful"[37] because of its overly romantic view of fans and the counter-hegemonic potential of fan culture. In spite of this limitation, it nevertheless established several important categories for understanding and evaluating fandom. The first-generation of fan scholars recognized that what most separates fans from popular audiences is the degree to which they engage in **cultural production** or the generation of semiotic, enunciative, and textual materials related to a specific media artifact.[38]

1   *Semiotic productivity* refers to the way fans use the semiotic (i.e. symbolic) resources in media texts to enhance the meaningfulness if their everyday lives. In the previous chapter, for instance, we discussed Janice Radway's study of romance novels, whose female readers often select only those stories and attend to only those themes that reaffirm feelings of self-worth.[39] Similarly, in her study of online fandom surrounding television soap operas, Nancy Baym found that *personalization* is among the chief interpretive practices of fans:

> One core practice in interpreting the soap is personalization, whereby viewers make the shows personally meaningful. They do this by putting themselves in the drama and identifying with its situations and characters. They also bring the drama into their own lives, making sense of the story in terms of the norms by which they make sense of their own experiences. This referencing from the world of the drama to the lives of viewers is the overriding way in which viewers relate to soaps.[40]

Henry Jenkins, drawing upon the work of Michel de Certeau, refers to this process of selective personalization by fans as *textual poaching*. Based on his study of science fiction fandoms, he too argues that fans promote their own meanings over those of producers as a way of drawing texts closer to the realm of lived experience.[41] Textual poaching should not be confused with Stuart Hall's notion of oppositional decoding explained in Chapter 10. Whereas oppositional reading adopts a reactionary stance to the text's preferred ideology, poaching is far more fluid and arises from fans asserting interpretive authority: their own right to make textual meanings. "For the fan," explains Jenkins, "reading becomes a kind of play, responsive only to its loosely structured rules and generating its own kind of pleasure."[42]

In addition to the notion of textual poaching, Jenkins is also interested in *rereading*, or the fact that fans repeatedly return to the same text again and again. Once a story's resolution is fully known, the reader no longer bears the same relation to that text. Instead of being motivated by form and the desire to resolve narrative mysteries, the reader may turn his or her attention to other interests, such as specific themes and characters.[43] The opportunity to focus so intensely on characters – to get to know them – allows for the development of *parasocial* relationships, in which fans form intimate bonds with media characters or personalities that, though inevitably one-sided, can produce outcomes similar to actual social relationships. Rereading, then, is an intensely personal mode of textual poaching that allows fans to build (parasocial) relationships with media characters or celebrities. Though, at first glance, this behavior may seem "fanatical," it is quite common today. Increasingly, MySpace users invite musicians, athletes, and other famous people to be their "friends." Some users go a step further, and leave personal messages on these celebrities' MySpace pages.

2 While semiotic productivity is primarily an internal and personal process, *enunciative productivity* is public and communal. Fans are rarely fans in isolation. Rather, they discuss and debate their shared interest in a media text at length. This can occur in person (i.e. face-to-face) through participation in local clubs and fan conventions, or it can occur remotely (i.e. virtually) through online chatrooms, listservs, and other electronic forums. Regardless of how participants "come together," they engage in similar (though certainly not identical) communication rituals or practices. Among the most common types of enunciative productivity or fan talk is *exegesis*: the careful attention to textual minutiae and hyper-detailed analysis of characters, themes, and plot developments. Close textual analysis can include a wide variety of interpretive activities such as judging the quality or emotional realism of a text, commenting on surprising plot twists, pointing out narrative and character inconsistencies or visual continuity goofs, highlighting seemingly trivial actions or events that have deeper meaning or relevance, and speculating about what will happen next. Exegetical energy is particularly high around texts with lengthy, complex storylines such as soaps or with mysterious, seemingly inexplicable phenomena such as *Twin Peaks*, *The X-Files*, or *Lost*. Regardless of text, however, analysis is designed to demonstrate textual mastery and fan knowledge, which in an informational economy such as a fan community, translates into prestige, reputation, and thus influence.[44]

Another way fans demonstrate textual knowledge and mastery, thereby heightening their cultural capital within a fan community, is by being the first to report "insider" information such as production schedules, future narrative events or arcs (termed *spoilers* by fans), actor contract disputes, and the like. Fan communities are often very hierarchical, and consequently newcomers or *neophytes* to a particular fandom may be verbally disciplined if they fail to follow communal norms or demonstrate proper respect for fan elders. Alternatively, the newbie–elder relationship may function in a more apprentice–mentor capacity, whereby the newcomer is initiated into the community by being taught its codes and customs. In her largely auto-ethnographic account of *Star Trek* fandom, Camille Bacon-Smith discusses the relatively structured phases of initiation she underwent, including being greeted by the *Star Trek* Welcommittee, meeting and getting to know members personally, and learning about fan-produced texts. It is to this third category that we now turn our attention.

3   The third category of fan production is *textual productivity*, which refers to the vast array of artistic, literary, educational, and entertaining cultural products that fans create. Games, character biographies, episode guides (for television shows), artwork, short films, fanzines, and fan fiction represent just a few of the fan-produced products common to fandom. In many ways, the products created by fans resemble the products generated by the mainstream media, fashion, and culture industries. The principal difference is that, while media texts are produced for profit, most fan texts are produced for pleasure, albeit often at considerable effort and financial expense to the fan. Though it is tempting to consider fan-produced media as simple, amateur, or childish, especially since fans rarely have access to state-of-the-art equipment to produce their products, it can rival and even exceed mainstream media products in creativity, originality, aesthetic quality, and overall production values. In his study of online *South Park* fandom, for instance, Ott noted the sophistication of *Babylon Park*, an animated spoof that combined the elaborate storylines of *Babylon 5* with the fart jokes, general character style, and stop-motion technique of *South Park*.[45] Ott also mentions the 3D images produced by a fan at sweeet.com, many of which were parodies of movie posters involving *South Park* characters, as an example of creative fan artwork (Figure 11.2). A more recent type of fan art – referred to simply as "vids" – entails the splicing together of clips from films and television shows to create video montages, which tell stories that differ in theme or perspective from the original text. The fans, known as "vidders,"

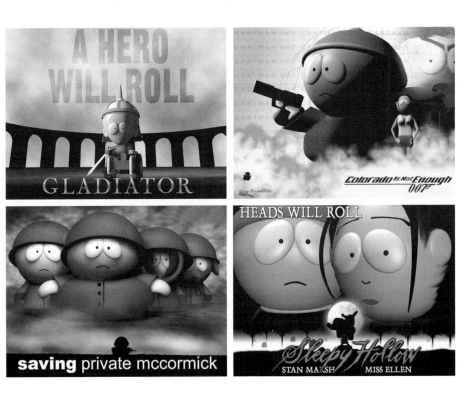

Figure 11.2
Fan artwork: South Park movie poster parodies.

who produce these montages demonstrate their creative and artistic abilities through audio and video editing rather than filming. "Experienced vidders," notes Mazar, "hold formal and informal workshops to help others learn these skills," allowing more and more fans to become cultural producers.[46]

Perhaps the most studied form of fans' textual productivity is fan fiction. *Fan fiction*, or fanfic for short, is a literary genre in which fans write unauthorized stories that expand upon the storyworld (characters or setting) of a mainstream media text, such as a novel, film, or television show.[47] "Writing stories about characters of a favorite television program," explains Rhiannon Bury, "is a means of extending the meanings and pleasures of the primary text."[48] Fan fiction is typically written by women and often revolves around science-fiction texts such as *Blake's 7*, *Dr Who*, *Smallville*, *Heroes*, *Battlestar Galactica*, or *Stargate: SG1*. Since fan fiction is not sanctioned by the companies that hold the copyrights to the media texts used as the basis for its stories, and it is commonly published online or in fan magazines, most fanfic is illegal. Despite clear copyright infringement, fan fiction tends to be ignored or, at least, tolerated by media companies, however. They recognize that it is produced by their most loyal fans, a group they do not want to alienate. The transgressive character of fan fiction, then, has less to do with its legal status and more to do with how it is specifically functioning for the fans who write it. Fans appropriate and rework media texts they love as a way of making those texts better address their own needs and social agenda.[49] To illustrate this process, we briefly examine two popular subcategories of fan fiction, Mary Sue and slash.

Mary Sue is a sub-genre of fan fiction in which the author/fan inserts herself as a character into the storyworld of a popular media text. Such stories are referred to as "Mary Sues" because it was the name of the central female character in Paula Smith's famous parody of this sub-genre titled, "A Trekkie's Tale."[50] Though the content of Mary Sue fan fiction is infinitely diverse, the underlying form of the stories is overwhelmingly predictable. With few exceptions, Mary Sue characters are adolescents, who are either related to or romantically involved with one of the principal characters from the original media text. An author/fan of a Mary Sue writing about the storyworld of *Stargate: Atlantis*, for instance, might introduce a young female character who is romantically involved with Col. John Shepherd. In addition to being closely linked to one of the primary characters, Mary Sues are almost always beautiful, beloved by the other characters, and extremely intelligent. She is also central to the narrative action, and usually saves the day before meeting an untimely death at the story's end. Mary Sues are, for most fan writers, the first fan fictions they write. Because they are seen as beginning attempts at fan writing, they are widely denigrated even within the fan communities that produced them. But, nonetheless, they serve an import cultural function for the women who write them.

According to fandom scholar Camille Bacon-Smith, Mary Sue stories are a way for their authors to confront the painful memories and experiences of adolescence, when they were teased for interests (i.e. science-fiction and action adventure) and behaviors (i.e. non-seductive fashion and non-subordinate attitudes) deemed too "masculine." Mary Sue stories rewrite and hence recode childhood experiences by creating "perfect" female characters that are both competent *and* well liked, intelligent, *and* desirable. They fulfill an emotional need for their authors by creating a cultural model of the ideal woman with which fans can identify.[51] Often, as fan writers "mature," they stop writing Mary Sues and begin writing other forms of fan fiction. One of these forms, which is generally regarded by media scholars as a far more subversive sub-genre of fan fiction, is known as slash.

Slash, like Mary Sue fan fiction, appropriates the characters and storyworld of a popular (and, again, often science-fiction) text for personal ends. But in contrast to Mary Sues, slash fan fiction does not insert the author as a character in the story. It does, however, feature two or more of the main characters from a popular media text in a romantic and often explicitly sexual relationship that they do not, in fact, have in the original (or "canon") text. This sub-genre is referred to as *slash* because the stories are identified by the first name or initial of each the paired lovers, separated by a "/." Slash fiction centers exclusively on the relationship between same-sex (usually male) characters.[52] It emerged in the 1970s when *Star Trek* fans began writing erotic stories about the relationship between Captain Kirk and his first officer, Mr. Spock. Although slash fiction was dominated by Kirk/Spock stories early on, it has greatly diversified over the years. A few popular pairings today include Harry Potter and Draco Malfoy (*Harry Potter*), Xena and Gabrielle (*Xena: Warrior Princess*), and Frodo Baggins and Samwise Gamgee (*Lord of the Rings*). Slash stories are commonly accompanied by fan art, such as the Frodo/Sam image seen in Figure 11.3.

Figure 11.3
Hand-drawn fan slash image.

For the mostly heterosexual women who write it, slash fiction furnishes a vital outlet to envision, explore, and tell stories about romantic and sexual relationships in which the partners are powerful equals.[53] It is, notes Constance Penley, "an exemplary case of female appropriation of, resistance to, and negotiation with mass-produced culture."[54] In the specific case of *Buffy the Vampire Slayer* slash, like the snippet of Spike/Xander slash that begins this chapter, the figure of the vampire offers an additional "vehicle through which to encode subversive pleasures of sexuality and desire."[55] Because vampires, as with the central characters in many other science-fiction texts, are not quite human, slash writers have even more freedom to "imagine something akin to the liberating transgression of gender hierarchy John Stoltenberg describes: a refusal of fixed-object choices in favor of a fluidity of erotic identification."[56] In other words, fan fiction is not simply about producing alternate meanings and interpretations; it is also about experimenting with and producing alternate identities, about exploring the limits of who one is and what she or he can become.

Participatory media

Fans are not the only ones to use and interpret media in ways that simultaneously produce personal pleasures and symbolically or materially challenge the prevailing social order (i.e. hegemony). In the final section of this chapter, we look at a few of the ways ordinary people do so by examining participatory media. By **participatory media**, we mean those communication technologies that necessitate either *direct-user interaction* (DUI) or *user-created content* (UCC) to function. Digital video games are the most obvious example of DUI technology, and indeed when they began to garner serious academic attention in the 1980s it was largely due to interest in their unique *interactive* quality. Unlike more traditional communication technologies such as print, radio, television, and film, which allow for only limited user interaction, digital video games require direct and frequent inputs from users. Simply put, digital games oblige users to "play" them. Recently, scholars have begun to chart the specific pleasures that users derive from playing video games.[57] The three principal pleasures suggested by the literature in this arena are control, immersion, and performance.

1   Control. In 1990, psychologist Mihaly Csikszentmihalyi introduced the concept of *flow* to describe moments of optimal experience in life.[58] For Csikszentmihalyi, certain activities in life produce heightened states of enjoyment because they strike a delicate balance between being too easy (boredom) and being too difficult (anxiety). Basically, people achieve flow, an intense feeling of joy and creativity, when they feel challenged – pushed to their limits – by an activity, but not frustrated by it. Put another way, the experience of flow involves the paradox of control. One must feel that one has sufficiently control to obtain an objective, but never so much control that the activity stops being challenging. Digital games operate according to this same principle. They present an

opportunity for the gamer to experience control (quite literally concretized through a controller or joystick) without ever ceding complete control. Digital games are designed so that the better one becomes at playing them, the more challenging the task becomes; as soon as a player masters a skill, he advances to the "next level." By employing the paradox of control, digital games continuously produce extreme enjoyment.

2   Immersion. Given the frustrations and burdens of everyday life, we often evince a desire to escape from the "real" world into a land of pure wish fulfillment: a fact that partially accounts for the popularity of amusement and theme parks. Because of their interactive quality, digital games are especially effective at fostering elaborately simulated places in which we can forget our troubles and lose ourselves. When one becomes fully immersed in a digital game, the external world vanishes and the distinction between game and player fades away. The combined experience of total immersion and flow is frequently described by players as *being* "in the zone." If you have ever attempted to speak to a player when she is in the zone, you know how futile it is. Digital games are not, of course, the only media that allow for immersion. Recent research on the iPod, for instance, suggests that it creates a sonorous envelope in which one loses one's self in the sensorial enjoyment of music (*jouissance*).[59] Again, this is why people listening to their iPods in public appear to be in a different world.

3   Performance. Immersion in simulated worlds allows for yet another type of pleasure, the "experimentation with alternative identities. . . . The pleasure of leaving one's identity behind and taking on someone else's."[60] Role-playing digital games necessitate the creation of avatars (i.e. a computer user's unique representation of himself), and thus allow users to inhabit bodies or characters, if only virtually, and to adopt personas that may be drastically different from their non-gaming selves.[61] This type of "identity play" creates opportunities for users to escape the social structures that routinely discipline them (i.e. keep them in line) according to their gender, race, sexuality, and the way they look, sound, or dress. For some, this means not only trying out or experimenting with unfamiliar subjectivities, but also expressing actual desires and aspects of themselves that may not be accepted or acceptable in everyday life. The pleasure of performance, then, lies in its inventive, creative, and productive character. Unlike so much of our mediated environment, which by positioning us as (passive) consumers, tells us both who to be and how to be, role-play games (RPGs) foster imagination and self-creation. We tell them who and how we want to be.

Other popular DUI technologies include mobile devices such as cellular phones, personal digital assistants (PDAs), and handheld computers. Though such devices were used primarily for sending and receiving messages or storing and retrieving data early on, third-generation (3G) mobile telephony has created novel opportunities for interactive play. Mobile games such as *I Like Frank*, for instance, use mobile devices equipped with Global Positioning System (GPS) technology to allow players in the real city of Adelaide to interact with players in a virtual city who log on from around the world. The game, which interrogates the boundaries between "real" and "virtual" by requiring street players and online players to swap information, was created by Blast Theory, a London-based artists' group that mixes interactive media, art, and performance "to ask questions about the ideologies present in the information that envelops us."[62]

While DUI technologies require user interaction, the content – be it in the form of virtual environments or navigational maps – is still principally (though not exclusively) produced and distributed by large media conglomerates. Consequently, there are limits to the meanings it can generate and the uses to which it can be put. With UCC technologies or consumer-generated media (CGM), however, the possibilities are limitless. Before looking at few specific examples of UCC and the personal and social functions it serves, it is useful to chart its chief characteristics. A report prepared for the Organization for Economic Co-operation and Development (OECD) by Sacha Wunsch-Vincent and Graham Vickery of the Directorate for Science, Technology and Industry identifies three central characteristics of UCC: the material must be "published in some context" that is publically available, demonstrate "creative effort" through the production of original content or the sufficient adaptation of existing content, and be "created outside of professional routines and practices."[63] This definition is designed to include an array of material (i.e. text, image, audio, video) across platforms, including blogs, wikis (Wikipedia), podcasting, social networking sites (Facebook, MySpace), digital video (YouTube, MyVideo) and photography-sharing sites (Flickr, Snapfish, Ofoto), digital message boards and forums, and online feedback, while excluding email, bilateral instant messages, and commercial market material. Since it is impractical to discuss all of the UCC platforms mentioned above, we have chosen to limit our discussion to blogs.

Short for web log, a *blog* is an online site maintained by an individual or group that features time-dated postings of commentary and other material such as graphics, video, and links. Blogs, which appeared in the late 1990s and had exploded to nearly 55 million by 2007, typically fall into one of two categories: issue-oriented or personal diary. Issue-oriented blogs, explains alternative media scholar Cris Atton, "democratize what has long been the providence of the accredited expert (such as the professional politician and the journalist) by enabling the 'ordinary' contributions of people outside the elite groups that usually form the pool for opinion and comment" on the political and social concerns of the day.[64] Bloggers draw their authority not from professional credentials or expertise, but from their own personal, subjective experience with issues. Thus, they often tell stories using language and examples that relate to and resonate with their audience. Moreover, since issue-oriented blogs are largely opinion-driven and do not face the same organizational constraints as media institutions, they can tackle topics and issues considered taboo in mainstream journalism.

Not surprisingly, personal diary blogs, unlike issue-oriented blogs, tend to be about the person who writes them. In some cases, such blogs are mostly a means of promoting one's own artistic and creative abilities. Consider Bo Burnham, a teenager from Boston, who writes and performs his own songs. Eight months after posting two of his songs as videos on YouTube in 2006, Bo's videos had been "seen over ten million times worldwide."[65] On his website, Bo posts recent pictures, videos, tour dates, and even information on how to contact his manager should one want to book him. Bo's success, as well as that of internet celebrities, is significant, for, as Atton explains, "Participatory, amateur media production contests the concentration of institutional and professional media power and challenges the media monopoly on producing symbolic forms."[66] Though some personal diary blogs focus on self-promotion, others focus on self-expression through autobiographical writing. A study of an erotic story (available via the *Sehakia* website) by Al Kathar, a self-identified Muslim lesbian from Algeria, concluded that autobiographical writing can create "a space for agency within which counterhegemonic sexualities are asserted, and transgressive normative possibilities enacted."[67] These examples, though limited to blogs, reinforce previous research, which has concluded that UCC "leads to three cross-sectional trends: increased user autonomy, increased participation, and increased diversity."[68]

From digital video games to personal diary blogs, participatory media allows individuals to take risks and to produce experiences and content tailored to their own needs and desires. The pleasures that accompany such practices emerge in relation to personal expression and play. Commenting on the importance of play in our everyday lives, Henry Bial observes,

> We play to escape, to step out of everyday existence, if only for a moment, and to observe a different set of rules. We play to explore, to learn about ourselves and the world around us. . . . [P]lay is . . . the force of uncertainty which counter-balances the structure provided by ritual. Where ritual depends on repetition, play stresses innovation and creativity. Where ritual is predictable, play is contingent.[69]

Because play involves "a stepping out of 'real' life" for the joy of play itself,[70] in capitalist societies it has historically been constructed in opposition to *work*. Consequently, the choice to "play" at work carries a subversive potential all its own. The phrase "time is money" is a familiar refrain in corporate culture. It, along with other phrases like, "do that on your own time" or "I'm not paying you to . . . ," reinforce a strict separation of professional (work) and personal (play) time, implying that when one is at work, one's time is owned by another. In a capitalist system, time is a commodity and therefore a material resource. Thus, when workers "waste time" by surfing the internet, sending private emails, sharing vacation pictures, blogging, Facebooking, shopping online, or playing video games, they are subverting material resources. The personal and unsanctioned use of media at work both deconstructs the work/play binary and diminishes corporate profits. The very same uses of media that constitute transgressions in the workplace are, however, not transgressions in the home (or at least not in the same way). This observation serves as an important reminder of the first axiom of resistance (see Cultural Resistance, above): it is contextual.

Wasting time is, in effect, a type of stealing. Its influence on the corporate bottom line is no different than taking office supplies, making personal copies on the copy machine, or using an office computer to burn mix CDs for your friends. By some estimates, 75% of employees engage in office theft, which is believed to cost US businesses as much as $50 billion a year. We share this statistic not for the purpose of shaming employees, but to emphasize that – consistent with axiom four – resistance is cumulative in effect. In addition to wasting or stealing time through the personal use of media at work, media users also frequently steal media itself. It is estimated, for instance, that illegal music downloading outpaces legal music downloading 20 to 1, and that the average iPod or MP3 device contains 842 illegally copied songs.[71] Though much attention has been paid to the financial harm illegal downloading causes the music and film industries, far less attention has been paid to why illegal downloading occurs in the first place. The sheer ubiquity of the practice, especially in light of the serious risks involved (i.e. being sued, getting internet viruses, etc.), suggests to us that users must derive tremendous pleasure from it. More research is needed not just on the pleasures associated with media use, but also on the pleasures associated with its acquisition.

Conclusion

This chapter approached media from the newly emerging and still developing perspective of Media Erotics by illustrating the multitude of pleasures that audiences derive from media. Although the pleasures afforded by media frequently serve hegemonic interests, this chapter focused on the transgressive or counter-hegemonic pleasures associated with interpretive play, fandom and cultural production, and participatory media. In different ways, the practices and pleasures charted in this chapter all have material dimensions. Interpretive play entails the materiality of the body, and following its wishes and desires. Fandom involves the creation and circulation of material cultural products such as fan art and fan fiction. Finally, participatory media create opportunities for fully embodied material pleasures through the unique interactivity of digital games, as well as the subversion of material resources such as time. We close this chapter with two cautionary notes to students regarding the personal and critical pursuit of resistive pleasure. First, there is a tendency after studying the topic of resistance to see it in everything; such a move greatly weakens the force of the concept along with the transformative potential it holds. Second, there is a propensity to romanticize the role of resistance in society, thus underestimating hegemony and its capacity to co-opt and commodify resistance and to re-interpellate subjects.

MEDIA LAB 10: DOING EROTIC ANALYSIS

OBJECTIVE

The purpose of this lab is to heighten students understanding of Media Erotics by having them produce a fan text. The hope is that students will not merely describe or give an account of a transgressive pleasure, but experience such a pleasure.

ACTIVITY

- Divide the class into small groups of 4–5.
- Ask students to select a popular media text, and write a short fan fiction involving canon characters *or* select one character and develop an extended biography about that character and how he or she ended up where he or she is in the canon universe.
- After writing the fan fiction or bio, answer the following questions:
    1   In what ways, if any, was the act of cultural production pleasurable?
    2   How does fan fiction wrest control away from the original author in favor of the fan?
    3   In what ways does being a fan/cultural producer alter one's relationship to media?
    4   Do you think YouTube is a common site of resistive pleasures? Why or why not? Give several examples to support your position.

SUGGESTED READING

Aydemir, M. *Images of Bliss: Ejaculation, Masculinity, Meaning*. Minneapolis, MN: University of Minnesota Press, 2007.

Bacon-Smith, C. *Enterprising Women: Television Fandom and the Creation of Popular Myth*. Philadelphia, PA: University of Pennsylvania Press, 1992.

Bakhtin, M. *Rabelais and His World*. Translated by H. Iswolsky. Bloomington, IN: Indiana University Press, 1984.

Barthes, R. *The Pleasure of the Text*. Translated by R. Miller. New York: Hill and Wang, 1975.

Bataille, G. *Erotism: Death and Sensuality*. Translated by M. Dalwood. San Francisco, CA: City Lights Books, 1962.

Brooker, W. *Using the Force: Creativity, Community and* Star Wars *Fans*. New York: Continuum, 2002.

Butler, C. The Pleasures of the Experimental Text. In *Criticism and Critical Theory*, J. Hawthorn (ed.), pp. 129–39. London: Edward Arnold, 1984.

de Certeau, M. *The Practice of Everyday Life*. Translated by S. Rendall. Berkeley, CA: University of California Press, 1984.

Dhaenens, F., Van Bauwel, S., and Bilfereyst, D. Slashing the Fiction of Queer Theory: Slash Fiction, Queer Reading, and Transgressing the Boundaries of Screen Studies, Representations, and Audiences. *Journal of Communication Inquiry* 32, 2008, 335–47.

Douglas, M. *Purity and Danger: an Analysis of the Concepts of Pollution and Taboo*. New York: Routledge, 1966.

Fiske, J. *Understanding Popular Culture*. Boston, MA: Unwin Hyman, 1989.

Gray, J., Sandvoss, C., and Harrington, C.L. (eds) *Fandom: Identities and Communities in a Mediated World*. New York: New York University Press, 2007.

Hills, M. *Fan Cultures*. New York: Routledge, 2002.

Jenkins, H. *Textual Poachers: Television Fans & Participatory Culture*. New York: Routledge, 1992.

Jenkins, H. *Fans, Bloggers and Gamers: Exploring Participatory Culture*. New York: New York University Press, 2006.

Keft-Kennedy, V. Fantasising Masculinity in *Buffyverse* Slash Fiction: Sexuality, Violence, and the Vampire. *Nordic Journal of English Studies* 7, 2008, 49–80.

Kerr, A., Kücklich, J., and Brereton, P. New Media – New Pleasures? *International Journal of Cultural Studies* 9, 2006, 63–82.

Kristeva, J. *Powers of Horror: an Essay on Abjection*. Translated by L.S. Roudiez. New York: Columbia University Press, 1982.

Lewis, L.A. (ed.) *The Adoring Audience: Fan Culture and Popular Media*. New York: Routledge, 1992.

Mayné, G. *Eroticism in Georges Bataille and Henry Miller*. Birmingham, AL: Summa Publications, 1993.

O'Connor, B. and Klaus, E. Pleasure and Meaningful Discourse: an Overview of Research Ideas. *International Journal of Cultural Studies* 3, 2000, 369–87.

Ott, B.L. (Re)Locating Pleasure in Media Studies: Toward an Erotics of Reading. *Communication and Critical/Cultural Studies* 1, 2004, 194–212.

Ott, B.L. Television as Lover, Part I: Writing Dirty Theory. *Cultural Studies↔Critical Methodologies* 7, 2007, 26–47.

Ott, B.L. Television as Lover, Part II: Doing Auto[Erotic]Ethnography. *Cultural Studies↔Critical Methodologies* 7, 2007, 294–307.

Ott, B.L. The Pleasures of *South Park* (An Experiment in Media Erotics). In *Taking* South Park *Seriously*, J. Weinstock (ed.), pp. 39–58. Albany, NY: State University of New York Press, 2008.

Ott, B.L. and Herman, B.D. Mixed Messages: Resistance and Reappropriation in Rave Culture. *Western Journal of Communication* 67, 2000, 249–70.

Scodari, C. Resistance Re-Examined: Gender, Fan Practices, and Science Fiction Television. *Popular Communication* 1, 2003, 111–30.

Sontag, S. *Against Interpretation and Other Essays*. New York: Picador USA, 1961.

Stallybrass, P. and White, A. *The Politics and Poetics of Transgression*. Ithaca, NY: Cornell University Press, 1986.

Stam, R. *Subversive Pleasure: Bakhtin, Cultural Criticism, and Film*. Baltimore, MD: The Johns Hopkins University Press, 1989.

Taylor, T.L. Multiple Pleasures: Women and Online Gaming. *Convergence: the International Journal of Research into New Media Technologies* 9, 2003, 21–46.

Zukic, N. Webbing Sexual/Textual Agency in Autobiographical Narratives of Pleasure. *Text and Performance Quarterly* 28, 2008, 396–414.

NOTES

1. This is a brief excerpt from a *Buffy the Vampire*-inspired slash (Spike/Xander) story. Spurglie, Joined at the Hip, *All About Spike: Fanfiction that Explores Spike's Ambiguities*, www.allaboutspike.com/fic.html?id=497 (accessed December 14, 2008).

2. V. Keft-Kennedy, Fantasising Masculinity in *Buffyverse* Slash Fiction: Sexuality, Violence, and the Vampire, *Nordic Journal of English Studies* 7, 2008, 50.

3. R. Mazar, Slash Fiction/Fanfiction, in *The International Handbook of Virtual Learning Environments*, J. Weiss, J. Hunsinger, J. Nolan, and P.P. Trifonas (eds) (Dordrecht: Springer, 2006), 1141.

4. A. Ruddock, Media Audiences 2.0? Binge Drinking and Why Audiences Still Matter, *Sociology Compass* 2, 2008, 8.

5. M. Horkheimer and T.W. Adorno, *Dialectic of Enlightenment*, trans. J. Cumming (New York: Continuum, 2001), 144. Originally published by Querido of Amsterdam in 1947, the first English translation did not appear until 1972.

6. L. Mulvey, Visual Pleasure and Narrative Cinema, in *Feminism and Film Theory*, C. Penley (ed.) (New York: Routledge, 1988), 59. This essay was originally published in the autumn 1975 issue of the film journal *Screen*.

7. B. O'Connor and E. Klaus, Pleasure and Meaningful Discourse: an Overview of Research Ideas, *International Journal of Cultural Studies* 3, 2000, 370.

8. I. Ang, *Watching Dallas: Soap Opera and the Melodramatic Imagination* (New York: Routledge, 1985), 19.

9. O'Connor and Klaus, 375.

10. G. Mayné, *Eroticism in Georges Bataille and Henry Miller* (Birmingham, AL: Summa Publications 1993), 13.

11. G. Bataille, *Erotism: Death and Sensuality* (San Francisco, CA: City Lights Books, 1962), 29.

12. Bataille, 29–31; see also Mayné, 3.

13. B.L. Ott and B.D. Herman, Mixed Messages: Resistance and Reappropriation in Rave Culture, *Western Journal of Communication* 67, 2000, 251.

14. C. Barker, *Cultural Studies: Theory and Practice* (Thousand Oaks, CA: Sage Publications, 2000), 342.

15. L. Steiner, Oppositional Decoding as an Act of Resistance, *Critical Studies in Mass Communication* 5, 1988, 2.

16. M. de Certeau, *The Practice of Everyday Life*, trans. S. Rendall (Berkeley, CA: University of California Press, 1984), xix.

17. de Certeau, 30–1.

18. B. Brummett, *Rhetoric in Popular Culture*, 2nd edn (Thousand Oaks, CA: Sage Publications, 2006), 129.

19. A. Toffler, *The Third Wave* (New York: William Morrow and Company, 1980), 282–305.

20. U. Eco, *The Role of the Reader: Explorations in the Semiotics of Texts* (Bloomington, IN: Indiana University Press, 1979), 7, 4.

21. J. Fiske, *Understanding Popular Culture* (Boston, MA: Unwin Hyman, 1989), 54.

22. Fiske, *Understanding*, 50–1.

23. J. Fiske, *Reading the Popular* (New York: Routledge, 1989), 93.

24. Fiske, *Understanding*, 51.

25. J. Kristeva, *Powers of Horror: an Essay on Abjection*, trans. L.S. Roudiez (New York: Columbia University Press, 1982), 4.

26. M. Bakhtin, *Rabelais and His World*, trans. H. Iswolsky (Cambridge, MA: MIT Press), 19.

27. J. Fiske, *Television Culture* (London: Methuen, 1987), 243.

28. R. Rorty, *Contingency, Irony, and Solidarity* (Cambridge: Cambridge University Press, 1989), 74.

29. V. Turner, *The Ritual Process: Structure and Anti-Structure* (Ithaca, NY: Cornell University Press, 1969), 95.

30. Turner, 128.

31. J.B. Harms and D.R. Dickens, Postmodern Media Studies: Analysis or Symptom?, *Critical Studies in Mass Communication* 13, 1996, 222.

32. J. Fiske, Postmodernism and Television, in *Mass Media and Society*, J. Curran and M. Gurevitch (eds) (New York: Edward Arnold, 1992), 60.

33. J. Baudrillard, *The Consumer Society: Myths and Structures*, trans. C. Turner (Thousand Oaks, CA: Sage Publications, 1998), 34.

34. J. Baudrillard, *In the Shadow of the Silent Majorities*, trans. P. Foss, J. Johnston, and P. Patton (New York: Semiotext(e), 1983), 43–4.

35. De Certeau, 169.

36. J. Fiske, The Cultural Economy of Fandom, in *The Adoring Audience: Fan Culture and Popular Media*, L.A. Lewis (ed.) (New York: Routledge, 1992), 30.

37. J. Gray (ed.), *Fandom: Identities and Communities in a Mediated World* (New York: New York University Press, 2007), 1.

38. Fiske, The Cultural Economy of Fandom, 37.

39. J.A. Radway, *Reading the Romance: Women, Patriarchy, and Popular Literature* (Chapel Hill, NC: University of North Carolina Press, 1984), 184.

40. N.K. Baym, *Tune In, Log On: Soaps, Fandom, and Online Community* (Thousand Oaks, CA: Sage Publications), 71.

41. H. Jenkins, *Textual Poachers: Television Fans & Participatory Culture* (New York: Routledge, 1992), 18, 34, 53.

42. H. Jenkins, Star Trek Rerun, Reread, Rewritten, in *Fans, Bloggers, Gamers: Exploring Participatory Culture* (New York University Press, 2006), 39.

43. Jenkins, *Textual Poachers* 67.

44. H. Jenkins, "Do You Enjoy Making the Rest of Us Feel Stupid?": alt.tv.twinpeaks, the Trickster Author, and Viewer Master, in *Full of Secrets: Critical Approaches to Twin Peaks*, D. Lavery (ed.) (Detroit, MI: Wayne State University Press, 1995), 59.

45. B.L. Ott, "Oh My God, They Digitized Kenny!" Travels in the *South Park* Cybercommunity v4.0, in *Prime Time Animation: Television Animation and American Culture*, C.A. Stabile and M. Harrison (ed.) (New York: Routledge, 2003), 228–9.

46. Mazar, 1148.

47. Mazar, 1141.

48. R. Bury, A Critical Eye for the Queer Text: Reading and Writing Slash Fiction on (the) Line, in *The International Handbook of Virtual Learning Environments*, J. Weiss, J. Hunsinger, J. Nolan,

and P.P. Trifonas (eds) (Dordtrecht: Springer, 2006), 1152.

49. Jenkins, *Textual Poachers*, 102.

50. C. Bacon-Smith, *Enterprising Women: Television Fandom and the Creation of Popular Myth* (Philadelphia, PA: University of Pennsylvania Press, 1992), 94.

51. Bacon-Smith, 102.

52. Keft-Kennedy, 49; see also Mazar, 1147.

53. Bacon-Smith, 249.

54. C. Penley, Feminism, Psychoanalysis, and the Study of Popular Culture, in *Cultural Studies*, L. Grossberg, C. Nelson, and P. Treichler (eds) (New York: Routledge, 1992), 492.

55. Keft-Kennedy, 50.

56. Jenkins, *Textual Poachers*, 189.

57. A. Kerr, J. Kucklich, and P. Brereton, New Media – New Pleasures?, *International Journal of Cultural Studies* 9, 2006, 63–82.

58. M. Csikszentmihalyi, *Flow: The Psychology of Optimal Experience* (New York: Harper & Row, Publishers, 1990).

59. J. Gunn and M.M. Hall, Stick it in Your Ear: The Psychodynamics of iPod Enjoyment, *Communication and Critical/Cultural Studies* 5, 2008, 135–57.

60. Kerr *et al.*, 74.

61. T.L. Taylor, Multiple Pleasures: Women and Online Gaming, *Convergence* 9, 2003, 26; see also S. Turkle, *Life on Screen: Identity in the Age of the Internet* (New York: Touchstone, 1995), 177–96.

62. Blast Theory, *About Blast Theory*, www.blasttheory.co.uk/bt/about.html (accessed December 14, 2008).

63. Working Party on the Information Economy, *Participative Web: User-Created Content* (2007), 8, www.oecd.org/dataoecd/57/14/38393115.pdf (accessed December 14, 2008).

64. C. Atton, Current Issues in Alternative Media Research, *Sociology Compass* 7, 2007, 21; see also H. Hewitt, *Blog: Understanding the Information Reformation That's Changing Your World* (Nashville, TN: Thomas Nelson, 2005), 71.

65. Welcome to BoBurhmam.com, http://boburnham.com/ (accessed December 10, 2008).

66. Atton, 21.

67. N. Zukic, Webbing Sexual/Textual Agency in Autobiographical Narratives of Pleasure, *Text and Performance Quarterly* 28, 2008, 397.

68. Working Party on the Information Economy, *Participative Web: User-Created Content* (2007), 35, www.oecd.org/dataoecd/57/14/38393115.pdf (accessed December 14, 2008).

69. H. Bial, Play, in *The Performance Studies Reader*, H. Bial (ed.) (New York: Routledge, 2004), 115.

70. J. Huizinga, *Homo Ludens: a Study of the Play Element in Culture* (Boston, MA: Beacon Press, 1950), 8.

71. D. Sabbagh, Average Teenager's iPod has 800 Illegal Music Tracks, *Times Online*, June 16, 2008.

12 Ecological Analysis

Technologies fundamentally influence the ways in which we communicate. Take, for instance, the rise of digital MP3 players and mobile telephony: two communication technologies that share a number of similar characteristics. Both are highly portable and mobile, allowing us to enjoy *our* favorite music or to talk with *our* closest friends virtually anywhere and anytime. Both technologies are also highly customizable, allowing us to create *our* own music playlists as well as unique ring tones for each of *our* friends. In emphasizing "our" in the previous sentences, we are trying to highlight that iPods and cell phones foster a very specific type of connection and sociability, namely one that is *intensely personal*. In connecting us to *our* favorite music and friends, these technologies increasingly divorce us from the "social" by transforming even the most public and social spaces into very personal and private ones. Anyone who has been made uncomfortable by overhearing an extremely personal cell phone conversation can attest to just how oblivious the user was of his or her social surroundings. Given the way that digital music players and phones privilege the personal over the social, it is hardly surprising that sociologists such as Robert Putnam have observed a dramatic decline in community over the past decade.[1] These technologies emphasize our own needs and desires over others'.

One consequence of the shift from the social to the personal, especially in public, appears to be an increased callousness toward strangers, whom we impatiently honk at on the highway or huff at in the grocery store line. We all, of course, know that such behavior is not very sociable, and indeed, we may even feel guilty after we engage in it. Guilt over our insensitivity toward others may, in fact, be fairly common in society today. One way of judging the accuracy of this hypothesis is by examining our public discourse to see if it contains symbolic resources that address such guilt. During the decade of the 1990s, just as communication technologies were beginning to alter the character of our interactions, the television show *Seinfeld* attained an unprecedented popularity. The show was famously about "nothing": just four friends living in New York City. But its central theme, which was explicitly dramatized in the series' finale when the foursome was imprisoned for failing to assist a man who was being robbed, concerned the lack of consideration for others. In retrospect, it appears that *Seinfeld*'s popularity was due, at least in part, to its capacity to make us laugh at ourselves and our own foibles. The dual role that media play in creating our environment and helping us to function within it can best be assessed from the perspective of Media Ecology.

Media Ecology: an Overview

In 1999, *Biography*, a television show on the Arts and Entertainment (A&E) cable channel, counted down the 100 most influential people of the past 1,000 years. The 4-hour, world-premier special was broadcast on October 10 and 11. To create this remarkable list, which included such renowned figures as Albert Einstein, Karl Marx, and Sigmund Freud, A&E polled 360 noted scholars, scientists, and artists. Their responses along with individual ballots cast through *Biography*'s website were, then, evaluated by A&E's editorial board, who eventually settled on a rank-ordered list. Sitting atop the list as the single most influential person in 1,000 years was Johannes Gutenberg, the inventor of moveable type mechanical printing. Gutenberg was awarded top honors because the printing press was felt to have more profoundly transformed the world than any other invention, discovery, or action by a world leader. Regardless of whether or not you agree with *Biography*'s pick, it signals the central influence of communication technologies on society.

The printing press's revolutionary and transformative role in society raises an interesting question. Are communication technologies merely an aspect of our cultural environment, or are they, in fact, environments themselves? Increasingly, scholars have begun to view media (i.e. communication technologies) *as* environments, a perspective now known as **Media Ecology**. Neil Postman coined the phrase in 1970 to highlight that we live *in* communication environments, and that those environments reflect the communication technologies that are dominant in a particular historical moment. Elaborating on the goal of Media Ecology, Postman wrote:

> Its intention is to study the interaction between people and their communications technology. More particularly, media ecology looks into the matter of how media of communication affect human perception, understanding, feeling, and value; and how our interaction with media facilitates or impedes our chances of survival. The word ecology suggests the study of environments: their structure, content, and impact on people in their daily lives.[2]

To promote and advance the study of media from this perspective, Postman established the now famous program in Media Ecology at New York University in 1971. Since the founding of the NYU program, Media Ecology has flourished. Today, it is characterized by multiple approaches. In this chapter, we examine two approaches in particular, both of which in their own way take seriously the idea of "media as environment." The first approach, equipment for living, focuses on the prevailing symbolic forms that comprise our environment. The second approach, medium theory, views each medium as its own type of setting or environment.[3]

Equipment for Living

The idea that messages, media and otherwise, afford individuals symbolic resources for confronting and resolving the anxieties they face in their everyday lives originated with twentieth-century literary critic and philosopher Kenneth Burke. He advanced this idea in an essay titled "Literature as Equipment for Living," which was originally published in the magazine *Direction* in 1938. Burke begins his famous essay with a discussion of proverbs, noting that proverbs are really just literary devices for naming typical, recurrent situations. A popular proverb like "birds of a feather flock together," for instance, simply names the fact that people who have like tastes commonly associate with one another. But because proverbs describe recurring situations, they offer a means for quickly sizing up a "type" of situation and developing a strategy to respond to it. If you attend a party in which a select group of people has congregated in one corner, then the "birds" proverb provides a way of admonishing the group for having excluded you. Verbally lumping the individuals together and then disparaging them for drinking too much, behaving badly, or dressing poorly is a particularly effective way of resolving the anxiety of having been excluded. For Burke, proverbs were just succinct instances of how literature in general functions as "stylistic medicine" for everyday problems.

Thus, for Burke, various literary forms are themselves ways of naming recurring social situations, thereby providing readers with symbolic resources for addressing those situations in their real lives. The theory of literature (or really any type of discourse) as **equipment for living**, which Burke also called sociological criticism, is rooted in the idea of symbolic action. Burke believed that symbolic actions can produce the same effect as material ones. "*The reading of a book on the attaining of success*," explains Burke, "*is in itself the symbolic attaining of that success*,"[4] which is why the reader is unlikely to take any actions to attain success beyond reading the book. One of the reasons why literature and other art forms function as symbolic action for audiences is because the producer of art created it as a means of dealing with some challenge (i.e. recurring social situation) in his or her own life. Authors write books, Burke believed, as a way of "coming to terms" with (i.e. symbolically confronting and resolving) difficulties in their own lives. Though a prolific writer, Burke wrote only one novel, *Towards a Better Life*, in his lifetime. He wrote the book in 1931, just 2 years before he married Elizabeth Batterman, the sister of his first wife, Lily Mary Batterman. In the story, Burke's narrator undergoes moments of extreme discomfiture only for the theme of resurgence to be explicitly proclaimed. Perhaps himself aware of the symbolic connection to his own life years later, in the 1965 preface to the second edition, Burke wrote, "Often, a closer look at . . . texts will make it appear that, however roundabout, they are modes of symbolic action classifiable as rituals of resurgence, transcendence, rebirth. . . . My . . . study of various literary texts, viewed as modes of 'symbolic action,' has convinced me that this book is to be classed among the many rituals of rebirth that mark our fiction."[5]

One of the most common recurring situations in the human condition is guilt. According to Burke, every aspect of our lives is governed by values and rules, which he refers to as **hierarchy** or order. **Guilt** is the condition that arises every time we violate hierarchy. Because we all participate in multiple hierarchies, which often have conflicting rules, it is impossible to keep all the rules all the time. Consequently, guilt is ubiquitous. Imagine the following scenario: your best friend is celebrating her 21st birthday and wants you to join her for the festivities that evening. But you have an exam the next day that is worth 30% of your grade in a class you need to graduate. One set of rules (hierarchy) is telling you to go have fun with your friend, while another set is saying you should stay home and study. Ultimately, you will have to violate one of these hierarchies, which will cause you to feel guilty. Because guilt is profoundly disquieting and discomforting, we have developed an array of symbolic strategies for ridding ourselves of it. Burke calls this process the pollution–purification–redemption cycle (Table 12.1), and it offers three different means of addressing guilt: transcendence, mortification, and victimage.

Transcendence is not so much a way of resolving guilt (as mortification and victimage are) as it is a way of avoiding guilt by appealing to a new hierarchy or third perspective in which the two conflicting hierarchies cease to be in opposition.[6] Rather than celebrating with your friend, you decide to stay in and study after all. You rationalize your decision not by placing the exam ahead of your friend, an action sure to lead to guilt, but by reminding yourself that your friend values family above all else and that your family is struggling to pay your way through school. Poof: your guilt is gone. *Mortification*, a second means of dealing with guilt, requires a symbolical act of atonement such as confession or self-sacrifice.[7] Perhaps you

Table 12.1   Kenneth Burke's pollution–purification–redemption cycle

	Pollution	Purification	Redemption
Description	The violation of order	The purging or punishment of guilt	The restoration of purity
Symbolic act	Sin→guilt	Transcendance, mortification, or victimage	Absolution→rebirth

decide to celebrate with your friend instead of studying for your exam, which you subsequently fail. This leads to feelings of guilt about your choice. As a means of relieving your guilt, you punish yourself by swearing off beer, which just so happens to be your favorite beverage in the whole wide world, for an entire year. Though your abstinence lasts only 2 days, you nevertheless feel as though you have paid a heavy price and your guilt subsides. Self-flagellation is another a form of atonement, though a bit more masochistic one than confession or sacrifice.

A third strategy for addressing guilt – and the one that most directly concerns us as media critics – is victimage. *Victimage* is a form of scapegoating in which the guilty party transfers his or her guilt onto another party. To the extent that a character in a novel, television show, or film is guilty of "sin" (i.e. any violation of hierarchy) similar to our own, that character may serve as a surrogate for our own guilt. The resolution of the character's guilt is, through symbolic action, the resolution of our own. Burke argued that the two archetypical symbolic forms, tragedy and comedy, both provide equipment for living. The ways they equip us to resolve guilt, however, vary greatly. *Tragedy* is a form of drama in which the protagonist, the tragic hero, experiences a reversal of fortune as a result of some mistake or error in judgment. The tragic hero's inevitable demise (usually death) is symbolic equipment for audiences to the extent that they identify with the hero and his/her error. Herman Mellville's *Moby Dick* is a well-known tragedy, in which Captain Ahab, the tragic hero, ultimately dooms both himself and his crew because of his monomaniacal obsession. Most of us have, at one point or another, been obsessed about someone or something. If it ended badly, it was likely a source of guilt for us. Ahab or a similar character, however, can purge that guilt by vicariously "paying the price" for us.

Comedy, by contrast, traces the buffoonery of its central character, the comic fool, who is reinstated into the community after being shown the error of his/her ways. In the opinion of one of the authors of this text, one of the greatest comic fools in history is Peter Griffin, the crude and dimwitted father of the Griffin family on the television show *Family Guy*. When Peter's doltish behavior inevitably causes things to go horribly awry, he must be taught his error, so that it can be corrected and he may be accepted again by his family and/or friends. Since most of us are not that much brighter than Peter Griffin, we frequently engage in stupid behavior that has negative consequences. If, hypothetically speaking, you recklessly drank too much alcohol one evening and then vomited on the seat of your best friend's car, you would likely feel badly about it . . . at least after you sobered up. Peter aids in resolving such guilt by reminding us that we all throw up on other people's car (couch, bed, or pant leg). Who among us, after all, has not done something totally idiotic? Watching someone else make poor choices and then seeing that person corrected serves as our own admonishment to avoid errors like pitching our pop tarts (i.e. vomiting) in the future.[8] Burke viewed comedy as a particularly humane way of resolving guilt because it recognizes that "to err is human" and therefore calls for the tolerant reinstatement of the fool in society, rather than for his or her tragic punishment.[9]

Tragedy and comedy are very broad (generic) forms and subsequently can function as symbolic equipment for a wide variety of situations (types of guilt) over time. But Burke also recognized that societies continuously face social problems that are unique to particular historical moments, and therefore must continually develop new, specialized discursive forms to address them. Noting the contextual character of form, Burke wrote, "the conventional forms of one age are as resolutely shunned by another."[10] Following the end of the Cold War and collapse of the former Soviet Union, for instance, there was a noticeable decline in films like *Firefox* (1982), *War Games* (1983), *The Day After* (1983), *Red Dawn* (1984), and *Threads* (1984) that addressed anxieties over mutually assured destruction. The aim of sociological criticism, then, is "to identify the modes of discourse enjoying currency in a society and to link discourse to the real situations for which it is symbolic equipment."[11] An excellent example of this practice in media studies is Barry Brummett's study of haunted house (note: not horror) films. Based upon analysis of *The Shining* (1980), *The Amityville Horror* (1979), *The Hearse* (1980), *The Haunting* (1963), and *The Uninvited* (1944), Brummett notes that haunted house films stage "horrors" that help us cope with real (if unconscious) ones. Specifically, he argues that haunted house films help equip us to confront feelings of disorientation, the fear of the unpredictable and shocking, and the idea of death. One of the most interesting and insightful aspects of Brummett's study is that it shows that haunted house films provide symbolic equipment for audiences at both the level of form/content and medium.[12] The medium itself, though oft overlooked, is of vital importance to understanding the role of media in society, and thus the central focus of the next section.

Medium Theory

Like equipment for living, medium theory is an ecological approach to studying media, and therefore concerns the character of our social environment at a particular time and in a given place. But whereas equipment for living concerns the symbolic *forms* that comprise our social environment, medium theory concerns the material *technologies* that are our social environment. If we adopt "sending a package" as a metaphor for communication, the contents of the package would represent the *message*, the shape and size of the packaging would represent the *form*, and the means by which it was delivered would represent the *medium*. Historically, media scholars have focused far more on the message and its form than on the medium. What difference, after all, does it make if the package was delivered by a truck or a horse? Seemingly little, unless the message happened to be fresh fruit, the packaging a mesh bag, and it was being delivered from halfway around the world . . . oh, and did we mention the truck is refrigerated? In this instance, the medium makes a world of difference (especially to one's taste buds). Medium theory posits that the mode or technology of communication *always* makes a world of difference, or, to adopt Marshall McLuhan's famous aphorism, "the medium *is* the message." Scholars who employ this approach are quick to point out that studying communication technologies is important precisely because we typically do not think about them, which means that we are largely oblivious to their influence and effects.

The central premise of **medium theory** is that each medium of communication "has relatively fixed characteristics that influence communication in a particular manner: regardless of the content elements and regardless of the particular manipulation of production variables."[13] Thus, the primary aim of medium scholars is to identify the features of a medium that distinguishes it physiologically as well as psychologically from other media.[14] Medium theory can be utilized at either a micro- (single-situation) or macro-level (social). At a micro-level, medium theory might ask, for instance, what are the consequences of breaking up with your significant other in person versus via text message? Even if the message was identical (e.g. "I can't stand you. I never want to see you again. And you smell funny!"), the medium would matter. By contrast, macro-level medium theory asks questions such as what senses are activated, what degree of interactivity exists, how many people can receive the same message, and at what speed? Our concern in this chapter is with macro-level medium theory, which we examine by discussing three of its most prominent theorists: Harold Innis, Marshal McLuhan, and Walter Ong.

Harold A. Innis (1894–1952)

Harold Adams Innis was a professor of political economy at the University of Toronto, where his interest in economic monopolies would eventually lead to the study of information monopolies. The exercise of political power within society, Innis argued, is influenced by the unique character of the communication media that dominate the dissemination of information. Hence, information monopolies can be diffused or reconfigured by the development and spread of new media. The printing press, for instance, is regarded as having had a democratizing effect because it diminished the privileged position held by religious scribes and undermined the medieval Church's monopoly over religious information and ultimately over salvation.[15] Even though the content of the scriptures had not changed, the change in medium – from an elite class of scribes that painstakingly reproduced scripture by hand to the efficient mass reproduction of scripture by the printing press – fundamentally altered the public's relation to the Bible. As the scriptures became widely available and literacy spread among the masses, they no longer relied as heavily upon the Church to interpret religious doctrine for them.

Innis's interest in the relation among monopolies of knowledge, political power, and technologies of communication in society is most fully explored in his 1950 book, *Empire and Communications*, which was based on a series of lectures he delivered at Oxford University in 1948. It is here that Innis introduced his now famous distinction between time-biased and space-biased media, arguing that most communication media are inclined (i.e. biased) toward either enduring for long historical periods or being moved easily across vast distances.[16] "Media that emphasize time," according to Innis, "are those that are durable in character, such as parchment, clay, and stone."[17] **Time-biased media** are characteristic of tribal or oral civilizations. Because their production utilizes heavy materials and is frequently labor intensive (e.g. carving and hand-writing), they reach only a limited audience. Politically and organizationally, civilizations based on such media are usually decentralized and hierarchical.[18] Since time-biased media do not allow for efficient or easy communication over great distances, the various communities that comprise such civilizations tend to be relatively independent and autonomous. As it is difficult for a leader located in one tribal area to communicate with other tribal areas, it is also more difficult to exert direct political influence and control. Meanwhile, leadership *within* a particular tribal region or community is exceedingly hierarchical because knowledge is tied to tradition, which is preserved by community elders or religious figures.

Whereas time-biased media favor religion and political stability, **space-biased media** are inclined toward secularism, materialism, and rapid social change. They are typically lighter in character, less durable, and more ephemeral than time-biased media.[19] Space-biased media such as papyrus, paper, television, radio, and newspapers can reach many people over long distances, and thus support centralized systems of government that are less hierarchical. Because societies built upon space-biased media can communicate easily over distance, it is easier for a government located in one place (i.e. highly centralized) to govern far-away places. At the same time, because knowledge is not controlled by a select few, the structure of government itself is more egalitarian, which in turn fosters rational deliberation and democratic debate. Innis's interest in the bias of media informed his analysis of the Egyptian, Babylonian, Greek, and Roman empires in *Empire and Communications*. Since empires are characterized by rule over large areas for long periods of time, Innis believed that empires had to strike a careful balance between media biased toward space and time. He wrote:

> Large-scale political organizations such as empires must be considered from the standpoint of two dimensions, those of space and time, and persist by overcoming the bias of media which over-emphasize either direction. They have tended to flourish under conditions in which civilization reflects the influence of more than one medium and in which the bias of one medium towards decentralization is offset by the bias of another medium towards centralization.[20]

To more fully understand this process, it is helpful to look at his specific analysis of a particular empire. We have selected his discussion of the Egyptian empire, as it furnishes a fertile example.

Innis begins his discussion of the ebb and flow of the Egyptian empire by reflecting on the importance of the Nile, and its role in agricultural production and trade. Though this may seem like an odd place to begin an analysis of the relation between media and empire, Innis's discussion of the Nile moves quickly from the water itself to the necessity of creating a calendar that could accurately predict the river's annual floods. The first such calendar, which relied upon astronomy to reconcile the lunar calendar with the solar year, imposed Ra – the Sun god – as the supreme author of the universe. From roughly 2895 to 2540 BC, this "divinely inspired" calendar affirmed an absolute monarchy in which the Pharaoh – by controlling knowledge associated with the calendar – was elevated to the status of a god. The rigidly hierarchical character of society at this time was reflected in the dominant communication medium, pictorial hieroglyphic writing on stone. These sacred engravings functioned to consolidate power, allowing the Pharaoh to establish authority and control over all arable land. This authority was perhaps most evident in the construction of the pyramids and elaborate burial rites of the Pharaohs, which "suggested that the people expected the same miracles from the dead as from the living king."[21]

Over time, difficulties in the sidereal year created irregularities in the calendar, which the priests exploited to challenge the authority of the Pharaoh, who was lowered in status from an individual godhead to the Son of Ra. Eventually, the absolute monarch was replaced by a royal family when the clergy of Helkiopolis established a more contemporary calendar and imposed it on Egypt.[22] This shift in power led to the development of a more feudal society that ceded authority to local administrators and clergy. "The profound disturbances in Egyptian civilization involved in the shift from absolute monarchy to a more democratic organization," Innis noted, "coincides with a shift in emphasis on stone as a medium of communication or as a basis of prestige, as shown in the pyramids, to an emphasis on papyrus."[23] As power was increasingly decentralized, the necessity for administrative communications increased. This led to the development of new forms of writing that were more secular and less like the sacred symbols used in hieroglyphics, a development that broadened literacy and brought even more change. In an effort to resist this change and re-centralize power, the scribes were elevated to the upper classes, which included priests and nobility. Though this re-centralization was successful in re-monopolizing knowledge over writing and thus accurate predictions about the Nile, it caused problems for ruling over a space that had grown quite large. Consequently, Innis argued, the new monopoly over writing defeated efforts to solve the problem of space and gradually cost Egypt its empire.[24] The ideas introduced by Innis in *Empire and Communications* would eventually be extended by a fellow professor at the University of Toronto, Marshall McLuhan.

Marshall McLuhan (1911–1980)

Herbert Marshall McLuhan began his academic career teaching English at St. Louis University in 1937. He continued teaching there even as he worked on his graduate degrees at University of Cambridge, England. McLuhan earned his PhD in 1942 after completing his dissertation on the historical development of the verbal arts or *trivium* (rhetoric, dialectic, and grammar). Prior to leaving St. Louis University for a position at a Canadian institution in 1944, McLuhan would direct Walter Ong's Master's thesis and introduce him to the topic on which he would later write his doctoral dissertation under Perry Miller's direction.[25] A few years later, McLuhan took up residence in Toronto, where he was influenced by the economist Harold Innis, and served for several years as chairperson for the Ford Foundation Seminar on Culture and Communication. During that time, McLuhan published his first book, a broad-ranging study of popular culture, titled *The Mechanical Bride: Folklore of Industrial Man.* But it was another book, *The Gutenberg Galaxy: The Making of Typographic Man* (1962), that established McLuhan as a major scholar of medium theory.

The Gutenberg Galaxy is a sustained study of not only the printing press's influence on European culture, but also on human consciousness itself. According to McLuhan, technologies create unique technological environments that modify our "*forms* of thought and the organization of experience in society and politics."[26] For McLuhan, moveable-type printing constituted a decisive break from the oral societies of the past and produced "Gutenberg man:" a subject who was characterized by rational, linear thought processes. The cognitive reorganization of humans was accompanied by an equally dramatic social reorganization, not the least of which included the creation of *publics.* Prior to the development of mass printing, there was no way to create publics on a national scale, and indeed, what we call "nations" could not, McLuhan argues, have preceded Gutenberg's invention. For both individuals and publics, the printing press fostered a visually oriented self-consciousness, which isolated the visual faculty from the other senses and affirmed the principles of uniformity and continuity. Linking technologies to specific senses was one of McLuhan's key contributions to media studies. In his view, each medium is an extension of human senses, limbs, or processes, and therefore of ourselves.[27]

Since different communication technologies privilege different senses, the prevalence of certain technologies at any given historical moment contributes to our overall *sensory balance.* Based on the idea of sensory balance, McLuhan argues all of human history can be divided into three major epochs or periods: oral, writing/print, and electronic. In each of these periods, what matters in not the content delivered by media, but the character of the medium itself. To illustrate this point, McLuhan adopts the example of electric light in chapter one of his most famous book, *Understanding Media: The Extensions of Man* (1964). He explained:

> The electric light is pure information. It is a medium without a message, as it were[.] . . . Whether the light is being used for brain surgery or night baseball is a matter of indifference. It could be argued that these activities are in some way the "content" of the electric light, since they could not exist without the electric light. This fact merely underlines the point that "the medium is the message" because it is the medium that shapes and controls the scale and form of human association and action.[28]

In the remainder of the book, McLuhan proceeds to identify the unique characteristics of various media using his distinction between hot and cool media as a broad template.

A **hot medium** is one that "extends a single sense in 'high definition,'" while a **cool medium** is "low definition" because it is "high in participation or completion by the audience."[29] For McLuhan, the distinction is not so much an either/or, as it is a spectrum for evaluating the degree to which media are low or high in participation. Media such as radio, photographs, film, and the phonetic alphabet are relatively hot, while media such as television, telephones, speech, and cartoons are comparatively cool. This distinction can be a confusing one, especially if one is encountering it for the first time. To underscore the point McLuhan is making, it is helpful to consider his inspiration. Paul Levinson offers this insightful history:

> McLuhan's invocation of hot and cool derived from jazz slang for brassy, big band music that overpowers and intoxicates the soul (hot) versus wispy, tinkly stretches of sound that intrigue and seduce the psyche (cool). The brassiness of the big band bounces off us, knocks us out—we neither embrace it nor are immersed in it—in contrast to the cool tones that breeze through us and bid our senses to follow like the Pied Piper.[30]

So, whereas hot media fully satiate the senses (at least those that they engage), cool media have less clarity, depth, and vividness, and therefore invite our involvement; they ask us to fill in the details. Film is a hot medium because it asks very little from us, supplying all the necessary input. Television is cool, by contrast, because it is incomplete, less overwhelming than cinema, and more fleeting. The distinction between hot and cool media has been criticized in recent years as being too sweeping in scope. McLuhan, much like Innis, tended to take a very expansive view of history and culture: an approach that, while very useful in charting broad patterns, potentially misses the subtleties of various communication technologies.

Walter J. Ong (1912–2003)

If Marshall McLuhan's work is characterized by its breadth and generalizations, Walter J. Ong's work is defined by its historical depth and specificity. A Jesuit Catholic priest, Ong spent most of his academic career at St. Louis University as Professor of Humanities in Psychiatry and then William E. Haren Professor of English. He had earned his doctorate degree in English from Harvard University in 1955 after completing his dissertation on the French logician Peter Ramus. Ong's dissertation would lead the publication of *Ramus, Method, and the Decay of Dialogue: From the Art of Discourse to the Art of Reason* in 1958 in which he argued that the emergence of a visualist print culture enabled a new, mathematical state of mind in the Middle Ages. In his 1967 *The Presence of the Word: Some Prolegomena for Cultural and Religious History*, which was based upon his Terry Lectures delivered at Yale in 1964, Ong turns to the "word" – man's [sic] primary medium of communication – and its successive stages or transformations: (1) oral or oral-aural, (2) script (alphabet and print), and (3) electronic.[31] In that work, Ong explores the phenomenon of (word as) sound, arguing that it "is more real or existential than other sense objects [such as sight]" because it (i.e. the sensory experience of hearing) is a happening in time that, though evanescent, produces a feeling of liveliness.[32]

Ong's most in-depth study of **orality** or "thought and its verbal expression,"[33] however, comes in his 1982 book, *Orality and Literacy: The Technologizing of the Word*. The most popular of Ong's writings, *Orality and Literacy* has been translated into more than 10 languages. It explores the profound changes to society and human consciousness that accompanied the shift from orality to **literacy** or the technologies of writing and print in Ancient Greece. For Ong, primary oral cultures or voice-and-ear cultures are ones that have no known literate modes of communication. Nine psychodynamics characterize such cultures. Specifically, thought and expression are: (1) additive rather than subordinative, with ideas piled one upon the next; (2) aggregative rather than analytic, in which clusters of words aid in memory; (3) redundant or "copious" to keep the listener oriented; (4) conservative or traditionalist to preserve the passing along of knowledge; (5) close to the human lifeworld, as abstraction is not easily recalled; (6) agonistically toned so as to encourage intellectual combat and test ideas; (7) empathic and participatory rather than objectively distanced, which fosters communal identification; (8) homeostatic or concerned with the present more than the past; and (9) situational rather than abstract, for memory is biased toward that which is concrete.[34]

As a consequence of these psychodynamics, people in oral cultures do not know history the way people in literate and electronic cultures do. In oral cultures, one is constantly losing contact with the past because of the fleeting character of speech. Since nothing is recorded or written down in primary orality, there is no way to look anything up. Thus, the only way to learn something other than through direct experience is to ask another living person. If there is no one who experienced or can recall what one wishes to know, then that information or knowledge is lost. This is, of course, quite different than in literature cultures, where technologies of writing and print allow for the storage and retrieval of knowledge (e.g. libraries). The transition from orality to literacy also shifted our sensory experience of the world from predominantly one of sound, which is group-oriented, to one of sight, which is individually oriented. Reading is, after all, an inward, isolated, introverted practice. Memory also decreased in importance with the rise of literacy, as events could now be recorded for posterity. Today, of course, virtually anything can be looked up on the internet in a matter of seconds. For Ong though, electronic media such as telephones, radio, motion pictures, television, and computers have given rise to "secondary orality" by restoring the strong group sense associated with the spoken word. He did not see the new orality as identical to primary orality, however, and noted that, "secondary orality generates a sense for groups immeasurably larger than those of primary oral culture: McLuhan's 'global village'."[35] Ong stopped short of identifying the psychodynamics and social impacts on thought of secondary orality, as the electronic revolution was still in its infancy.[36] Drawing on the work of recent medium theorists, our aim in the final section is to chart the key features and logics of secondary orality.

Charting the Third Wave

There is, as of yet, no consensus on precisely what to call contemporary culture. It has variously been referred to as postmodern, electronic, digital, secondary orality, and the *third wave*. We have settled on the last of these phrases, which was coined by futurologist Alvin Toffler in 1980,[37] because despite the diverse terminological preferences of medium theorists, they all seem to agree that if history is measured according to communication technologies, then we now inhabit the third stage of human history. Furthermore, as a dramatic swelling or disturbance that moves through space and time, and ends with the transfer of energy, the "wave" metaphor is especially apt. For most scholars, the social changes that characterize the transition from print culture to third-wave culture are no less striking and significant than those marking the shift from orality to literacy. The changes wrought by the rise of new information technologies such as television and computers are nothing short of paradigmatic: a fundamental restructuring of social life and human consciousness. In this section, we begin by identifying the central features of third-wave media, and then consider how repeated exposure to those features fosters a unique way of perceiving, knowing, and being.

Characteristics of third-wave media

1   Nonlinear/decentered. Third-wave media are *nonlinear* in structure, meaning that they typically do not have a prescribed beginning or ending. Consequently, media users can enter (or exit) the text (i.e. content or message) at any point and then move from that point to any other point. The printed word, by contrast, is highly linear, leading the reader along a sequential and predetermined path. While printed material only makes sense when read in accordance with the prescribed order, it is not at all uncommon to listen to songs on an iPod at random. Indeed, most MP3 players are equipped with a shuffle function. Similarly, television, which has often been described as an endless flow of images, and the internet, which is highly decentered, do not require the user to start and end in specific places to have meaningful experiences. The unique hypertextual structure of the internet allows users to jump easily to personal points of interest without following a preset sequence of points.

2   Dynamic/indeterminate. Third-wave media are both *dynamic* or perpetually unfinished and *indeterminate* or endlessly mutable. Printed material such as newspapers and book are very difficult to update and tend therefore to be highly static. Alternatively, television and the internet continuously create and add new episodes and webpages. Moreover, the traversal function or means of moving between textons – the smallest unit of meaningful textuality – is marked by instability. On television and the internet, the relationship among textons is in constant flux, as TV programming schedules are reshuffled and hyperlinks are

updated. Printed material is not only linear, it is also fixed. The *arrangement* of textons does not change. The information on page 18, for instance, is always followed by the information on page 19 in a printed manuscript. Thus, the structure of information in third-wave media is unstable as well as nonlinear.

3   Collaborative/interactive. Whereas print media entail the dissemination of single-authored messages to more or less passive receivers, third-wave media foster *collaborative* production. Perhaps the most obvious example of this capacity on the internet is Wikipedia, where information can be added or altered by users. Blogs operate in a similar manner, allowing users to both contribute and respond to others. Since third-wave media are nonlinear, users must make choices and actively input those choices through interface devices such as keyboards, joysticks, or remote controls to experience a medium's content. In a very real sense, the user is a co-creator of the content by giving it a particular form and structure. Third-wave media have begun to collapse the old boundaries between producer and consumer, sender and receiver, author and reader. To engage with third-wave media is itself an act of authorship.

4   Image/iconicity. One of the principal traits of third-wave media is the implementation of simple and easily identifiable visual signs. Though the words on a page are also visual signs, they are not quickly and easily processed. The linear structure of language necessitates that signs (i.e. individual words) be processed temporally or literally in time. Images function differently, however. Because the signs (i.e. lines, shapes, colors) that comprise images are not sequential, they can be processed simultaneously, which allows images to communicate complex messages clearly and efficiently. The windows environment typical of computers today replaced the early DOS environment for precisely that reason. Through metonymy, desktop icons quickly convey meanings or ideas that are considerably more complex.

Logics of third-wave media

The traits of non-linear/decentered, dynamic/indeterminate, collaborative/interactive, and image/iconicity all serve to distinguish third-wave media and culture from the print-based culture of modernity. The rise of third-wave media and corresponding decline of print media have resulted in a series of seismic social and cultural changes. In the remainder of this chapter, we consider how third-wave media are remaking human consciousness by examining the four key logics that underlie the new information technologies.

1   Associative/spatial. The highly linear character of print media favors a mode of information processing rooted in causality and temporality. It invites us to make sense of our world in terms of scientific rationalism, where actions and events have direct, measurable consequences. Indeed, the scientific method is designed to allow scientists to conduct experiments that determine causality (such as how

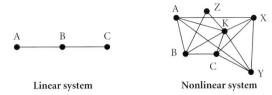

Figure 12.1
Linear and nonlinear
systems.

Linear system   Nonlinear system

objects move) in the physical world. In contrast to traditional print media, third-wave media are structured as nonlinear networks, which invite lateral connections and favor *associational* logic.[38] In a linear system, moving from point A to point C demands passage through point B. But in a nonlinear system, there are multiple channels for moving from point A to point C, many of which do not involve point B at all (see Figure 12.1).

Repeated exposure to nonlinear systems such as third-wave media trains the mind to perceive the world spatially rather than temporally: to see the connection among individual nodal points (or textons) as relational rather than causal. For philosopher Mark Taylor linear systems produce grids, while nonlinear systems produce networks.[39] The difference between the two is evident in the architecture that employs these concepts (see Figures 12.2 and 12.3). In a grid, there are centers, straight lines, and a rational use of space; in a network, there are flows, curves, and aesthetic (non-rational) spaces.

The nonlinear, relational, associative logic of third-wave media is evident in the practice of *surfing*. One can channel surf on television, station surf on radio, web surf online, and even crowd surf at concerts. With each generation, surfing becomes an increasingly common way of navigating media and the world. Studies of remote control use, for instance, have found that young viewers are far more likely than older viewers are to "zap:" to switch from one channel to another during a program.[40] Fundamentally, surfing is about surface and "gap jumping" rather than depth and following a straight line. Thanks to the hypertextual structure of the internet, one can jump directly to required information by using a search engine like Google instead of following an outdated linear structure like the Dewey Decimal System.[41] In *Playing the Future*, media guru Douglas Rushkoff argues that it is no accident that snowboarding emerged when it did. Snowboarders have internalized the logic of surfing, which they literally perform as they navigate their way down a mountain; for Rushkoff, skiing reflects the old linear logic of print and snowboarding the new nonlinear logic of third-wave media.[42]

2   Provisional/adaptable. A second key logic underlying third-wave media is provisionality/adaptability. The rise of anti-essentialist and anti-foundational philosophy, which rejects correspondence theories of truth, partially accounts for the increase in contingent and conditional thinking. As Richard Rorty explains in *Contingency, Irony, and Solidarity*, "Truth cannot be out there – exist independently of the human mind – because sentences [i.e. language] cannot

Figure 12.2
Seagram Building
and grid architecture.
PHILIP GENDREAU/
BETTMANN/CORBIS.

Figure 12.3
Guggenheim
Museum and
network
architecture.
IAN DAGNAL/ALAMY.

so exist, or be out there. The [physical] world is out there, but descriptions of the world are not."[43] Since there is no natural connection, no necessary correspondence, between language (a fully human construction) and the physical word, linguistic description or visual depiction of the world is always an approximation, a particular point of view. As Kenneth Burke succinctly put it, "Every way of seeing is also a way of not seeing: a focus on object A involves a neglect of object B"[44] Third-wave media have been central to this (re)cognition by collapsing physical space, and exposing audiences to multiple perspectives and points of view. In a global world, it is increasingly difficult to cling to the idea that one has access to ultimate truth because one literally sees the many truths of a situation. The dynamic, indeterminate, multi-perspectival, global character of third-wave media all function to train the mind to see "facts" as provisional. As a result, young people today tend to be more adaptable to change, as change is a common feature of their cultural environment.

3   Prosumerly. Whereas print media privilege a logic of consumption and passive reception, third-wave media promote a logic production and active creation. By "productive," we do not mean to suggest that the logic of third-wave media is worthwhile and the logic of print media worthless. Rather, we are suggesting that third-wave media "produces" something new and unintended by its "original" author/creator. Given the collaborative/interactive quality of third-wave media, users take on the role of author and creator; they "produce" texts, meanings, and experiences that are uniquely theirs. Though audiences have always been central to the interpretive process, third-wave media make user

collaboration explicit and central, rather than hidden and peripheral.[45] This logic is an especially valuable one in an age of fragmentation and information over-load, as it allows users to (re)combine cultural fragments and textons in ways that aid them in confronting and resolving the challenges of everyday living.

4   Decisiveness. One of the greatest challenges faced by individuals today is the sheer volume of information they must confront. Changes in the production, flow, and format of information have led to an unprecedented explosion of infor-mation.[46] In 1989, Richard Saul Wurman noted that "A weekday edition of *The New York Times* contains more information than the average person was likely to come across in a lifetime in seventeenth-century England," adding that, "More new information has been produced in the last 30 years than in the previous 5,000."[47] With so many signs (re)circulating in society, it is more important that ever the people be able to process information quickly. The logic of decisive-ness is embedded in the iconicity of third-wave media. Repeated exposure to icons, which create meaning through visual metonymy, fosters a logic of reduc-tion and immediate assessment over extended exposition. Contemporary cul-ture increasingly invites people to make snap judgments about what to watch, to stay on a website or to move on, to answer the phone or not, and to open and read an email or delete it. There is, then, a strong connection between the perspective of equipment for living and medium theory, for as media technologies change, they also reform human consciousness in ways that function as equip-ment for living.

Conclusion

The conclusion to the eleventh and final perspective, Ecological analysis, is in many ways a fitting conclusion to the book as a whole. Media Ecology is, after all, about seeing the big picture, about understanding the way that media both help us live our lives, by confronting its many challenges, and shape our lives by influencing how we process and make sense of our social world. Despite their obvious differ-ences, equipment for living and medium theory are both concerned with broad pat-terns, with our cultural environment and the experiences it entails. The latter perspective, medium theory, has for many years been unfairly criticized as deter-minist, as suggesting too strong a link between communication technologies and the structure and character of society. But it is precisely that relationship which medium theory seeks to understand, not simply to accept uncritically. Medium the-ory does not claim the social changes fueled by communication technologies are causal or unidirectional. It simply insists that the underlying form (technologies) of our social environment is as consequential as the content (messages). And just as society cannot be reduced exclusively to form or content, nor can critical media studies be reduced to solitary, universal perspective. We hope the many perspect-ives presented here affirm that.

MEDIA LAB 11: DOING ECOLOGICAL ANALYSIS

OBJECTIVE

The chief aim of this lab is affirm the principles of Media Ecology by furnishing students with an opportunity to examine the symbolic equipments of a media text and the features and logics of a specific medium.

ACTIVITY

- Divide the class into small groups of 4–5.
- Equipment for Living: show the *South Park* episode, "Over Logging," and then answer the following questions.
  1   What social anxiety does this episode stage?
  2   Who is the comic fool and how is he shown the error of his ways?
  3   What symbolic resources does the episode provide for confronting the social anxiety it stages?
- Medium Theory: invite students to select a contemporary communication technology such as the cell phone and then answer the following questions:
  1   What are the key characteristics of this technology?
  2   What "logics" do those characteristics foster?

SUGGESTED READING

Altheide, D.L. and Snow, R.P. *Media Worlds in the Postjournalism Era*. New York: Aldine de Gruyter, 1991.

Angus, I. *Primal Scenes of Communication: Communication, Consumerism, and Social Movements*. Albany, NY: State University of New York Press, 2000.

Brummett, B. Burke's Representative Anecdote as a Method in Media Criticism. *Critical Studies in Mass Communication* 1, 1984, 161–76.

Brummett, B. Electric Literature as Equipment for Living: Haunted House Films. *Critical Studies in Mass Communication* 9, 1985, 247–61.

Burke, K. Literature as Equipment for Living. In *The Philosophy of Literary Form: Studies in Symbolic Action*, pp. 293–304. Baton Rouge, LA: Louisiana State University Press, 1941.

Castells, M., Fernández-Ardèvol, M., Qiu, J.L., and Sey, A. *Mobile Communication and Society: A Global Perspective*. Cambridge, MA: The MIT Press, 2007.

Chesebro, J.W. and Bertelsen, D.A. *Analyzing Media: Communication Technologies as Symbolic and Cognitive Systems*. New York: Guildford Press, 1996.

Gronbeck, B.E., Farrell, T.J., and Soukup, P.A. (eds) *Media Consciousness, and Culture: Explorations of Walter Ong's Thought*. Newbury Park, CA: Sage Publications, 1991.

Havelock, E.A. *Preface to Plato*. Cambridge, MA: Harvard University Press, 1982.

Havelock, E.A. *The Muse Learns to Write: Reflections on Orality and Literacy from Antiquity to the Present*. New Haven, CT: Yale University Press, 1988.

Innis, H.A. *The Bias of Communication*. Toronto: University of Toronto Press, 1964.

Innis, H.A. *Empire and Communications*. Toronto: University of Toronto Press, 1972.

Levinson, P. *The Soft Edge: a Natural History and Future of the Information Revolution*. New York: Routledge, 1997.

Levinson, P. *Digital McLuhan: a Guide to the Information Millennium*. New York: Routledge, 1999.

Manovich, L. *The Language of New Media*. Cambridge, MA: The MIT Press, 2001.

McLuhan, M. *The Gutenberg Galaxy: The Making of Typographic Man*. Toronto: University of Toronto Press, 1962.

McLuhan, M. *Understanding Media: The Extensions of Man*. New York: McGraw-Hill Book Company, 1964.

McLuhan, M. and Powers, B.R. *The Global Village: Transformations in World Life and Media in the 21st Century*. New York: Oxford University Press, 1989.

Meyrowitz, J. *No Sense of Place: The Impact of Electronic Media on Social Behavior*. New York: Oxford University Press, 1985.

Meyrowitz, J. Medium Theory. In *Communication Theory Today*, Crowley, D. and Mitchell, D. (eds), pp. 50–77. Stanford, CA: Stanford University Press, 1994.

Meyrowitz, J. Taking McLuhan and 'Medium Theory' Seriously: Technological Change and the Evolution of Education. In *Technology and the Future of Schooling: Ninety-fifth Yearbook of the National Society for the Study of Education. Part II*, S.T. Kerr (ed.), 73–110. Chicago, IL: University of Chicago Press, 1996.

Meyrowitz, J. Multiple Media Literacies. *Journal of Communication* 48, 1998, 96–108.

Ong, W.J. *Orality and Literacy: The Technologizing of the Word*. New York: Routledge, 1982.

Ong, W.J. *The Presence of the Word: Some Prolegomena for Cultural and Religious History*. Binghamton, NY: Global Publications, 2000.

Postman, N. The Reformed English Curriculum. In *High School 1980: The Shape of the Future in American Secondary Education*, A.C. Eurich (ed.), pp. 160–8. New York: Pitman Publishing Corporation, 1970.

Postman. N. *The Disappearance of Childhood*. New York: Vintage Books, 1982.

Postman, N. *Technopoly: The Surrender of Culture to Technology*. New York: Alfred A. Knopf, 1992.

Stephens, M. *The Rise of the Image the Fall of the Word*. New York: Oxford University Press, 1998.

NOTES

1. R.D. Putnam, *Bowling Alone: the Collapse and Revival of American Community* (New York: Simon & Schuster, 2000).

2. N. Postman, The Reformed English Curriculum, *High School 1980: The Shape of the Future in American Secondary Education*, A.C. Eurich (ed.) (New York: Pitman Publishing Corporation, 1970), 161.

3. J. Meyrowitz, Multiple Media Literacies, *Journal of Communication* 48, 1998, 103.

4. K. Burke, Literature as Equipment for Living, in *The Philosophy of Literary Form: Studies in Symbolic Action* (Baton Rouge, LA: Louisiana State University Press, 1941), 299.

5. K. Burke, *Towards a Better Life: Being a Series of Epistles or Declamations* (Berkeley, CA: University of California Press, 1966), vii, vi.

6. K. Burke, *Attitudes Toward History*, 3rd edn (Berkeley, CA: University of California Press, 1984), 336.

7. M.P. Moore, To Execute Capital Punishment: the Mortification and Scapegoating of Illinois Governor George Ryan, *Western Journal of Communication* 70, 2006, 312. In Burke's words,

"Mortification is the scrupulous and deliberate clamping of limitation upon the self." See K. Burke, *Permanence and Change: an Anatomy of Purpose*, revised edn (Los Altos, CA: Hermes Publications, 1954), 289.

8. Burke, *Attitudes*, 41.
9. B. Brummett, Burkean Comedy and Tragedy, Illustrated in Reactions to the Arrest of John Delorean, *Central States Speech Journal* 35, 1984, 220.
10. K. Burke, *Counter-Statement* (Los Altos, CA: Hermes Publications, 1931), 139.
11. B. Brummett, Burke's Representative Anecdote as a Method in Media Criticism, *Critical Studies in Mass Communication* 1, 1984, 161.
12. B. Brummett, Electric Literature as Equipment for Living: Haunted House Films, *Critical Studies in Mass Communication* 2, 1985, 247–61.
13. Meyrowitz, Multiple, 103.
14. J. Meyrowitz, Medium Theory, in *Communication Theory Today*, D. Crowley and D. Mitchell (eds) (Stanford, CA: Stanford University Press, 1994), 50.
15. Meyrowitz, Medium Theory, 51.
16. Meyrowitz, Medium Theory, 52.
17. H.A. Innis, *Empire and Communications* (Toronto: University of Toronto Press, 1972), 7.
18. I. Angus, *Primal Scenes of Communication: Communication, Consumerism, and Social Movement* (Albany, NY: State University of New York, 2000), 20.
19. Innis, 7.
20. Innis, 7.
21. Innis, 14.
22. Innis, 15.
23. Innis, 15.
24. Innis, 25.
25. T.J. Farrell, An Overview of Walter Ong's Work, *Media, Consciousness, and Culture: Explorations of Walter Ong's Thought*, B.E. Gronbeck, T.J. Farrell, and P.A. Soukup (eds) (Newbury Park, CA: Sage Publications, 1991), 27.
26. M. McLuhan, *The Gutenberg Galaxy: the Making of Typographic Man* (Toronto: University of Toronto Press, 1962), 1.
27. Meyrowitz, Medium Theory, 52.

28. M. McLuhan, *Understanding Media: the Extensions of Man* (New York: McGraw-Hill Book Company, 1964), 8–9.
29. McLuhan, *Understanding Media*, 22–3.
30. P. Levinson, *Digital McLuhan: a Guide to the Information Millennium* (New York: Routledge, 1999), 106.
31. W.J. Ong, *The Presence of the Word: Some Prolegomena for Cultural and Religious History* (Binghamton, NY: Global Publications, 2000), 17.
32. Ong, *The Presence*, 111.
33. W.J. Ong, *Orality and Literacy: The Technologizing of the Word* (New York: Routledge, 1982), 1.
34. Ong, *Orality*, 37–50.
35. Ong, *Orality*, 136.
36. B.E. Gronbeck, The Rhetorical Studies Tradition and Walter J. Ong: Oral-Literacy Theories of Mediation, Culture, and Consciousness, *Media, Consciousness, and Culture: Explorations of Walter Ong's Thought*, B.E. Gronbeck, T.J. Farrell, and P.A. Soukup (eds) (Newbury Park, CA: Sage Publications, 1991), 15.
37. A. Toffler, *The Third Wave* (New York: William Morrow and Company, 1980).
38. D.D. Cali, The Logic of the Link: The Associative Paradigm in Communication Criticism, *Critical Studies in Media Communication* 17, 2000, 401.
39. M.C. Taylor, *The Moment of Complexity: Emerging Network Culture* (Chicago, IL: University of Chicago Press, 2001), 19–46.
40. R.V. Bellamy Jr and J.R. Walker, *Television and the Remote Control: Grazing on a Vast Wasteland* (New York: Guilford Press, 1996), 97; see also J.W. Chesebro and D.A. Bertelsen, *Analyzing Media: Communication Technologies as Symbolic and Cognitive Systems* (New York: Guildford Press, 1996), 134.
41. On this point, see M. Heim, *The Metaphysics of Virtual Reality* (Oxford: Oxford University Press, 1993), 34–9.
42. D. Rushkoff, *Playing the Future: How Kids' Culture Can Teach Us to Thrive in an Age of Chaos* (New York: HarperCollins, 1996), 15–16.
43. R. Rorty. *Contingency, Irony, and Solidarity* (New York: Cambridge University Press, 1989), 5.

44. K. Burke, *Permanence and Change: an Anatomy of Purpose*, 3rd edn (Berkeley, CA: University of California Press, 1954), 49.

45. B.L. Ott and B. Bonnstetter, "We're at Now, Now": *Spaceballs* as Parodic Tourism, *Southern Journal of Communication* 72, 2007, 322.

46. B.L. Ott, *The Small Screen: How Television Equips Us to Live in the Information Age* (Malden, MA: Blackwell Publishing, 2007), 29.

47. R.S. Wurman, *Information Anxiety* (New York: Doubleday, 1989), 34–5.

13 Conclusion: the Partial Pachyderm

We begin with a rather obscure American poet: John Godfrey Saxe. Saxe was born in Vermont in 1816 and worked throughout his life as a lawyer and newspaper editor in addition to writing poetry. His most famous rhyme (indeed, his only famous piece of work at all) is a poem titled "The Blind Men and the Elephant," a retelling of a classic Indian fable. The poem opens in India with six blind men approaching an elephant in order to better understand what the animal looks like as a whole. The fact that these men, presumably, have lived their entire lives in India but have never encountered an elephant prior to this occasion is not addressed. The first man approaches the elephant and, feeling the side of the creature with his hands, proclaims to the others that the elephant is best understood as something like a living wall: rough, hard, and very large. The second man, eager to join the first, happens to grasp onto the elephant's tusk instead of its side. As a result, he loudly disputes the first man's claim and says that the elephant is *really* more like a spear: smooth, pointy, and sharp. Each of the other four men approach the elephant in succession, and each provides his own interpretation of what an elephant *really* looks like: a snake (when grasping the animal's trunk), a tree (when touching its legs), a fan (when caressing its large ears), and a rope (when holding onto its tale). An argument ensues. Saxe concludes the poem by imparting a moral to the reader regarding the pitfalls of perception:

> So oft in theologic wars,
> The disputants, I ween,
> Rail on in utter ignorance
> At what each other mean,
> *And prate about an Elephant*
> *Not one of them have seen!*[1]

At this point you may be asking, what does an elephant have to do with approaches to critical media studies? Beyond the fact that both can, in certain circumstances, crush an eager individual new to the field, Saxe's poem provides an important allegory for a metatheoretical approach to media studies. If we replace the word "theologic" with "theoretical" in Saxe's concluding stanza, we arrive at a fairly useful warning for anyone engaging in the critical study of contemporary media. Despite what the individual theorists addressed in this book may think, no single approach covered in these pages is the correct or best interpretation of this strange creature we call the media. Instead, each represents one way of grasping the media to better understand a certain part. Marxist analysis, Rhetorical analysis, and Reception analysis can each only tell us so much about the role of the media in society, and confusing any individual part for the whole only closes down inquiry, misrepresents phenomena, and stunts the growth of the field overall.

Thus, we conclude this theoretical adventure by looking again at the widely disparate approaches to media studies in an attempt to synthesize them into an entire "elephant." The fact that each approach "discovers" a different part of the mass media does not mean that they are all distinct or mutually exclusive. We contend that a critical understanding of the media is useful to the extent that it recognizes the interconnectedness of the various approaches and traditions represented here. Useful knowledge comes from the understanding that all of the parts of the media, from tusk to tail, are deeply intertwined and influence one another. Only by recognizing this fact can we begin to think of ways to apply the critique of media to issues of media reform. Toward this end, the first part of this concluding chapter provides a critical overview of the different approaches discussed in this book, with particular attention on their intersections and various combinations. The second extends these critical ideas to the ways in which individuals are transforming how we interact with the mass media through pedagogy, activism, and new media outlets.

Critical Media Studies: an Overview

We opened this textbook by considering the very basic function of the media as a source of knowledge for human beings. Much of what we know about the world we live in comes to us in mediated forms, rather than through the direct experience of different phenomena. At this point, if you have read through our entire book (or even if you only poached from select chapters), you now know something about the mass media that you didn't know before. An understanding of Erotic analysis, for example, came to you not by ruminating on a bodily response you had to media text, but *through* the medium of this very book. In an image-saturated society like our own, the acquisition of knowledge through the media is becoming more and more common. As such, it is important to understand the multiple, often conflicting ways of analyzing the mass media. We divided this analysis into three parts: theories of media industries, media messages, and media audiences.

Approaches to media industries

If pressed to identify the legs of our mass media elephant, we would be tempted to offer the various theoretical approaches to media industries as a possible answer. As the oldest and longest-standing strand of critical media studies (dating back to the work of the Frankfurt School in 1923), approaches to media industries are often the base of the traditions that followed them, if only as implied and "incorrect" perspectives that more recent traditions respond to and critique. To say that these approaches are the "base" of critical media studies is not to imply that they are any more or less correct than the other approaches. Instead, approaches to media industries represent the first time scholars and theorists took the mass media as a serious or important force in everyday life. As such, these perspectives inaugurated the discipline of critical media studies and deserve to be called the base of contemporary critique and analysis. We divide the study of industries into three different approaches: Marxist analysis, Organizational analysis, and Pragmatic analysis.

Marxist analysis. The section on media industries began with Marxist analysis, or a focus on the role of economic exchange and the profit-motive on the structure of the media industry and the content that mass outlets produce. Following the canonical work of Karl Marx, Marxist scholars look at the ways in which the economic base of a society influences – or, in classic/vulgar Marxism, actually determines – the make-up of its cultural superstructure. Marxist media critics contend that those who control the means of media production (the Big Five corporations that own the vast majority of media outlets) shape the look and form of media content to secure their continued profit and economic domination. In addition to this ever-present goal, carried out through strategies of profit maximization like cross-promotional networks and the logic of safety, the capitalist profit-motive and the media content it inspires have important consequences for our daily lives. Marxist scholars reveal how the economic logic of media industries, in turn, restricts the possibility of variation and diversity in media content. This is a vital connection between Marxist scholars and the ideological work of Cultural analysis (Chapter 6). Though Marxist critics disagree with their Cultural counterparts over the *source* and primacy of ideological power, or the ability to enforce one's personal interpretation as the standard for "reality," both camps agree that the concept of ideology is an important lens of interpretation when it comes to studying the mass media.

Organizational analysis. The next chapter in the media industries section, Organizational analysis, concentrated on the ways that the matrix of hierarchies and relationships present in any media industry influences the production of its media content. In other words, Organizational media scholars contend that the economy is but one factor in a larger nexus of interconnected pieces that make up a media industry. The chapter undertook an in-depth case study of contemporary news organizations as a way of understanding this perspective. The news, far from standing as an objective account of the most important events happening on any given day, is in fact shaped by the norms and practices of the organization that produces it. The fact that a newspaper must fill its pages every day regardless of the day's actual events, or the fact that a journalist covers and reports on a particular beat even if nothing really happens in that sphere of society, begins to point out how issues of process and professionalization color the supposedly factual news. Organizational analysis is an important extension of Marxist analysis because it reveals how an industry, though based in economic necessity, can begin to run on its own cultural conventions somewhat divorced from the capitalist profit-motive.

Pragmatic analysis. We concluded the section on media industries with Pragmatic analysis, an original perspective by which to assess the federal and self-regulation of these industries. While many authors consider this very important area of analysis through the lenses of politics or history, we feel that the philosophy of pragmatism and its focus on consequences and contingencies is an appropriate and fruitful lens of assessment. By evaluating a media regulation – be it the US Telecommunications Act of 1996 or the broadcast of indecent content – through pragmatic standards of truth or "goodness," scholars can come to a better understanding of quality media control in contemporary life. This chapter also considered the always-current debate over violence in the media as an important case study in Pragmatic analysis, especially because so much of the debate relies upon the perceived effect of mediated violence on children. Though the debate is long from over, we hope that other scholars find our particular application of Pragmatic philosophy to be a productive springboard for the way we understand media regulation in the years to come.

Approaches to media messages

The next content section, on media messages, could be likened to the body of our theoretical elephant. When people refer to "the mass media" in casual conversation, they are often referring to the variety and circulation of media messages and images: in a word, texts. Textual analysis has represented the bulk of critical media studies throughout its history in academic institutions around the world, but the project of understanding how the mass media paint reality is a complicated one, housing many different theoretical perspectives. Thus, while a close inspection of our creature's hide reveals a rough, bumpy, and diverse surface, these peaks and valleys are unified in their approach to analyzing issues of media representation and its subsequent influence. We divide our study of messages into five different approaches: Rhetorical analysis, Cultural analysis, Psychoanalytic analysis, Feminist analysis, and Queer analysis.

Rhetorical analysis. The first approach we considered in understanding media messages is Rhetorical analysis, the study of how the artful and purposeful combination of signs works to move audiences toward particular ends. In their most basic form, all texts can be conceived of as an association of signifying words and images. By understanding their specific combination, as well as noticing what signs are not present in the text, Rhetorical critics reveal how a text functions to persuade audiences to feel certain ways or to undertake particular actions. Although this approach dates back to the ancient Greek art of oratory, this chapter presented a number of different ways to understand the association between signs: clusters, form, genre, narrative, and affect. The textual "building block" approach of Rhetorical analysis outlined in this chapter is its key contribution to other areas of media studies. The critique of sexual representation taken up in Queer analysis, for example, would not be possible without first understanding *how* a text comes to signify and represent sexuality in the first place.

Cultural analysis. One of the longest-standing traditions of media analysis is the study of how texts embody and transmit ideology, the primary focus of Cultural analysis and the academic "interdiscipline" of Cultural studies. Ideology and the various forms it takes – myth, doxa, and hegemony – are implicit in any culture, and media texts are a primary site of ideological construction and reinforcement. Cultural studies scholars, in turn, deconstruct texts for the ways that they normalize relations of power between ideological subjects, which marks Cultural studies as the first of the many political approaches to media texts we cover in this book. This chapter focused primarily on the media representation of class and race as a way of practically understanding this approach, but in reality Cultural studies is interested in media representations associated with any axis of social power: race, class, gender, sexuality, age, disability, etc. In this way, the Cultural studies focus on the textual negotiation of power between social groups becomes a crucial framework in both Feminist and Queer analysis (Chapters 8 and 9, respectively). In addition, Cultural studies' tendency to elevate subordinate groups also becomes an important way to center media audiences, a project fully developed in Reception analysis (Chapter 10). Because of these various connections with other traditions, Cultural analysis and Cultural studies are virtual juggernauts in the field of critical media studies.

Psychoanalytic analysis. The midpoint in our discussion of media messages delved into the esoteric world of Psychoanalytic theories of desire and their convergence with film studies. Like Marxist analysis of the media, Psychoanalytic analysis adapts theories from an outside discipline into the realm of critical media studies. The formative theories of psychoanalysts Sigmund Freud and Jacques Lacan became a way for media scholars to understand how human desire and a shared compulsion toward wholeness manifest in relation to the movie theater and the cinematic image. Though perhaps the most theoretically obtuse of all the approaches discussed in this section, Psychoanalytic analysis provides a truly unique perspective on the role of desire and bodily pleasure in the consumption of film. This chapter diverges from other perspectives by deemphasizing the meaning of symbols and instead concentrating on why filmic texts may appeal to us on an unconscious level through the notions of regression, scopophilia, and fantasy. As a result, we can see echoes of psychoanalysis in Erotic analysis (Chapter 11) and its own focus on the audience's bodily "cruising" of texts.

Feminist analysis. The next approach we considered as a way of understanding media messages was Feminist analysis. A Feminist approach to media concentrates on how texts represent ideological categories of gender as biological or natural constants. Feminists seek to disrupt systems of sexism and patriarchal power that reify gender roles and privilege the needs, desires, and interests of men in society to the detriment of women. "Feminism" is a historically fluid term often contested and demonized in the popular consciousness, and this chapter demonstrates the complexity of Feminist analysis through its consideration of stereotypical media representations of both femininity *and* masculinity and the role of the postfeminist sensibility in contemporary media. These two concepts are important to a general Feminist analysis of media, but the various specific strands of feminist theory not discussed here (including Womanism, Ecofeminism, and Power Feminism, among others) provide an arsenal of critical tools for media scholars. These strands of feminism also become critical intersections with other political projects like Cultural studies and Queer theory (Chapters 6 and 9).

Queer analysis. The final chapter in the section on media messages looks at the approach of Queer analysis. Like Feminists with gender, Queer theorists analyze the ways in which media texts represent and normalize issues of sexuality as a basis for critique and social transformation. The political project of Queer theory intentionally eschews easy definition. It is the embodiment of a disruptive and elusive ambiguity that shatters social binaries and the ideological powers they maintain; "queerness" is a radical rejection of categories in relation to sexuality. This chapter looked at the notion of queerness in two different ways. The first considered stereotypical representations of heterosexuality and homosexuality in the media, looking at how each supported systems of heteronormativity that, in turn, render the categories coherent. The second used the work of Michel Foucault and Judith Butler to problematize the very notion of an individual sexuality at all. Taken together, these two sections give some form to a purposefully formless approach, and in them we can see the critical overlap between Queer analysis and other political projects (Cultural and Feminist analysis).

Approaches to media audiences

Recalling our elephant metaphor again, approaches to understanding media audiences would likely form the various appendages of our theoretical beast. Widespread, serious studies of the audience did not really begin in earnest until the 1970s, and in many ways these approaches represent the most shifting and mutable areas of study today. In fact, the final two chapters in this section represent our own syntheses of widely disparate theories into coherent traditions of audience studies. This indicates that approaches to media audiences are more fluid and ill-defined than their industry or textual counterparts. At the same time, we contend that audience studies are more uniquely communicative than either industry- or message-based approaches because they bring to the fore all of the classic aspects of human communication: signs and symbols, of course, but also feedback, perception, and environment. This is why we associate audience approaches with the ears, tail, and trunk of our elephant. These are the dynamic, shifting appendages that mark the elephant as a unique creature. We divide our study of audiences into three different approaches: Reception analysis, Erotic analysis, and Ecological analysis.

Reception analysis. Our first approach to the audience is Reception analysis, a tradition that takes the audience as the primary site of meaning-making in relation to the media. Rather than consider the economic underpinnings of a media text or investigate the power relations it reinscribes, reception scholars seek to understand the meanings that actual individuals make out of the media texts they consume everyday. They recognize that media producers may intend a text to mean something in particular, but they also point out that audiences may understand it in a radically different way. This chapter considered many different theories of meaning – including the encoding/decoding process, polysemy/polyvalence, and interpretive communities – before looking at the ethnographic method as a primary means of gathering data regarding audience perception. Reception theorists and ethnographers both challenge the traditional understanding of the audiences as a passive, vulnerable mass at the whims of the media, and lay the foundation for the type of work on individual pleasure central to Erotic analysis (Chapter 11).

Erotic analysis. The second approach to the audience we considered, and one that is original to this book, is called Erotic analysis. Erotic analysis takes the notion of pleasure as its central component in attempting to understand how audiences consume media. Positioning themselves in opposition to Marxist approaches to media, scholars employing an Erotic perspective understand pleasure as a powerfully resistive force. This chapter outlined three forms of audience pleasures and their resistive potential. The first, Barthes's notion of *jouissance* and the six forms of interpretive play which produce it, looked at how individuals "cruise" texts for bodily pleasure instead of "reading" texts for meaning. The second, the productive work of fandom and textual appropriation, analyzed how fans take media texts and refashion them to serve their own, personal needs. The third, participatory media and interactive technologies, considered how media technologies and outlets (iPods and MySpace, for example) fulfill particular needs in audiences and allow for the infinite possibility of play and meaning. Each erotic engagement of the media provides a form of resistance that, while fleeting, ultimately allows the user to escape the system of meanings and power outlined by all of the other critical perspectives. As such, Erotic analysis is a comment upon and important derivation from classic conceptions of the audience and the entire field of media studies.

Ecological analysis. We concluded the section on media audiences with another original synthesis of work on the media we call Ecological analysis. Media Ecologists consider how the media are not merely aspects or parts of our contemporary environment, but how media *are* our environment. Functioning as both symbolic and material resources, media are deeply and intricately connected to our lived experiences. This chapter covered two forms of media ecology: equipment for living and medium theory. Burke's theory of equipment for living explains how we can use the media to symbolically resolve guilt and conflict in our own lives, and medium theory (here represented by the work of Innis, McLuhan, and Ong) reveals how

changes in communication technology literally rewrite the means of human interaction and our understanding of reality. Perhaps the "broadest" approach, Ecological
analysis provides a novel way of understanding issues of media industry and representation. For example, while a Marxist may claim that economic factors direct the
media, a media ecologist would say that our very notion of the nation state (and
therefore the economy) is a result of the media technology of our age. Media influence
the very look and logic of the world in which we live.

Applied Media Studies

As we've just reviewed, this textbook outlines eleven different approaches to the
critical study of media. Now it is time to see what we can *do* with them. We've seen
inklings of application in the media labs at the end of every chapter, but, really,
what can we do in the world outside of the classroom with these theories? Why do
they matter, and what is the point of a class on critical media studies anyway? This
section, on the translation of media studies into social action, supplies three possible "things" to do with media theory: education, resistance, and reform. Each course
of action grounds the abstract understanding of media theory in political struggles
for meaning and change. As the novelist and poet Edith Wharton famously wrote,
"There are two ways of spreading light: to be the candle or the mirror that reflects
it."[2] If we consider the theoretical traditions outlined in these pages as the candles
of critical media studies (and the light our understanding of media), then the following three projects are the various ways of potentially acting as mirrors.

Media literacy

Media literacy is a difficult concept to pin down. Broadly, it refers to any learning opportunity that increases an individual's understanding of how the mass
media function. W. James Potter frames media literacy as a source of individual
empowerment:

> Becoming more media literate gives you a much clearer perspective to see the
> border between your real world and the world manufactured by the media. When
> you are media literate, you have clear maps to help you navigate better in the media
> world so that you can get to those experiences and information you want without
> becoming distracted by those things that are harmful to you.[3]

To be media literate, then, is to possess the dual understandings of how the mass
media function *and* how those modes of operation have bearing on one's daily life.
The critical awareness of the media and the interactions between individuals and
wider cultures connoted by the term "media literacy" are becoming increasingly

important as society relies more and more on media to transmit information or share values.

In reviewing current literature in the field, two major themes or conceptions of media literacy become apparent. The first is an emphasis on media *production* as a way of learning about how mass media generate and circulate messages. This interpretation of media literacy often takes the form of adolescent educational programs that allow young adults to record their own media messages. In creating their own media texts, adolescents learn about the kinds of decisions which all media creators face: how to tell a story, how to represent an idea, how to attract an audience, etc. The experience, especially if supplemented with critical inquiry or reflection, educates young people about the constraints of media production and its subsequent influence on representation and reception. A school's morning announcements or radio station can serve as an important learning site for understanding how to prioritize newsworthy information or build a station identity.[4] Classroom video projects reveal to young film makers how processes like editing change the ways audiences interpret messages.[5] Whatever the medium, this type of media literacy encourages young people to view the media as an active, participatory social outlet rather than as a distant, confusing network beyond their control. It also supplies them with a cursory understanding of how the media operates as a symbolic or cultural form.

Such an understanding of the symbolic codes, logics, and powers present in the media is central to the second major approach to media literacy. In this frame, media literacy represents the acquisition of explicitly critical tools in relation to aspects of media production, circulation, and reception. This textbook is firmly in line with this second strand of media literacy. By equipping you with different perspectives regarding power in the media (economic, ideological, or otherwise), this book increases your ability to understand the media in all its various forms and functions. You are now, in some ways, media literate: congratulations! Moreover, you are probably reading this text because you are enrolled in a college class organized around the theme of the media. Classes like your own are becoming increasingly common around the world and show much success in teaching students to carefully discern the structures and effects of contemporary media.[6] Likewise, recent studies show that general audience instruction in these kinds of critical perspectives can partially reduce stereotypical ideas of race and gender.[7] In short, then, this type of media literacy, inside or outside of the classroom, focuses on teaching the ideas one might conceive of as the "critical media tradition" in higher education.

Although this second approach to literacy is perhaps more cerebral or scholarly than the concurrent, "hands-on" focus of the production route, both interpretations represent the real-world application of critical media theories in appropriate contexts. The original generation of media content and the creation of college media courses are both productive responses to theoretical understandings of the media. Both represent important nodes of convergence between knowledge of the media and the *dissemination* of knowledge of the media. Overall, it may be best to understand media literacy projects as the distillation of abstract theory into concrete, localized activities and seminars, educating individuals on why the media matters (or should matter) to them.

Culture jamming

Near the end of his most widely known work, *Society of the Spectacle*, Guy Debord makes a curious statement on the role of plagiarism in contemporary culture:

> Ideas improve. The meaning of words participates in the involvement. Plagiarism is necessary. Progress implies it. It embraces an author's phrase, makes use of his expressions, erases a false idea, and replaces it with the right idea.[8]

Debord's interpretation of plagiarism as the appropriation and refashioning of pre-existing signs into the "right idea" is at the heart of the second area of media application we consider: culture jamming. **Culture jamming** is the use of familiar media symbols and channels to reveal and overturn the consumerist, capitalist ideologies they embody. Like media literacy, culture jamming is difficult to describe succinctly, and many scholars conceive of it in different ways. For example, Michael R. Solomon positions it as a strategy "that aims to disrupt efforts by the corporate world to dominate our cultural landscape."[9] Tim Jordan calls jamming "an attempt to reverse and transgress the meaning of cultural codes whose primary aim is to persuade us to buy something or be someone," a sort of "semiotic terrorism."[10] In all cases, culture jamming refers to the individual or organized effort to turn mass media messages against the media itself.

The organization Adbusters is perhaps the most visible example of culture jamming. A self-proclaimed "global network of artists, activists, writers, pranksters, students, educators and entrepreneurs" whose aim it is to "topple existing power structures and forge a major shift in the way we live in the 21st century,"[11] the Canadian-based Adbusters culture jams primarily through advertisement parody. For example, in the "Spoof Ads" section on the organization's website, users can browse a variety of images which call into question the social importance or benevolence of corporations. One features a runner in fluorescent Nike apparel sipping on a large convenience-store soda. The accompanying tagline, following the curve of a huge day-glo Nike "swoosh," reads "Just Douche It." Another ad depicts a hospital operating room with a patient open on the table. In the foreground of the ad, a heart monitor reveals the familiar McDonald's Golden Arches imbedded in the jagged cardiac line. These "subvertisments," as the organization calls them, refashion familiar media codes and symbols to criticize big business practices.

However, in her 2004 article "Pranking Rhetoric: 'Culture Jamming' as Media Activism," Christine Harold questions the effectiveness of parody as a jamming form.[12] Pointing out that parody "perpetuates a commitment to rhetorical binaries [and] the hierarchical form it supposedly wants to upset,"[13] she instead proposes "pranking" as an effective form of culture jamming. Media pranking, or actions that "playfully and provocatively [fold] existing cultural forms in on themselves,"[14] disrupts the *original/commentary* dichotomy that parody relies upon and inspires a deeper reflection in those who witness it. Harold cites the famous Barbie/G.I. Joe computer chip switch as an example of pranking. Just before the winter holiday shopping season of 1989, media pranksters referring to themselves the Barbie Liberation Organization purchased hundreds of electronic "talking" Barbie and G.I. Joe dolls. Members of the BLO spent weeks removing the talking computer chips from the figures and switching them so that the Barbie dolls played messages of death and destruction while the G.I. Joes discussed shopping and fashion. The group then proceeded to return every doll to the store, causing a very confusing Christmas morning for thousand of American children. To make sure their prank reached the maximum number of audiences, the BLO included messages inside the packing of each returned doll that urged consumers to contact their local media about the switch. The organization also prepared news packages about their work and intentions and disseminated them to local news outlets when the prank broke. Harold contends that this kind of pranking, whose coherent message only comes later and with much reflection, serves to subvert media resources far more effectively than exercises in parody.

At the same time, some scholars continue to see parody as an important form of culture jamming, especially in relation to "jamming" other forms of culture like the political sphere. In her 2007 article "Political Culture Jamming: The Dissident Humor of *The Daily Show With Jon Stewart*," Jamie Warner argues that the satirical form of Comedy Central's *The Daily Show* jams the branding practices inherent to US politics.[15] Because politicians have begun to employ the same kinds of marketing and image-management strategies of corporate advertisers, Warner contends that culture jamming can be equally applied to the political landscape as an effective means of critique. Jon Stewart's "fake" news program uses the same production conventions as "real" news programs (graphic montages, interviews, and packaged stories with correspondents), but it juxtaposes this form with humorous and scathingly critical interpretations of global politics. This creates a sense of incongruity between form and content, an important platform from which viewers can understand the conflation of marketing and politics in contemporary society. Drawing upon the work of Cultural studies scholar Stuart Hall, Warner claims that any type of incongruity is powerful because it represents danger, taboo, and threats to the cultural order. In essence, parody *is* powerful because it taps into and challenges our unquestioned ideas about the symbolic world in which we live.

Obviously, the debate over the power of parody in relation to culture jamming is ongoing. What is important to glean from these examples for the purposes of this chapter is the very *active* nature of culture jamming itself. If approaches to media theory provide the ability to critique mass media industries, texts and reception practices, then culture jamming is the messy and living fusion of all these perspectives into real-world activism and action. Culture jamming efforts, especially widespread ones like the Barbie prank or *The Daily Show*, which reach many people, extend the highly academic work of media scholars into the public sphere and daily life. Though far less organized or sanctioned (or even, in some instances, legal) than media literacy programs, culture jamming is also far more visible, dynamic, and exciting in most instances. Culture jamming is an important link between the realm of ideas and the realm of action, and it represents some of the most vibrant phenomena in media studies today.

Media reform

The summer of 2003 will go down in history as host to one of the most significant examples of widespread citizen involvement in governmental media policy ever.[16] Alarmed by Federal Communications Commission (FCC) deregulatory policies and galvanized by watchdog groups like Free Press and MoveOn.org (in addition to publicly dissenting members of the FCC itself), millions of Americans opposed what they saw as reckless and dangerous moves by the FCC to promote increased monopoly ownership of media industries. Journalists and Hollywood union members also voiced their discontent with the FCC's free-market logic, claiming that journalistic integrity and media content suffer when fewer companies own more media outlets. In many cases the FCC, which had anticipated an easy fight for deregulation against a largely apathetic public, found themselves ducking out of public meetings and avoiding an increasingly angry citizenry. Responding to this sudden spike in policy interests among everyday individuals, the Senate overturned the FCC's rules changes in September 2003 by a 55:40 vote. In late June 2004, the Third Circuit Court of Appeals in Philadelphia reinforced the Senate's position when it soundly rejected the FCC's attempts to deregulate the industry.[17]

The events of 2003 represent the most recent example of a growing citizen interest in media reform. **Media reform** refers to any efforts by citizens and citizens' interest groups to effect change in the structure and operation of mass media industries. Although the issues involved in media reform are wide, they usually concentrate on increased transparency of media operation and increased accountability of industries to matters of public interest (see Chapter 4, Pragmatic Analysis, for a discussion of the role of public interest in the media). In the words of Robert W. McChesney, President of Free Press and vehement supporter of media reform, once people understand "media as a policy issue . . . all bets are off. Organized people can defeat organized money."[18] Thus, media reform represents somewhat of a median between practices of media literacy and culture jamming. It blends together the structured and organized channels of media literacy with the radical zeal and spirit of culture jamming.

One of the most apparent manifestations of contemporary media reform is the current increase of alternative media outlets. For example, the growing Indymedia movement represents more than 150 global and fairly autonomous Independent Media Centers networked though a central online hub, all of which operate community-based newspapers and other sources of alternative information.[19] In relying on contemporary media technologies like the internet, the Indymedia network "enables activists to appropriate the technologies of globalization to promote access to citizen-produced content."[20] At the same time, the rise of "citizen journalism," or the increase of blogs and other online resources where citizens directly report to other citizens about the state of their world, signals growing dissatisfaction with traditional media outlets and the impulse toward more democratic forms of media.

However, the focus on media policy is still central to many media-reform movements. Rather than attempt to catalog all of the important policy battles in the last 30 years, we choose to concentrate on the fight for low-power radio (low-power FM, LPFM) as a representative case study of this kind of work. Throughout the 1990s the broadcast of (sometimes pirate) community-based radio programs over short distances on LPFM frequencies became the site of a political struggle between local citizens and the radio industry, especially after the Telecommunications Act of 1996 increased industry control and content standardization.[21] In January 2000 the chair of the FCC, William Kennard, approved a program that would extend broadcast licenses to 1,000 LPFM stations in an effort to quell the amount of illegal broadcasting and better represent local communities. Local broadcasters jumped at the chance to be licensed, and more than 3,000 had applied for LPFM licensure by the fall of 2003.[22] However, industry heavyweights like Clear Channel Communications effectively lobbied Congress to block the emerging LPFM movement, claiming that the proliferation of community radio signals would jam their own signals. Congress responded to these industry concerns by passing the Radio Preservation Act in 2000. The act limited the FCC's ability to license LPFM stations by reducing the number of available frequencies, as no LPFM could broadcast within three frequencies of a high-power station. Although a Congressional study found that industry claims of signal jamming were questionable, and despite the lobbying efforts of grassroots media campaigns like the Prometheus Radio Project of Philadelphia,[23] the interests of the industry ultimately prevailed.

In his article "Rationalizing Dissent? Challenging Conditions of Low-Power FM Radio," John Hamilton traces this evolution of LPFM and adds that FCC restrictions on surviving local radio broadcast content – such as a ban on supporting political candidates or a 36-hour per week broadcast requirement – "restricts and channels LPFM into highly rationalized forms to preserve the current commercial dominance of radio broadcasting."[24] Implicitly or explicitly requiring the remaining LPFM stations to adhere to the rules of the industry heavyweights "in effect turn[s] LPFM into a farm league for commercial broadcasting,"[25] rather than allowing LPFM to flourish and serve community needs. However, he also notes that LPFM advocates continue to struggle against the FCC, citing court cases in 2002 that struck down an FCC regulation that barred those who had broadcast illegally prior to 2000 from applying for a new, legal license. As a result, Hamilton invokes cultural critic Raymond Williams's understanding of the "long revolution" as a guiding heuristic in understanding LPFM reform, advocating a far-reaching view of the dialectical struggle between radio industry and reformists as an endless struggle of give and take. In a historical battle that seems to favor industry over community, Hamilton's ultimate conclusion provides the kind of raw hope that the media reform movement thrives upon.

By inaugurating alternative media and constantly challenging entrenched media policies through legal battles and awareness campaigns, media reformers represent the most ambitious application of critical media theory. The efforts of media reformists teach us all that the media is not some overwhelming system impossible to comprehend, but rather a complex field of interests and needs which we can creatively engage in order to build a better tomorrow. Drawing upon media education programs and the "semiotic terrorism" of culture jammers, media reformers are applying their nuanced understanding of media to utterly transform the mediated world in which all of us live. Theirs is a battle over symbols *and* the wires that transmit them, representations *and* the laws that shape them.

As a result, we can see in media reform the point that underlies any application of media theory (and, indeed, the purpose of this concluding chapter): everything in a mediated world is deeply, profoundly interconnected. Knowledge, activism, understanding, and participation are all facets of living in an image-saturated world that cannot afford to ignore one another. Only by understanding the links that exist between nodes in the mediascape, as well as the intersections that *can be made* with the proper training, can any of us hope to begin to talk about the media creature. Only by understanding each part of this elephant as necessarily incomplete but ultimately important can we train the animal to serve our needs at the dawn of the twenty-first century.

SUGGESTED READING

Carducci, V. Culture Jamming: a Sociological Perspective. *Journal of Consumer Culture* 6, 2006, 116–38.

Duran, R.L., Yousman, B., Walsh, K.M., and Longshore, M.A. Holistic Media Education: as Assessment of the Effectiveness of a College Course in Media Literacy. *Communication Quarterly* 56, 2008, 49–68.

Gibson, T.A. WARNING—The Existing Media System May Be Toxic to Your Health: Health Communication and the Politics of Media Reform. *Journal of Applied Communication Research* 35, 2007, 125–32.

Harold, C. Pranking Rhetoric: "Culture Jamming" as Media Activism. *Critical Studies in Media Communication* 21, 2004, 189–211.

Livingstone, S. Engaging With Media—a Matter of Literacy? *Communication, Culture & Critique* 1, 2008, 51–62.

McChesney, R.W., Newman, R., and Scott, B. (eds) *The Future of Media: Resistance and Reform in the 21ˢᵗ Century*. New York: Seven Stories Press, 2005.

Stengrim, L.A. Negotiating Postmodern Democracy, Political Activism, and Knowledge Production: Indymedia's Grassroots and e-Savvy Answer to Media Oligopoly. *Communication and Critical/Cultural Studies* 2, 2005, 281–304.

Vatikiotis, P. Communication Theory and Alternative Media. *Westminster Papers in Communication and Culture* 2, 2005, 4–29.

Warner, J. Political Culture Jamming: The Dissident Humor of *The Daily Show With John Stewart. Popular Communication* 5, 2007, 17–36.

Potter, W.J. *Media Literacy*, 4th edn. Thousand Oaks, CA: Sage Publications, 2008.

NOTES

1. J.G. Saxe, The Blind Men and the Elephant: a Hindoo Fable, in *The Poetical Works of John Godfrey Saxe, Household Edition* (New York: Houghton, Mifflin and Company, 1882), 112.

2. E. Wharton, Vesalius in Zante, in *Artemis to Actaeon and Other Verse* (New York: Charles Scribner's Sons, 1909), 23.

3. W.J. Potter, *Media Literacy*, 4th edn (Thousand Oaks, CA: Sage Publications, 2008), 9.

4. For a good summary of literacy strategies in relation to radio, see L. Burton, I Heard it on the Radio: Broadcasting in the Classroom, *Screen Education* 50, 2008, 68–73.

5. For a recent example of this kind of video project, see S. Sobers, Consequences and Coincidences: a Case Study of Experimental Play in Media Literacy, *Journal of Media Practice* 9, 2008, 53–66.

6. See R.L. Duran, B. Yousman, K.M. Walsh, and M.A. Longshore, Holistic Media Education: as Assessment of the Effectiveness of a College Course in Media Literacy, *Communication Quarterly* 56, 2008, 49–68.

7. S. Ramasubramanian, Media-Based Strategies to Reduce Racial Stereotypes Activated by News Stories, *Journalism & Mass Communication Quarterly* 84, 2007, 249–64; T. Reichert, M. S. LaTour, J.J. Lambiase, and M. Adkins, A Test of Media Literacy Effects and Sexual Objectification in Advertising, *Journal of Current Issues and Research in Advertising* 29, 2007, 81–92.

8. G. Debord, *Society of the Spectacle*, trans. unknown (Detroit, MI: Black and Red, 1983), 207.

9. M.R. Solomon, *Conquering Consumerspace: Marketing Strategies for a Branded World* (New York: American Management Association, 2003), 208.

10. T. Jordan, *Activism! Direct Action, Hacktivism and the Future of Society* (London: Reaktion Books, 2002), 102.

11. About Adbusters, *Adbusters*, www.adbusters.org/about/adbusters (accessed December 13, 2008).

12. C. Harold, Pranking Rhetoric: "Culture Jamming" as Media Activism, *Critical Studies in Media Communication* 21, 2004, 189–211.

13. Harold, 191.

14. Harold, 191.

15. J. Warner, Political Culture Jamming: The Dissident Humor of *The Daily Show With John Stewart, Popular Communication* 5, 2007, 17–36.

16. For an excellent comprehensive summary of the events surrounding citizen involvement in media policy in 2003, see R.W. McChesney, Media Policy Goes to Main Street: The Uprising of 2003, *The Communication Review* 7, 2004, 223–58.

17. S. Labaton, Court Orders F.C.C. to Rethink New Rules on Growth of Media, *The New York Times*, June 25, 2004, A1.

18. R.W. McChesney, The Emerging Struggle for a Free Press, in *The Future of Media: Resistance and Reform in the 21ˢᵗ Century*, R.W. McChesney, R. Newman, and B. Scott (eds), 9–20 (New York: Seven Stories Press, 2005), 19.

19. L.A Stengrim, Negotiating Postmodern Democracy, Political Activism, and Knowledge Production: Indymedia's Grassroots and e-Savvy Answer to Media Oligopoly, *Communication and Critical/Cultural Studies* 2, 2005, 281–304.

20. Stengrim, 283.

21. J. Hamilton, Rationalizing Dissent? Challenging Conditions of Low-Power FM Radio, *Critical Studies in Media Communication* 21, 2004, 44–63.

22. M. Connors, A High Powered Battle, *The News Media and the Law* 27, 2003, 44–5.

23. McChesney, Media Policy Goes to Main Street.

24. Hamilton, 50.

25. Hamilton, 54.

Glossary

aesthetics—The meaningfulness of art (and life) as apprehended through the senses; the beauty of art and the sensual enjoyment it engenders.

affects—The feelings, moods, emotions, and passions that arise in relation to direct sensory data.

aggressor effect—The hypothesis that repeated exposure to representations of violence increases aggressive behavior on the part of audiences.

American Dream—The unquestioned assumption that hard work leads to success, and that success is measured in terms of economic wealth.

apparatus theory—An early Psychoanalytic approach to film that claims the actual environment and machinery of the cinema activates a number of desires within spectators.

assimilation—The process of "white washing" ethnic diversity by de-historicizing cultural difference.

base (in Marxist theory)—The underlying economic and material conditions of society.

bystander effect—The hypothesis that repeated exposure to representations of violence promotes increased callousness about violence directed at others.

catharsis effect—The hypothesis that repeated exposure to representations of violence functions as an outlet for pent-up aggressive drives in the individual.

closed text—A text that is structured to elicit a particular, usually singular, response from audiences.

clusters—The way individual signs are associated and dissociated with one another.

code—A set of rules that govern the use of visual and linguistic signs within a culture.

code of ethics—A self-imposed set of rules that outline the ethical strivings of a particular media outlet.

concentration—An organizational state in which the ownership and control of an entire industry, such as the mass media, is dominated by just a few companies.

conglomeration—The corporate practice of accumulating multiple, though not necessarily media, companies and businesses through startups, mergers, buyouts, and takeovers.

connotation—The cultural meaning of a text; second-order signification.

consequences—The clear effects of a given regulation on society at large.

conspicuous consumption—The belief that one can attain the kind of happiness or completeness often conceived of as upper class through the purchase of material goods and services.

contingencies—The unique contextual and historical factors that influence regulatory decisions.

conventions—The norms that govern the technical and creative choices made by workers in the execution of their duties, art, or craft.

cool media—Communication technologies that are high in participation or completion by the audience (e.g. television, telephone, cartoons).

copyright—The legal granting of exclusive control of a creative work to that work's creator.

critical studies—An umbrella term used to describe an array of theoretical perspectives, which, though diverse, are united by their skeptical attitude, humanistic approach, political assessment, and activist orientation.

cruising—The interpretive practice of reading with one's body.

cultural production—The generation of semiotic, enunciative, and textual materials related to a specific media artifact by fans of that artifact.

Cultural studies—An interdisciplinary approach to the study of culture that seeks to understand how relations of power are enacted, reified, and challenged.

culture—The collection of artifacts, practices, and beliefs of a particular group of people at a particular historical moment, supported by symbolic systems and directed by ideology.

culture jamming—The use of familiar media symbols and channels to reveal and overturn the consumerist, capitalist ideologies they embody.

decoding—The process of using a code to decipher a message and assess meaning.

denotation—The literal meaning of a text; first-order signification.

desire—An appetite for something that promises enjoyment, satisfaction, and pleasure in its attainment.

difference—The depiction of others who are subordinate to, but a source of pleasure for, US American tourists and consumers.

digital rights management—Any software program that media industries employ to control the distribution and use of digital intellectual property.

discursive construction—A social construction made invisible, natural, normal, and indeed "biological" by its discursive aspects.

doxa—Cultural knowledge that is accepted as common sense; the realm of the taken-for-granted.

encoding—The process of creating a meaningful message according to a particular code.

encryption—The digital scrambling of a message such that it can only be read by using an appropriately correlated decoding program.

equipment for living—The idea that public discourse provides audiences with symbolic resources for confronting the anxieties and difficulties of their own lives.

essentialism—The belief that cultural distinctions such as masculinity and femininity are inherent, universal, and natural.

ethnography—A qualitative research method that employs observation to understand cultural phenomenon from the perspective of the members of that culture.

exclusion—The symbolical annihilation of various cultural groups through erasure or under-representation.

exoticism—Images of foreign lands and bodies that romanticize or mystify other cultures.

fandom—Organized communities or subcultures comprised of persons who share a special affinity for or attachment to a media text, which they, in turn, express through their participation in communal practices (fan fiction, etc.) and events (conventions).

fantasy—A mental representation of conscious or unconscious wish fulfillment.

feminism—A political project that explores the diverse ways men and women are socially empowered or disempowered.

fetishism—The psychic structuring of an object or person as a source of sexual pleasure.

form—The creation and satisfaction of desire.

gender—The culturally constructed differences (tastes, roles, activities, etc.) between men and women.

gender performativity—The idea that gender, rather than a coherent component of identity incorporated through socialization, is in fact a bodily performance of discourse that exists only because people believe it is significant.

genre—A type, kind, or class of messages that share distinctive and identifiable aesthetic, stylistic, substantive, and/or ideological conventions.

glass ceiling—An invisible barrier sustained by gendered workplace policies that restricts women from being promoted equally to men.

guilt—The emotional condition that arises every time we violate hierarchy.

hegemony—The process by which one ideology subverts other competing ideologies and gains cultural dominance.

hermeneutic depth—The critical recognition of multiple meanings in a text as the source of its overall meaning.

heteronormativity—A system of inequality that perpetuates a binary understanding of heterosexuality and homosexuality in which heterosexuality is privileged.

hierarchy—The social rules by which we play.

historical materialism—The underlying method of Marxism.

historical violence—Representations of violence that invite self-reflection and social consciousness.

hot media—Communication technologies that extend a single sense in high definition (e.g. radio, photographs, and films).

hyper-real violence—Representations of violence that are stylized and appeal to hyper-realism, but are shorn of any critical reflexivity.

iconic sign—A sign that structurally resembles the object for which it stands.

ideology—A system of ideas that unconsciously shapes and constrains our beliefs and behaviors.

Imaginary—The pre-linguistic realm (similar to the Freudian pre-Oedipal, pleasurable stage) where the infant feels whole and connected to everything via the bond to the mother.

indecency—Any material that is morally unfit for general distribution or broadcast.

indexical sign—A sign that conveys meaning through cause or association.

informational bias—The journalistic predisposition that governs how a story is structured and told; four common informational biases are *dramatized*, *personalized*, *fragmented*, and *authority-disorder*.

integration—An ownership pattern in which the subsidiary companies or branches within a corporation are strategically interrelated; integration can be *vertical* (within a media industry) or *horizontal* (across media industries).

interpellation—The process by which individuals are turned into ideological subjects.

interpretive communities—Groups who interpret texts similarly because they share similar social positions and experiences.

interpretive play—An improvisational mode of reading that ignores dominant interpretive codes in favor of pursuing immediate bodily desires.

jouissance—A radically disruptive pleasure; an elusive and ecstatic pleasure that destabilizes culture/subjectivity.

journalistic beats—The places and institutions where news is regularly expected to occur.

lack—A psychoanalytic concept that describes the gap separating Imaginary pleasures and lived reality.

libel—Printed statements that falsely impugn or defame a person's character.

literacy—The technologies of writing and print.

male gaze—The cinema's frequent positioning of women as objects coded for strong visual and erotic impact.

Marxism—A theory and social movement rooted in the idea that "society is the history of class struggles."

mass media—Communication technologies that have the potential to reach a large audience in remote locations.

Media Ecology—An approach that views communication technologies as environments.

Media Erotics—An approach that explores the array of resistive pleasures that audiences derive from media by examining the various sensuous, creative, and transgressive ways in which persons use and experience media.

media literacy—Any learning opportunity that increases an individual's understanding of how the mass media function.

media reform—Any effort by citizens and citizens' interest groups to effect change in the structure and operation of mass media industries.

medium—Middle; that which comes between two things.

medium theory—The idea that each medium (technology) of communication promotes a particular type of consciousness.

multinationalism—A corporate presence in multiple countries, allowing for the production and distribution of media products on a global scale.

myth—A sacred story or "type of speech" that reaffirms and reproduces ideology in relation to an object.

narrative—The visual or verbal retelling of a series of events, real or fictitious, that occur in (often chronological) succession.

news—The media product produced by the organization structures and practices of journalism.

news agencies—Corporations that produce and sell stories to other news providers or non-profit cooperatives, which work with large media companies to generate news centrally and distribute it locally.

objectivity—The reporting of facts in an impartial manner.

obscenity—Illegal, sexually explicit material that lacks literary, artistic, political, or scientific value.

Oedipus complex—A mental structuring that takes the raw libidinal materials of the oral, anal, and phallic stages and splits them into conscious and unconscious desires.

open text—A text that is structured to call for active participation of the behalf of audiences in the production of meaning.

orality—Thought and its verbal expression.

organizational culture—The set(s) of norms and customs, artifacts and events, and values and assumptions that emerge as a consequence of organizational members' communicative practices.

organizations—A system (network) of ordered relationships and coordinated activities directed toward specific goals.

othering—The process of marginalizing minorities by defining them in relationship to the majority, which is assumed to be the norm.

participatory media—Communication technologies that necessitate either *direct-user interaction* (DUI) or *user-created content* (UCC) to function.

patriarchy—A system of social relationships in which women's interests are subordinated to those of men.

phallocentrism—A social condition in which images or representations of the penis carry connotations of power and dominance.

plaisir—A hegemonic pleasure; a comfortable and comforting pleasure that reproduces dominant culture/subjectivity.

pleasure principle—The uncontrollable human drive to satisfy desire.

polysemy—The notion that a text is open to multiple interpretations and meanings.

polyvalence—The notion that a text has a relatively unified meaning that is valued differently by different audiences.

postfeminism—A conceptual shift within the popular understanding of feminism from an emphasis on the systemic oppression of all women to the empowerment of individual women.

postmodernity—The historical epoch that began to emerge in the 1960s as the economic mode of production in most Western societies slowly shifted from goods-based manufacturing to information-based services.

pragmatism—The branch of philosophy that assesses truth in terms of effect, outcome, and practicality.

press release—A strategically prepared written or recorded statement produced for news organizations to announce something that claims to be newsworthy.

profanity—An utterance that is abusive, irreverent, or vulgar.

professional culture—The set(s) of norms and customs, artifacts and events, and values and assumptions that emerge as a consequence of formal training (i.e. education, apprenticeships, internships, etc.), membership and participation (i.e. professional associations, conferences, workshops, licenses, etc.), and recognition (i.e. industry awards and honors) within a profession.

professionalization—The process by which an individual with free will and choice is transformed (i.e. socialized) into an ideological subject (i.e. professional) whose behaviors and actions reaffirm one's status as a professional.

professionals—Individuals who possess expertise in a particular area or field that allows them to accomplish the distinctive tasks of their position.

profit-motive—The continuous desire to increase capital.

punditry—News that is pre-packaged by politicians and their communication consultants (i.e. press advisors and public relations managers) to promote a favorable image of a politician and her or his specific policy initiatives.

Queer theory—An interdisciplinary perspective that seeks to disrupt socially constructed systems of meaning surrounding human sexuality.

reality principle—The constant curbing of desire according to possibility, law, or social convention.

Reception theory—An approach that stresses audience interpretation as the primary site of meaning-making.

relativism—The belief that diverse approaches and theories related to a given subject are all equally correct.

representation—The manner in which various social and cultural groups are depicted in the media.

repression—The process of mentally containing our desires below conscious recognition or expression.

resistance—Any symbolic or material practice that challenges, subverts, or suspends the cultural codes, rules, or norms, which through their everyday operation create, sustain, and naturalize the prevailing social structure in a particular space and time.

resistive reading—The active, audience-based creation of textual meaning that is contrary to the meaning intended by the text's author, creator, or producer.

rhetoric—The ancient art of persuasion; the use of symbols by humans to influence and move other humans.

ritualistic violence—Representations of violence that are spectacular, gory, exaggerated, hyper-masculine, and adrenaline-pumping.

scopophilia—The pleasure that comes from the process of looking.

semiology—Ferdinand de Saussure's approach to the study of signs.

semiotic—Charles Sanders Peirce's quasi-scientific approach to the study of signs.

sex—The innate, biological differentiation (anatomy, reproduction, hormones, etc.) between men and women.

sexism—Discrimination based upon a person's biological sex.

sexual othering—The process of stigmatizing homosexuality (or really any non-heterosexual practice) as abnormal.

sexuality—An enduring emotional, romantic, or sexual attraction toward others based upon their gender or sex.

sign—Something that invites someone to think of something other than itself.

signified—The mental concept evoked by the signifier.

signifier—The material form (sound-image) of a sign as perceived by the senses.

signifying system—Roland Barthes's approach to the study of signs.

slander—Speech that falsely impugns or defames a person's character.

socialization—The process by which persons – both individually and collectively – learn, adopt, and internalize the prevailing cultural beliefs, values, and norms of a society.

space-biased media—Ephemeral media such as paper and television.

stereotype—A misleading and reductionistic representation of a cultural group.

strategic ambiguity—The intentional decision to craft a vague, semantically rich text that is purposefully open to multiple interpretations.

structuralism—The view, largely popularized by the anthropologist Claude Lévi-Strauss, that each element in a cultural system derives its meaning in relation to other elements in that system.

structure of feeling—The sum of the subtle and nuanced aspects of a historical culture, those aspects not obviously or completely captured in the artifacts of a society.

superstructure (in Marxist theory)—Social consciousness, as encoded in institutions such as culture (art and media), religion, education, politics, and the judicial system.

symbol—A sign that is linked to its corresponding object purely by social convention or agreement.

Symbolic—The realm or the cultural plane of language, social meanings, and relationships.

text—A set of signs working together to produce a relatively unified effect.

theory—An explanatory and interpretive tool that simultaneously enables and limits our understanding of the particular social product, practice, or process under investigation.

time-biased media—Durable media such as stone or clay.

token—An exception to a social rule that affirms the correctness of an ideology.

unconscious—The structure within the psyche (i.e. mind) that keeps trying to make its desires felt while remaining continually repressed.

victim effect—The hypothesis that repeated exposure to representations of violence promotes increased fearfulness of violence.

visibility—The degree to which various social or cultural groups are present in the media.

voyeurism—The process of experiencing pleasure by watching a desired object or person from a distance.

Index